WHEN THE ALMOND TREE BLOSSOMS

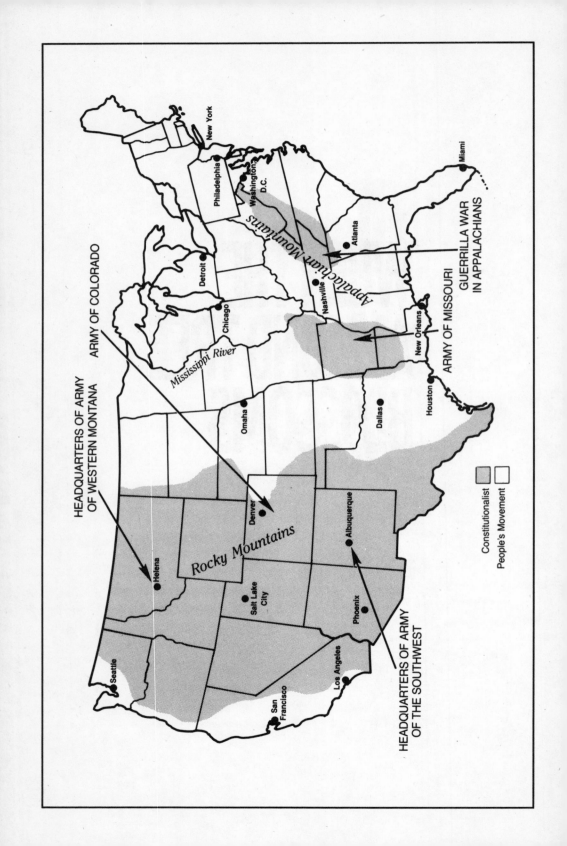

WHEN THE ALMOND TREE BLOSSOMS

DAVID AIKMAN

WORD PUBLISHING
Dallas·London·Vancouver·Melbourne

Library of Congress Cataloging-in-Publication Data

Aikman, David, 1944–
    When the almond tree blossoms / David Aikman.
      p.   cm.
    ISBN 0–8499–0962–7
    I. Title.
    PS3551.I37W49   1993
    813'.54—dc20   92–38340
                                              CIP

Printed in the United States of America

34569 LBM 987654321

Acknowledgments

Many people provided advice and encouragement during the writing and editing of this book. Space and time constraints make it impossible for me to mention everyone I should, so I ask forgiveness in advance of any I have inexcusably omitted.

My first debt of gratitude is to Kip Jordon, my publisher, whose faith and enthusiasm for the book never flagged from our very first discussion of it. If all publishers were as gracious in dealing with their authors as Kip and his associates at Word Inc., the psychiatric profession might quickly sink into recession. Nancy Norris, Words's wondrous project editor, demonstrated Job's patience, Talleyrand's diplomacy and Stakhanov's work appetite in coaxing the manuscript through the complex editing process. My debt to her is enormous.

Great thanks to Harold Fickett, my editor, who performed some excellent, and vitally needed manuscript surgery.

I could never have attempted the story without the outstanding input of U.S. military officers, both serving and retired. I am very grateful to Brian Zimmer, who explained to me firsthand the wonderful features of his native Montana. Dave Stockwell, Robin Cathcart, Tom Burgess, Tony Stewart, and Andy O'Meara offered me not just assistance but fine friendship too. Brigadier General Richard S. Sweet, Sr. USA (Ret.), offered me invaluable help and hospitality, as did Charles A. Krohn, along with the counsel of Jim Bambery, Bill Baxter, and Robert Helvey, colonels all, now retired.

Joseph Zwilling helped me enormously in learning about St. Patrick's Cathedral and some Roman Catholic details. Liam Sarsfield was a genius at contacts, Lela Gilbert offered wise and kind advice, Michele Clark was impeccable on detail, and the donor of the rare Fulleylove and Kelman will be gratefully remembered for a very long time.

Years ago, Robert R. Gottlieb, now executive vice-president of the William Morris Agency, contacted me in Jerusalem and asked: "Have you ever thought of writing a book?" Thank you, Robert, for watering the seeds that grew into this Almond Tree.

When men are afraid of heights
and dangers in the streets;
when the almond tree blossoms
and the grasshopper drags himself along
and desire no longer is stirred.
Then man goes to his eternal home
and mourners go about the streets.

Ecclesiastes 12:5 NIV

It has long been a grave question whether any government, not too strong for the liberties of its people, can be
strong enough to maintain its existence in great emergencies.

Abraham Lincoln

1

The Rendezvous

November 25, 1998. Aboard the USS Massachusetts, *twelve miles off the New England coast*

A moment earlier Gresham had been peering into the forbidding gloom of the North Atlantic. Now the scope had cleared the surface, and he was staring just over the top of the rolling New England swell. At first, with the scope on low power searching backward into the ocean, he could pick out nothing but the clouds racing over the waves, the sea and the sky all but inseparable beneath the moonless canopy of night. But as he continued wheeling around, adrenaline suddenly surged into the pit of his stomach. There, over the submarine's three-mile horizon, but still tantalizingly close, was the intermittent flash of Highland Light, the *Massachusetts's* final—and riskiest—navigational reference point.

The brightest and oldest of Cape Cod's lighthouses, its welcoming beam had been sighted gratefully by lost or storm-threatened mariners ever since 1797. Just behind the light was the faint glow of Provincetown, the site of the Pilgrims' lonely landfall in 1620.

"Quartermaster, no close contacts periscope depth. Highland Light abeam, Captain," Gresham reported.

"I'll take a look," Rush, the captain, said, moving to the scope so quickly that Gresham had to jump out of the way. Gripping the handles as though the scope might somehow leap out of his hands, Rush took the instrument through a complete circle of the horizon, his pale lips pursed.

The rendezvous boat was still not in sight. They had ten minutes for it to appear. Rush silently released the scope's handles and moved away for Gresham to take them back.

A silence came over the control center, or "con," of the submarine as each man made ready for surfacing. Reynolds, quartermaster of the watch, wiped sweat from his face. Rodriguez, the burly chief of the watch, kept craning his neck in all directions as though impatient for someone to give him an order. Stevens was dead still and seemed to be rehearsing in his mind the various evolutions the submarine would pass through before finally surfacing. Roberts had adopted what Gresham dubbed his "supercilious look," an expression which implied that he, of all people, was not going to display tension or fear.

Gresham concentrated harder on his search, slowly wheeling the scope around. Then he saw it, hovering for half a second above the horizon before being engulfed by a swell. There could be no mistake: a red light over a white light over a red light, the lower light just slightly out of alignment. He kept his feet on exactly the same spot and his wrist muscles taut on the handles. There, again.

"Quartermaster, mark bearing periscope two," he called out hoarsely, his throat suddenly dry.

"Bearing one seven zero."

"Captain, one contact, red over white over red, bearing one seven zero, over the horizon."

"Very well."

There could be no doubt that they had found the Constitutionalist boat, a trawler out of Boston with the standard identification lights of a fishing boat. There was no possibility of mere coincidence. The vessel was well away from the main trawling areas and obviously not moving purposefully in any direction. And then there was the positioning of the lower red light, just slightly—but deliberately— misaligned.

"Helmsman, left five degrees, all ahead two-thirds." Rush's next order pushed the forward speed of the *Massachusetts*, still only at periscope depth, to nearly seventeen knots, fast enough, Gresham thought wryly, to water-ski behind. It was essential to get within surfacing distance of the trawler as soon as possible. Every minute spent in enemy waters was dangerous. The last clear intelligence picture Hawaii had managed to cross-transmit via a friendly Liberian freighter in the South Atlantic was of a dozen or so Russian Romeo-class fast attack submarines on picket duty along the American east coast.

"How does he look now?" Rush asked.

Gresham had not moved his eyes away from the scope while the con rustled with the preparations for surfacing. But now his fatigue was attacking again. He blinked and rubbed his eyes hard, remembering with an effort what he was supposed to be doing.

The three lights of the trawler were no longer bobbing up and down below the horizon, but now hung steadily above. The *Massachusetts* was closing fast. He made another sweep of the horizon to ensure that no other vessels were in sight, then switched to the high-powered scope to take a closer look at the Constitutionalist vessel. The navigation lights, powerfully magnified, momentarily blinded him. He winced. Obviously, they could also be seen from the Cape Cod shore, he reflected, and probably from the beach itself. There was most likely a People's Militia unit in Provincetown. What if some off-duty sergeant just happened to be walking the beach this morning in the footsteps of Thoreau?

"Target approximately two miles," Gresham reported after a long pause. Rush grunted impatiently.

Daylight was coming on fast now. The moonless Atlantic night was yielding to the first fingers of gray dawn infiltrating westwards above the clouds. The swell still surged around the periscope in dark masses, but it too had acquired the blank grayness of a morning sea. In another twenty minutes it would be light enough to read a newspaper, light enough, too, for the navigator/bombardier of a Russian Bear reconnaissance plane to spot the submarine from his ten-thousand-foot perch.

"Chief of the Boat, assemble small-boat party in the air regeneration room." Rush did not want any detail left to the last few minutes of the rendezvous. "Ensure every man is properly equipped with foul-weather gear and life jacket," he went on. This time he was speaking not over a regular MC channel, but into the "growler," the bulky, sound-powered headset always used in battle conditions. "See that the men are armed."

Gresham frowned. Rush's precaution was entirely sound. If the other side had somehow gotten wind of the rendezvous, they would do everything possible to capture the submarine intact. The function of the small-boat party would be simply to hold off a boarding attempt from the trawler long enough to seal all hatches and crash-dive the boat. In that event, of course, the entire small-boat party would be captured or killed.

"Chris, that means you too." Rush was speaking to him directly now, having pushed aside the growler. "For heaven's sake, man," he added, catching Gresham's frown, "the whole thing could be a setup. What if the boat's full of Ivan's thugs, or even some of the People's Militia? You don't think they'd blow us up, do you, if they could get their hands on this beauty intact? Get yourself an Uzi from the armory!"

Rush's irritability shook Gresham once again out of his encroaching torpor. He had, of course, considered the possibility, however extreme it was, that either Russian or People's Movement intelligence might have penetrated the command structure of the Constitutionalists so completely that neither Hawaii nor Montana was aware of it. But it was only now that he realized he might have to fight for his life against an attempt by hostile commandos or sailors to board the *Massachusetts*. *How absurd that would be,* he thought.

"One thousand yards, Captain." The quartermaster of the watch, trained especially on the periscope, had now taken over to count off the distance from the trawler before surfacing. Gresham was waiting until the surfacing maneuvers were well under way and it was time to go aft to join the small-boat party.

"Con, ECM, what's the traffic?" Rush directed his query to the radio and electronic countermeasures operator. Out at sea, prowling the limitless oceans, the three surviving Ohio-class submarines had only one real worry: that a Russian fast-attack submarine might detect one of them before the American vessels had become aware of the other's presence. But surfaced, out of its natural element, the most sophisticated submarine became pathetically vulnerable.

"Radar, con. No surface or air traffic, Captain. We have Boston and Connecticut radio stations, but it seems to be quiet there."

"Very well. Copy all local radio channels. I want a transcript of Boston's WGBH seven o'clock news broadcast."

"Radio, con, will copy."

"Eight hundred yards, Captain."

"Very well."

Rush now flicked his MC switch calmly and spoke on the open channel. "Prepare to surface," he said simply.

"Prepare to surface, maneuvering, con, aye," came back the inverted acknowledgment from maneuvering, whose actions were decisive in the surfacing of the submarine. Simultaneously, in every part of the boat, men were stirring to life, donning their sound-powered phones and taking up positions close to the complex controls that had to be activated in perfect coordination for the huge submarine to rise smoothly out of the water. Gresham felt a slight new chill in the air as the ventilation systems were changed from the recycling of the submarine's own air to direct intake from the surface through the snorkel atop the sail. One by one the key departments of the boat reported the precise status of the submarine, as though presenting it to Rush for his final inspection. When he had acknowledged all the reports, he turned to the diving officer. "Surface the ship," he said quietly.

"Surface the ship, aye."

"Chief of the Watch"—on the number-one MC—"surface, surface, surface."

At this last command the chief of the watch sounded the diving alarm three times. For Gresham this was invariably a spine-tingling moment. No matter how many times he had been through the operation, or how placid the practice had been in peacetime, the strident "aooga . . . aooga . . . aooga" of the klaxon never failed to convey a sense of urgency and immediate danger. All over the boat men hurriedly opened valves, watched dials, and waited for key sequences to be completed.

"Chief of the Watch, blow the forward group," ordered Rush.

A high-pitched hissing sound, like that of a leaking tire, now whistled through the con as air under three thousand pounds of pressure blasted into the *Massachusetts*'s ballast tanks to expel the seawater from them.

As order followed order to complete the precise surfacing evolutions, Quartermaster of the Watch Reynolds positioned himself
on the ladder just below the lower hatch in the sail, the streamlined
structure rising above the deck that used to be called a "conning
tower" in old, World War II-era submarines. It was his task to confirm whether the pressure in the boat had been equalized with that
of the atmosphere outside. In case the barometers were not functioning properly, the quartermaster of the watch had a convenient
visual device to double-check. He would observe the movement of
smoke from a lighted cigarette. A downward flow meant that the
pressure in the boat was less than outside. An upward flow meant
the opposite.

"No airflow," Reynolds reported. Rush was still impassive.
"Open the upper hatch."

Gresham did not stay to observe the three seamen and an officer scurry up the ladder to the bridge. He quickly went aft to join the
small-boat party in the air-regeneration room.

There, amid the "scrubbers" that turned acrid carbon dioxide
back into remarkably pure, breathable air, six men were already
bundled in camouflage-colored foul-weather jackets and life vests.
As he was handed his own jacket and vest, Gresham glanced sideways at the chief of the boat, Remowitz. An unusually short, stubby
man, at forty-six he was the oldest person aboard the submarine. He
had an ugly temper, and Gresham didn't like working closely with
him. This time, though, he was grinning, grasping a holstered pistol
with one hand and handing Gresham a black Uzi submachine gun
with the other. He was obviously eager for action and in exceptionally high spirits. The other men in the boat party seemed to have
picked up his ebullience, too.

Slinging the Uzi over his shoulder, Gresham set his hands and
feet on the ladder leading up to the aft hatch. Someone had already
opened it a crack, and Gresham was soon pushing it up against the
stiff breeze coming off the ocean.

Icy spray splashed his face as he braced himself on the
slightly rolling deck. Looking up and taking his bearings, he saw
that the trawler was much closer than when he had left the con,
probably no farther than two hundred yards off. It was riding high

and uncomfortably in the swell, pitching down in the troughs of the waves, then rearing angrily up on the crests.

Only two figures were visible aboard the vessel, leaning over the railings behind the bridge. Through his binoculars they looked surprisingly young to Gresham, possibly still in their teens. Both seemed to be grinning as they chatted to each other.

Just then a small boat appeared from behind the trawler's hull, bearing down fast upon the submarine in a wide arc—a Boston whaler. The propellers of the powerful outboard motors sometimes flailed wildly at the air as the boat roared and thumped its way over the tops of the swell. A man in oilskins was at the helm in the stern. In the bow was an older-looking man, lean of face and bearded, who stood bolt upright, holding on to the bow rail. Behind him were two others, one also standing in the boat's midships, feet spread apart as if to enjoy the violent ride. The fourth man was sitting down and clinging with both hands to one side, looking distinctly unwell. *That would be the photographer*, Gresham thought.

Moving his binoculars back to the trawler, Gresham noticed that one of the two men behind the bridge was pointing excitedly to the sail of the submarine and yelling something to his companion. When he followed their gaze, Gresham understood. Probably neither of them had seen the Stars and Stripes flown publicly since the outbreak of the civil war, and it was now snapping in the breeze from a mast on the bridge of the *Massachusetts*.

The whaler throttled back as it approached the midships of the submarine from the stern. As it came abeam, the older-looking man in the bow deftly threw a line to Gresham's small-boat party. It was caught by a sailor and quickly secured. The whaler bounced alongside the submarine, and the bearded, thin-looking man grasped the outstretched arm of a sailor and hauled himself up to the deck of the *Massachusetts*. He steadied himself in the slight swell, noticed Gresham standing a few feet away, and took a few steps toward him.

"Welcome aboard," Gresham said, smiling and stretching out his hand. "Commander Gresham, United States Navy. I'm the executive officer of the USS *Massachusetts*."

"Harfritz, Boston area," said the other, his eyes twinkling with pleasure. "Welcome home." He half-turned to the whaler and pointed to the crouching figure amidships. "Tom, Charlie, help Mike out quickly. Wait till he's safely on deck before handing up his gear."

Three more of the small-boat party scurried past Gresham and Harfritz to lend assistance to the photographer who was half-hoisted, half-dragged out of the whaler. Once aboard the submarine, the man made no attempt to get up. He sat on the deck with his feet spread wide apart and his head bent as low as he could bend it. After breathing in deeply, though, he seemed to revive a little and hauled himself up shakily with the help of a sailor. Slowly he began taking his cameras out of his equipment bag.

"He can use as many of my men as he needs," Gresham said, turning back to Harfritz. Then he turned to the photographer. "How are you feeling?"

"Not . . . good," came the slow, choking response.

"Can you still do the job?"

The photographer straightened himself with immense effort and staggered to his feet. He grimaced, but there was a hint of a grin at the corner of his mouth.

"I'll finish this if it kills me," he replied, ". . . and it may."

"What's your name?" asked Gresham.

"Haines. Mike Haines."

"Okay, Mike, my men are yours. Just tell them what you want them to do."

"Right, thanks." The photographer took a breath and went on hoarsely. "Look, before we do anything else, the authentication shots get top priority. That's to be sure we have at least a few usable pics in case we get interrupted. I want today's *Boston Globe*—the outside pages—held up across this, whatever it's called," and he pointed to the sail behind Gresham, "so that we can confirm the date of the picture." He then reached into his bag and pulled out a tightly folded newspaper.

The photographer seemed to recover from his seasickness now and moved fast. After shooting several closeup frames of the *Boston Globe* fastened to the sail, he retreated slowly backward toward the bow of the submarine, shooting as he went, a sailor moving behind him to ensure he didn't slip.

Suddenly there was a shout from the bridge.

14

"Aircraft approaching, bearing one nine five! Abort mission! All hands below deck!"

Gresham whirled around instinctively, half-expecting to see a fighter swooping down to strafe them. But the sky was clear. Thank God. At least their radar had picked it up first. It could be a straightforward passenger aircraft on a flight from Europe. But a multi-engined propeller aircraft spelled serious trouble; that would almost certainly be a Russian patrol plane. They would probably know for sure before the submarine was fully submerged again.

The photographer, followed by the sailor who had been assisting him, was now half-running, half-lurching back toward the submarine's midships, where two sailors were nervously holding the bobbing whaler alongside. Cramming his cameras back into the equipment bag, he swung it on the whaler. The helmsman caught it. Then as the second whaler crewman grabbed one of his arms, he threw himself into the small boat and landed heavily amidships.

Harfritz leaped in after him, barely in time, as the helmsman gunned the outboard motor and was already shifting into forward gear as the nose came round away from the submarine.

As the whaler roared off, the klaxon sounded raspingly from the sail of the *Massachusetts* and the chief of the watch's voice boomed out over the speaker system: "Emergency deep! Emergency deep!"

Remowitz rushed past Gresham to the aft hatch with the two sailors who had been holding the whaler, then disappeared below deck. The ocean was already foaming angrily over the bow section of the submarine's hull as if jealous of the boat's brief flirtation with the surface, and the *Massachusetts* was surging forward under full reactor power. Gresham walked briskly back to the hatch and put his feet on the second rung of the ladder before pausing to cup his ear to the wind one final time.

Then he heard it. Still distant and half-muffled by the roaring wake of the submarine as it sank lower into the Atlantic was the high-pitched, whining drone of turboprop aircraft engines. There was no mistaking it. The plane approaching them from the north was a Russian Bear antisubmarine reconnaissance bomber.

2

The Parade

November 26, 1998, Thanksgiving Day, New York City

*D*ouglas Richfield had decided to stand on the raised plaza in front of the General Motors Building. Once there he was close to the corner of Fifth Avenue and Fifty-eighth Street and thus exposed to the cruel east wind that bullied its way into midtown from across the East River. His beige windbreaker ill prepared him for the season, especially since he would be forced to stay virtually immobile in one place for two hours. But the exposed position also had some value. He would not be caught by the crowds when the parade was over and everyone began streaming down Fifth Avenue to the bus stops and other exit routes. He had managed to get a police pass from the Protocol Department for the Fifty-eighth Street checkpoint. If the parade went on for too long, he could plead ill health and walk back to his apartment on East Seventy-first Street.

He dug his hands deeper into the windbreaker's pockets, trying at the same time to sink his head between his shoulder blades. It wasn't much use. The wind cuffed him mercilessly with icy gusts to his back and his neck, mocking his poor judgment in failing to check the weather forecasts. He tried jogging in place, but that didn't help either. Besides, it might attract attention to him, not a good idea when he was so conspicuously close to the special guests in the Plaza Hotel, not to mention the reviewing stand itself. It would be galling to have to identify himself to some sour-faced Public Security agent, or, even worse, to the foul-mouthed thugs who tended to fill out the ranks of the People's Militia, all leather jackets, blue armbands and, frequently, the red headband of the real radicals. He'd have to endure meekly at least an abrasive questioning and possibly an official warning. The incident might go down on his record, and he would have some explaining to do at City Hall. It was always better not to be conspicuous.

Five miles of Fifth Avenue had been cordoned off for the march, from 108th Street to 23d Street. As with all official parades during the past fourteen months of the new regime, the precise route had been carefully selected for its political symbolism. Harlem, for example, had been an obvious starting point. The marchers had grown slowly numb in the wind as Preston Northwood, secretary of the National Executive Committee of the People's Movement and its most silver-tongued apologist, had thundered away about the evil of Harlem's past and the brilliance of its future as a showcase of social and economic planning in the New Era.

"Before the overthrow of the old system," he declaimed, "these streets knew nothing but the filth and refuse of racist and sexist exploitation. Drugs, alcoholism, prostitution, and decay held sway here. Today, we have already removed the filth. Tomorrow, a glorious new culture and society will arise, one from which the American people, rising up as one to claim their true birthright, will have banned all political, economic, gender, and racial exploitation and oppression. Instead of the drab, grim tenements that landlord greed had permitted to decay, color and brightness will return to these once-blighted streets."

Cynics in Northwood's audience sneered privately at the unintended double entendre of his use of the noun *color*. You had to be extremely careful how you used the word *color*. The National Executive Committee itself was endlessly debating whether to stop using the term "people of color" to denote nonwhite minorities. The better-educated Asian-Americans tended to object strenuously, and some of the most militant African-Americans in the movement were no longer happy either. Asian-Americans had more complicated reasons for objecting to the phrase. They resented the idea that everyone who was not white automatically belonged to a single category, including other minorities they themselves felt uncomfortable with.

As for the "filth" not many people would have argued with Northwood's harsh description. In one of the earliest acts of the new regime, several thousand of the most retrograde and socially dangerous elements of Harlem and the South Bronx had been rounded up and sent to reeducation camps. They were the chronically unemployed, the druggies, the winos, the violently insane, and the professional beggars. In the past they had festooned the street corners or stared hostilely and alcoholicly from rundown stoops at passersby. As for their being "removed," well, that was a euphemism for deportation. Most had gone to the camps and mines of Alaska, which many people expected soon to be handed back peacefully to Russian sovereignty.

The main reviewing stand had been set up just a few blocks down the avenue from where Richfield was standing. Construction crews had hastily assembled temporary bleachers in front of the Channel Gardens to accommodate VIPs, luminaries like Stan Rutledge, chairman of the National Executive Committee, and the other nine members (apart from Preston Northwood). The senior Russian Kommandatura representative would be there too, but discreetly. A lot of Americans, even in New York where the People's Movement held sway most decisively, were not happy at having Russians of any political stripe assisting their entry into the New Era. It was better simply to keep them out of sight, if possible, which was why the Kommandatura had been tucked away on Governor's Island in New York Harbor.

Douglas decided just to endure the cold as meekly as he could. He didn't want to draw attention to himself, even here among the crowds watching the parade. Ever since he'd landed the City Hall position just nine months earlier, he had kept a clean record and skillfully navigated the various political shoals of the New York municipal government. He'd gotten the job because of his role as an organizer early on in the People's Movement, during the Chicago rent riots back in 1995. By definition that involvement meant he was trusted by the People's Movement as they struggled to fit together the building blocks of the New Era, as the revolutionary regime that controlled his part of the United States liked to refer to its rule. He had been an "activist," he was clearly "progressive," and he could be trusted, it was assumed, to defend the new regime.

He was well built, fit from hiking and jogging, and six feet tall. The People's Movement at first wanted him to be part of the emerging People's Militia squads, but he disliked strong-arm tactics and so was assigned instead to the education committee. There he thought up slogans, composed political broadsheets, and discovered how quickly one could translate single-issue anger into almost fanatical support for a broad political cause.

Richfield was only twenty-eight, and his job in the Protocol Department gave him access to some of the most interesting people and events in the New Era. He wasn't listed by the Public Security Bureau or People's Militia as a "watchable," and none of his close friends or relatives had been in trouble or gone off to the Constitutionalists in the West. Better yet, he didn't think he was on any of the Constitutionalist hit lists. After all, he was a small fry, and although the city was crawling with Constitutionalist agents, he didn't think he was important enough for anyone to want to do him harm. As assistant adviser for protocol, his rank was technically quite low. What made his job fun was his access to the National Executive Committee of the People's Movement in Rockefeller Center and to the Russian Kommandatura on Governor's Island. He had a laid-back personality and liked people; much of his time was spent smoothing feathers that had been ruffled in the infighting between the factions of the coalition that constituted the People's Movement.

Douglas could also count on some extra perks because of his position: additional ration coupons if he or his friends were in need of life's ordinary, trivial necessities—coffee, sugar, fresh fruit, fresh meat, or even lightbulbs and flashlight batteries that were almost impossible to come by through normal channels. He had built up contacts in the key departments of City Hall, people who would always pass on confidential information on which stores still had these items in stock. All things considered, it wasn't much use having extra coupons if you couldn't find the things you needed.

Of course, there was a price to pay for such privileges, as there always was for any relief from the privations and anxieties of life within the People's Movement. For Richfield, that price was not the outright betrayal of his friends and associates, as it was, for example, in the case of PSB informers. But it was a tedious burden neverthe-less. Part of the obligation for his comfortable City Hall position re-quired him to spend hours propping up the public facade of the regime's official activities: parades, cultural minority conventions, rallies to denounce the bad -isms (sexism, racism, culturalism, etc.), and welcoming ceremonies for sympathetic groups and political del-egations from abroad. City Hall functionaries were required to at-tend all public events. Those who failed to show were reported to their supervisors for punitive action.

Loud peals of deep-throated laughter now caught his attention on the other side of Fifth Avenue, toward the Grand Army Plaza. They seemed to come from a cluster of turquoise military greatcoats and peaked caps. *Interesting,* Douglas thought, *Russian officers.* As far as he could tell there were six or seven, and two or three were red-faced from what had probably been a long, liquid lunch with People's Movement officials at the Plaza. The hotel was favored by the regime as a lodging for important foreign delegations. It was probably the only place in New York where you could find a decent steak, and salads were available at any time of year. As far as Richfield could recall, this was the first time that Russian military personnel had attended a public event in uniform in Manhattan. Most of the area immediately in front of the hotel had been roped off and was now protected by a cordon of tough-looking militiamen and militiawomen in their standard leather jackets and armbands. The Russian officers were congregated behind them.

Officially, a small Russian military contingent was based in New York Harbor on Governor's Island as part of the terms of the Strate-gic Reordering Treaty that had been signed by the president the pre-vious year. The unit was in charge of coordinating and monitoring the stand-down of all American strategic nuclear facilities.

Over the officers' heads, three camera and sound crews—twelve people in all, including producers and assistants—were perched uncertainly on a makeshift scaffold some ten feet above the ground. All of them wore thick, down-filled coats with hoods that seemed to protect them from the biting wind. The street crowds were thin, embarrassingly so for a Thanksgiving Day parade, and the cameras were uncertain as to what they should be showing. Most

New Yorkers had tired of the endless security checks imposed by the militia. The bombings of buildings by Constitutionalist agents early on in the war had made people wary of unnecessary travel in the city. Moreover, at one or two earlier parades in New York and Washington, Constitutionalist sympathizers had pushed up subversive placards in front of the television cameras. The militia had quickly torn down these signs of protest and arrested and beaten the protesters. It made for a certain tension.

The Russian officers were craning their heads up Fifth Avenue now, and Richfield saw all three television crews swing their cameras in the same direction. The buzz of conversation in the crowd around him temporarily subsided, and between gusts of wind, Richfield caught the approaching rhythmic boom of bass drums and the rattling of side drums. It would be a minute or so before the first ranks of the marchers would come abreast of the Plaza Hotel.

As the drums got louder, Richfield was also able to pick out the melody being played by the approaching October Youth League, a zealous Maoist group. It was the "Internationale," the anthem of Marxist revolutionaries for more than a century. The front ranks of the marchers were behind the band, which was itself preceded by three police cars abreast with flashing lights and two single files of twelve PSB officers each on both sides of the road. Behind them were about thirty marchers, most wearing leather jackets or trench coats, all bearing the blue armband of the militia.

Richfield watched them closely as they approached. They instantly reminded him of two photographs he had seen before the civil war. One had been in a pictorial history of the U.S. in the 1960s and showed a paunchy southern sheriff standing in a street and blocking the way of a civil rights march. Sunglasses had concealed the eyes, but Richfield had been struck by the paunch, the arrogant set of the jaw, and the near-smile playing at the corners of the man's mouth. The other photo had been in a book about Soviet Jewish refuseniks in the 1970s. The poorly focused, grainy picture had obviously been taken in a hurry and furtively. Yet the faces had stood out like arabesques in marble: KGB plainclothesmen breaking up an unauthorized artists' exhibition in Kiev. There was the same arrogance, the same set of the jaw, the same sneer, and even the same paunch. *Perhaps,* Richfield wondered, *men who operated in the twilight fringes of official violence shared common genetic markers*. He suddenly felt a chill and wasn't sure if it was from the thought or the wind.

Not far behind the October Youth League came an assortment of civic groups with placards denoting their various affiliations. A group of clergy came marching by, their clerical collars contrasting sharply with the casual dress everyone else was wearing. Richfield recognized an Episcopal bishop from California and a Roman Catholic prelate from the Midwest. FAITH FOR EQUALITY, PEACE, AND JUSTICE read one of the banners carried by two young-looking priests. Just behind the priests was a contingent of television and movie stars. In the middle of the line of marchers were the two heroines from the People's Movement's quasi-official soap opera, "Our Lives and Our Future." With some skill, because there was just enough criticism of the regime in the dialogue to provide a touch of realism, the series examined tough issues that ordinary people were encountering during the civil war: the perpetual shortages, the rationing, and the endless militancy of the regime. By echoing street-level complaints and then addressing them, often with self-deprecating humor, the authorities had invented a clever device for venting discontent and addressing the serious issues behind it. The actresses were pretty and smiled unself-consciously. Douglas found himself reminded once again of his early enthusiasm for the People's Movement and for what it was trying to accomplish.

The actresses were followed by a wide variety of social groups trying to identify themselves, at least by the banners they were carrying, with the New Era: LAWYERS FOR JUSTICE AND PROGRESS, EMPLOYERS FOR FAIR WAGES, and—somewhat jarringly for Douglas—CLERGY FOR HUMAN DECENCY. Richfield was about to ask another bystander what the clergy had been advocating before they discovered human decency, but he held his tongue. Unapproved political humor that mocked any part of the program of the New Era was highly dangerous. In public, it could lead to arrest.

Richfield shivered again and pressed his arms closer to his side to keep warm. Glancing about him for a familiar face, he spotted

Esther Garcia, his boss's assistant, who had taken a conspicuous position on the General Motors Plaza closer to Fifth Avenue. She at least was dressed for the occasion, padded out with a dark-blue, down-filled coat, her black, wavy hair tucked away beneath a maroon woolen beret.

He caught her eye and she nodded at him, picking her way through the crowd toward him. She was a good soul, a Puerto Rican. Richfield could easily imagine her bustling about as a floor manager for Sears, where she had held a job in the old days. No one quite knew how she landed in New York's Protocol Department. Esther was a skillful administrator and wasn't affected by the cynicism and sourness of most of the officials with whom she worked. *Odd,* Richfield thought, *how smoothly some people had glided from good pre-civil war jobs to positions that now clearly aided the war effort of one side or other.*

"Aren't you cold?" asked Esther, as solicitous as ever, seeing him shiver.

"What does it look like?" Richfield grimaced and shook from head to toe as he answered.

"Well, at least this won't be a very long one," she replied, ignoring the sarcasm. "It's supposed to end in less than two hours."

"Right, by that time I'll be as blue as a militia armband."

"Well, Douglas," asked Esther after a silence between them, "are the Constitutionalists going to try anything today?"

"Not likely, Esther. I'll bet there are enough militia and plainclothes PSB agents to arrest everyone in midtown right now."

He looked sideways and found Esther eyeing him carefully. Where were her loyalties? She was working for an important agency of the People's Movement, but she never did more than what was needed to perform the job competently. He wondered if she despised him because of his work. Did she resent his privileges, his comfortable way of moving between City Hall, Governor's Island, and Rockefeller Center?

Esther's eyes met his glance, and she immediately broke into his thoughts. "Douglas, you're so serious today," she said with a sudden burst of laughter. "I thought you enjoyed attending parades. Isn't that what you said?" She was teasing him now, and he grinned back.

"I don't *choose* to go to any parade," he replied, "and I didn't choose to stand in a freezing cold wind to watch a Thanksgiving parade today, either. Nor did you. There are a lot of things we do that we don't choose to do."

She ignored the comment and came back with another question.

"Have you ever thought back to when all this began?"

"What do you mean, all this?"

"Douglas, you crazy man," she said with another peal of laughter. "When the civil war began, when the Gulf crisis and the Washington Uprising took place. Or the economic collapse? Don't tell me you've forgotten," she teased. "You're supposed to know all that stuff and hand it out to visiting delegations. You know," she went on, conspiratorially now, "my parents and their friends used to talk about what they were doing when Kennedy was shot, like it was the most indelible thing in their minds, something they all shared. I was only five when that happened, but it was pretty scary even for a kindergartener. A lot of my friends don't remember that. Do you suppose people talk about last year's surrender in the Gulf?"

"I don't know what people talk about," Douglas replied carefully, cordially.

"Well, I do," Esther retorted. "They talk about children and jobs and waiting in line and getting time off." Richfield knew she was deliberately provoking him now, but he let her go on. He wondered what she was getting at.

"All I mean is this: Have you ever thought how different your life would be today, if, say, there hadn't been a surrender, if there hadn't been a reordering treaty, if . . . if"—Esther momentarily stumbled, aware of the tricky path she was taking—"if all those things hadn't happened in Washington, if "—now she became almost triumphant—"if we didn't have a People's Movement?"

Richfield was perplexed, not knowing whether to be serious or laugh, not wanting to put her down or agree with her tone either. She was making fun of him in a friendly way, but he found himself feeling increasingly insecure and embarrassed. Why couldn't people mind their own business? He decided to delay his reponse.

"If you really want to know," he replied at last, in a low, patient tone, as though he were addressing a child, "I was too busy in Chicago to think much when the Washington Uprising took place. Leanna Greene was speaking to a group meeting of 'committee' representatives, and she said flatly she expected a civil war. She asked whose side we were going to be on."

"You mean Leanna Greene of the National Executive Committee?"

"Right."

"What did you say?" asked Esther, pressing her attack.

"I said I would be on the progressive side of history." Douglas reddened as he said it. It sounded phony. You said that sort of thing in political meetings, not to friends. To his relief, Esther seemed eager to tell her own story.

"I was visiting my family in Puerto Rico," she said without being asked. "My dad said he didn't think the People's Movement would be able to hold power unless someone outside helped them. He thought the Russians would probably come sooner or later. Frankly, my dad never understood the Russians. I think he still thinks they're Communist or something." She laughed. Then, more seriously, she added, "But he still talks a lot about Castro."

Esther wasn't smiling now. "He said many things that I won't tell you—except one. He said that there would be a civil war if the president ever signed a treaty with the Russians that looked like a surrender."

"When did he say that? After the Treaty of Paris?"

"No, before, in July, after the troops had gone to the Gulf but before the surrender."

"You mean he knew before August that the U.S. had lost the big one? What made him so smart?"

"His brother was shot by Castro."

There was a sting to Esther's answer that brought a chill into the conversation.

"I'm sorry," Douglas said.

"History's strange, isn't it," she resumed. "How might things have been if Hopkins hadn't been president. If Truman or even Reagan had been around? Would either of them have signed the Strategic Reordering Treaty? Would they have allowed the Russian observers at our missile and bomber bases? Do you think they would have just given in as easily as Hopkins?"

"I don't see what they could have done differently," Douglas said noncommittally. "By the end of Reagan's second term, Congress was refusing to fund any more arms programs. When Bush came in, the fall of the Soviet Union ensured massive cutbacks in defense. How could we know that the Russian military kept testing and developing new systems? With Yeltsin in charge, the military didn't seem to matter very much. Remember Senator Winfield? He was pretty eloquent when it came to streamlining our military. If *he* could support that, a conservative southern senator, what luck would a pro-military president have had?"

Just ahead of Douglas and Esther a man in the crowd quickly turned his head back, as though listening in on the conversation. To Esther, Richfield motioned toward the man with his eyes and fell silent for a while. *Great,* he thought, *you can't talk anywhere without somebody eavesdropping.* Neither Esther nor Douglas had committed any great indiscretion, or so Richfield thought.

One of the banners bobbing by suddenly caught his attention. LONG LIVE THE NEW INTERNATIONALISM, it read. It was carried by two men in the new khaki uniforms of the American People's Army. Richfield turned to Esther, who was looking at the same placard. "Have you seen that one before?" he asked quietly.

"No," she said.

"Do you think it means what I think it means?"

Esther turned her face half toward him with a curious expression on her face. "You mean like the Connies have maybe been doing a little better than we thought?"

"Right. That might also explain those turquoise greatcoats in front of the Plaza Hotel."

Esther knew what he was implying. She knew of the rumors that the National Executive Committee was debating asking the Russians for military assistance. For all their zeal, the regular army soldiers who had come over to the People's Movement and the hastily trained troops raised from the inner-city poor had proved no match for the steady professionals of the U.S. Army who had followed Lucius Hodges from Fort Hood, Texas, to the West. The Maoist radicals in the People's Movement had promised to raise and train a new army employing Chinese-style guerrilla tactics—"an army of the

27

people for the people," as the catch phrase went—but no one had devised a strategy capable of trouncing first-rate, highly motivated troops.

"I don't know," Esther said, responding to Richfield's allusion to the Russian officers. Then she asked, as though she were changing the subject, "Do you know if the Chinese are attending the parade today?"

"You mean their U.N. mission?"

"Yes."

"Of course. Every U.N. delegation has sent representatives. Well, almost every one. The Japanese have rather prominent places this time, by the way. They sent their foreign minister. Rather interesting. The Israelis all came down with the flu, which seems to afflict them regularly around Thanksgiving and whenever a parade is scheduled. The Canadians came up with some excuse or other. Rather bold of them, I think. As for the Chinese, I saw a seating plan for them on the reviewing stand at Rockefeller Center. Why shouldn't they show up?"

Esther leaned her head coquettishly to one side and didn't immediately answer. She looked sideways at Richfield and smiled mischievously.

"Douglas," she said with mock seriousness, "promise you won't get me into trouble if I tell you why I asked?"

"Quit it, Esther," he said. "We've run through most of the world at different times, but I can't recall ever laying a bureaucratic trip on you before. What's up?"

"The friendship treaty, Douglas."

"Oh, yeah, that treaty," he said with a false laugh. He hadn't a clue what she was talking about, but he decided to see if he could bluff his way through. "Didn't they ratify that last week?" It was a wild stab—and completely off target.

"Noooo, they haven't signed it yet. Not ours. We don't have one with the Chinese—and we aren't likely to get one. Our revolutionaries don't trust them for abandoning Maoism. And the Russians . . . Moscow desperately wants Beijing to join Russia and the People's America in an alliance that would also attract the Japanese. The Russians are wooing them like they're the boss's daughter. I don't know how much of this is true. It came my way from a friend of a friend. Just letting you know in advance, okay?"

"Sure, go ahead."

"She says someone she knows saw a copy of the *Jerusalem Post* from about a week ago. According to the story the Russians have been having talks with the Chinese in Moscow. Something about spheres of influence over Australia and New Zealand. The *Post* also said that it seemed the Chinese don't think the American People's Army is doing very well out West against Hodges. The Chinese keep asking the Russians why they haven't used nuclear weapons against the Constitutionalists or the provisional government in Hawaii. All the Russians say is that it's not their policy to use nuclear weapons. The Chinese evidently believe that the Connies may have some strategic missiles in Hawaii or even a missile submarine or two."

Just then, Esther nudged Richfield with her elbow. "Douglas," she whispered, "look over to your right. Bremer's here."

Alarmed by the earlier eavesdropper and Esther's tone, Richfield began to feel uneasy. As casually as he could, he turned his head and, sure enough, Bremer was just a few feet away, almost within earshot, watching them both with a silly kind of smile on his face.

Bremer, senior protocol adviser, was seldom without his smile. Early in life he had discovered it was a powerful weapon to keep others on the defensive. They learned quickly that it seldom meant friendliness and masked a whole array of other thoughts. Was he being cheerful, cynical, or just sneering? Sometimes it was hard, no, impossible to tell. Genuinely good-natured people felt uncomfortable in Bremer's presence, quickly discerning his insincerity. The smile kept people off-balance. Was the obviously concealed hostility toward them, others, or just the world in general?

Douglas and most of Bremer's colleagues had learned to be completely impassive when Bremer was around, neither humoring the man nor provoking him. It was the best defense against his dangerous hostility. Esther alone had shown the courage to be indignant at Bremer, rejecting his clumsy advances with a loud Latin flourish.

As soon as he saw that Douglas and Esther had spotted him, Bremer edged toward them through the crowd.

"A great day for confidential tête-à-têtes, isn't it?" he said in his most unctuous voice, the false grin glued to his mouth like dentures. "I'm glad to see you're both here, but where's your enthusiasm, your attention? Did you see the October Youth League? Weren't they terrific?"

Douglas resented Bremer's way of posing questions that forced people either to agree with him or sound awkwardly at variance with his view. He decided to ignore the question.

"Walter," he replied jovially, "aren't you freezing? Even in this windbreaker I'm shivering."

"Yeah, it's cold all right. But you haven't answered me. What about that band? Stunning, don't you think?"

"To be frank, Walter, I couldn't see very much of the parade from here. There are a lot of people in front."

Bremer frowned but didn't pursue the issue. He nudged closer, squeezed between them, put his arms around them, and pulled the three of them into a conspiratorial huddle. Douglas forced himself not to wince. He noticed Esther instinctively draw back, too. Bremer had been drinking, and the bourbon was stale on his breath.

"This is for your ears only," he said, his voice barely a murmur. "The PSB says there's a special alert out in Manhattan today for someone the People's authorities and our Russian friends have been trying to locate for months. I think you two need to know because, if this nasty guy is in the neighborhood, the PSB wants him picked up without advertising his arrest. D'you get me?"

"If he's such a troublemaker," Douglas rather rashly interjected, "why don't they just track him down?"

"Because there's a lot of antipopular elements around this city that might want to stop him from getting arrested. I'll tell you this much. He's dangerous, and we could probably shorten the war if he were caught. He's been hiding somewhere in Manhattan, the PSB thinks, and they're close. They think he'll try to get out of the city. But let's just say he's very, very difficult to hide."

"Why?" asked Richfield involuntarily.

"Because he's got a very bad limp. An old war wound. He's pretty easy to spot on the street."

"Who is he, Walter?" It was Esther speaking. Momentarily charmed by the closeness generated by his huddle, Bremer replied immediately. "Marcus. Daniel Marcus. But this is absolutely, 100 percent confidential. No one is going to hear this name other than you two, and if it gets out that you've told anyone, you'll both get one-way tickets to Alaska, or worse, I promise you. Fact is, he's probably moving around under a whole dictionary of aliases."

Douglas desperately wanted to get away from Bremer. The man's bourbon breath was nauseating. "Walter," he said as benignly as he could, "this is intriguing, but do you think we could talk about it away from all these people? It's awkward around here."

"Good idea. Let's move back to the doorway." So saying, he turned around and walked back with them to the showroom window of the General Motors Building.

"Walter," Douglas asked, as all three looked at the sole car in the showroom, "what's so special about this guy? The city's full of Constitutionalist agents. They're being hauled in all the time."

"I'll tell you what's so special about him. The PSB thinks he's a gold mine of information on the pre-civil war Ohio-class submarine program. That's all I can say for now. Think the Russkies accounted for all the subs in the old U.S. Navy? Think again. Marcus may know a thing or two, if you follow me. It might do wonders for your careers if you could help bring the guy in."

"I see," said Douglas, eager to end Bremer's lecture. "The trick is to pick the guy up without a fuss and with as few people as possible knowing about it? Okay, but what happens if we spot him? Do we try to wrestle him to the ground or just whistle for the nearest militia patrol?"

Walter looked at Richfield sharply, not sure whether he was being made fun of. He sneered, "Douglas, it's not worth your job or your life to mess up a scene with Marcus. If you see him, keep a safe distance and just follow him. He'll probably have friends covering him. Find out where he goes and phone the PSB. But not just any number— this one." He handed a piece of paper to Richfield. "The militia are not always the smartest citizens of the New Era. There's a good chance they'd bungle it, and they're not above being bribed."

"What makes you think either of us is likely to spot this man?" Richfield asked sharply.

"No one is likely to spot him, but the PSB figures that with his heavy limp, if he's moving across town, he's likely to do so where the crowds are thicker and he's not so noticeable. It's a guess, of course, but you two are pretty centrally located in Manhattan. If nothing happens, forget I ever told you about him and don't ever mention him again. Even to me. Bye. Enjoy the parade." With that, he grinned smugly and sauntered slowly off through the crowd down Fifth Avenue.

"Yuck," Esther burst out when Bremer was safely out of earshot. "That man makes me sick. What does he think we are, spare-time spycatchers during holiday parades? Do you think I'm going to creep around New York looking for guys with a limp and then go rushing off to phone up some PSB spook?"

"Easy, Esther, take it easy," Douglas said quietly but hastily. "I don't like Bremer any more than you do—"

"What do you care about him?" Esther testily interrupted. "Has he tried to get you into his apartment for a political talk? He just makes me sick."

Richfield was silent. He didn't like it that Esther was getting angry and raising her voice. It could get them both into trouble if someone were eavesdropping.

The parade was ending and the final tired, bedraggled groups were heading past with neither the strains of a band nor the curiosity of the crowd to egg them on. The spectators had thinned out considerably, and the ubiquitous militia squads were less in evidence. There was no sign of Bremer, and Richfield, scanning the faces of those around him, saw no one he recognized. He judged it was close enough to the time when he could legitimately quit the field and return to his warm apartment.

He decided to make his way through the Fifty-eighth Street checkpoint. He could walk to Lexington and take the subway to Seventy-second Street. He detested the subway, but it seemed a better alternative than walking in this chilly weather. He wasn't sure why he disliked the subway so much, but he thought it had to do, ironically, with the improvements the People's Movement had brought to it. Subway crime was almost nonexistent because there were both on-duty and off-duty militia on every train and, sometimes, it seemed in every car. Muggers or thieves of any kind weren't just arrested; they were first beaten and then arrested. Thus, the New York subway was now safer and cleaner than it had probably been in its century-long existence. But Richfield was uncomfortable on the subway, due in part to the unwritten rule of silence that had descended upon the system. In the old days, you avoided danger by avoiding eye contact with strangers, lest a glance evoke a physical confrontation. But at least friends talked to one another. Now, as the trains rattled and boomed their way through the tunnels under the city, nobody talked. And the silence was oppressive. Still, esthetically, New York City under the People's Movement was a vast improvement from the old days.

Along with the virtual elimination of street crime had come the complete disappearance of graffiti. Of course, there were practical political reasons for this. Since the civil war had begun, graffiti was no longer just resentful, angry markings by poor people in places of maximum public visibility. It was also often politically subversive. On balance Richfield thought he preferred the city in its People's Movement guise.

On his way out of Fifth Avenue, Douglas thought the south sidewalk of Fifty-eighth Street looked freer of pedestrians than his own side, and he started to cross the street. Traffic, of course, had been sealed off hours earlier. There was a pleasant, almost relaxed mood in the streets running into Fifth Avenue. The absence of cars and trucks and the usual pedestrian throngs cut the city down to a more humane, habitable size.

Before he had gone more than a few yards, a roar of shouting and singing suddenly ricocheted out from a knot of a dozen or so young men on the north side of the General Motors Plaza, several yards from where Richfield had been standing to review the parade. The sudden noise of their voices startled the others on the street, too. Conversation halted, heads turned.

From the sound of it the men were drunk. Yet, if so, how had they managed to remain so sober until this moment? During his entire conversation with Esther there had been no hint of drinking or

33

rowdiness close by. Bremer would certainly have noticed it—and probably reported it—if there had been. People drank a lot in private, but in public it was plain stupid to appear drunk. The "committees" were harsher on drugs, street crime, and public drunkenness than on almost anything else. As on the subways, the militia attacked first, then arrested, then interrogated. "It's not Miranda's laws," National Executive Committee Secretary Northwood had once said after a number of complaints about militia brutality, "but then it was only the rich and their lackeys who got anything out of that legalistic morass anyway. If it keeps the streets safe, people will accept it."

The drunks were boisterous now, picking mock arguments with each other and hurling insults to four militiamen standing on the other side of the street. All four immediately approached the group and ordered them to be quiet. But the shouting didn't abate. In fact, if anything, the mockery of the militia became more ribald.

The militiamen lost their tempers. Drawing their nightsticks, they charged into the throng and tried to seize the ringleader of the shouting. But the man's companions, warmly dressed and apparently quite drunk, responded with obscenities and a belligerence that sent the militiamen reeling. As whistles blew and radios crackled with calls for reinforcements, other nearby militia groups, New York police, and plainclothes PSB agents came running to the General Motors Plaza. The troublemakers were attacked by some twenty or so law enforcement officers, most of them militia toughs using their nightsticks.

Though the drunken youths fought back with a verve and skill that sent several of their blue-armbanded assailants flying, it was not a fair match. In minutes the sheer numbers of the militia had overwhelmed the rioting youths. The shouting died down almost as quickly as it had started and was replaced by low curses and groans. The troublemakers, beaten unconscious or tightly handcuffed, lay upon the pavement like beached whales, surrounded by panting militia. There was blood on the plaza. Several militia were injured and sitting or lying nearby, attended to by their comrades.

Richfield had kept his distance when the fight broke out. He had seen the militia in action before and had no wish to be around when they were fighting anyone. As the crowd quickly scattered away from the fracas, he moved back onto the sidewalk of Fifty-eighth Street. He thought it likely that the authorities would cordon off several blocks around the incident as soon as they could, and he didn't want to get caught in it. If he moved quickly enough, he might be able to pass through the checkpoint halfway down Fifty-eighth Street before the barricades went up. He was confident his Kommandatura pass and the parade pass would ease his way through the checkpoint even if the militia were now more vigilant because of the incident. He was cold, tired, and depressed. He wanted to get home as quickly as he could.

So, evidently, did others. Barely ten yards in front of him, an elderly couple was shuffling along as quickly as they could in the same direction. As the three of them came up to the two lines of trestle barricades sealing off the street and the sidewalk, the oddity of the situation struck Richfield forcefully. The narrow gap in the barricade, barely large enough for one person to squeeze through, was unguarded. It was clear why: the two militiamen who had been on duty there had sprinted off to join their comrades battling it out at the General Motors Plaza.

The elderly couple passed the barricades and accelerated from a shuffle to a surprisingly brisk stride for two people presumably in their sixties or seventies. Curious, Douglas quickened his own pace, came abreast of them, and started to engage them in friendly conversation.

"Not a good idea to get caught in a street fight, is it?" he said by way of an opener. The elderly man, nearer him, looked irritatedly at Richfield for a moment but didn't respond. The woman all but jumped as she walked when Richfield was abreast of her and speaking. She was clutching her companion's arm but turned her face fully toward Douglas after he had spoken. The features were even, the eyes dark and set deeply in her face. A lock of thick, salt-and-pepper hair had escaped from beneath the brim of a willowy green hat and was bobbing on her forehead as she walked. But it was her eyebrows that caught Richfield by surprise. They were thick and bushy, more like a man's than a woman's.

A few seconds passed as Douglas continued to walk with the couple, wondering whether to leave them alone or pursue the attempted conversation. He decided not to embarrass them and dropped back a few yards. As he did so, it occurred to him that the elderly lady wasn't moving at all like most women her age would. Her stride was long, the clutch of her arm on her companion seemed awkward. She was, well, odd. Then, as all three turned left on Madison toward Fifty-ninth Street, it suddenly struck Richfield what else was odd about the woman. Despite her brisk pace she was quite clearly limping.

A few seconds later it all came together for Richfield. Bremer's words came tumbling back into his mind. Of course, the *limp*.

Marcus. It had to be. The woman didn't look like an old woman, much less walk like one. Bremer, more cunning than he seemed, had even said something about a diversion. Obviously, the whole point of the drunken troublemakers challenging the militia had been to draw the militiamen away from the checkpoints and enable Marcus and his companion to pass through them unchallenged. The Constitutionalists must have wanted to protect Marcus at any cost, Richfield thought, if they were prepared to put twelve of their number at risk to help him get away.

Richfield knew what Bremer expected him to do. It would be the simplest matter to slip to a call box, dial the number on Bremer's piece of paper, and let the PSB do the rest. But something in Richfield told him not only not to do that, but to stay with the "couple" as long as he could without compromising his identity or rousing their suspicions. Perhaps it was the distaste for the militia he had felt when they waded into the gang of rowdy, drunken youths. Perhaps it was just an exhaustion with political obligations, with the perpetual psychological pressure to be vigilant on behalf of the regime. Richfield knew that he wasn't going to call Bremer's number just yet.

They were already halfway up the block to Fifty-ninth Street when Richfield made his decision, and he deliberately allowed the disguised Marcus and his companion to gain a distance on him. He crossed to the other side of Madison and moved up in tandem with the posing couple. He carefully dodged into a store when the couple crossed the avenue a few moments later and went around the corner, east along Fifty-ninth Street. As soon as they were out of sight,

Richfield quickly headed for the same intersection and followed. His pulse was racing now, as though he himself were on the run rather than the limping fugitive in front of him, the most wanted man in the files of the PSB.

But as Richfield rounded the corner after the couple, he froze. Marcus and his companion had gone only about twenty yards up the block, but they had been stopped by two militia as part of an apparently random and arbitrary check of pedestrians. Marcus himself seemed to be reacting to the confrontation in a low-key manner, his tapping left foot the only indication of any nervousness. But the companion, instead of quietly submitting to the check and handing the documents that presumably had been forged well enough to get by, was becoming argumentative and blustery. Edging as inconspicuously as possible up to within a few feet of them, Richfield tried to look casual in order to allay any suspicions by the militiamen. The smaller and younger of the two militiamen was attempting, with surprising good nature, to mollify the "old man," Marcus's companion, and to prevent the altercation from becoming more serious.

"I don't care who you think you are, where you say you're going, or how old you are," the more senior militiaman was saying, "let's see some identification."

"And I don't care who *you* are," the elderly man replied, "because you don't have the right to stop citizens on the street without grounds and subject them to an interrogation."

"See this," said the militiaman with a sneer, pointing to his blue armband. "This means People's Militia. I can do what I like to people like you who want to play a street lawyer's game. Now show me some I.D.—NOW!" An angry militiaman meant only one thing: The scene was going to get ugly real fast.

The next sequence of events occurred so quickly that even Richfield, who was within feet of the scene, couldn't recall later exactly how it unfolded. Probably both militiamen feared that Marcus and his companion were armed. As the elderly man began to reach into his jacket, the militiaman suddenly pulled out his pistol, jumped into a crouch position with the weapon aimed at him, and shouted "Freeze!"

37

Had he been just three feet further away, Marcus's companion would have been forced to comply. But the militiaman was too close, and his adversary swung out the hand that had reached into his jacket, grabbed the pistol's barrel in one sweeping move, and tried to pull it from the militiaman. Two shots cracked out in rapid succession. The man crumpled slowly to the ground. "Run, man, for God's sake run," he shouted hoarsely before a third shot smashed into his chest and silenced him. Marcus, suddenly jolted from his pose of cronelike passivity by the shots, tried to gallop away as fast as his limp would permit him. To Douglas he seemed to be skittering with remarkable agility, grabbing at his dress to help him run faster and swinging his arms wildly to increase his speed.

He almost made it to the corner of Park Avenue where he could have dodged out of the line of fire, at least for a few more seconds. But the older militiaman had become deadly calm during the second or two that Marcus had made his run. Quickly and professionally adjusting his crouch, he drew a careful bead on the skittering fugitive and fired three more shots in succession. Long skirt billowing, willowy green hat tumbling, arms flailing futilely for support as he careened through the air, Marcus fell with a terrible clattering thud onto the sidewalk.

When the first shots rang out, Douglas had not run or dived for cover as others around him did. Oblivious to any sense of personal danger, he found himself running hard on the heels of the two militiamen to the spot where Marcus was now lying, face down, a dark puddle spreading rapidly out from his chest and head. The militiamen were panting from exertion and combat fear, and Richfield's own heart was thumping wildly in his chest. The smaller of the two men turned Marcus over, feeling for a pulse, and then searched the pockets for some identification. "Some chick," he said with a disgusted sarcasm as the angular sprawl of Marcus's body made it obvious that the corpse was a man in woman's clothing. "Damn fool," was all the other man would say. "Damn fool."

"Sure, Jim, it was pretty stupid of him to try to take your gun. But we may not have been so smart dropping him like that. You think this pair was just some ordinary gay couple taking a stroll across town 'cause there's nothing better to do on Thanksgiving? And they just got nervous because they don't like being pestered by the People's Militia? No way. I'll bet my next paycheck that we've gotten a fugitive here, probably with connections to the Connies. How's the other guy? He still alive?"

They both looked back at the body of Marcus's companion, now lying as immobile as the paving stones on which he lay.

"Fat chance," said Jim. "I dropped him with three shots from about three feet. Hey, you!"—and he spun around to talk to Richfield, who had been listening to the exchange from just behind them both. "If you don't want the same medicine, get out of here!"

Douglas obediently backed away, turned slowly around, and walked back toward Madison as calmly as his shaking legs would let him. A safe distance off, he turned around again to look back at the scene. The militiamen were now rifling through the pockets of Marcus's companion. Douglas watched for a minute, then leaned against a doorway trying to decide what to do. His only impulse was to move as far away from the scene of the shootings as quickly as he could.

But he tried to leave too late. Two police cars, lights flashing, now blocked the street in front of him, and nobody was being allowed through without showing their credentials and giving their accounts of what had been seen. Turning around, he saw that the two militiamen still completing their initial investigation of the dead suspects had themselves been joined by a trio of plainclothesmen.

Richfield cursed under his breath and resumed a careful and deliberate walk toward the two police cruisers parked across the road. One by one a small knot of pedestrians was being funneled through a makeshift checkpoint. As his turn came around, Douglas reached into his windbreaker with a slow, casual movement that he had practiced innumerable times. From a special pocket he pulled a laminated identity card that he kept separate from his regular credentials. As the policeman scowled routinely at him and the other pedestrians moving through the checkpoint, Richfield pulled out the larger-than-usual document and placed it with gravity in the officer's hands. The thick, purple letters were in both Russian and English: KOMMANDATURA ONLY.

3

The Library

*R*ichfield gazed up at the great portico of the New York Public Library. At the top of the twenty-seven steps and stretched out a hundred feet between the two bronze lions lay John Jacob Astor's greatest gift to the world: eleven million books, a legacy of nations and cultures both ancient and modern, a repository of human wisdom and folly.

Douglas had always loved this building with its solid, Edwardian grandeur and the exhilarating sense of intellectual freedom and opportunity he had always associated with it. Sometimes, while researching for the University of Chicago Ph.D. that he had never completed, he had stopped by the library on visits to New York. He'd been fascinated, as generations of sociology majors before him had, with Marx's theory of alienation, and the New York Public Library had a rich treasury of secondary literature on the subject. The South Reading Room for Richfield exuded at times an almost intoxicating sense of the power of knowledge and intelligence.

But the People's Movement had not felt so warmly toward the institution from the moment it had taken over the city fifteen months earlier. Most of the eleven-member National Executive Committee could find no good reason for closing the institution. After all, though some of them seemed obsessed with the idea of revolution, there was enough lingering dislike of old-style dictatorships among the others to make them uncomfortable with introducing crude censorship into American life. "Reactionaries should be permitted to study, even publish," Elroy Robinson, vice-chair of

41

the National Executive Committee and commander of the People's Militia, had said in an early meeting of the coalition's leaders. "If they study, they may learn a little about the grotesque system we've just abolished. If they publish some antipopular ideas for a small group of readers, it won't affect the masses, and our activists will just be more on their toes philosophically and tactically." So at first the library had been kept open.

What caused the authorities to change their attitude was not an outpouring of anti-People's Movement books; not one had appeared so far. The local "committees" that supervised the printing plants saw to that. Rather, it was the library's transformation into a subtle bastion of intellectual subversion against the authorities. Readers left neatly folded notes denouncing the regime in the books they borrowed. Librarians went out of their way to suggest titles that contradicted the philosophy of the New Era. Worse, from a security point of view, the Public Security Bureau was convinced that Constitutionalist agents were using the library as a drop-off point. A note would be left between preagreed pages of an obscure, out-of-date reference volume, for example, and the contact would know where to find it. So passes were required for all users, just to keep tabs on the ebb and flow of people through the building. Everyone had to register upon entering. In addition PSB agents posed as readers to monitor the activities of the users. Stan Rutledge, chair of the National Executive Committee, had even devised a glib rationalization for the restrictions. "There is absolutely nothing sacred about freedom of information," he said, "when it can be used to undermine social progress."

The library remained open for the same number of hours each week as before, but the registration requirement and the need to have a pass in order to use the library had discouraged many people from coming. Also, as a result of the Great Cleanup, the same sweeping purge of New York that had eliminated crime from the subway, the front terrace had been cleared of the flotsam and jetsam of New York citizenry that used to frequent it. To obtain a pass one needed authorization from a local "committee" or a bona fide scholarly or professional institution. Applicants then had to be photographed, intimidatingly in the Public Security Bureau's Intelligence Division in the downtown Municipal Building. Technically, virtually anyone could obtain a pass, excepting felons and fugitives, but few people were willing to brave the intimidating procedure.

Douglas had a pass, of course. The Protocol Department could get him virtually any privilege except those limited to an exceptionally high level. But it brought a knot to his stomach to walk up these steps under the view of two sour-faced militiamen at the top of the terrace and without the comforting presence of the swirl of indolent humanity that in happier times had frequented the entryway.

Douglas took a deep breath and made his way toward the entrance, a shabby brown briefcase in hand. He was stopped routinely by a militiaman who asked for his I.D. and library permit and wanted to look inside his briefcase. It was a cursory inspection; the real examination would come inside the building itself.

Rain from an autumnal squall had splattered the marble floor just inside the heavy glass doors. Dirty gray footprints had been tracked in all directions from the center of the main lobby. Douglas noticed this even before he was stopped at a chest-high table just inside the main doors. Two officials sat behind it. A thin wooden screen extending from the floor to the edge of the table concealed from visitors the PSB photographs of wanted or suspected Constitutionalist agents, as well as an alarm button and a pistol resting on a small shelf just above knee level. The height of the table was deliberate: it gave the officials an initial psychological advantage over all but extremely tall visitors to the building.

The screen in front of the table was joined to a wooden barrier that extended in a rough semicircle around the entrance doors, cupping them, as if to protect the library from the unwelcome. A narrow passage through the wooden barrier to the right of the examination table was controlled by an electrically operated wooden arm.

Richfield stood in front of the table and found himself looking up at a surly woman in a blue workshirt. As he reached into his briefcase for the documents he needed, he noted her appearance more closely. Her hair fell severely down both sides of her face from a part in the middle and was cropped just below the ears. No one would ever accuse her of "lookism," the epithet sometimes hissed at women and even men who dressed too fashionably in public.

To the woman's left, fidgeting back and forth on his stool, was a pimply young Hispanic with long, dirty hair and sideburns. Dandruff lay scattered on the collar and shoulders of his denim jacket, which bore the Red Stars, the new flag of the People's Movement, fifty stars outlined in white on a blue background. He seemed uncertain whether to continue reading a copy of the regime's own daily, *The People's Voice,* or pay attention to the library's sparse flow of visitors.

"What's the poypose of your visit to the librerry?" the woman said in her best Brooklynese.

"Research for a political discussion at City Hall," Douglas replied slowly. In these situations it was best to speak confidently and with a certain arrogance.

"I.D.," she demanded.

Richfield pulled out the red plastic internal I.D., which the People's Movement had issued to everyone in its area of control, and his approved library card. He decided not to produce his Kommandatura pass for the time being. He made a point of wearing an indifferent, impersonal expression.

"What is the subject of your political research?" asked Cropped Hair as she handed the passport to Pimply Face to double-check. She was beginning to practice the boring-in approach. Richfield felt sweat beads form on his forehead and upper lip. He scratched his neck and replied, "We're studying Marx's writings about New York and America during the civil war period. We're working up a new sociology of New York in the New Era."

"Well, what kinds of books are you going to be looking at?" the woman asked.

"Marx's works, secondary sources on Marx, discussions of the theory of the Asiatic mode of production, that sort of thing," he replied.

"The Asiatic mode of production? That's a lie about Marx that revisionists and reactionaries have been trying to peddle to show that Marx's theories were not universal. What's that got to do with New York City, anyway?" She was sneering again.

"Well, it's just possible," Douglas responded, sweating with both fury and nervousness now, "that Marx's writings about America may have made the same kinds of distinctions between

44

American bourgeois society and European bourgeois society that he made between European feudalism and the Asiatic mode of production."

"That's totally speculative," said the woman. "Don't they know that in City Hall?"

Inwardly, something was snapping in Richfield. From her own brand of revolutionary zeal, this militant was essentially defining what was and what was not legitimate scholarly research. But he decided not to argue. If he did, he might not get into the library at all.

He shrugged. "Well, I'm the only one who's actually studied Marx in an academic setting before, so I was asked to provide the research framework for the project."

Cropped Hair looked at him coolly, deciding whether to pursue the topic. She decided not to.

"Sign here," she ordered. "Your I.D. and library card numbers, too." Richfield picked up the ballpoint and filled out the requisite information in the registration book.

On cue Pimply Face pressed a button under the table and the electronic arm retracted.

It was a long, slow walk from the main lobby to the reading room on the third floor. Douglas was careful neither to hurry nor dawdle. Either action might draw the attention of the militiamen who were patrolling every floor of the library.

Once in the reading room he headed straight for the card catalog. He could have used the computerized index, but there were problems with it. Library users were sometimes monitored. And the electronic catalog didn't let you browse through different titles and authors the way you could with the card index.

If Richfield had enjoyed anything about his graduate research at the University of Chicago, it had been the very freedom to speculate which the uncouth gatekeeper was now telling him was unacceptable. What right did this woman or anyone else have to dictate dogmatically what academic theories were or were not true? Douglas had taken it for granted that the regime would not interfere either in the topics people studied or in the theories accepted currently in any given academic area. Now he was truly irritated. It was hard, if not impossible, now to research his assigned topic with any sense of confidence or pride. He was angry, and a prickly heat was spreading up his back and over his shoulders.

He was so engrossed in his continuing annoyance and with trying to focus his mind once more on his research project, that at first he didn't notice what was going on around him. There were probably about thirty readers in the room, and there had been the usual low buzz of conversation between the staff at the central desk and people making inquiries. But now a complete hush had descended upon the room. He looked up to see everyone's attention directed to a red-faced information clerk and a young woman. A loud and nasty altercation had just broken out between them. Richfield was only a few feet from the clerk, who was facing him, and heard everything the man was saying. As other readers paused to eavesdrop, the woman's voice became audible too.

"I don't care what organization you belong to," the clerk was saying in a whining tone, "if they won't let you have this book in the South Hall, there is nothing we can do about it here. You're not authorized to use it!"

From where Richfield was leaning over the catalog drawers, all he could see of the woman was straight, brunette hair descending to her shoulders, a dark brown raincoat, and calf-high boots. Douglas guessed that she was probably in her early twenties.

"Listen," she said, her voice low and clear, but rising now with anger, "this book is in the card catalog. There is absolutely nothing on the card that says it is restricted for public security reasons or that only committee activists and others are permitted to read it. Your own regulations say—here, read them!"—and she thrust a copy of the standard "Instructions to Readers" in front of the clerk's face— "that *all* library resources are available to readers except those in the special collections. So why am I being denied access? Am I a criminal, a Constitutionalist spy?"

"You better watch your mouth around here, lady." The clerk's face became blotchy and his hands trembled. "We've got our own rules in this library, and we aren't going to bend them for you. If you want to argue, I'll call the militia and have you removed."

The woman suddenly stiffened at this, and Richfield wondered if she were going to hit him. Richfield knew the clerk could activate

an alarm from the library floor and summon militia and PSB agents.
He could tell them that a deliberate provocation was being staged by
enemy agents. The PSB would likely seal off the entire library. The
readers would not be permitted to leave until the PSB was satisfied
with their identification and proved their innocence of any possible
wrongdoing. Suddenly Douglas's rage at having his research questioned and at the imposition of *any* restrictions to information and
knowledge went off in him. It was outrageous that a free, public library should have control over what could and could not be used by
ordinary readers.

Impulsively, he closed the card catalog drawer and strode confidently toward the information desk and the clerk. He pulled out his
Kommandatura pass, holding it up just long enough for the clerk to
see the purple word "Kommandatura" but not actually handing it
over for inspection.

"Kommandatura, Municipal Protocol, Richfield," Douglas said
slowly and in a low voice, facing the clerk and paying no attention to
the girl. "I'm very sorry to interrupt you, sir," he said, "but it's essential that there be no disturbance in this library." He leaned forward
so his whisper would be audible only to the clerk and the young
woman. "We have certain elements under surveillance," he said with
just the right mixture of gravity and conspiratorial friendliness. "As
for you, committee member"—and he turned for the first time to
face the woman squarely—"you must leave the library now. I'll have
to make a routine report on this incident. If you don't leave immediately, I'm afraid you may be arrested and questioned. Please follow
me."

With that he curtly nodded to the woman and the clerk, turned
on his heel, and walked briskly toward the door.

The clerk looked stunned and uncertain. The woman seemed
startled for a moment, but on seeing the clerk's hesitancy she quickly
regained her composure. Pausing only to look at Richfield, she
turned around and followed Douglas out of the catalog room.

For an agonizing moment Richfield wasn't sure whether his
ploy would work. Should the woman or the clerk openly challenge
his credentials, he knew that both he and she would be in serious
trouble, especially him.

But she didn't hesitate. As Richfield turned the corner, he heard the swish of her nylon raincoat as she strode to catch up with him.

He didn't dare turn around to look at her. His heart was pounding furiously as he approached the checkpoint and Cropped Hair and Pimply Face.

To his relief they were both hunched over the papers of another prospective library user. The exit on the right-hand side of the lobby was only a magnetic book detector and a guard who examined purses and briefcases.

As Richfield pushed the door release bar to leave the building, he turned around to take a quick look back. The woman was only a few feet behind him and was holding up her purse for the guard's examination. She gave no indication of any connection with Douglas, but as he walked slowly ahead, he heard her high-heel shoes on the library's front steps following him down to Fifth Avenue.

Richfield turned north toward Forty-second Street, waited for the pedestrian light, and crossed over to a store window on the street facing the north end of the library. He stopped and watched the reflection of the storefront glass to see whether the woman was still there. She was. She was walking slowly, trying not to overtake him. A surveillance expert wouldn't suspect that the two had anything to do with each other.

Douglas's pulse was still racing. He was nauseated at the thought of being involved in yet another public dragnet of possible suspicious persons. But some affronted sense of justice and truth had also surfaced. There was something heinous in telling people what kind of academic research they could or could not do in a library specifically made available to the public.

From his quick glance at the woman's face in the library, Richfield had noticed that she was very pretty. From all appearances she didn't suspect him of an elaborate attempt at picking her up. There were as many compulsive philanderers in New York under the People's Movement as there had been in earlier times. They were just less open about it. Virtually none of them would risk a labor camp in Alaska just to pick up a woman in a place as closely watched as the library, no matter how attractive she might be.

Douglas wondered about his own behavior and allowed his thoughts to swish around for a few seconds before deciding what to do next. He noticed in the window's reflection that the woman had casually followed him across the street and then moved off to his left.

It was an electronics store, one of the few places in Manhattan where ordinary people could still buy Japanese and other imported goods like stereos and computers. There were "committee stores," heavily subsidized and virtually secret outlets for luxury purchases by People's Movement officials above a certain grade and Russian Kommandatura officers above the rank of major.

Here at Fifth Avenue Electronics privilege or rank didn't pay for the goods, just money. The prices were ferocious. Richfield had heard of a handful of extremely wealthy people who had escaped the People's Movement assaults on accumulated wealth by cooperating with the regime on some matter or other. Fifth Avenue Electronics, in fact, was one of the few places where one could still publicly flaunt one's wealth. Ordinary people could only stare at the splendor in the windows like nineteenth-century street urchins ogling a Christmas feast through a tavern window. The collapse of both world trade and the domestic economy after the depression of 1994 had virtually ended the mass marketing of quality consumer goods.

Richfield watched the woman out of the corner of his eye for a few seconds. He waited until a couple standing between them had moved on, then he slowly shuffled over to her.

"Can I buy you a cup of coffee?" He felt suddenly flush again as he asked the question. "I know a place two blocks from here where they serve the real stuff. It's not too crowded either."

He didn't look directly at her as he spoke, but stared and scrutinized her reflection in the window.

The woman allowed the hint of a smile to curl the corners of her mouth. "Okay," she said with a quiet decisiveness, as though it was the most natural thing in the world to be invited for coffee by a stranger who had rescued her from certain trouble in the New York Public Library.

Richfield looked briefly at his watch and turned around as if he were an out-of-towner getting his bearings. He wanted to be sure no one was watching them, even though he thought it unlikely that the library clerk, if he were having misgivings about the incident, had called for militia or PSB action. Satisfied that neither he nor the woman was being followed, he walked with her a block up Fifth Avenue and turned left on Forty-third Street.

The coffee shop he had in mind was about a third of the way down the block, and its entrance was almost concealed by a large dry-cleaning store on one side and an office furniture outlet on the other. The door to the shop was eight steps below ground.

Once inside Douglas had to adjust to the dark; there was almost no natural light, and the owner had not bothered to replace two of the main fluorescent tubes that had burned out. There was a counter on the right; the rest of the area was a long, narrow room with a center aisle and booths on each side that swept back into the dark.

A middle-aged, unshaven man—the manager or owner—was talking in low tones to a customer seated at the counter. As Richfield and the woman entered, he stopped talking, eyed them both carefully, and waited until they had moved to the back and taken a table that faced the door. There was nobody else in the restaurant.

"Excuse me a moment," the woman said and disappeared into the ladies' room. She moved with poise, each foot seeming to pause for a fraction of a second as though to ensure her fleet step. Her hair, trimmed neatly to shoulder length, swung lightly with each movement of her body. Her raincoat was high-collared, a fashion that had come around in the early nineties, and it all but concealed a black or dark brown—Richfield couldn't quite tell in the poor light—turtleneck sweater. Her face was broad, but pleasantly rounded; there was the suggestion of an impishness in the quick movement of her cheeks. Her mouth was wide and generous with perfect teeth. Her nose, completely straight, was set between high cheekbones. Her face was not just pretty, Richfield now realized, it was exquisitely beautiful.

But it was the woman's eyes that made the greatest impression as he watched her return. Even in the gloom of the coffee shop, they appeared enormous.

She placed her raincoat over the back of the chair next to hers. Level with Richfield now, and looking intently into his face, she waited several seconds before saying anything. Then she smiled and momentarily dazzled Douglas.

"I'm Rachel," she said quietly but with a gentleness that hinted at gratitude for what had taken place.

"Douglas Richfield."

"What you did was both risky and brave, and it got me out of quite a fix. Thank you. Why did you do it? You're obviously not with the PSB."

Douglas was a little embarrassed in spite of himself. "What makes you so certain?" was all he could say.

Rachel laughed. "It was obvious as soon as we got out of the South Hall. If you'd been PSB, you'd have had some backup or a partner. I'm surprised the clerk didn't have the street smarts to grasp that."

"All right, so it wasn't the world's most brilliantly planned maneuver. But it got you out of trouble, didn't it?"

Rachel became quite tender now. "Yes, it did," she said softly. "Go on."

"I work at City Hall in the Protocol Department. The only reason I was in the library was to do some research on Marxism that might actually have been of some interest. I don't normally stick my neck out like that. I did what I did because that Medusa at the entrance virtually told me what I could or could not research. When that little bureaucrat in the catalog room was refusing you access to material and was threatening to denounce you for socially hostile behavior, I had to do something. I've been through one of those dragnets—in Macy's, of all places—and it isn't fun.

Even as he said this, Richfield's normal instinct of prudence caught up with him. He had no idea who this woman was. Being too open could yet be his undoing. She could be working for anybody—the Kommandatura, the PSB, the Constitutionalists, some maverick organization—and he was being much too talkative.

"Well," he continued awkwardly, "I just didn't want to have to put up with that sort of hassle again. If I'd taken the time to think about it, I probably wouldn't have chanced it."

"I'm glad you did," Rachel said quietly.

"Thanks." Douglas looked down at the table before going on. "What do you do?" he asked, looking back at her again.

"I work for the Caleb Foundation."

Richfield's expression betrayed his ignorance.

"It's a philanthropic Jewish organization."

"What does it do?" Richfield persisted.

"We help make arrangements for Jewish people to emigrate to Israel."

"Emigrate? Is that still possible?" Richfield had heard of a few people occasionally being permitted to leave for Israel after paying enormous fees/ransoms/bribes. He had never met anyone familiar with the program.

Before Rachel could reply, the coffee shop manager approached them. He was unshaven, grubby, as most coffee shop or restaurant proprietors were these days. "Coffee?" he inquired in a wheezing, off-handed voice.

"Yes, two, with cream and sugar," Richfield replied without asking Rachel. He didn't want the man lingering at the table and possibly asking questions.

"Forget the cream," the man said breathily. "I haven't seen any for weeks, but you lucked out on the sugar. We got some in from Brooklyn yesterday."

"Good. Thanks." Richfield hoped the man would leave without asking them if they wanted anything else, and he did.

Neither of them said anything while the coffee was being served. Richfield was grateful for the opportunity to gather his thoughts. Rachel's presence drew them out. Her face seemed to swim in front of him. But his survival instinct warned him against trusting her.

When the manager had grumpily asked for and received his money, Douglas looked up to see Rachel watching him almost severely. Her lips were pursed. She glanced down at her coffee, stirred it idly for a few moments, then looked over her shoulder at the rest of the coffee shop.

"Look," she said finally, "we've just met and I don't know you. You work for the city and you have Kommandatura clearance. You're kosher with the People's Movement and the PSB. For all I know, you may even be on a committee. You risked your neck to get me out of a tight spot in the library, but to be brutally honest I'm taking a chance by having coffee with you. I appreciate what you did. I just want to make it clear that I'm pretty careful these days whom I sit down and talk with."

Richfield drew in his breath slowly. How could he lighten the conversation enough for both of them? All sorts of political alarms were sounding in the back of his mind. What if . . .

But even as he sifted through these warnings, he came to regard them as out of place. Had he not already risked his neck by impulsively obstructing her possible arrest, and if the library decided to follow up the case, it would be a simple matter to identify him and track him down. He had already bought the horse, as it were, and now was checking its teeth after the purchase. If he was in big trouble, then he might as well enjoy the company of the cause of it for a few minutes. If she was a PSB agent—not very likely—he was dead. But if she was an agent for the Constitutionalists, well, then she was the one who was in trouble, because she seemed to like him enough to want to know him a little. He found himself smiling at the idea.

"How long have you worked at Protocol?" she asked, her pleasant demeanor returning.

"A little over a year."

"You travel?"

"Not really. Occasionally. I've been to Chicago and Detroit with visiting delegations, but most of the delegation work is around here. I did get to go to New Orleans last February."

"You must meet some really interesting people. You're very lucky. Especially for someone so . . . so young and impulsive." She looked at him slyly as she said this and then raised a long-fingered hand to her mouth to cover her own embarrassment.

Richfield found his inhibitions melting.

"Oh, they're not really that interesting, most of them. I mean, my job's not that great. Who can get excited about giving tours to Cuban bodybuilders and Chinese textile officials? My dad used to be a school principal, and he'd always complain about the endless tours he'd have to organize for visiting educators or local politicians. Now I know how he felt."

"Yeah, but how would you like to *be* a Cuban bodybuilder?" She laughed with a hint of coquettishness, then shook her head in mock disapproval of the idea.

Richfield laughed in spite of himself, causing the coffee shop manager to turn briefly and look back from his counter. Rachel's hair swung out elegantly again. "What else do you do?" she asked.

"Well, let's see, I get to go to parades, and I mean *all* parades. You name the occasion, the Protocol Department is there. That part isn't voluntary."

Rachel laughed again. "I can imagine," she said. "How about the Thanksgiving Parade the day before yesterday?"

The question jolted Richfield, bringing to mind the sickening image of Marcus clawing futilely at the air as the militiaman's bullets tore into his back and neck. He grew cautious again.

"Yes, I was there. As you probably know, the Russian liaison commander was there. The marching groups were the same as usual. It was over by 3:30."

"Where were you standing?"

"The General Motors Building."

"You mean opposite the Plaza Hotel?"

"Yes."

"So you must have seen everything that happened."

What did she mean? Could she have heard about either incident—or both of them—from her own contacts? He was not anxious to let her know anything at this stage, if he could avoid it.

"I had a very good view of everything," he said noncommittally.

"Yes, I'm sure you did," she said, leaning forward and speaking so softly that Richfield had difficultly hearing her. "But I don't mean that. What *really* happened? I heard a rumor that some people provoked the militia."

Richfield felt awkward. If he denied the rumor, it would be tantamount to cutting off their conversation. But "antistate rumor mongering" was an offense with a mandatory five-year labor camp sentence. Under the law a rumor was defined as the passing on of any information that had not been officially confirmed by the authorities of the People's Movement, even if the information itself were factually accurate.

He sipped his coffee a moment before replying, trying to gain time. So far it had been Rachel who had taken most of the chances, not just by skating on thin ice in the library, but by following Richfield to

54

the coffee shop and then volunteering information to him for which she could be arrested if Richfield chose to report her. Yet psychologically, it was Douglas, not Rachel, who was on the defensive.

"Okay," he said, somewhat brusquely after a pause, "there was a demonstration. For obvious reasons I can't tell you about it. Anyway, I only saw the beginning."

"Why did you leave early?" Rachel interrupted.

"Hold it. You sound like the library clerk." He didn't like people who pushed him when he was talking. He looked at Rachel almost fiercely.

She smiled contritely and looked him straight in the face. "I'm sorry," she said, "I can steamroll people when I'm really interested in something. There's no need for you to answer if you'd rather not."

But Richfield now saw the incident as an opportunity for him to regain the initiative, to grasp the direction of the conversation. He spoke slowly and carefully. "Because," he said, "I couldn't stand people being beaten and trussed up like the turkeys no one can afford anymore for Thanksgiving Day."

Rachel's lips trembled a little and the color drained from her face. She looked down abruptly, and Douglas wondered if he had gone too far. He certainly didn't know where he was now. Why had she become so frightened?

He decided to change the subject altogether. "Listen," he said placatingly and gently, "I'm sorry if I sounded like I was going to jump down your throat every time you ask what might seem to you like a simple question. I'll calm down. Could we talk about you for a second?"

"Of course," she said quietly.

"Okay, then, it's my turn to be naive. How come the authorities allow a private foundation to keep on operating?"

"Well, it's not as though we're a conglomerate," Rachel replied with a laugh, grateful for the change of direction. "There are just two of us, the president and me. My job is to verify the applications of those people who want to emigrate. I have to prove that their leaving won't have a negative effect on the People's Movement or the war effort. Basically, I try to prove how progressive they were in the old days."

"And the president? What does he do? Type out the research?"

"Orville? Goodness, no, you'd never catch him near a typewriter or a computer. He wouldn't even know how to turn one on."

"I've known about the emigration programs," Richfield followed up, "but they've always puzzled me. Why do the authorities allow anyone to leave? Isn't border control one of the cardinal doctrines of this and every other progressive regime in history? The Maoists and the radicals in the People's Movement talk a lot about proletarian borders, but my impression is that they'd like total control of our borders, given the civil war."

"Maybe you don't know," Rachel responded, "that the Communist countries of Eastern Europe from the 1950s onwards were willing to let certain people emigrate legally as long as some wealthy organization was willing to pay a fee for them. It was an ongoing ransom system. East Germany made a lot of hard currency out of it, as did Cuba during the sixties and seventies. There was even a price tariff. A schoolteacher would require $15,000, but a scientist would fetch $40,000 or more. Usually, the West German government paid up, but sometimes there were deals through Sweden or one of the neutral countries."

"But why would the People's Movement go along with such a program, to Israel, of all places?"

"Money, Douglas, money. Each emigrant is charged a 'processing fee' before being issued an exit permit. This can be as much as several thousand dollars per person. Naturally, payment has—"

"Come on," interrupted Douglas, almost vehemently, "no one is permitted to have more than $20,000 in any bank account. You know as well as I do that all accounts with more than that were confiscated last fall."

"The accounts were frozen, not confiscated," Rachel said, correcting him. "The fact is, the regime simply hasn't figured out what to do with all of the wealth it has confiscated. Meanwhile, until it does, it permits prospective emigrants to sign over very large amounts of frozen securities as part of the processing fee. Don't forget, a lot of people in this country still hold assets in the independent countries that still claim to be capitalist—Japan, Australia, New Zealand, Chile, any of them."

"Doesn't that generate resentment from the people who aren't eligible for emigration?" Douglas had heard senior People's Movement officials complain about this.

"Of course it does. Many Jews hate it. It's humiliating for us to be told that the program is a privilege when we regard it as an inalienable Zionist right. The non-Jews hate it because they can't go. And a lot of people in the People's Movement don't like it because it stirs up some ugly anti-Semitism. Of course the fascists in Moscow think it's just fine if progressives in America approve of an emigration program to Israel. They've been saying for years that Zionists and Freemasons control the world."

"Careful, Rachel," Richfield cautioned quietly but sympathetically, gesturing to her with a slight movement of his hand to lower her voice. Though no one else had come into the coffee shop since they first sat down, the proprietor had glanced back as Rachel's voice had grown louder and more intense. Richfield, facing the door, could see him, but Rachel couldn't. There was some tension between them as Rachel thought Richfield was objecting to her comments rather than warning her against being overheard. When she realized what he was doing, she relaxed a little.

"Tell me about Orville," Richfield asked. "What's he like?"

"Have you heard of the Marcus family? They were very well known before the civil war."

"Orville is a Marcus?"

"Yes, Orville Marcus. Does that surprise you?"

"Do you spell it M-A-R-C-U-S?"

"Yes, why? Do you know something about the family?" Rachel asked, suddenly serious and intent.

"No, I've never heard of them."

Rachel looked puzzled. "Never heard of them?" she said. "It's only one of the most famous names in retail outlets in America, even if you never hear their name mentioned these days."

"There are a lot of things that suddenly appear and disappear from the public limelight these days," Douglas said, doing his best Groucho Marx impersonation. "You can't tell the politicians from the magicians, if you know what I mean," and he flicked an imaginary cigar and flexed his eyebrows.

Rachel laughed, grateful for the dry, risky joke. "First of all," Rachel said, deciding to continue the story, "the family was one of the wealthiest in America. Old man Aaron Marcus was a billionaire; he owned hundreds of stores across the country. Sadly for him, only one of his four sons, Joseph, showed any interest in the family business. When the civil war began, he was in Switzerland and he hasn't shown any interest in returning. Orville, the eldest, was the family idealist, a real soft touch for good causes, and he gave generously. Of course, he had plenty to give away. Aaron didn't want his sons to work as hard as he had. Orville was particularly drawn to work with Jewish organizations. After the Washington Uprising he could easily have hopped off to Hawaii on any private aircraft. But he chose not to. I've often asked him why he didn't go, and he's always said that he felt he was supposed to be here. He's quite determined about it.

"The second son, Marvin, is different. His politics were always somewhere to the left of Lenin, and he hated anyone who disagreed with him. He took every cause extremely personally. When the People's Movement came along, Marvin found his life's cause, and he's never looked back. The odd thing is, he hasn't gotten very far politically, which may be why you haven't heard of him. The last I heard, he was the state chairman for Massachusetts. In nonpolitical life he's been teaching sociology at Harvard. Some people think he's been held back by the bad political background of his brothers."

"By Joseph, maybe," interjected Richfield, whose Protocol job had given him a keen sense of the way political pedigrees helped or harmed people, "but hardly Orville, whom the authorities obviously find a rather useful person to work with. What about the third brother?"

"Douglas, I'm sorry, I really can't discuss him. Please don't ask me about him."

"Look, maybe it sounds as though I'm being a little too nosy," he said patiently, "but there's a very good reason for my asking. Besides, you started filling me in on the Marcus family. What's so special about the fourth son? You can at least tell me his name."

Rachel was silent for a few seconds. Douglas didn't press her, but drank up the rest of his coffee and kept his eye on the proprietor at the counter. The man was busy talking to the other customer.

"All right," Rachel said finally, but in a brisk, almost cold tone that shook Richfield a bit. Was she closing off the friendship he felt had begun to grow between them?

"Daniel Marcus was in the navy," she said in a flat voice, as though citing an obituary. "His present whereabouts are unknown."

"Meaning he's in Hawaii, on the run, or rotting in a PSB cell in the Tombs," commented Richfield brutally. "Isn't that what 'whereabouts unknown' usually means?"

Rachel winced, and Richfield realized that he had touched a nerve. "I'm sorry," he said, "that was very insensitive of me. What I meant was, Daniel was—or is—a lot more distasteful to the authorities than Joseph, whom I gather the Russian spooks haven't gone after in Switzerland at the request of the People's Movement. If he had any rank, he would be in a reeducation camp—or worse, mining in Alaska. He can't be a fugitive or I would have seen a wanted notice for him myself. Protocol receives every major fugitive listing that comes up. They even test us on them."

Rachel looked sharply at him, once again gauging how much she could trust him.

"Did you know," she said slowly, "that there are some fugitives who are so politically sensitive the authorities can't publicly acknowledge they're even looking for them?"

"You mean Constitutionalist agents?" replied Richfield quietly.

"Yes, but not just only them."

Richfield was becoming exasperated again. He didn't want to antagonize Rachel, much less bully her into telling him what she knew but had to keep silent about. Yet an instinct told him he needed to know more about Daniel Marcus than what Walter Bremer had half-drunkenly let out. He also felt that, though she appeared reluctant to discuss the matter, Rachel also seemed eager that he should know certain things about Marcus. He took a different tack.

"All right," Richfield said matter-of-factly, "let's approach this in a way that doesn't complicate things any more than it has to. You said Daniel Marcus was in the navy. Was he well known or something? If his brothers are anything to go by, he probably wasn't an underachiever."

"He was brilliant," Rachel said, "but I shouldn't tell you anything about him that you can't access yourself."

"Let me help you out. In Protocol we have virtually every biographical manual ever printed. Not just the old Who's Who volumes. Too many People's Movement VIPs were too prominent in the old days, and we have to know who they were. I could dig up Daniel Marcus if he was as distinguished as you imply, but why don't you save me the trouble and fill me in now?"

Rachel looked dubious for a moment, then relented. "All right," she said unenthusiastically, "this much is, or at least was, public knowledge. Marcus enlisted in the navy. Enlisted, mind you. He could have stood on his head all the way through Annapolis, of course, but he had an ornery streak about him. Maybe he didn't want to go through life on Daddy's coattails; maybe he just wanted to be original.

"At any rate, he signed on in the late sixties and joined the SEALs, you know, naval commandos. He served three tours in Vietnam, was made an officer in spite of himself, and was decorated several times. He was also badly wounded. His left leg was almost severed by a mortar shell, and he's walked with a limp ever since.

"In spite of this, he talked them out of a medical discharge and got himself transferred to submarines. Of course, he never served at sea. But after attending the Naval Postgraduate School at Monterey and the Naval War College, he earned a reputation as an expert on submarine strategy and wrote extensively about it."

"So far, seems to me," Richfield commented, "he was living up to the family reputation of superachievers."

"Marcus gained notoriety outside the navy during a controversy over defense strategy in the early 1990s. The newspaper leaks were incomplete, of course, but it seems he advocated a no-surrender policy for the nation's Trident submarines in the event of a military collapse."

"How do you mean, 'no-surrender'? Were the Tridents supposed to scuttle themselves?" The idea struck Richfield as absurd, and he made no attempt to conceal his skepticism.

Rachel, who had ignored his earlier comment, responded calmly, "No, they were under orders not to accept surrender commands even if they were authenticated as coming from the commander-in-chief, the president himself. The speculation at the time was that the subs would somehow operate independently until an alternative National Command Authority was reestablished. We never heard the whole version because the issue sort of disappeared from the press after a few weeks. I think they called the proposal the Almond something or other."

"What's so significant about almonds?" Douglas asked.

"Daniel was some kind of Bible student. He used biblical references in a lot of his codes, including his worst-case scenarios. I think almond is a reference from Ecclesiastes, something about the rise and fall of nations. Considering the premise of the Almond Project, that's not such a big step in logic."

Richfield felt a chill as Rachel filled in the background of the man he had seen gunned down in the street just two days earlier. He still wanted to know why Marcus had been so important to the authorities.

"But that was nearly a decade ago," Douglas said. "Why would a series of speculative articles about submarine strategy interest the PSB in their author today, particularly if he wasn't a line officer, just some kind of desktop strategist?"

Rachel suppressed her impatience, and Richfield glimpsed the steely resolve behind her softness. "Look," she said firmly, "you're the last person I'd expect to have to lead through this mystery by the nose. Hasn't it seemed a little odd to you that the authorities have never proven that the most important and dangerous element in the entire U.S. strategic equation, the Ohio-class submarines—the Tridents—were ever captured or destroyed?"

Douglas challenged her, "Don't you remember the big deal that was made of the *Mississippi* off the coast of Madagascar? Half the Russian Indian Ocean fleet was there. Someone even filmed it. The papers played it up for weeks. Those folks on Governor's Island, the Kommandatura, even looked for a while as if they could tell a joke or two. Didn't Admiral Korneev say that the sinking of the *Mississippi* signified the end of any hope the Constitutionalists had to threaten either the New Era in America or the emerging global entente?"

"Boilerplate, Douglas. Nothing but smoke and mirrors. You really display an amazing incapacity to go beyond the surface of that gobbledygook. Did Korneev, or anyone, actually say that the

Tridents had been wiped out, or did he say something that most people would presume to mean the same thing?"

Stung by the sharpness of her rebuke, Richfield was tempted to lash back with a rather heavy-handed sarcasm. But his need to hear out the Marcus story overrode his pride, and he held back. Slowly he began to realize how naive he had truly been, and he reddened.

Rachel knew she'd been harsh. "I'm sorry," she said, "you didn't deserve that."

"Not to worry," he said, recovering. "Go on with the story."

"Well, there isn't a lot to say," she said. "I'm not the world authority on Daniel Marcus, and," lowering her voice, she said, "I think we've both taken enough risks today without pushing our luck in areas that aren't the sort of things reasonable citizens talk about."

She looked at her watch. Once again a certain briskness, one that Richfield dreaded, came into her manner. "I'm sorry," she said, "I've got to go. There's a pile of work waiting for me at the foundation, even if they won't let me do my job in the library."

She started to move her chair out and gather up her coat. Keeping his eyes firmly on hers, Richfield pulled his trump card. "What would you say," he asked her, "if I told you that Marcus is dead?"

Rachel went pale. "How could you know that? You told me you never heard of the Marcus family."

"Two days ago, as I left the General Motors Plaza and the melee began, I found myself following an elderly couple, one of whom had a limp, the woman. I can't tell you exactly why I felt that this limping person wasn't what he—she—purported to be, but they walked unimpeded through the Fifty-eighth Street checkpoint. I had already heard the name 'Marcus,' and I knew that the PSB and the Russians especially were desperate to find him. I'd never seen his photo, but the information about his limp, coupled with the obviously male features of the 'woman,' registered immediately. It was Marcus.

"He didn't get as far as Park Avenue. They were stopped by the militia in what I guess was a random check, and the other man said the wrong thing to one of the militia. He might also have been trying to shoot his way out of the trap. Well, he was shot, and Marcus tried to run. The limp, the dress. He was hit by three bullets, two in the back and one in the neck.

"I know for certain he was dead, because one of the militiamen started bawling the other out for messing up the arrest. The stupid, crazy thing is that the militia had no idea who they had stumbled across. They probably still don't know. I'm sure I'm the only person who knows who it was and saw him shot."

"Oh, God." Rachel covered her face with her hands. Richfield stopped.

"You say this man, dressed as a woman, had a limp?" Rachel asked. She didn't wait for his answer but continued in a hurried, frightened voice. "It's fair to assume after all the fighting that a lot of people in New York have limps and that some of them are wanted by the authorities. How could you be sure it was Daniel?"

"Because someone—I won't say who—specifically told me during the parade that there was a massive search going on for one Daniel Marcus, a man with a limp, that there might be a diversion to help him escape, and that the authorities couldn't let the People's Militia or the regular police know who it was they wanted so badly. I'm sorry, Rachel, I'm really sorry. I can see how close you feel to the family."

"I have to leave," was all Rachel said in response, as she abruptly got up from her chair and put her raincoat on. "Please leave with me. I don't want to let them have anything to remember us by."

It was getting dark as the two of them climbed the steps to street level. The wind had begun to blow, and Richfield shivered. He noticed that Rachel was buttoning up the top of her high-collared raincoat too, and had drawn from her pocket a brown felt hat that perfectly matched it. She turned to say good-bye to him, and her face was calm, even tender now.

Richfield, his hands in his pockets, wasn't sure how they should part, but he realized that neither of them should stay in the same spot for more than a few seconds. Many of the midtown streets had video cameras deployed at key intersections, and there were routine inspections of the tapes to check for fugitives or others under search warrants. "Is there a chance we can see each other again?" he asked, a slight frown betraying both frustration at the circumstance of their meeting and anxiety over whether he would see her again.

"It depends," she said simply. "Not on me, or on you, but on them. It wouldn't be too smart for either of us to go back to the library for several weeks at least, if at all. You'll need to lie low at work for a while to find out whether you're under surveillance. As will I. Let me do the contacting. I won't have any trouble finding you, but I think I ought to be the one to decide if the occasion is or isn't safe. Oh, one last thing. Did either of those militiamen know who you were?"

"My name was taken along with everyone else in the street once they blocked off both exits. But they can't have the slightest idea I know who the dead man is."

"Probably not, but no doubt you'll get the once-over. You can protect yourself though. Everything I told you about Marcus is public knowledge. Whatever you do, don't forget that. One other thing. Don't worry too much about the PSB. It'll take five more years of brutalization before they're up to snuff as sleuths. Shalom."

With that Rachel turned and walked off toward the West Side, her heels clipping the grimy sidewalk. Richfield tried not to stare after her in case the surveillance was on, but he was both puzzled and confused. Who were the good guys?

4

Ponomarev

*P*onomarev opened the window that looked out onto Central Park just enough to let some fresh air circulate. The sitting room felt a little too tropical as he entered in his pale blue bathrobe. He was surprised. He'd stayed at New York hotels before—though never previously at the Plaza—and they always seemed to judge the temperature perfectly. But, of course, as so many Americans had pointed out to Ponomarev when he had been serving at the Soviet Mission to the U.N. during the 1980s, capitalism always did manage to make the comfort industry work better than socialism did.

He padded over to the television and turned it on. The number of channels he'd been familiar with on his previous visit years earlier had dropped precipitously. The cable networks and CNN had been taken over by the People's Movement, and the three traditional networks had shrunk to two because of economic pressures.

There was a shuffling outside the door, evidently in response to the noise of the television in the room, then a knock. "Yes," he said sharply. It was only 6:30 A.M. What would anyone want at this hour?

After a few seconds of silence Ponomarev repeated, "Come in." Then, remembering suddenly, he switched to Russian. "*Zakhodite*," then, slowly and deliberately, as though speaking to a simpleton, "*zakhod-i-te*."

The door opened just enough for a plump, balding head to poke around it and scan the room. It was Sergei Gusev, his aide. Unimaginative but thorough, attentive to the point of servility, phlegmatic but efficient, Gusev's useful qualities were so evident they were frequently annoying.

65

"Well, what is it, Gusev?" Ponomarev's voice rattled with impatience.

"I know it's very early, Alexei Ilyich, but most people are up well before dawn the day after they arrive here from the Motherland. When I heard you already moving around, I thought you might like to look at the morning papers. Would you like to order breakfast now?"

"Gusev, thank you for the thought. But I've spent about fifteen years in and out of some rather fine hotels around the world, and I think I know how to order breakfast."

"All right, Alexei Ilyich. I'll just leave the newspapers on the coffee table. If you need me, I'm in Room 715."

Twenty-five minutes later Ponomarev was dressed, shaved, splashed with an expensive French eau de toilette, and halfway through his first cup of coffee. Room service had managed to come up with his favorite breakfast, eggs Benedict, and he was savoring it over the Metro section of the *New York Times*. He summoned Gusev to get some early phone calls done.

There were the usual reports of small robberies, arrests of "suspected enemy infiltrators" (that is, Constitutionalist agents), new public works projects (which meant reminders of the regime's efforts to reduce unemployment), and an occasional murder. Ponomarev had observed with a smirk that the murder rate in American cities under People's Movement control had declined drastically since the emergency regulations brought in shortly after the Washington Uprising. Possession of a handgun without a permit was punishable by a mandatory ten years' imprisonment. Nowadays the majority of murders were knifings in gang fights. The Great Cleanup of the city had also removed the bulk of the hard-core criminal element.

The Russian's practiced eye, after scanning the entire paper, nevertheless quickly focused on a small item buried close to the back of the metro section: "Two Wounded Suspects Still Not Identified." It read as follows:

> Manhattan. Two suspected hostile agents, one of them shot dead in midtown Manhattan after last Thursday's Thanksgiving Day parade, had still not been identified by late Sunday, city officials said.

The suspects, who sources said were shot as they attempted to flee a militia patrol, were believed to be fugitives. Both were white males, approximately in their early fifties. One of the suspects was dressed as a woman.

City sources said they had not so far been able to check the photographs and fingerprints of the slain suspect against existing fugitive and "watch" lists. A Public Security Bureau spokesman would say only that the case was still under investigation.

The incident brings to a total of 174 the number of suspected hostile agents slain by militia forces in the city after attempting to avoid arrest since the beginning of this year.

Ponomarev didn't know whether to laugh or splutter with fury. He decided to laugh. "Dressed as a woman!" he repeated out loud with a roar. "Only the *New York Times* could leave a reader so uncertain. Is the story about the accidental shooting of Manhattan's leading drag queen or the hunting down of two desperate Constitutionalist agents? Gusev, you absolutely must read this!" Then, remembering that his aide was on the phone in the bedroom, his mood switched to one of quiet fury.

Traitors, he thought. *Subversive but clever meddlers, those people at the* Times. A tiny, four-paragraph news item manages to announce to the world that (1) city authorities are too incompetent to identify two obviously important Constitutionalist agents after three days; (2) the PSB isn't offering any help to the city; (3) the trigger-happy People's Militia is shooting suspects dead in the street at the rate of one every other day. Well, he reflected, if that's how these ardent lefties want to run their press in this war, let them learn the hard way that it's going to be an uphill battle. It certainly doesn't make my job any simpler.

But something about the story nagged at Ponomarev. He was trained to tug at the smallest details, and like a small boy with a passion for untying knots, he never liked to let go of a problem until he could clearly see how to untangle it. Gusev reappeared from the bedroom with the look of a well-trained retriever. He was ready to be dispatched on whatever project his superior might devise.

"Sergei," said Ponomarev cheerfully, "take a look at this piece and tell me what you think." Gusev relished these moments:

Ponomarev thinking rapidly through a problem or a decision and allowing him the opportunity to inject his own comment or two.

"Well, I don't think the man in the woman's clothes was a regular transvestite. I understand some of the committee people, despite their official positions, are not very friendly toward gays and lesbians. Why would they run unless they had something to hide?"

"Exactly. And what else did you notice?"

Gusev looked embarrassed and read the article again slowly. "Well," he began tentatively, "they don't say which of the two suspects was killed, the regular man or the one dressed as a woman."

"Good thinking, Gusev! You are exactly right, and that is an enormous advantage to us. What would you say if I told you that one of the two suspects—we don't yet know whether the dead one or the surviving one—was probably Daniel Marcus, the very man we have been looking for?"

"But Alexei Ilyich, how can you possibly know that?"

"I don't, of course, but neither do other readers of this newspaper who are highly sympathetic to Marcus. If Marcus was involved, and if he is the one who survived the shooting, then we've hit the jackpot. By the way, Sergei, haven't you always wanted a vacation in southern Florida? You just may get to do that before too long."

"I'm sorry, Alexei Ilyich, I don't understand. I thought we had two tasks to accomplish here."

"Of course, Sergei, of course. But if Marcus is in hand, then it is only a matter of time before he obliges us with the information we need to track down those rogue submarines. Who knows? He may also be able to lead us to whichever of those circus clowns on the National Executive Committee has been having serious loyalty problems."

"Excuse me again, Alexei Ilyich, but what if Marcus was one of those two suspects in the article, only he was the one the militia killed?"

Ponomarev narrowed his eyes. "Well, that, of course, would be inconvenient to us." He paused to spread some marmalade on a piece of toast. "But exactly how inconvenient would really depend on how many people were aware of it. A dead man may not really be dead until everyone agrees that he is two meters under the soil. Our challenge today and for the next several weeks, Sergei, may be to lean on the good name of Marcus, dead or alive, without so much as breathing our intentions to the incompetent and mole-ridden PSB or those Constitutionalist jackals."

Gusev twitched nervously at these last words and pointed to the ceiling lamp with an exaggerated but silent facial grimace. He didn't like the idea of being bugged by the security services of a regime they were supposed to be working with.

Ponomarev roared with laughter and cruelly mimicked Gusev's action. "Sergei," he said pityingly, as though to someone chronically naive about life, "the People's Movement did not invite the Russian Foreign Intelligence Service to assist them with a serious security and espionage problem because they like us or admire us, much less because they agree with our views on the origins of the universe. Privately, they detest us and everything we stand for. Behind our backs they call us Russian fascists.

"Publicly, it is a different matter. The only reason they do not criticize either Zhelenovsky or our patriotic ideals is that they desperately need us. Now please inform my security detail that I will be downstairs in twenty minutes ready to go to Rockefeller Center. Tell them I'll walk."

"Isn't that a bit dangerous, Alexei Ilyich?"

"No more so than getting into a limousine with darkened windows outside a hotel in which, it seems, half of our general staff appears to be frolicking these days. I'll see you down there."

With that Ponomarev returned to the *New York Times* and the regime's *People's Voice*, methodically reading and rereading every important article and making notes on them, quickly deciding which pieces he would ignore.

He had been right about the discomfort the People's Movement felt in bringing Ponomarev over, essentially as a counterespionage specialist, to do the work their own security forces had proven incompetent to do. The Russians had broken the back of the American military in Iran and forced the U.S. president to sign an arms-control agreement so humiliating that it amounted to nothing less than a strategic surrender. The Senate had refused to ratify the Strategic Reordering Treaty, as the agreement was called, and, enraged but prepared for this development, the People's Movement had led a mob that simultaneously overran both Capitol Hill and the White House. Only explicit Russian threats to the safety of the fifty thousand U.S. POWs held in camps in Iran deterred U.S. Special Operations Command from launching a counterattack that would have recaptured Washington within two weeks of the uprising. A quasi-fascist Russia helped install a leftist American regime in power in Washington. It was not something the People's Movement liked to boast about.

But Ponomarev had taken the switch in stride. It was he who had insisted on having at least temporary offices in Rockefeller Center rather than within the drab setting of the Russian Mission to the U.N. on Sixtieth Street. During his second U.N. tour in the early 1980s, Ponomarev had spent a lot of time in the electronically secure "Residency" of the KGB, deep within the mission. There he had coordinated work for the KGB's Directorate S, a department of the First Chief Directorate that was responsible for training "illegals," deep-cover Soviet agents who posed as U.S. citizens. It had been a fascinating job and had brought him into much closer contact with ordinary American life than even the normal work of a KGB agent posing as a diplomat would have done. But the U.N. mission site was such a conspicuous base, he knew that Constitutionalist agents would quickly tag everyone entering or leaving. And even if they didn't, he couldn't be sure that the notoriously leaky PSB might not slip information to the other side. No, it would be much better that his particular mission to the U.S. have its own set of offices completely unconnected with anything else Russian in the city. Besides, at thirty-nine, sensing even greater power ahead for himself, he wanted to be close to the new decision makers in America.

The People's Movement had at first resisted the idea fiercely. Why should any foreign intelligence organization, they asked, have an entire floor inside the RCA Building, the location of the National Executive Committee and its various staff operations? Ponomarev had replied with three reasons when RFIS Chairman Kuzmin had himself brought up the American objections. First, the RCA building was one of the few People's Movement-occupied structures that was probably as secure as one could find under conditions of civil war. Second, Ponomarev regarded it as essential to stress the one-time-only nature of his current assignment and its intimate connection with the National Executive Committee of the People's Movement. Third, when Ponomarev wanted to interview People's Movement officials or liaise with PSB counterparts, he didn't want to trail across town in a convoy every time he did so. Reluctantly, and over the objections of senior PSB officials, the National Executive Committee had given in.

It was a brisk, sunny day as Ponomarev left the Plaza through the Fifty-eighth Street exit—escorted by four Russian intelligence security personnel, a liaison agent from the PSB, and Gusev. All six wanted to form a phalanx around him, as though he were a rock star liable to be mobbed at any moment. But Ponomarev insisted on a more casual deployment at a stroll's pace. He was confident the Constitutionalists hadn't gotten wind of his presence or his objectives, yet he had no desire to hand them a public notice of his arrival. He'd insisted that his Russian guards vary their dress instead of looking like B-movie heavies in their leather coats.

Moving off Fifth Avenue onto Fiftieth Street, the group came to a checkpoint that sealed off Rockefeller Plaza and the entire RCA complex from the rest of the city. A semi-permanent, glass-enclosed guardhouse was the only way pedestrians had access to the building. Visitors were required to present their passes through a narrow slot in the bulletproof glass and speak into a microphone. Fortunately, Ponomarev was spared the humiliation of having to identify himself personally. The PSB official with him showed his own pass, was admitted into some sort of holding area where he evidently spoke with the guards inside for a few minutes, and opened the door for the group to enter. Once in the guardhouse each man, including Ponomarev, had his I.D. examined, was searched thoroughly by two PSB officials in plainclothes, and then asked to move into a second holding area.

Gusev was about to object to this humiliating examination on Ponomarev's behalf, but the PSB escort spoke first. "I regret this complicated procedure," he said, "but all first-time visitors have to go through it. Once you're inside the building, security will issue passes to you and your designated aides. You will have to show these at the guardhouse each time you arrive, but you'll no longer be searched.

We've made allowances for your guards to keep their Makarov pistols. No one else, including you, will be permitted to carry a weapon into this security area unless you specifically apply for a permit to do so. I think you know why."

Interesting, thought Ponomarev. *This man isn't such a dolt if he knows about the Makarov 9mm.* But Ponomarev could hardly restrain his smile as he strolled the last few yards from the guardhouse to the main entrance of the RCA Building. On his earlier visits to America in pre-civil war days or during his tours in New York, he had visited the building many times. He loved the Rainbow Room and its air of 1940s-era glittery romance, and he had spent several pleasant evenings there with an attractive secretary from the Soviet mission while he was recovering from his painful divorce.

He particularly enjoyed the sense of comfort and opulence that the building's massive and ornate lobby inevitably gave off. He'd been amused to learn that the elaborate murals by José Maria Sert had been ordered by archcapitalist John D. Rockefeller to replace those by the Mexican revolutionary painter Diego Rivera when the Mexican proved unwilling to modify a panel portraying a heroic Lenin. He paused again amid the art deco to enjoy the multiple ironies. Here was a monument to capitalism, conceived and erected during the first global crisis of capitalism in the 1930s. Now it had been taken over by a utopian leftist regime in the second great crisis of capitalism. And here he was, intelligence envoy of an anti-socialist regime in the country where Lenin was born. Life was far more unbelievable than fiction.

Ponomarev left his bodyguards in the lobby and took the elevator to the thirty-fourth floor with Gusev, his PSB escort, and another PSB official who had joined them in the lobby and introduced himself as Hawkins. The man had a badly pitted face, as though he had survived smallpox as a child, and wore a turtleneck sweater. Ponomarev wondered what the conspicuous informality was supposed to mean.

Nothing outside the elevator on Ponomarev's floor indicated any connection with Russia or anything remotely concerned with intelligence matters. A plain black sign on the double glass doors read Educational Programs Administration, a purposefully bland title.

There was nothing inside the reception area to distinguish the operation from hundreds of typical bureaucratic—or in the old days business—organizations throughout New York. A tall and handsome-featured African-American woman sat behind the beige marble receptionist desk. Two long Swedish-style leather couches were set at right angles around a square glass coffee table on which there were a handful of out-of-date magazines. The lithograph landscape on the wall was almost a self-parody: "Ducks over the Chesapeake at Sunset," number 28/300.

Hawkins introduced Ponomarev and Gusev to the receptionist, then stretched out a hand to say good-bye to the two men. "I know you have plenty to do, and I don't need to be in your way. I have an office in this building five floors above you. Mr. Rutledge has personally requested that I be your liaison with the Public Security Bureau during your stay in America."

"Thank you," said Ponomarev politely. "I'm grateful for all of your assistance so far. May I ask, the young man who escorted us into the building, one of yours, I don't remember his name . . ."

"Weikert. He's been assigned to ensure that you run into no ground-level bureaucratic obstacles, militia inspections on the street, and so on. You'll find him very useful. Of course, if you think he'll be a hindrance to your operation, then . . ."

"No, no, I'm sure he'll be just fine."

"Okay, then I'll leave you here. Look forward to hearing from you. And good luck." With that Hawkins turned quickly and left through the glass doors. The receptionist waited until he had boarded an elevator, then she locked both glass doors from the inside. On her way back she walked past Ponomarev and Gusev, saying "Follow me, please," and led them down a corridor to the left and into what appeared to be a small office kitchen. Opening a drawer, she pressed four numbered keys in a rapid sequence. Immediately, an entire section of the kitchen cabinet swung back to reveal a continuation of the original corridor with offices opening off it.

"Not bad, Gusev, not bad," said Ponomarev with a smile of wry admiration for the operation that the Foreign Intelligence Service had set up in advance of Ponomarev's arrival.

The receptionist permitted herself a modest smile. "Your reputation for punctiliousness preceded you, Alexei Ilyich," she said in perfect Russian, breaking into a smile herself.

For the first time Ponomarev was genuinely taken by surprise. "Are you . . . one of ours?"

"Yes. I may not look like it, but I am. My name is Natalya Frederikovna Fedorova, daughter of an African-American family that emigrated to Russia—the Soviet Union, actually—in the 1950s and widow of Igor Yevgenevich Fedorova. I think you knew him."

"Knew him!" Ponomarov exclaimed. "He was one of my closest friends and a first-rate officer! When he died in Turkey I was heartsick. I had heard about you, of course, always in glowing terms. It is an honor for me that you have been assigned here."

"I requested it."

"Then even more so. Sergei Mikhailovich here also knew Igor quite well and admired him as I do."

Gusev nodded warmly.

Ponomarev added, "I feel excellently equipped already. Now, if you can show me my *real* office and explain whatever I need to know about communications, I am eager to get moving."

"Certainly, Alexei Ilyich." Natalya, a wonderful African-American Natalya, as Ponomarev kept thinking to himself, led the two men down the corridor to an office at the very end. She took out a key, opened the door, and showed Ponomarev into a spacious, corner office with a fine view southward down Manhattan and westward toward the Hudson.

Apart from a love seat and two armchairs around the obligatory coffee table, the sole piece of visible furniture in the room was a large, finely polished, kidney-shaped table, probably of cherry wood. There was a single phone on it, but behind it, not one, but two identical leather desk chairs.

Gusev cackled as soon as he saw them. "Alexei Ilyich," he said, "whoever set up this office was intimately familiar with your methods. How many people from the old First Chief Directorate know that you always like to have a second person behind the desk when you question people?"

Genuinely warmed by the efficiency with which the entire operation had been handled so far, Ponomarev felt jet lag begin to lap at the edges of his alertness, but he decided he could hold it at bay. He wanted to move ahead quickly on a hunch that had started fermenting in his mind about the *New York Times* article.

"Natalya," he said warmly and briskly. "I know that it's going to be a pleasure to work with you. Do you have to sit out there in the reception room all day or can you work with me?"

"I have a backup who usually helps with research and verification here in the back area. She can handle virtually all of her checking work out front, and I know she won't mind doing that."

"Good. I have a priority assignment for you and Gusev. Sergei, show Natalya the *New York Times* piece about the shooting last Thursday. Then call up Hawkins and apologize to him that you forgot to present him with the two bottles of Stolichnaya vodka that I brought over yesterday. Ask if you can deliver it to him right away. He'll be very happy, of course, and will ask you if there's anything he can do for you in return. Say no, thanks, everything is under control, but you might want to call for some routine checking an hour or so later. About an hour after you have delivered the vodka, call him up again. Ask if I can interview the two militiamen who shot the fugitive after the Thanksgiving parade. If he questions you, say that I'm trying to establish characteristic behavior patterns for Constitutionalist agents or for fugitives when they are confronted at a checkpoint.

"Natalya, call in Weikert and tell him how grateful you are he's been assigned to us. Don't ask him for any favors. What I really want to know is what he thinks of Hawkins and who the power holders are in his outfit. He looks thoroughly professional, which is good. We don't want some third-rate ideologist messing things up for us.

"By the way I assume that we have at least three completely different phone numbers in here. Use one for the up-front stuff, that is, if we're calling on behalf of the Educational Programs Administration and the other two for all of our own work. Obviously the PSB has all of our numbers, but I'd like to get them accustomed to using just one. If absolutely necessary, and only if so, the highest officials of the National Executive Committee may reach us on the third number.

"Before you get moving on that, let me have the civil war status report from the Residency and any other materials I'll need to get through. Oh, and, sorry to have to ask you about this, but does that phony kitchen have the means to produce a cup of coffee?"

"I'll get that first, Alexei Ilyich. And don't worry, I'm not offended to be asked to make coffee. Igor told me that when you were both in Turkey, you made some of the best coffee in the Middle East." She laughed charmingly at the recollection, then added, "but I'll show Sergei Mikhailovich how everything works."

Gusev, accustomed to being teased but perennially uncomfortable about it, reddened slightly as he followed her out of Ponomarev's office.

On the twelfth floor of New York's Municipal Building at One Centre Street, Douglas was in a self-pitying mood. He'd squirmed in his chair for an hour earlier in the morning as the study group had hacked through the material it had gathered for the new sociology of New York. Because Richfield hadn't gone back to the library after his dramatic rescue of Rachel, he wasn't very well prepared. His sympathy for the overall objectives of the People's Movement hadn't extended to the determination of its leaders to force everyone to fit some aspect or other of Marxist philosophy. He'd borrowed some books from a couple of friends on Sunday, reread his University of Chicago notes, and done his best to digest what he could about the topic. The problem was his heart just wasn't in it.

His heart, in fact, was still strangely warmed by his encounter with Rachel. For several hours after their meeting he thought or at least imagined there were traces of her fragrance on his right wrist. He had, after all, shaken hands with her. Her image—fragrant, sensual and charming—had fluttered into and out of his mind at different times all weekend long, each time disturbing his equilibrium. As coldly and detached as he could, he had tried to analyze the phenomenon.

All of his life he had heard clichés about people having "chemistry," but he had never known what it meant other than that some people generally get along with certain kinds of people better than they do with others. Now he found that whenever he thought of Rachel an indefinable reaction occurred within him—an elation, an uncertainty. He didn't mind it, but it bothered him that he seemed to have no control over it. Rachel, someone he had barely spent forty minutes with, had somehow managed to affect the very molecules of his being.

The odd thing was that Douglas had known women whose appearance turned most men's heads faster than Rachel's would. Even these days, when makeup was hard to find, one could still meet some extremely good-looking women. Some of them found their way now and then to the Protocol Department on some pretext or other. New York's city officials were known to have more direct access than most people to both the necessities and the luxuries of living. They seemed to know their way around, and Richfield could count at least two occasions, perhaps three, when an attractive woman had implied that a relationship was his for the asking if he could provide access to the more luxurious goods in the city. Douglas was not so scrupulous a People's Movement activist that he hadn't been tempted by the transaction. But, in the end, he was put off by the hardness in these people, however physically appealing they were. Why would anyone want to take up with a woman whose sole motivation for a "romantic" relationship was to find a way to the head of the line?

Rachel was so different from this kind of woman. Why? Her paradoxical personality excited him. She was tough-minded and unsentimental about her business affairs, but charmingly tender-hearted when touched in an area of her ordinary humanity.

As the group discussion on the sociology of New York droned on, Richfield had found himself wrestling with these thoughts and drifting away from the discussion.

"You're getting very vague, Douglas," said the supervisor, a long-term committee propagandist, when his efforts to sum up one or other exploratory line in the discussion had ended lackadaisically. She was right, of course, but who cared?

Back at his desk for his normal job after the meeting, he was quickly distracted by a heavy workload. A Swedish and a Peruvian delegation were in town as guests of the People's Movement, and they wanted to meet the mayor and at least one member of the

National Committee. A Russian journalist wanted to interview his countrymen at the Russian Komandatura on Governor's Island. Academics from Boston needed help meeting with grassroots committee people in Harlem. Richfield could slough off some of the requests to other officials, especially those from journalists. Generally, though, word had gotten out that the official press office of the National Executive Committee was so unhelpful and so physically remote, tucked away somewhere in the RCA Building, that either you could never reach the people who supposedly worked there, or, if you could, they were of no help at all. As a result much of the press business ended up in the Protocol Department. Richfield had discovered what efficiency experts had often noted: If you're available to be bothered, somebody is going to bother you.

To add to his sense of beleaguerment, Bremer had dropped by that morning and casually let him know that the man they were looking for during the Thanksgiving parade had been caught by the militia. "That Marcus fellow?" Richfield asked with genuine surprise, but he bit his tongue before blurting out that he had seen the shooting. "How did it happen?"

"Oh, one chance in a million. A random militia I.D. check on the street. It was just after I told you and Esther about him. Took place close to where you were. I'm surprised you didn't see it."

"Why would I? The militia are questioning people all the time."

"Yeah, but they don't always shoot at the people they talk to."

"I thought you said he was caught."

"Well, he was, wise guy. But there was some shooting too. I don't know exactly what happened. Anyway, that's one less of their guys to worry about."

"But wouldn't it make quite a difference if he were alive or dead? I mean, didn't you say that he had some information or something?"

Bremer's face changed into a sickly smile, a sign to Richfield that it was time to back off. So far, though, he hadn't asked anything out of the ordinary.

"We're keeping track of things quite well these days, aren't we?" said Bremer greasily. "It'd be nice if you were always so attentive." But he didn't answer the question and slunk off.

Richfield now had a momentary stab of fear. What if it had gotten back to Bremer that Richfield had been stopped by the militia in the same street as the Marcus shooting? How close was Bremer to the PSB? Who had gotten the story wrong? Had someone at the PSB deliberately misled Bremer over what had happened, or just misinterpreted information passed on by the militia? Or was the militia purposefully withholding the details of the incident from the PSB because it feared embarrassment over a grossly mishandled arrest?

Just then the phone rang. It was Esther.

"Greetings, wise one," he told her cheerily. "I suppose you've called to invite me to lunch. It's getting close to that time."

"Douglas, that would be just fine any other day of the week, but today you have a more important invitation than mine."

"What's that?"

"They want you over at the RCA Building right away."

"Who wants me over there?"

"A guy called Weikert from the PSB called. He said there's a routine investigation going on, and the man in charge wants to see you. You're to be at the main checkpoint off Fifth Avenue and identify yourself at the guardhouse."

"If it's so routine, how come I get zero notice to show up?"

"Search me, I'm just the messenger. Bremer passed the message on."

"Bremer? Did he say anything else other than I'm to go?"

"No, but he said you were to drop whatever you were doing and get there immediately. It's pretty urgent. Douglas," she said with a soothing laugh, conscious of the tension in Richfield's voice, "you must've hit the jackpot. Let me see, now, you're the head of a gun-smuggling ring. No, you're going to be promoted to chief of protocol for Chairperson Stan Rutledge. No, maybe they're going to send you off on liaison duty to Cancun. Look, don't worry, you'll be back in a couple of hours. Maybe they'll even give you something to eat. Enjoy."

"Thanks, Esther, I'll give you a full report."

But he *was* worried.

❖ ❖ ❖

Richfield presented himself to the same guardhouse through which Ponomarev had passed a few hours earlier. He had decided on the bored approach. As languidly as he could, he produced both his Protocol Department and his Kommandatura passes for inspection through the slot in the bulletproof glass. The outer door was quickly opened, and Richfield was admitted. He raised his arms for the pat-down weapons search before he was even asked to do so, as though being searched were so normal he responded to it automatically. A guard took the Kommandatura pass from him, registered it on a computer with a bar-code reader, and then handed back a large plastic pass with the words "RCA BUILDING VISITOR" in large red letters on it.

"Wear this at all times in the building," the guard instructed him, "and return it when you leave. We'll give you back your Kommandatura pass in exchange." A button was then pressed to open the door to the rear holding area, and after that another was activated to open the rear door of the guardhouse.

Stepping out, Richfield found himself facing a man wearing a thick, somewhat creased, brown polyester suit, a cream-colored shirt, and a striped brown tie. He was in his mid-thirties, with thinning blond hair and deep rings under his eyes. Why do plainclothes policemen all look alike? Richfield found himself asking.

"Weikert," said the man, extending his hand in an unexpectedly friendly manner. "Public Security Bureau. I'm to take you upstairs."

"Thank you." Richfield decided not to betray any curiosity, but he was bursting with it. Who on earth in the RCA Building would want to meet him? He'd been in the building a few times on routine business, but he had always dealt with lower-level National Executive Committee bureaucrats, who tended to be brusque and arrogant. Now someone was pretending to take a special interest in him.

He followed Weikert into the lobby past the second checkpoint where his pass was scrutinized. As the elevator soared effortlessly to the thirty-fourth floor, it occurred to Richfield that the machinery and the entire building were better maintained and cleaner than any other government office he had been in since the beginning of the civil war. Weikert, professional and discreet, made no effort at conversation.

Natalya was in the reception area when they arrived at the offices of the Educational Programs Administration, and she had been expecting him. "Good afternoon," she said warmly. "May I take your coat? The deputy has asked me to bring you straight into his office."

That accent, Richfield thought, his ear accustomed to detect regional and educational differences in the hundreds of people he met each month, *it's certainly not from the Bronx or Harlem or the South. Sort of British. Odd, for an African-American, unless she's spent a few years outside the States.* As she walked in front of him down the corridor, through the kitchen into the second corridor and then into Ponomarev's office, her walk seemed more European than American, possible French. Her posture was impeccable.

Natalya knocked lightly twice on the open door, then stopped just inside the room. "Mr. Deputy Director," she said with a warm, confident voice, "Mr. Douglas Richfield."

Ponomarev rose from one of the two armchairs beside the coffee table and reached out to Richfield to shake hands. "Welcome and thank you so much for coming. I'm sorry to interrupt your day's work for this, but I think you'll come to understand why in a moment. Natalya, bring Mr. Richfield a cup of coffee, and bring me a cigar while you're about it. Please sit down, Douglas."

This was getting weird. A tall, handsome African-American woman with a British accent called Natalya and a man who was obviously not American-born but spoke with a British accent were treating Richfield as though he were an honored guest. What on earth did the "thanks for coming" mean? Had there been any option not to come?

Sitting down on the couch at a right angle to Ponomarev, Douglas saw that his host was looking intently at a lavishly illustrated book on birds and sipping coffee from a large mug with the inscription: "New Orleans Dixieland Jazz Festival, 1983."

"I'm fond of the hawfinch," Ponomarev said casually, as though he and Richfield were chatting about someone they had known for years. "It has one of the most elegant courtship manners of any of the Passeriformes. It's colorful without being too exotic, and its great conical bill can crack a cherry stone."

Richfield leaned over to observe a quarter-page painting of a perching bird with orange-yellow, white, and dark gray plumage. "You don't find them outside of Europe and Asia," Ponomarev went on, "but I think I once saw one in Turkey. Are you fond of birds, Douglas?"

"Well, I've never studied them. I had a roommate in college who spent his vacations wandering around the country looking for any species he had never seen previously."

"It's such a shame none of us can do that now, isn't it? War, and especially civil war, always deals nature and nature watchers a bad hand, doesn't it?"

Douglas had never met anyone like this. What was his name, and what was he deputy director of? And why was he wasting his own and Richfield's time prattling on about birds?

Ponomarev went on, "When I was in India, I took a real liking to the myna bird. They're nosy, inquisitive chaps, but they're so rewarding to get to know. A good friend of mine had one, and they used to chat together in the morning before he had to dress, shave, and go to work. My friend, that is." And Ponomarev laughed agreeably at his own joke.

Douglas felt sheer politeness was forcing him to launch a conversational gambit of his own. He knew it was exactly what the other man wanted, but he also knew that if he started inquiring what he had been called to Rockefeller Center for, he might be in for a subtle cat-and-mouse game. The whole scene was too strange for him to find his bearings. It reminded him of the deliberate disordering of reality he had seen in some avant-garde films, like those made by Federico Fellini in the sixties.

"Have you spent much time in India?" he asked.

"Enough to know the country rather well. I think the only state I never visited was Uttar Pradesh." He was silent. The ball had been skillfully lobbed back to Richfield.

This was getting exasperating. Natalya came in with the coffee. Richfield wondered if her timing had been prearranged with his host, but he resisted the idea as paranoia. More time was spent pouring the cream—real cream!—and sugar, and then waiting for Ponomarev to go through the laborious process of cutting and lighting a cigar.

"I hope this doesn't upset you," he said.

He smiled so warmly at Richfield as he spoke that Douglas couldn't tell him that cigar smoke tended to nauseate him. "I'll survive," he replied with a grin, relaxing a little for the first time.

Ponomarev closed his book, leaned back in his chair, and took several long puffs on his cigar. Then, without looking at Richfield, he threw out the first challenge. "What do you know about those two Constitutionalist agents in the shooting incident you witnessed last Thursday?"

Finally, the point, Richfield thought. He had been preparing for this.

"You mean the elderly couple who were questioned by the militia?"

"Richfield!" Ponomarev's tone suddenly turned cold and stinging. "You were stopped by a police patrol less than a minute after shots were fired by a militiaman at a fleeing suspect. Don't insult my intelligence by saying that you neither heard nor saw anything. We've identified all twenty people checked by the police on the street when it was cordoned off, and we've shown photographs to the militiamen who did the shooting. Your face was the only one either of them recognized. One of them said that you came right up behind him as he was checking the fugitive who tried to run away. At that point the man was apparently sprawled in a pool of blood all over the sidewalk. Did you have any idea who he was?"

Ponomarev now turned around in his chair and looked intently into Richfield's face.

Once again Douglas was startled. "No . . . not for sure."

Ponomarev still stared intently at him. But the momentary hesitation in reply by Richfield was all he had needed.

"You knew the woman flying through the air as she was shot wasn't a woman at all, didn't you? And you knew he was Daniel Marcus, didn't you? Now why?"

"Because of the limp."

"And who told you about the limp?"

Richfield paused momentarily. Did this man know Bremer had told him? Probably. After all it was Bremer who asked Esther to pass the summons on to Richfield to come here in the first place. As long as he could keep Esther out of the equation. She hadn't been around when the shooting started.

"Steve Bremer," he finally said, his lips and his mouth dry.

Now Ponomarev hesitated. He blinked twice, took a pen and notebook out of his pocket, and quickly wrote something in the notebook. He turned back to Richfield and asked, "Do you know whether Marcus is dead or alive today?"

"No," said Richfield with conviction. Technically, it was true; he didn't know. He hadn't examined the body, hadn't seen any death certificate, and Bremer had implied that the outcome wasn't clear either. But if he had to bet his life on it, he'd say without hesitating that Marcus was dead.

He'd lied, and he didn't feel good about it, except for one thing. It now gave him one solid advantage over this cigar-smoking foreigner who was playing nasty psychological games with him.

Ponomarev suddenly relaxed. He puffed quickly on his cigar, put it in an ashtray, and called out, "Natalya! Please ask Gusev to join me."

Natalya? Gusev? Who were these people? Richfield felt himself exploding inside. "Look, you've asked me a lot of questions," he blurted out. "Now would you mind if I returned the favor? First, what is all this about? Second, are you Russian or something?"

Ponomarev roared with good-humored laughter, picked up his cigar, and smiled broadly at Richfield.

"Yes, we're Russian. Forgive me for not putting all of the cards on the table. I'm sure you'll understand why we don't always do that in this business. You can call me Alexei. I won't burden you with the last name because Americans invariably have trouble with it. You ask what this is all about. That's reasonable. Let's just say that Chairman Rutledge, I mean Chair*person*"—he snickered as he said this—"considers us helpful and has asked us to assist the PSB in a matter or two. And I'm delighted to help if I can. Ah, Sergei," he interrupted himself as Gusev quietly entered, scrutinizing Richfield as he did so, "meet Douglas Richfield. Douglas, this is my assistant Sergei Gusev." Richfield rose awkwardly from the couch to shake hands with Gusev, who smiled slightly and sat in the chair beside his boss.

"Okay," said Richfield, assembling his wits for whatever was going to come next, "now where do I fit in with all this?"

"Oh, that's simple," replied Ponomarev looking at him intently again. "We want you to work for us."

5

The Recruiting

Work for whom?" Richfield struggled to stall for time. Then he re-membered the title Natalya had first mentioned, the deputy director.

"I've barely been in this office half an hour," he continued, snatching at the initiative, "and you're trying to recruit me for some-thing. How do I know who you are? You sound Russian. You say you're Russian. But the sign on the door says 'Educational Administration' or something like that. You're obviously in the intelligence business. Are you deputy director of the Russian Foreign Intelligence Service?"

It was a bold response, and Ponomarev raised his eyebrow with a slight smirk at Gusev. Gusev nodded toward the two chairs behind Ponomarev's desk and looked inquiringly at his boss. Ponomarev shook his head, facing Richfield the whole time.

"Not bad for the Protocol Department. You could turn out to be quite useful," he said with deliberate condescension. "No, I'm not deputy director of the Foreign Intelligence Service, but I'm high up in one of the main departments. I've told you my first name, Alexei, and because you're full of youthful curiosity this afternoon, I'll tell you that my middle name is Ilyich. In Russia—perhaps you don't know this—in polite conversation people address each other by first name and their father's name, the patronymic. I don't mind in the least if you call me Alexei Ilyich."

Richfield felt his blood pressure rising by the second. This con-ceited, sneering apparatchik, probably no more than ten years older than himself, was patronizing him. Why had he fallen for all those lines about myna birds and Uttar Pradesh?

He stood up. "I'm sorry, I can't help you, Alexei Ilyich," he said briskly. "I have a lot to do back at the Protocol Department this afternoon, and I don't think they'll appreciate it if I don't show up. I'm sure you can find someone more qualified to assist you. Why don't you have the PSB lend you one of their men? Thank you for the coffee. May I leave?"

Richfield expected some response from the two men, perhaps a protest or a reluctant good-bye of their own, but Gusev and Ponomarev just sat there coldly, looking at the American and waiting for him to move.

Douglas felt uneasy. What if they decided to be unpleasant? If he shouted, no one was likely to help him. Russia's Foreign Intelligence Service, after all, was only in the RCA Building because the People's Movement at the highest level had approved its being here. He decided to try to negotiate his way out. If that didn't work, he'd make for the door as quickly as he could.

"I don't think you have a legal basis for detaining me. If I had committed a crime, no doubt the Public Security Bureau would have wanted to see me. So, excuse me; it was nice to meet you."

He didn't need any directions. He knew he had to go back down the corridor, through the kitchen, down another corridor to the reception, and out. But as he stepped briskly out of Ponomarev's office, a sudden chill came over him. Although the corridor was in front of him, there was no kitchen, no door, just a wall. They'd done something to block off the kitchen while he had been sitting in the Russian's office. He went to the wall and banged on it; it sounded hollow. Douglas was getting a creepy, almost panicky feeling. A moment later his fear turned into anger.

He turned around defiantly and marched back into Ponomarev's office. Both Russians were now sitting in the two chairs behind the desk. Ponomarev was on the phone.

"Look, if this is some kind of game you're playing," Richfield said, "I think it's pretty sick. Would you mind getting someone to show me out?"

Ponomarev looked at him steadily and showed no emotion as he talked in Russian into the phone.

Gusev now became the friendly one. "I'm so sorry, Mr. Richfield," he said soothingly, rising from his chair and approaching Douglas with a repentant look. "My superior only came in from

Russia yesterday, and I think he's very tired. He is—how do you say it?—very eager sometimes. We certainly understand that you have other business back at your office. I will ask Natalya to show you the way out."

Douglas turned back to watch the corridor, hoping to see how Natalya would arrive. To his amazement the wall swung back on noiseless bearings, revealing once more the cheerful kitchen he'd originally entered through. Natalya walked in smartly, friendly as ever.

"Natalya, please show Mr. Richfield the way out," said Gusev. "He has to return to the Protocol Department."

Natalya smiled guilelessly at Richfield as though they'd known each other all their lives. Despite Gusev and the chilling Alexei for whom she worked, he couldn't help liking her. "There's just one thing all visitors have to do, Mr. Richfield, if you don't mind," she said. "Will you please register in our visitors' book? I don't think you did that on the way in."

"Sure, no problem." Richfield was just eager to get out. He pulled out a pen to sign even before she had the book ready. It was a standard sign-in book: name, organization, time in, time out, person visited, reason for visit, signature.

"What was the purpose of my visit?" Richfield asked Natalya, who was watching him fill in the entries.

"Well, I don't know what you discussed. Perhaps you'd better just write in 'discussion.' That should cover it."

"Thanks," said Richfield gratefully.

"Now I'll call the people downstairs and have an escort come to take you back to the guardhouse. I'm sure you understand the building's security system."

"Yes, of course." It was irritating, but protesting wouldn't do much good, Richfield thought. Natalya punched a four-digit extension on the phone and said, "Please ask Mr. Weikert to come up to the thirty-fourth floor. Thanks." To Richfield she added, "It'll be a minute or two. Have a seat if you like."

Douglas suddenly felt very tired and very hungry. It was nearly three o'clock and he'd had no lunch and not much for breakfast. The combination of the political discussion, Bremer's nasty little comments, and now this "recruitment" at the Education Administration, or whatever it was, had knotted up his insides. The strong, European-style coffee hadn't helped either.

But his reverie was interrupted. Natalya's phone rang and he heard her say, "He can't do it now? Isn't there someone else who can come? Our visitor needs to return to his office right away. . . . Twenty minutes! Can't you do any better than that? . . . Okay. The reception doors may be locked, so buzz when you get here."

Natalya turned to Richfield with an embarrassed expression. "I'm very sorry," she said, "but our regular liaison officer, the gentleman who escorted you here, has been called away on urgent business and won't be back for some twenty minutes or so. Unfortunately, there isn't anyone else who can cover for him. Should I call your office for you?"

"Yes, please," Douglas responded. Giving her the phone number, he said, "Please tell Esther Garcia that I'm still at the RCA Building and hope to be back in about an hour. Also, I'd like to know if there are any messages for me."

Natalya was on the line with Esther quickly and sounded as though Douglas and she were already the closest of friends. Douglas grinned to himself as he wondered what Esther made of the voice at the other end of the line—friendly, vaguely British, and seemingly impressed with Douglas Richfield. Natalya's ebullience helped lighten the gloomy mood that had stolen upon him since his ugly confrontation with Ponomarev.

"He also asks if there are any messages," Natalya was saying, repeating Esther's response for Douglas's benefit: "The Cuban mission to the U.N. . . . Right . . . right . . . the Kaylip Foundation. How do you spell that? . . . C-A-L-E-B. Okay. Any message? Okay, I'll pass that on: 555-2100."

Douglas's pulse quickened. That could only be Rachel. It was bold of her. Douglas knew from contacts in the PSB that the Protocol Department lines weren't generally tapped, but he suspected that a borderline group like the Caleb Foundation, with its links to people seeking emigration to Israel and to Israeli representatives themselves, would be under close surveillance much, if not all, of the time. Still, a call to the Protocol Department was plausible.

"I think you got all that," Natalya said perkily. "Now, my guess is that you're absolutely starving since you didn't have any lunch. We're much too small here to have a cafeteria, but I think we've got some pizza in the refrigerator. Would you like me to warm a piece for you in the microwave?"

"That'd be real nice of you. Thanks." Douglas was genuinely touched. This pleasant woman, an African-American who had a Russian name and spoke perfect Russian, was offering him the first no-strings-attached kindness he had encountered since entering this highly secretive outpost of the Russian KGB, alias the "Educational Programs Administration."

Natalya was off and back in three minutes with his pizza and a fresh mug of coffee. The pizza was good, and Douglas felt better. There was even a slight lessening in his anger toward Ponomarev. He'd almost forgotten about his escort, Weikert, when this polyester-suited servant of the New Era arrived.

"Good, we wondered where you'd gone," Natalya said.

"I was on an errand for Mr. Ponomarev. He asked me to deliver this back to him." Weikert handed Natalya a legal-sized brown envelope. She took it, looking carefully back at him and then at Richfield.

"I'll give it to him now and be right back. Please wait here with Mr. Richfield until I return."

As she hastened down the corridor, Douglas tried to draw Weikert into conversation. "Do you usually work here?" he asked carefully.

"You mean in this building? Sometimes, but mostly my work takes me all over town."

"How's the PSB as an employer?" Richfield pursued, adopting a we're-all-family tone.

"Pretty good, I'd say, at least compared with what I did before the civil war."

"What was that?"

"Anti-drug stuff. DEA. It got messy at times."

"You mean you were a federal agent?" asked Richfield, his curiosity aroused, "and they employed you at the PSB?"

Weikert looked embarrassed and protected himself with a prop-aganda comeback. "Many employees of the federal government before the New Era tried to serve the people and not just the interests of the ruling class," he intoned, paraphrasing Stan Rutledge.

But Richfield was skeptical. Hardly any federal agents, whether Treasury Department, FBI, or Justice Department, had stayed around in the People's Movement areas of control, much less volunteered for service in the New Era. Weikert must have had deep and clandestine links to radical politics or some other intelligence organization to be in his present job.

Natalya returned but looked crestfallen. "Mr. Weikert," she said with apparent embarrassment, "would you mind staying a little longer, or maybe coming back after we've called you again? Mr. Ponomarev has some more business to discuss with Mr. Richfield and asks if you'll wait for them to complete it. If you prefer, of course, you may want to go back to your office and wait for us to call again. I'm very sorry." And she seemed so.

She turned to Douglas. "Mr. Richfield, Alexei Ilyich asks that you please come to his office. He says something has come up, and he needs your input."

She looked uncomfortable. This new demand from Ponomarev would probably aggravate Douglas. For a moment he debated refusing to see Ponomarev again and asking Weikert to escort him out of the building immediately.

But there was something unnerving about Weikert. Tired-looking and expressionless in his rumpled brown polyester and his garish, faded yellow shirt, Richfield doubted that Weikert would defy Ponomarev's "request." The man might be more than just a liaison agent with the Russians; he might be a deep-cover agent originally run by Moscow back during the Cold War days.

Thus Douglas followed Natalya down the corridor, into the kitchen, through the false wall into the other corridor, and back into Ponomarev's office like a schoolboy being taken to the principal's office. At least, he thought as he entered, he had now heard the deputy director's last name. He would try using it.

This time the Russian was sitting at the desk, wearing eyeglasses, and perusing a thin sheaf of papers, presumably from the envelope Weikert had just brought in. Gusev was sitting next to him, taking notes on a legal pad. They looked for all the world like they were doing their homework together at the kitchen table. Was Ponomarev gay? He doubted it. The Russians were intolerant of homosexuals.

"Please sit down, Mr. Richfield. I'm sorry we've had to bother you again, but since you were still here when this information arrived, we wanted to talk to you as soon as we could rather than request your office send you back." It was Gusev, playing the good cop in what seemed to Richfield to be a rather transparent version of the old routine. "I know that you had hard feelings during our first conversation, and I hope we can get over those now. The problem is that Alexei Ilyich did not have the time to explain to you why we think you could be of enormous service to your government, your country, and to world peace if you were willing to help us. Would you be so kind and permit Alexei Ilyich to discuss those points now?"

"He's free to discuss anything he wants, and I'm free to continue to say no to whatever it is he wants me to do."

"Exactly. We certainly understand your point of view." Richfield was sullen, but Gusev's respectful tone and his quaintly polite English disarmed some of his resentment.

Ponomarev had taken off his reading glasses during Gusev's last remarks and had pressed his fingers together in front of his face as though praying, his eyes focused speculatively on some distant point. He appeared oblivious to Gusev's efforts to put Douglas in a more receptive mood. Either the guy has extraordinarily thick skin, Richfield thought, or he operates on a plane of ruthlessness beyond anything I've ever experienced.

"Douglas," Ponomarev began, "have you ever reflected on how seriously unstable the world is? I mean even now, despite the Treaty of Paris—the Strategic Reordering Treaty—despite our good relations with your government. Despite the fact, of course, that we assume the People's Movement will eventually rule all of America."

Weird question, Douglas thought. "As far as I can see, the world has never been stable for more than a few years at a time. I'd say it's probably more stable now than, say, a couple of decades ago."

"You would? May I ask why?"

"Because," said Richfield, "there's no cold war, there's no serious hot war between the major powers, and the only military conflict anywhere is the civil war in this country. Since no one else is involved in that, I'd assume things could be a lot worse around the world."

"How do you know nobody else is involved?"

"What are you talking about? You Russians aren't helping us, although I know there's been some talk both here and in Moscow that you might get involved at some point. Who else would be involved?"

"The Chinese, perhaps."

"The Chinese! That's ridiculous. They're strictly neutral."

"The Chinese are an enigmatic people. They operate in a different timeframe from other countries. They think ahead in half-centuries and centuries, whereas you and we can barely master a couple of years at a time, much less a decade. There is one thing you can always be certain of about the Chinese, though, and that is that they don't like to be dependent on anyone else's favor. We learned that the hard way in the 1950s.

"There is another thing about the Chinese: they do not like to have unfriendly powers on either side of them. We, as you know, have rather good relations now with the Japanese. When Ushihara became prime minister and abrogated Japan's security treaty with your country, before our troops clashed with yours in Iran, of course, he made good on a threat he and other Japanese patriots had made earlier, namely to make Japanese microchip and other advanced technology available to us instead of to America. That was very helpful. And when President Zhelenovsky wisely decided to return the Kurile Islands to Japan—though he was much criticized for that at home by some of his supporters—that established something like an alliance between Russia and Japan. Who would have thought of it? The very country that decimated our fleet in the Straits of Tsushima in 1905 would one day be helping us back on our feet.

"The Chinese are very uncomfortable about this. Though it may seem ridiculous to you that the Chinese could intervene in the civil war in your country on the side of the Constitutionalist forces and against the People's Movement, it is a very real possibility to us."

Douglas had not suspected this side of Ponomarev. The Russian's passion for international politics had made him interesting to listen to, even eloquent.

Ponomarev paused as though, having launched a deep thrust in his argument in one direction, he wanted to reinforce his final push with a different approach. "The danger of a Chinese decision to favor the Constitutionalists," he went on, "is a real one to us, though not exactly an immediate one. It would be a long time before they could provide anything other than token military assistance. Nevertheless, I don't think I need to stress further how serious a blow it would be to the credibility of your government, and perhaps even its long-term viability, if a world power like China supported your opponents.

"But let's come to what I consider the most unstable element in the world scene. Douglas, I'm going to be very blunt with you. What you have no doubt picked up as rumors, that there are three Ohio-class nuclear ballistic missile submarines still at large in the oceans and loyal to the Constitutionalists, is true. They exist. We don't say so publicly, but we know they are there, and we have been trying very hard to find them. The man you saw shot last week on Fifty-ninth Street, Daniel Marcus, is the one who knows where they are, or at least, where, at some point, they can be found. At the moment we cannot find out from him what he knows about these submarines and where they secretly resupply with food and other items. He is in a coma and we don't know when he'll come out of it."

Liar, Richfield thought. *You know as well as I do that he's dead. But that's okay. It's something I have on you that you don't know about.*

"I am authorized to tell you that President Zhelenovsky has agreed with Chairperson Rutledge that capturing or destroying these submarines must be the priority of all cooperative activity between our two countries. Marcus may not be able to talk quite as quickly as we had hoped, and we cannot afford the luxury of awaiting his recovery. It is therefore essential that we pursue every means to find out where these submarines are reprovisioning and perhaps even permitting their crews to rest. Are you following me so far?"

Richfield had a disturbing feeling that Ponomarev was coming around to the issue of Richfield's involvement. He was now very curious about the Russian's agenda. He wanted his interlocutor to put as many cards as possible on the table before he had to play any of his own.

"How can you be so sure," he asked, "that the submarines are really out there? You admit you don't know where they are. What if they've been scuttled over the Marianas Trench and their crews have now vanished into a hundred different locations around the world? There are countries that would protect these people."

"That is a good question and a good point, though we do know the names of the crews," responded Ponomarev enthusiastically. "There are two reasons why we do not think that has happened. First, the submarines are the ultimate trump card of the Constitutionalists. Apart from a handful of ships in Hawaii and maybe a fast-attack submarine or two, we have located, disabled, or turned over to the People's Movement virtually every vessel in the former U.S. Navy. The seventy-two Trident-D missiles aboard these three submarines thus constitute a deadly and potentially decisive independent nuclear deterrent for the Constitutionalists. As long as the subs are out there, General Hodges in Montana and so-called President Verazzano in Hawaii know that the People's Movement will not use either nuclear or chemical-biological weaponry against the Constitutionalist forces. Even if only one of the submarines survives operationally, it's inconceivable that the Constitutionalists would throw away such a valuable strategic trump. Besides, when you scuttle an object that is 560 feet long and 16,000 tons in weight, it is not always certain that some evidence of it won't surface at some point, literally, in this case.

"The second reason is more technical. I suspect that Steve Bremer gave you some information about Project Almond, the devilish scheme that Daniel Marcus dreamed up. Marcus was clever enough—and he is a clever man—to foresee the possibility of a strategic showdown, possibly even a defeat, for America's military forces. Now it's just one of the peculiar facts of history that the Trident submarine is the most perfectly concealable doomsday weapon that mankind has ever devised. The missiles of just one submarine could devastate forty or more Russian cities, including the obvious targets of Moscow, St. Petersburg, Ekaterinenburg, and Nizhny Novgorod. Yet even if you know which quadrant of the ocean these submarines are patroling, it is virtually impossible to find them.

"We believe that Marcus established several remote resupply bases for each submarine. We have no idea what is involved, but it could range from the absolutely basic—a warehouse, let's say, in a sparsely inhabited area—to a cavernous repair shop concealed in any of the thousands of coastal inlets around the globe. We are a major world power—no, we are the sole major world power today—yet it might take years to locate these places and root them out."

While Ponomarev spoke, Gusev took methodical notes like an old-fashioned law clerk. *Who else does Gusev report to?* Richfield wondered.

"To put it simply," Ponomarev said, obviously closing in on the point of this long preamble, "we need access to the highest Constitutionalist leadership to discover as much as we can about the Almond Project." He paused, looking carefully but not aggressively at Douglas.

Here was another chance to deflect his aim, Richfield thought. "I'm sure the Public Security Bureau has already deployed its agents to this end," Douglas said matter-of-factly.

"They have certainly tried to discover what they can," Ponomarev replied with a sigh approaching exasperation, "but regrettably not to great effect. The PSB was originally established as an agency to protect the People's Movement itself from infiltration. It is, in essence, a counterespionage unit. In this work it has not done badly, considering its lack of professionalism in general. But it is regrettably inexperienced in old-fashioned espionage and infiltration techniques. I hope I am not showing disrespect to your government if I say that the other side appears to have had more success in penetrating the People's Movement than vice versa."

"What do you mean?" Douglas was astounded at this remark and found himself momentarily playing the role of a wounded People's Movement activist.

"We at the Foreign Intelligence Service in Moscow for some time have been certain that there is a mole at the very highest level of the People's Movement, possibly within the National Executive Committee itself."

Douglas exploded. "You've got to be kidding! All those people were involved in the People's Movement when it was a grassroots movement before the civil war. How could any of them be working for the Constitutionalists? Don't you think that the PSB has carefully verified the backgrounds and activities of all NEC members?"

"Of course," said Ponomarev calmly. "The PSB may not be the most effective intelligence agency the world has ever seen, but it is not entirely stupid, I agree. Its chief problem is inexperience. But that is not the point. You can, for example, monitor a colony of rabbits for weeks and still miss several moments of conception. The baby rabbits keep being born."

"I'm sorry," said Richfield with some impatience, "but I don't see the connection between rabbits and Constitutionalist spies."

"You don't? Suppose I told you that there was circumstantial evidence of Constitutionalist advance knowledge of People's Movement military or security operations in about two out of every three cases decided at meetings of the National Executive Committee. We know who attends these meetings, we monitor their activities, and yet the leaks still occur." The last sentence was expressed with disgust, as though it was tedious for Ponomarev to have to deal with this problem.

Richfield had been alerted to something Ponomarev had said. "You mean that your agents monitor NEC meetings?"

"*We* don't monitor these meetings. The PSB does. But we work closely with the PSB, and they naturally provide us with the essential information that we need. In addition, in case you may have forgotten, Chairperson Rutledge personally requested President Zhelenovsky to provide the resources of our not-inexperienced First Chief Directorate to assist the PSB in remedying this deplorable situation." Ponomarev was becoming sarcastic again, and Richfield decided not to pursue this line of curiosity.

"So then," Douglas said, "you regard catching this Constitutionalist mole, whoever he or she is, as connected in some way with information about Operation Almond?"

"Project Almond," Ponomarev corrected him. "Yes. At present, I do not surmise that if we found the mole, he or she would then lead us to the well from which we could draw up all we needed on the renegade submarines. But I suspect that if we could penetrate the Constitutionalists at a sufficiently high level, we could, at one stroke, uncover enough details of Almond to close down the project and find the trail leading to our mole."

Gusev, jotting down furiously as much as he could of Ponomarev's speech and Richfield's reply, smirked from time to time at Ponomarev's figures of speech. He seemed particularly to like the rabbits and moles.

So far, Ponomarev had spoken in background generalities. Richfield knew intuitively that sooner or later he would circle back to the issue of his involvement. He resented the thought of having to argue his way out of the room again. Anyway, where was Weikert? Surely he'd arrived by now and could escort Richfield out of this sinister office, which was making him feel more claustrophobic by the minute.

But Ponomarev seemed to have come to the end of his remarks. He had leaned forward on the desk several times to emphasize a point as he talked, but now he pushed himself back from the desk, leaned back in his chair, and placed his feet on the desk.

This abrupt posturing had an immediate impact upon Richfield. From one point of view it was rude. Richfield was technically a guest in Ponomarev's office; the two men were anything but bosom buddies. From another point of view Ponomarev's maneuver suddenly relaxed the atmosphere in the room.

Richfield was about to collect himself, rise, and say good-bye with a sigh of relief when he saw Gusev picking out from under his pile of legal-sized notes the typed pages that Ponomarev had been perusing earlier.

"As we understand it, Mr. Richfield," Gusev began, for all the world a charming country lawyer advising a local landowner's son, "your father died a few years ago and your mother remarried and now lives in East Orange, New Jersey. Is that correct?"

"Yes, but what's that got to do with what we've just been discussing?" Richfield said testily.

"Oh, nothing. I just wanted to be sure the biographical information on you was correct. And you have a sister, three years younger, who dropped out of graduate school, just like you, and now works at the New Jersey Department of Motor Vehicles. Correct?"

"Yes, but what's that got to do with anything? I'm the one you want to talk to, not them."

Richfield was becoming angry and a bit careless. He had inadvertently conceded some sort of right to Ponomarev and Gusev to question him.

"Yes, that's quite right. We certainly don't want to disturb your mother and your sister. It's you we really hope will help us out." Gusev was now slipping quietly but inexorably into the steely tone that Ponomarev had adopted when Richfield was in the office the first time. It was devilish. The two men were alternating the good-cop-bad-cop routine, deliberately confusing their target as to which one, at any time, was "good." Richfield began to feel like a man who had just had a second opinion confirm his cancer.

"Now, if I'm not mistaken," Gusev went on as though assessing an insurance claim, "your mother and sister actually live together at 1460 Maypole Avenue, South Orange. Is that correct?"

Richfield was getting very angry and hot now. "You know, you Russians can be pretty dumb in your heavy-handedness," he interrupted Gusev. "You're presumably telling me about my mother and sister to impress me with your information-gathering techniques. Next thing you'll tell me the title of my prize-winning poem about turtles in the third grade. Hey, aren't you all just terrific? So what is this supposed to prove, that the PSB has done its flat-footed best to provide its good buddies with warehouses full of useless biographical information?"

There was a chill in the air after this blast by Richfield. The American felt cornered, and all three men knew it.

Gusev eyed him calmly and coldly, untroubled by the outburst. Ponomarev, still leaning back in his own chair, hands clasped behind his head, merely narrowed his eyes slightly. He had been rocking gently in the plush leather seat, but now he was quite still.

Gusev shot him a glance, and he nodded imperceptibly in response. Gusev let a slight pause hang in the air and then went on. "No, Mr. Richfield," he said, almost sighing at the need to explain it all, "we aren't particularly interested in impressing you with our knowledge of your life. You're intelligent enough not to need impressing in that way. What we want to impress you with is our familiarity with your closest family members."

"You what?" shouted Richfield. "What kind of rock did you people crawl out from under?"

Gusev merely shrugged at this and looked down at his information sheet on Richfield. Ponomarev now took up the dialogue.

"Yes, we in the intelligence business are cold-blooded, always have been, always will be," he observed, as though announcing that his family profession was plumbing. "The bottom line, as they used to say in the old days, is that we do what we have to do to get information. Douglas, this is very serious. This isn't a game. I'm talking about the direction of history itself. Do you want a world where war has been largely banished, where there is some order, some predictability in life, or do you a world constantly at war with itself? Does it give you a thrill to think of your own country struggling through another half-decade, perhaps, of civil war, with all of the carnage, brutality, and misery that war brings? I believe that if we can cut off this submarine game quickly and clean up the performance of the PSB in catching spies, we can bring an end to the war before the Chinese have a chance to get involved.

"Your country and mine, of course, have different ideas on how to organize our economies and our societies. In an ironic way we have completely changed positions ideologically. But we can coexist, perhaps even come to respect each other a little. The point is that we must bring an end to the conflict. You, Douglas, are in an absolutely unique position to help us do that."

"What am I supposed to do," Douglas asked, "march off to Montana and announce that I'm looking for anyone who can help me pinpoint some submarines and uncover a spy in New York? They'd really put out the welcome mat for me, wouldn't they?"

To Richfield's surprise and annoyance, his sarcasm didn't make a dent on Ponomarev's equanimity. Gusev fidgeted a little, bored now with the dialogue. Douglas, he and Ponomarev both now intuitively sensed, was tiring. But he still had to make one more effort to evade their net.

"Suppose I refuse," he asked defiantly. "Suppose I walk out of here, go straight to my superiors in the Protocol Department, and complain that the Russian Foreign Intelligence Service is threatening my family in order to force me to work for them?"

"Douglas, you're not serious, are you?" Ponomarev asked. "There are two good reasons why you should take advantage of this opportunity to participate in the making of history. The first is the excitement, the satisfaction, of taking part in a great venture to bring an end—successfully for your side, *our* side—to this civil war. The second is, to be blunt, that the PSB has already given us the authority to secure your cooperation. I suppose I have to be painfully blunt because you seem not to grasp this. You will without question cooperate with us. I don't want to spell out how, because it's unpleasant and you're smart enough not to need me to. Now, it's getting late and we're all getting a bit tired, so could we get to the details?"

Douglas felt nothing but despair. It was a horrible sensation, being trapped, being swept along by a current that would not let him rest or take his bearings, that insisted he keep up with the flow. With each minute sealing his fate and his inevitable participation in Ponomarev's emerging scheme, Richfield became more determined to conceal his feelings. All right, if this was naked coercion, the implied threats to his mother and sister, then he would submit to *force majeure,* for their sake. But Ponomarev would not have his mind and soul.

"I understand," he said. "But what good am I to you? I don't know squat about spying. What use could I be?"

Gusev stopped writing momentarily and turned for a quick moment toward Ponomarev. It was the question they had both been waiting for. Ponomarev allowed a slight smile to turn the corners of his mouth. Douglas had surrendered, and he and the Russians now knew it. What he also knew, but they didn't, was that in cornering him to pursue a goal he already believed in, they were invading the floating world of conscience. Ponomarev and Gusev, after years of exploiting the weaknesses of others, had lost all sense of what this was. Their cynicism had blinded them to its reality and its power to take vengeance on those who violated it.

"Good," said Ponomarev smugly, "good. I'm glad we don't have to spend any more time on the preliminaries. Actually, it's very simple. We are going to take advantage of the one indisputable asset you have. You're an unknown. There is nothing about your training, your behavior, or your professional experience that would lead anyone to think of you as a likely agent for one side or other. The fact that you joined the People's Movement early on is also an advantage. We know that you're already somewhat disappointed in what has happened under the People's Movement's rule. We will need very little imagination to build up a convincing legend for you."

"A legend?"

"A legend is the invented background of the person a spy is pretending to be. In your case we don't have to invent your background. It is already ideal for our purposes. You merely have to simulate a motivation in order to get yourself recruited by Constitutionalist agents."

How does he know I don't feel that motivation? Richfield asked himself. But his words were different.

"You can't be serious!" he protested.

Ponomarev showed signs of annoyance. "I hope I don't have to tell you again that this is not a game," he said coldly. "In fact, even the PSB has figured out where the largest concentration of Constitutionalist agents and sympathizers hang out in Manhattan. You probably wouldn't be surprised—Greenwich Village. It attracts transients, wanderers, petty thieves, drug addicts, old-fashioned hippies, nonconformists of every shape, and thousands of people who don't like any kind of government, especially this one. To bump into those among them who are working actively for the Constitutionalists would take only patience, perseverance, and the smallest amount of luck.

"What you have to do, in fact, is very simple. Meet one or more of these agents, convince them that you're a genuine defector from the regime, and ask if they can smuggle you to Montana. Once you're there . . ."

"Excuse me," Richfield interrupted, "but if this is so simple, why can't you just get one of your regulars to do it? For that matter how come the PSB hasn't done this a dozen times already?"

"They've tried. How often they've succeeded, I won't tell you, for obvious reasons. Let's just put it this way. From several points of view you are better equipped and prepared to execute this mission than anyone currently available. Is that satisfactory to you?"

"Sure, but would you lay out the mission for me?"

"Certainly. But first, let me give you an idea of what you may be in for once you get into the Constitutionalist areas. We know that there are crossovers from no man's land every day. The vast majority are either locals or part of the general migration from small towns and suburbs in the Midwest. It is very unusual for someone to walk into Constitutionalist headquarters straight from New York, so to speak, and straight from a People's Movement job. Your advantage is that you're not so senior as to arouse suspicion about your motives for defecting, but you're senior enough to have information about the way the People's Movement operates. They will pay a lot of attention to you.

"You will, of course, be interrogated and debriefed as soon as you arrive in Montana. Your objective will be to ensure that you tell your story directly to the highest-ranking intelligence official. Only when you are sure that you aren't dealing with some junior-level screening should you let it be known that you saw Marcus arrested after a shootout in Manhattan. This information will be extremely important to General Hodges, and they will probe you meticulously about it. What you are to tell them is that you have heard that Marcus is alive and being held somewhere—you don't know where—you think maybe New York City.

"After that you're to cooperate eagerly with whatever they suggest to you. It is my hunch that they will try to recruit you as one of their agents and send you back here to find where Marcus is, so that their own agents can either rescue him or kill him before he talks to us. Meanwhile, you will use every means at your disposal while in Montana to uncover this despicable mole feeding at the same table as the National Executive Committee of the People's Movement. Before long, I suspect, they will ask you to return to New York to work for them. You must appear very reluctant to do so because of the dangers involved, but you must allow yourself to be persuaded. Once you are back here, of course, we will talk again. Is your mission clear so far?"

"Sure, except for the details. What if they don't ask me to work for them? What am I supposed to do then?"

"If they don't recruit you, then you must do whatever you can to get back here. Sooner or later an opportunity will arise. Take it. It's clear that you don't think highly of us, but you ought to know that the Russian Foreign Intelligence Service has no interest in needless repression. If, through no fault of your own, you are unable to come up with any information, or if they simply decide you aren't useful to them, we will not hold you responsible. In fact, it will be as though we had never met. Naturally, this pleasant arrangement will be null and void if we learn later that you've been telling stories in Montana about meetings with foreigners in the RCA Building. You understand, don't you, that you are to reveal absolutely nothing about us or this contact? Let me say only that if you break this confidentiality in any way, we will have ways, even in the Constitutionalist areas, of finding out." Ponomarev's face was controlled, brittle. He went on more slowly now. "It would be regrettable, but we might have to pass on to you some tragic news, perhaps your mother's sad passing in a car accident, or your sister's deplorable gang rape. Heaven forbid that any of these nightmarish events should befall anyone in your family. How terrible that would be."

Richfield looked at Ponomarev expressionlessly. Was it conceivable, he wondered, that the same man who rhapsodized about myna birds and world peace could, just as casually, threaten to murder or rape?

Ponomarev was watching Richfield closely and accurately guessed his thoughts. "Please don't get sentimental, Douglas. You're young, but not so young that you haven't seen some violent sides to the reality of life. Have you ever read Machiavelli? You should. He is the most realistic judge of political character who ever lived. He said, 'It's questionable whether it is better to be loved than to be feared, or the other way around. But if we have to choose, it is far safer to be feared than to be loved.' Fear has shown itself to be a reliable way of motivating people, perhaps not ideal, but certainly more dependable than love. I could choose to debate your own somewhat half-baked morality against mine, and I think you would be surprised to discover that mine is both more consistent and more likely to accomplish its objectives. But let us leave that conversation for another time."

Richfield was completely still. The one thing he would not permit Ponomarev to achieve was domination over his thoughts. With a supreme effort of self-control, he forced himself to return to the details of the operation. "What makes you so sure," he asked, "that the Constitutionalists here will be willing to recruit me, much less help me get to Montana?"

"I am not sure at all," Ponomarev replied with surprising candor. "But I think that when the right Constitutionalist agents hear about you, with your background in the People's Movement, they will not treat you like any old disgruntled New Yorker looking for some civil war excitement. They will make serious efforts to make use of you. That means getting you out of the city as quickly and safely as possible.

"Obviously, they will check you out here, your job in the Protocol Department and so forth. They will want to know why someone with a comfortable bureaucratic slot in the People's Movement suddenly chooses to defect to them. Well, we've hit upon a good legend for that. You are going to be fired from your City Hall job."

"What?" Richfield spluttered.

"Don't worry, the PSB, of course, knows that we're 'borrowing' you and understands what is going on. Your immediate supervisor, Bremer, will be told that the PSB has requisitioned you for a special mission. Technically, he will fire you and pass the word to your colleagues that you fell afoul of the law during a drunken fracas on Thanksgiving Day. Your firing will be easy for the other side to check out. By the way our own people and the PSB will be keeping track of your movements as you get started here. We'll obviously stay out of your way, but we'll be around—just in case.

"It will probably take a few days, maybe even a week or two before the Constitutionalists feel comfortable enough with you to make a decision on getting you out of town. Once that happens you'll be completely on your own. But I don't have any doubt about your ability to succeed at this mission. Your own—and your family's—survival instincts are quite well developed, in my view."

"How am I supposed to survive financially? What about my ration card? With my job gone I won't have it after the end of next month."

Ponomarev sighed as though he were having to cope with a spoiled four-year-old.

"Obviously," he said, his voice indicating irritation, "we don't think you can do a very good job if you are actually starving. The PSB has a special fund for these circumstances and will pay your next three months' rent, no matter how quickly you get the job done. That's a very small way of saying thanks. You share an apartment with someone, don't you?"

Richfield knew it was a fake question; Ponomarev had most of the details of Richfield's professional and daily life in front of him in the report that Weikert had delivered. But he played along.

"Yes, I share an apartment with a militiaman. How much of this is he allowed to know?"

"Nothing. He gets the same information from you that the Constitutionalists get. If you have any trouble from him, let us know and we'll have the PSB shut him up. You can continue to see your old friends. In fact, if you don't, people might start to wonder why. You've probably complained to them at different times about your colleagues and your bosses—people always do—so if you lose your job, it shouldn't be so unlikely to them. Tell them you're looking for another job in the city and you think you can get one. Do you have a regular girlfriend?"

"No."

"Good. Then there will be less explaining to do. And don't start any new romances. People in love have a boring compulsion to tell each other the truth, and we wouldn't want that to happen."

Did Ponomarev know about Rachel? Douglas doubted it. It was true that he had signed in at the library, but people generally didn't bother to sign out, and it was unlikely that the clerk from whom he'd rescued Rachel had remembered his name or had reported the incident to security. People tried to stay out of incidents.

"There's one thing we haven't discussed. How am I supposed to keep in touch with you?"

"Gusev." Ponomarev turned to his aide, who looked up from the sheets of paper he was rapidly filling up with Russian. Gusev drew a small green notebook out of his inside coat pocket, opened it, and read aloud, "One-zero-nine . . . one-two-two-four. Mr. Richfield, please don't forget this number, but don't write it down either. Please repeat it."

"One-zero-nine . . . one-two-two-four."

"Again, please."

"One-zero-nine . . . one-two-two-four."

"Good, Mr. Richfield. We will test you again just before you leave."

Ponomarev took over once more. "Do you have any more questions?" he asked.

"Yes. How soon should I start wandering around the Village?"

"Obviously not right after leaving this building," Ponomarev half-chuckled. Give it twenty-four hours or so, and don't give the impression that that's all you have to do in the city. Gusev will give you some cash before you go to make up for the next two or three paychecks you won't be getting."

Pensively, Douglas asked, "What guarantee do I have that no harm will come to my mother and my sister if it takes me longer than you think to get back here from Montana?"

"You have our word that everything will be fine as long as we are certain you have not betrayed your mission."

Your word? Richfield thought. The value of that trust had yet to be determined. Douglas asked a last question, "How often should I contact you?"

"You shouldn't try to reach us at all before you leave Manhattan, unless it's an emergency. The phone number should be used only after you return from Montana."

"Okay," Richfield said after a pause. "I think that should cover me until someone lines me up against a wall and offers me a blindfold. I assume you'll have some way of getting the ration cards to me without my having to come back here?"

"Of course," said Gusev. "We'll put them in your mailbox. Natalya will provide you with some money before you leave. After that you're on your own. Now, just one thing. What's the phone number you need to know?"

"One-zero-uh . . . uh . . . one-two-two-four."

"No, it's one-zero-nine. Think of January 1909. For one-two-two-four, think of twelve months and two years. Again, please."

"One-zero-nine . . . one-two-two-four."

"Again."

"One-zero-nine . . . one-two-two-four." This was getting tedious, but Richfield sensed that just as unhappy experiences sometimes etch themselves indelibly into one's memory as much as pleasant ones, he would never forget this number.

Ponomarev and Gusev both rose from their chairs, evidently satisfied that they had accomplished with Richfield what was necessary. Ponomarev seemed to suppress a certain gleefulness, probably because he realized how tired and docile Richfield had become. He extended his hand to Douglas, and the reluctant "agent" shook it perfunctorily.

"I know you would not have volunteered for this assignment," Ponomarev said bluntly, "and I know that you resent me and our organization deeply. Fortunately, I am quite certain that these feelings will not interfere with your effectiveness. It may be that what you see of life now in the next few weeks will make you more appreciative of what we are trying to accomplish. Your own decisions of the past two years confirm that you yourself wished to be rid of the old society and its corrupt and ineffective ways of dealing with social and economic problems. That is why you joined the People's Movement. Perhaps at the outset you didn't grasp the implications of changing an entire society, an entire nation, from the bottom up. It is a painful, sometimes violent task. But if you are to do it, you must be resolute until the very end. Otherwise, the fine ideals and goals that launched you on this intrepid course will be compromised and betrayed, not by the enemy, but by your own fecklessness and inconstancy. If you'll indulge me just one more quotation from Machiavelli, which I paraphrase a little. He said a prince 'should appear merciful, faithful, humane, religious, upright, and so forth, but with such an attitude of mind that, if you actually need to be the opposite of this, you can be quite capable of being that opposite.'"

With no further ceremony Gusev shepherded Richfield out of Ponomarev's office into the corridor, which was open once again to the kitchen and the corridor beyond. As he traversed the kitchen, the idea of *Alice in Wonderland* flitted across Richfield's mind. *Yes,* he thought, *this is a sort of Wonderland world, a fantasy behind strange walls that is inescapably real, unpredictable, and nightmarish.*

Perhaps there was a deeper reality beyond Ponomarev's, he speculated, one that neither he nor Machiavelli knew. He toyed with this idea for the few seconds it took to get to the reception area. It was oddly comforting, a ray of genuine sunlight in the morally gloomy cavern that Ponomarev had pulled him into. The idea had no basis in his own experience; it was pure speculation, but it had come to him freely from somewhere. Who knew the capacity of the heart to find hope amid despair?

109

In the reception area, Natalya handed him a small brown envelope and had a form for him to sign. Richfield did so mechanically and then looked into the envelope. It held thirty thousand dollars in one-hundred-dollar bills. After his rent was paid, it would last about three weeks, maybe four if he were careful. "Thank you, Mr. Richfield," Natalya said with a warm smile.

Weikert was waiting by the glass doors and opened them for him. Neither of them said a word as they descended and made their way through the checkpoint and the guardhouse. Once there, the PSB official simply said good-bye and went back into the RCA Building. Richfield, back in Rockefeller Plaza, looked for the first time at his watch. It was 3:57—not as late as he had expected it to be.

He felt emotionally sterile, numb. Was this how it was in China during the early Communist era in the 1950s? After being brainwashed, did a person feel just deadness inside, as though the entire psychological machinery had shut down?

The pedestrians on Fifth Avenue looked normal. Life for them had apparently gone on without Ponomarev and Machiavelli.

Richfield wanted, no, needed to talk to someone, anyone, who could jolt him back into the seminormality in which he lived prior to Ponomarev's coming. He couldn't go back to the Municipal Building. He wasn't allowed to say anything to his roommate—not that he would have wanted to.

He dreaded the idea of the blues bars of Greenwich Village. Everybody knew about the blues bars and how they served as outlets for resentment of much of the People's Movement. They were hotbeds of Constitutionalist sentiment. Bremer, who seemed to know more about PSB activities than the average PSB agent himself, had once said that the only reason the NEC didn't close the bars was that they were a magnet for people the PSB wanted to keep under surveillance.

Douglas picked up his pace as he walked, attempting to bolster his spirits both by physical activity and by observation of the ordinary passage of other people in this ever-heaving city. The blocks, the store windows (often dirty and poorly displayed these days), the militia patrols, the political slogans hanging across the avenue every now and then (remnants of the Thanksgiving parade) fluttered past as he headed aimlessly south. Suddenly he was conscious of where his feet, like a faithful dog trotting home, had taken him. He was standing in front of the steps of the New York Public Library. The lions stared at him, sentries of knowledge and maybe a little hope.

Of course. There was only one person who could help him make some sense of this. She would probably have an idea of how to get into the Village blues scene. Obviously he couldn't tell her about Ponomarev. The idea tantalized him, bringing relief from Ponomarev's corruption and generating a spark of the romantic. Thoughts of Rachel filled his mind and lifted his spirit.

6

The Second Recruitment

*R*ichfield quickened his pace past the library and headed toward the Garment District. He had to find a way to contact Rachel without alerting the PSB or Ponomarev. But how? He hadn't tried to confirm that he was being followed, but it was a safe assumption that he was. He dared not phone the Caleb Foundation; their line was almost certainly tapped. The safest way would be to find her.

Douglas needed to lose whoever was tailing him, find the Caleb Foundation, and intercept Rachel inconspicuously, perhaps as she was going home after work. Simple plan, he thought. Pulling it off was another matter. He needed to identify his tracker and to do so without alerting him (or her).

At the same time, should he find Rachel, what would he do if she snubbed him? Well, he had been humiliated by the Russians, the PSB, Bremer—what was one more person added to the list? He had to try.

The alluring smell of pretzels wafted from a street vendor's cart. On a whim Douglas stopped at the cart and used the moment to scan the sidewalk. A flash of moving cloth caught his peripheral vision. A block and a half away a middle-aged woman with dark glasses abruptly slowed her walk and paused to do a little window shopping. Her timing was a little off, and her actions struck Douglas as being clumsy and awkward. *Okay*, thought Douglas, *that's one. How many others are out there?*

As the mustached vendor handed him the pretzels and change, Douglas nonchalantly took in another area of the sidewalk.

He had heard that the PSB might put as many as a dozen tails on a person under blanket surveillance. Logically, though, Douglas wasn't that important, and he knew it, although the thought was somewhat flattering.

PSB agents were high-tech, as the old FBI had been. Agents were in touch with each other by radio, and their microphones could be concealed anywhere—a cuff, a lapel. "Martha," as Richfield dubbed his sunglassed follower, seemed to be scrutinizing everything in the store window. She probably wouldn't risk using her walkie-talkie as long as Douglas seemed to hover around the street vendor. But once he moved off, she would contact her partner.

While he pondered his next step, a bus came growling up to the curb, just a few feet from him. Richfield watched the exchange of old passengers for new ones. Street courtesy required that the passengers leaving the bus be allowed to exit first. Douglas almost smiled. He had seen this in a dozen movies. Would it work for him?

He waited until the first few passengers were climbing aboard and then moved away from the flow of the sidewalk traffic but parallel to the bus. A young African-American couple was climbing aboard, moving slowly as they maneuvered a baby seat between them.

Just as the couple began feeding coins into the fare machine and the driver reached for the lever to close the door, Richfield bounded for the bus steps. He landed heavily as the door was closing, bruising his arm.

"You idiot! What are you trying to do?" the driver shouted angrily.

"Sorry," Richfield said, apologizing as earnestly as he could, "I just remembered I had to be someplace ten minutes ago."

"Yeah, and you nearly lost an arm remembering. Take a seat, I've got a schedule to keep."

Douglas gratefully inched his way down the aisle filled with the blank faces of early rush-hour commuters. Through the arms and heads that blocked the view out of the bus's rear window, however, he saw "Martha," trench coat flapping, frantically running after the bus. She gave up the chase and stopped to talk into the cuff of her coat.

The bus lurched with a shift of the gears and accelerated. Douglas faced a new dilemma: When should he get off? The next stop might be too soon. "Martha" would see him. She might have alerted her partner to his sudden maneuver in time for the partner to board the bus at the next stop.

Yet he didn't dare stay on the bus too long. If his pursuers could summon the full PSB apparatus, they could blanket lower Fifth Avenue in twenty or thirty minutes. No, his best shot, he calculated, would be to get off two stops further on. The second agent was likely on the other side of Fifth Avenue from "Martha," and he'd have to get across the street to make it to the stop in time to board the bus.

The bus was weaving and shoving its way downtown now, the driver pulling it expertly through gaps in the buses and trucks that constituted the bulk of Manhattan's traffic these days. At the first stop, a block beyond an old Lord and Taylor's, Richfield watched anxiously as four passengers boarded: a rickety, white-haired old man who seemed to take forever to hoist himself up the stairs, two black teenagers, and a young Hispanic in his twenties. "Martha's" partner wasn't among the teenagers, and the old man wasn't a possibility. The Hispanic was problematic. Richfield hadn't seen him as the bus approached the stop and couldn't be sure where he came from. But the man paid no attention to him and seemed immersed in a paperback.

The bus was growling forward again, and Richfield tried to stay close to the rear door without appearing anxious to get off. At Thirty-seventh Street someone pressed the bell to get off. As the bus slowed down, Douglas took a notebook out of his coat and pretended to peruse it, trying to look like he was going to be aboard for a while.

The bus braked again with its usual abruptness. Four passengers got off, and two more boarded. Once again Douglas waited until the driver was about to close the doors. He hurled himself down the two steps to the street, unavoidably jolting other passengers as he did. Curses followed him out the door.

Richfield's heart was pounding. The Hispanic had not gotten off with him—he might have tried and just been too slow—and no one else seemed to be following him. He estimated he had about a minute to get off Fifth Avenue and disappear into the swelling crowds of late afternoon. Workers were pouring out of offices and stores, and Douglas melted gratefully among them as he quickly moved away from the avenue.

He'd have to double-back uptown. He didn't know where the Caleb Foundation was, and he didn't want to risk staying in the area if his trackers were close on his heels. Annoying as it was, he'd have to find a pay phone and then make his way to the foundation on foot, unless Rachel's building was in lower Manhattan.

He caught a train to Sixty-eighth Street, toyed briefly with the idea of going home to change clothes, but chose not to after thinking it through. His apartment would almost certainly be watched. It would be safest to contact Rachel as quickly as possible, then go out and buy something large and conspicuous, and bring it back to his apartment. At least he'd have a plausible explanation for what he had been doing between the time his trackers lost him and his return home.

The subway station at Sixty-eighth Street was not quite as dirty as most, perhaps a reflection of the still-elegant neighborhood it served. At a pay phone Richfield took out his diary and acted as though he were searching for a number. Then, after ensuring that no one was within earshot, he dialed information and found that the Caleb Foundation's address was 115B E. Seventieth Street. That was helpful. He could walk there and get back to Sixty-eighth Street fairly quickly.

Douglas wasn't sure how to approach the building. He was relieved to see that there were no large office buildings in the middle of the block. Still, it would be too risky simply to hover around the front door and gawk at whoever was entering or leaving it. He decided to stroll past, make a note of any activity, and take a position half a block away and on the other side of the street. He hoped that Rachel wouldn't be coming down the steps as he came by.

It was nearly five o'clock now, the normal end of the working day. There was a throng of visitors still milling around the front entrance to the building. Many of them were Orthodox Jews with large black hats and side curls, others wore skullcaps, and still others were no different from the average New Yorker. Richfield tried to look like another bored and fatigued New York commuter at the end of a weary day—that is, like he used to look before Ponomarev. Some of these people must be PSB, he surmised. Presumably, though, none of them knew who he was.

When he came to the front entrance, the only identifying mark on the door was a small, faded brass plaque that read CALEB FOUNDATION. The tenants, presumably, were modest about their name and organization. As buildings went in New York these days, it wasn't badly kept up. Lights were on in all floors except the top one. To judge by the movement he could see from the street, the rooms seemed crowded. Douglas crossed to the other side of Seventieth Street and looked around for a street vendor. They were everywhere about the city since the economic collapse a year earlier. He found one just down the next block and bought a cup of coffee and a copy of the *People's Voice*. He hoped that Rachel was in her office and not running an errand. Then again, as the coldness of the November night began to enfold the city, he hoped she wouldn't be staying late to finish some project or other. The encroaching darkness would help him blend in with the anonymity of the city after dark, but he doubted that he could loiter in the same spot for very long without attracting the PSB. He leaned back against the building, nursing his half-full paper coffee cup and glancing idly through his paper. He didn't have to lift his eyes to keep the Caleb Foundation under observation, but it was a tedious business to pretend to be giving his attention to the middle pages of the paper. Where was a *Times* when you needed one?

Ten minutes went by. Fifteen. Twenty-five. Finally half an hour passed. Douglas was feeling cold, doubtful, and not a little scared. How much longer could he pretend to be seriously challenged by the *People's Voice* under a New York street lamp without feeling ridiculous?

He shifted his weight, stretched, peered to his right, up Seventieth Street, and started for the fourth time to fold and unfold the newspaper. The coffee was long gone and he was losing concentration.

Douglas very nearly missed her. As he glanced back carelessly at the foundation for what seemed the hundredth time, he saw a woman step quickly off the bottom step of the foundation and walk briskly in the opposite direction. She was wearing a hat, and he wasn't sure at first whether it was Rachel. But the dark raincoat looked familiar, and she had on those elegant dark boots. What convinced him was her walk: self-confident, prancing, wonderfully feline.

Rachel was probably heading to the subway on Sixty-eighth Street or to a bus stop. If he didn't catch up with her quickly, she would be out of sight and unreachable. He had mentally rehearsed how he would approach her. He'd imagined walking past her and turning slightly, offering a witty greeting like, "I hope things are calmer back at the library this week." But as he saw her, the image that had stubbornly—and wondrously—taken root in his mind and preoccupied him since Saturday, came to mind again, and he threw all his planning to the winds. Douglas started running down the sidewalk across the street from her, oblivious to any curiosity he might attract. Impulsive? Foolish? He didn't care. He didn't care what they talked about once he caught up with her. He wanted urgently to see her again.

Within a block and a half he was just a few yards behind her. He jaywalked across the street, dodging the traffic riskily and provoking the drivers on his way. Then he was abreast of her.

"Rachel," he panted urgently.

She glared at him, startled, showing no sign of recognition, and looking annoyed. She kept on walking, slightly faster now. Douglas matched her pace. His heart was sinking. "Rachel," he said anxiously, "it's Douglas. The library." His tone was plaintive, but it didn't matter to him as much as that she might cut him off cold.

She stopped and smiled with embarrassment. "I'm sorry," she said radiantly. "I had a few things on my mind, and we've had some odd kinds of harassment at the foundation. I thought you might be part of that. What are you doing here?"

"I had to see you."

"Had to?"

"Yes. Remember what we talked about? Well, some pretty crazy things have happened since then. I really need your help."

Rachel frowned again and looked a little nervous. "All right," she said. "I don't have much time. I have to be somewhere at eight o'clock and I've got to get home first. Can we talk on the way? I'm heading for the subway but we can walk an extra block or two to give us some time."

The evening rush-hour crowds had filled the sidewalks, and they had to dodge knots of people continually. It was difficult to

118

talk without risking being overheard. Especially if it might be incriminating.

"I'm sorry you've been having trouble at the foundation. What sort of harassment has it been?"

She looked at him sharply, wondering how much to tell him.

"Oh, strange phone calls, stuff in the mailbox. I think you gathered that a lot of people don't like what we do. Some people in the NEC would even close us down if they could. Of course, others help."

"Would that end the emigration process to Israel?"

"Yes, but possibly much worse than that. Some of the leaders of the People's Movement are deeply anti-Semitic, but because Jews have traditionally supported progressive causes and were willing to back the movement, these sentiments didn't have much of a chance to surface. What hasn't helped is the increasing coziness of the Zhelenovsky regime in Russia with the NEC. You're not Jewish, so you can't know what it's like to feel that the ugliness and the hatred could emerge even in a country like America. We tend to forget that Germany had one of the best integrated Jewish communities in Europe before Hitler came along."

"How will you know?"

"Oh, it'll be clear, depending on what the NEC does. If they close us down, we'll know what to expect next. If they don't, that means we'll probably be safe for at least a year. Sometimes we get an idea of what goes on high up in the NEC."

"You do?" Richfield couldn't help but laugh. "We spend most of our lunch hours trying to figure out who does what to whom."

"But your liberty and possibly your lives don't depend on what happens in Rockefeller Center. Ours do," said Rachel seriously and very quietly as they dodged among the pedestrian traffic."

"Sorry," Douglas said, repenting, "I certainly didn't mean to be flippant. You could probably teach me a lot about national politics. But that's not what brought me here to ask for your help. This is difficult for me for reasons I can't get into, but how well do you know Greenwich Village?"

"Quite well. I go for the music. Don't you know it?"

"Well, given the place's reputation, they don't exactly encourage us to hang out around the Village. What music do you listen to, if you don't mind my asking?"

"Oh, jazz, blues, sometimes some ethnic groups. Why do you ask?"

"Because I want to dig a little into the blues scene, and I've no idea where to start."

Rachel's pace slowed and her eyes narrowed slightly. She stopped and asked him coolly, "Why the blues?"

It was the question Douglas had dreaded most hearing. What possible excuse could he give, without lying so elaborately? There was no reasonable explanation why he would suddenly want advice from a near-stranger on the blues scene in the Village.

"I want to meet some Constitutionalists," Richfield finally blurted out in a gap between the oncoming throngs after failing to think of a single convincing reason for his interest other than the truth.

"Yes, that much is obvious," Rachel said coldly. "But why?"

"Because I want to go to Montana."

"Well, that's a direct approach to winning the war. Nothing like a little ambition for getting a man ahead," she added sarcastically. She was detached, adversarial, frosty. It surprised Douglas. Mostly though, it provoked a deep inner fury with Ponomarev for forcing him into this diabolical situation.

They were rounding a corner, and Richfield was tongue-tied for a few seconds. Rachel gave him another jab. "Is the Protocol Department looking for new recruits out in the Bitterroot Mountains these days?" she asked.

"Rachel, believe one thing of me. If I were on any kind of mission for the People's Movement, why would I come to you for help? Nobody forced me to help you avoid certain arrest in the library. Besides, you could be working for anyone. I don't know. You may be taking a chance telling me anything, but I am too."

Rachel's eyes widened a little and softened, reminding Douglas of the impression she had made on him in the coffee shop as her features moved between her different moods and attitudes.

They were heading up Fifth Avenue now, and something of Douglas's anguish seemed to him to have gotten through to her. She was suspicious of him, but both his awkwardness with her and his obvious impulsiveness made him implausible as a spy or agent provocateur. She decided to draw him out.

"Douglas, I owe you one thing," she said, her voice less harsh: "I'm satisfied that what you did was really spontaneous, a bit crazy, in fact. Why you should surprise me two days later asking for help in a rather strange project, I'm not sure. Frankly, I'm suspicious. How do you know we're not being followed?"

"I don't," said Richfield sheepishly. "I surmised that the Caleb Foundation was under surveillance. It's obvious. But if you were personally being watched around the clock, I think that would have been apparent on Saturday, and I'm sure you weren't. I'm pretty sure that I'm not being watched, at least not now."

"What do you mean, 'not now'?" she asked anxiously.

"I . . . well, please don't ask me to tell you exactly. Rachel, believe me, I'm in a real fix and I'm not going to lie about anything to you. Look, I know that it's unreasonable of me to catch you on the run like this after work, asking subversive questions and not explaining the reasons. But I have absolutely nowhere else to turn. The other thing is, Rachel, I find you fascinating. Ever since I met you, you've been on my mind. I can't even do my job for daydreaming about you." He flushed and was immediately angry with himself for getting emotional.

But Rachel neither smirked nor scoffed. She stopped and looked at him with a puzzled expression. A slow smile grew at the corners of her mouth. "Douglas, you fool," she said with an impish tone that could melt a glacier. "You're not only impulsive and dangerously involved in something that you obviously shouldn't be trusted with, you're also romantic. What an amazing combination!" And she laughed good-naturedly as she strode forward again, with Douglas springing to follow.

She resumed, "Suppose I counsel you on the blues scene, not to mention hoofing it off to Montana. What assurance do I have that you won't end up hurting the Caleb Foundation? It obviously isn't your idea to take a sabbatical from Protocol and head west. I won't ask who's sending you—though it's clear that somebody in Rockefeller Center has gotten some hooks into you—but my inclination is it's not someone with friendly feelings toward us."

"Rachel, I can't give you any assurances. I'm in an impossible position. You're right, it certainly wasn't my idea to head west. About the only thing I can promise you is that if I ever hear of a policy change toward your foundation, I will alert you."

"How? By walking in the front door? By calling us? The PSB would have you in irons."

"Well, I don't know how I'd reach you without that risk, but there must be a way to contact you indirectly."

Rachel bit her lower lip in thought as they walked around Sixty-ninth Street yet again. "Okay," she said finally, "you can reach a friend of mine. Her name's Sherri. I'll write her phone number on the back of my card. If you want to reach me, phone her, and she'll tell you where to meet me. It's the only safe way. But don't hold on to the card. It could get both of us into serious trouble if it's found on you."

Rachel stopped at a phone booth, pulled a card out of her purse, and wrote the number on the back. She gave it to Douglas, and they walked to her subway stop.

As the minutes ticked away like seconds, they talked about her growing up in Israel and her father's work with the Soviet Jews. Richfield told her of his upbringing in New Jersey and his studies at Chicago. There was still some tension between them, and they steered clear of his involvement with the People's Movement and of her opinions of People's Movement politics. But a link was slowly forming between them, not necessarily a romantic one but a thread of commonality.

When they found themselves at the subway entrance, Rachel frowned. "I've got to go," she said.

"I know," he said, with a broad smile. "I'm sorry I've kept you. You've been wonderful. I wish we could get to know each other without the complications that our two lives seem to have gotten themselves into. All told, I bet we haven't spent more than half an hour together, but I'll remember these times forever, even if they're the only ones we have."

"Thank you, Douglas," she said, touched. "There's something about you that's quite different from most people. Our occupations and"—she paused, groping for the exact phrase—"political leanings may prevent us from getting to know or trust each other socially or professionally, but we both know there's more to life. Thank God! It would be terribly dull if there weren't.

"Before I leave, let me give you two bits of information. First, try Jake's, on Christopher Street, and ask if they've got Classic Coke. They won't, but ask anyway. Second, if my name ever crops up in any of your conversations with anybody in that place— or anybody else in this country, for that matter—I'll never speak to you again. Bye Doug."

He left her at the entrance to the subway. Energized more by the conversation than by the brisk walk, which was overshadowed only by the gentleness of their last few minutes together, Douglas could have walked all the way home—on air. But first, he had to get some things. He found an art supply store and bought half a dozen large, stiff, cardboard sheets in different colors and shapes. He tied them together and struggled out into the street with them. They looked cumbersome, and they were. The surveillance near his apartment couldn't miss him and would report that he was home and had done some shopping.

He was still elated over his meeting with Rachel as he opened his apartment door. Not even the sight of Kuzmic, his militiaman roommate, cavorting with a giggling, half-clothed female in the hallway between his bedroom and the kitchen could lessen Richfield's sense of surprising calm as he went wearily to bed.

Rested and still happy—a new sensation for him—Richfield spent the morning in unaccustomed ease, reading through the *New York Times* and even paying close attention to the *People's Voice*. He took out a fresh packet of ground coffee, one which he'd hidden from Kuzmic, and was enjoying his solitude when the phone rang.

It was Esther. Was he okay? They'd heard of his problem with the PSB and hoped he wasn't too discouraged. Was there anything she could do?

It was a simple conversation from a genuinely spontaneous, risk-taking person. It was typical of Esther. Although there were some decent folk among the others he knew in the Municipal Building, he didn't think any of them would have taken the chance to phone him, knowing his line was almost certainly tapped. But Esther walked boldly, never doing anything destructive or criminal. She avoided the black market, which virtually everyone, even in the Protocol Department, had wandered into at some point or other.

He was grateful, but he needed to keep the conversation short to keep her from getting a hint at his true activities. She seemed to understand his reticence, perhaps interpreting it as embarrassment, and she didn't stay long on the phone.

To prepare himself for the evening ahead, he took a sack lunch to Central Park. It gave him a delicious, almost guilty feeling to be away from work completely on a Tuesday, while the rest of the world was struggling through its week. This was like playing hooky from life itself. The park was nevertheless hardly less crowded than on a weekend. The homeless, the jobless, and the depressed snatched what comfort they could from this patch of countryside amid the heartland of the New Era. Richfield spent nearly an hour in the park, dressed warmly against the cold but enjoying the outdoors. Then, reluctantly, he returned to the apartment.

As Ponomarev had cannily anticipated, Kuzmic showed almost no curiosity about Richfield's situation. In fact, since he usually went on patrol duty at odd times, he hadn't bothered to inquire why Douglas was still hanging around the apartment long after it was time to go to work. Kuzmic was simple and churlish, given to a somewhat different idea of hygiene than his roommate.

Richfield spent much of the afternoon reviewing his material on the Constitutionalists. Everyone had heard of Hodges, the almost-mythic commander of the Army of Western Montana. So resonant was his name, in fact, that the People's Movement had gone to enormous lengths to try to blacken his character. He'd cheated at West Point, they said. He'd been a CIA informer at Oxford. He'd committed atrocities in Vietnam. He was a notorious womanizer. And so on. Richfield had read most of this material, some of it with limited circulation, but he'd wondered how Hodges had managed to organize one of the most formidable armies in American history if he had to carry around this collection of vices.

What Douglas wanted to put his finger on—and he doubted he could do this merely from newspaper clippings—was the appeal not just of Hodges but of the ideas he represented. As he admitted to himself, he'd never really given the matter much thought. Obviously not all Constitutionalists were bad, he realized, and some probably were fighting for a basically decent concept of America. But as a longtime backer of the People's Movement, he'd fallen into the habit of dismissing any serious opposition to the regime as reactionary, parochial, small-minded, bigoted, racist, homophobic, and fascist. Progress, after all, was what had distinguished American history, redressing the inherited wrongs of the past, experimenting with new directions of personal fulfillment, and doing away with negative attitudes toward people who were different.

Of course, Richfield had occasionally seen the contradictions. How could one espouse the ideal of multicultural tolerance, and portray as unregenerately wicked the Americans on the other side in the civil war who advocated a quaint, old-fashioned attitude toward the 1789 Constitution? Didn't the NEC claim worldwide solidarity with the oppressed peoples of the Third World and denounce Israel and the American Jews who supported those countries? Presumably, the Constitutionalists were coarse rednecks, racists, and bigots. But probably not all Constitutionalists were. Among the ones who weren't, were there not probably some very decent, honest, brave, and idealistic people? It was this last group, however small, that intrigued Richfield. After all, civil wars were over ideas and a way of life, not for territory. This second American Civil War wasn't over slavery or states' rights, (regardless of the People's Movement's rhetoric over economic slavery), so what was it that inspired either side? Douglas doubted he would find any answers before he entered the Village, but he wanted to convey a curiosity that was both open and genuine to the people who might get him to Montana.

He waited until dark before venturing out. From his previous visits to Greenwich Village, he had the impression that people dressed with a deliberate eccentricity. Neatness definitely counted. It was an expression of defiance toward the People's Movement's exercise of power.

Richfield dug out some old corduroy pants, a blue blazer that had once been fashionable, a red-and-white striped shirt, and a pair of thick-soled workingman's boots. He hadn't shaved, so the day's growth belied that he had a nice job.

He took the subway to Bleeker Street and ambled around Christopher Street, absorbing the mood in this notorious corner of the city. It wasn't a pretty sight. Nobody smiled. People avoided eye contact even more than New Yorkers generally did. The whole place looked like a training ground for militia rookies—everyone looked suspicious, menacing, or belligerent.

At first, he thought he had misunderstood Rachel. There wasn't a sign for a place called Jake's amid the neon glare of Christopher Street. He walked past the entrance twice before he found it. A single door, more like a back-alley door than an entrance to a cafe, held a small sign over a pane of mottled glass.

Grasping the handle, Douglas was surprised that it didn't turn. The door just swung open loosely in its dilapidated frame. Entering, he saw a small hallway. There was a door on the left, but it didn't seem to lead anywhere that Jake's customers were supposed to go. A hand-painted arrow at the end of the hall pointed left toward a stair-case that led to a basement area. Peering down from the top of the stairs, Richfield saw another door that presumably led to the cafe.

In earlier times the jazz clubs and cafes of the Village had been noisy, smoky places where you went to hear music, not to meet and chat. When the People's Movement had taken over New York, jazz lost out and the blues experienced a renaissance in both popularity and the quality of the performers. Most of the blues ca-fes and clubs competed for the most authentic, traditional, essen-tially African-American sound, even though nobody seemed to mind the performers' color. What counted were the sound and the words, especially the words. Audiences invariably joined the per-formers and invented their own lyrics, which tended to be subver-sive, antiregime, and bitter.

Douglas knew better than to look hesitant, so he took the stairs. The door had a small window through which he could barely make out the bar and the flicker of table candles. Suddenly a face appeared at the window and scrutinized him. The man was African-American and Richfield felt even more awkward. Was this one of the purely African-American cafes never visited by whites—not out of a sense of being prohibited, but out of a sense of being out of place?

The face disappeared and the door was abruptly pushed into Douglas. "What do you want?" the man asked. The tone was brusque, uninviting.

"I like blues," replied Richfield in a confident tone surprising himself. "I just want to listen to the music."

"Yeah, man. Do you know anyone?"

"If I did, why would you want to know?"

The man looked puzzled. "There's some room over at the bar, but you won't be able to see much," he said brusquely.

The cafe was dark. Even with the table candles—probably a fire-code violation—it was difficult to take in the scene. There were probably twenty or thirty tables that filled the room except for a small raised platform and the bar off to one side. The man at the window was right. You couldn't see much from the bar, because most of the cafe's customers were standing behind the tables watching the performance.

As Richfield grew accustomed to the lighting, he surveyed the crowd and was struck by the racial mix of the audience. There were as many whites as there were African-Americans and a few Hispanics and Asians. The crowd was pretty well mixed at their tables, not clustered in groups. That struck Douglas as unusual. He had expected homogeneous groups here and there.

Richfield had entered during a pause in the program. The performers had left the tiny stage, but they were meandering back, tie-less, coatless, and tired-looking. The lead singer was fortyish, large and balding. The others looked to be in their thirties, except for the keyboard player, who was considerably younger.

Without saying anything to the audience, the chatter died down, waiters scurried out from among the tables, and the lead singer took the mike out of the stand in front of him. A hush of expectancy filled the room. "This next number," he said, beaming at the audience with a cherubic smile, "is about how a certain gentleman out there in that mountain country spends a part of his daily time." The syllables flowed out slowly, punctuated by a dramatic aspiration of the consonants. The audience, well warmed up, laughed uninhibitedly, sharing in both the singer's humor and his subversive outlook. "We call it," and he paused again to look back and chuckle at the band, "'General Custer, He Ain't.'" Another roar of laughter, then silence as the singer two-threed the band into the number.

The man's timbre was nondescript, but his timing was exquisite, along with the solo acoustic guitar. From the first bars, always predictable in the twelve-bar blues routine, there was a feeling of coiled concentration among the players, an intense focus on tempo that didn't detract from the spontaneity of the instrumental fade-ins and fade-outs, especially by the guitar and keyboard.

The singer allowed two rounds of instrumental interlude and reprise, and then segued with the lyrics.

As the accompaniment embroidered the long, drawn-out final syllables, the entire room exploded in applause. "More! More!" "Yo! Tell it, brother!" "Bravo!" (in the plummy tones that might have more often been heard after the final act of a Verdi first night at the Met). But everything gave way to a whispered chant that gathered volume quickly. "Hod-ges," "Hod-ges," like a college cheerleading routine.

When the chant became dangerously loud, a man with a waiter's apron climbed onto the platform and hushed the audience with gestures that looked as though he was swatting down a fire. "Yeah, okay, that's great, folks. Thanks for the appreciation for Beaver Smith and his boys, but we'd like to stay in business, okay? Thanks, thanks . . ."

The man then whispered into the lead singer's ear, and Beaver Smith—presumably—looked worried at first, then laughed and pointed over to the bar.

The man in the apron came up to the bar next to Richfield and asked for a double scotch. "There's none left," the bartender replied. "Then give 'em bourbon," he replied.

Suddenly, Richfield remembered the rest of Rachel's instructions. On a whim, as the bartender was measuring out the bourbon, he asked, "Have you got any Classic Coke?" The bartender appeared not to hear the question and went on measuring the drink. "Hey," Richfield tried again, "have you got any Classic Coke?"

The bartender looked at him askance, this time without interrupting his pouring. "We haven't had any for months," he deadpanned back.

"It doesn't hurt to ask."

The bartender eyed him again. He pushed the double bourbon to the front of the bar and said, "Hold on." He disappeared through a door in the back of the bar.

Douglas felt a little nervous. He wasn't accustomed to terse conversations, especially when someone disappeared so suddenly afterward. It was too much like being with Ponomarev and Gusev. He hadn't ordered a drink yet, and he felt self-conscious sitting empty-handed while everyone around him had a glass of something. After a couple of minutes he asked a passing waiter for a cup of coffee. "Tell the bartender," the harassed man said abruptly.

He noticed the bartender at the entrance talking quietly to the doorman and pointing toward him. There was some mutual head-nodding, and the bartender went over to a thickset, scruffy, gray-haired man sitting at a table close to the back of the room. Again there was more pointing toward Richfield and whispered discussion.

Finally, the bartender returned. "Sorry, Mac, we don't have any Classic Coke," he told Richfield. "Sometimes there's guys here who know which bars and cafes still have it. See that guy in the back, the one with the gray hair? Maybe he can help you out."

"Thanks." Douglas was very nervous now. He tried to keep his movements relaxed as he threaded his way through the crowd, now becoming noisier again, to where the thickset man and a companion were watching him intently. Visions of Ponomarev and Gusev filled him with dread. He hoped they wouldn't interrogate him too closely.

"Mike says you'd like to find a certain product," said the gray-haired man. "Always interested in helping to meet the demand, aren't we, Willy?" His companion, a dark-haired man in his early twenties, smirked at the joke. "Siddown, young fella, and let's talk," he added. "I'm Fred. This is Willy. We're in the soft-drink business." He grinned at his own joke and Willy guffawed.

"I'm Doug. Nice to meet you guys," Richfield said, opting for the preferred no-surname style of talk.

"What's your work, Doug?" Fred didn't waste time on any formalities. Richfield found that he preferred this folksy approach to the Ponomarev cat-and-mouse game.

"I don't have one as of yesterday. I used to be a Protocol officer at City Hall."

Now Fred guffawed. "Protocol? That's a good one. All that curtsying and saluting." He was loud, and people were looking back to see what was going on. Richfield felt embarrassed and exposed.

"Not much curtsying these days," he said. "Monarchies are out down at City Hall. So is having a beer on Thanksgiving Day."

"Whad'ya mean? Had some trouble with the militia boys?" And he turned to Willy, who was looking very serious now.

"You could put it that way. They canned me for getting involved with some brawl near Fifth Avenue after the parade. Bunch of bull. The only part of it that is true was that I was at the parade and I did see a pretty big fight."

"Tell us about it. I guess I just don't get to attend parades like I used to."

Fred's tone was still bluff and hearty, but his voice level had dropped. Willy was quiet and watching Richfield intently.

"There was some fighting, pretty rough stuff, with the militia just kicking the life out of these guys, even though they fought back pretty hard. I left to get home before all the streets were shut down."

"Well, some days are rougher than others."

Willy finally asked Douglas, "Did anything else go on that got you into trouble?" It was an odd question, sort of a when-do-you-stop-beating-your-wife inquiry.

"Do you mean did anything else go on, or what other trouble did I get into?"

"Both."

Richfield perspired slightly. "Well, I didn't get into any other trouble." He paused. How much should he say? For that matter how much did Fred and Willy know about that afternoon, including the shooting of Marcus?

"And?" It was Fred now, not sounding as hearty as he was earlier. "I think Willy asked you two questions. You answered one."

Douglas recoiled. "Hey, guys, lighten up. I came over to talk about a rare, old classic, and you want a blow-by-blow account of the sights and sounds of Thanksgiving Day."

Willy rolled his eyes, and Fred leaned back in his chair. "Loosen up yourself, Douglas," he said. "Who are you to come waltzing into a place you've never been to before, ask a downright nosy question, and then clam up like some old nun at confession?"

Douglas froze. Part of him wanted to make a break for the door and get out of the Village as quickly as he could. Forget Ponomarev, Gusev, Bremer—even Rachel. But part of him knew that he'd hit the jackpot on getting to Montana, thanks to Rachel's guidance.

He reined in all of his instincts before replying, carefully. "I saw a shooting."

"Tell us what you saw," Fred said.

"An elderly couple—at least, that's what I thought they were at first—was leaving the parade site about the same time I was. We were all trying to put some distance between us and a street brawl between the militia and some rowdies. The couple was stopped by two militiamen and resisted arrest or something. Both of them were shot."

"How close were you to all this?"

"I was right behind them when they were stopped and just a few feet away when the first one was shot. The other one tried to run for it, but the militiaman shot him down as he ran. I saw him go down. I was close to the body when the militia shooed me off."

"You said you only thought they were an elderly couple. What makes you think they were anything other than that?"

"Because I saw them up close, and the one who tried to run for it was obviously a man dressed as a woman—maybe in his forties or fifties."

Both Fred and Willie studied Richfield for a few seconds. Finally, Fred asked, "Were you close enough to know how badly they were injured, or if they were both dead?"

"The first one was dead. He had three or four slugs in him at point-blank range."

"What about the fellow dressed as a woman? Do you think he made it?"

Richfield hesitated. "I don't know."

"Okay, Douglas," said Fred again, sighing slightly and resuming his former poker face. "You were saying something about Classic Coke earlier. That's pretty hard to find these days, but not exactly impossible. You've got a fancy job there—"

"Had."

"Okay, had a fancy job in City Hall. Why are you all of a sudden so eager to change professions?"

"It's a long story. Before they canned me, the work was driving me crazy. I figure if City Hall doesn't want me to work for them any more, well, maybe someone else could use me."

"Maybe they could. What do you have in mind?"

Douglas was perspiring freely now. He looked around and lowered his voice. "I was reading Horace Greely last night and thought I might look west," he said almost inaudibly.

"That much is already clear," said Fred dryly. "The question is, why would anyone there want you?"

Though Richfield had prepared himself for this question, its bluntness momentarily threw him. He took a deep breath and replied carefully, "Two reasons. First, because I've met everyone on the NEC, most of them quite recently. Second, because, like you, I think there might be some people there with a little curiosity about a certain cross-dressed man who was shot by the militia last Thursday."

Willy and Fred looked at each other for a moment. Willy asked Richfield, "Suppose someone out there decided they'd like to have you visit, could you be ready to go in forty-eight hours?"

"I could go tomorrow morning."

"I said forty-eight hours. Even if they wanted you next June, we'd still check you out. Come with us someplace a little more private."

The two men stood and ambled back to the bar. Douglas followed. A small door to the right said "Manager Only." Fred opened it and led them into a small, dimly lit room with a glass-covered desk, three chairs, and a couple of bookcases. He sat down behind the desk and motioned Douglas to a chair facing it.

He took some paper and a pen out and pushed them toward Douglas. Meanwhile, Willy locked the door behind them and took a position with his back to it.

"Write out your full name, date of birth, social security number, job title, and the names of three of your immediate superiors," said Fred. "Then write down exactly what I tell you."

Douglas filled out the personal details and handed it to Fred, who looked at it carefully. He waited, pen poised, for the rest of the assignment. Fred began, pausing occasionally for Richfield to write, "'I, Douglas Richfield, agree that I have consented of my own free will to ask for assistance in volunteering for service in the Army of Western Montana . . .'"

"Whaaat?" Douglas exclaimed, dumbfounded. "You want me to put my head in the noose?"

"I've already got my head in a noose. So has Willy. So do you, for that matter, just by being around us. Let's get that straight from the start. But we're not interested in your neck as much as ours. This is an insurance policy we like to have on file. Now just keep writing. 'And I also agree that, if required, I will make available to Constitutionalist forces any information, secret or otherwise, that I may have obtained in enemy-held areas.'"

Douglas wrote obediently, but he was shaken. Was this how the Constitutionalists welcomed potential defectors to their cause?

"Now write out your full name, along with your social security number, and sign it as you would a check."

Douglas did as he was told and watched Fred carefully proofread the document and place it with the first sheet.

Fred looked at his watch. "It's 10:20," he said. "Stay in the bar until 11:30, then leave alone and go to 21 Tenth Street. Press the buzzer for apartment 4C. When they ask who you are, say 'Diego.' Wait for further instructions after that."

7

The Road West

*I*t was 11:20 P.M. and a thin veil of chilling rain had descended upon Manhattan for the previous half-hour. It fell slowly, the light droplets gradually soaking everything. In the Village the few pedestrians left on the streets shivered and scampered to find a refuge.

For Douglas the last hour had passed slowly since putting his career, and perhaps his life, in the hands of the two agents Fred and Willy. Per their instructions he had left the small office before them, had waited ten minutes, and then left as casually as he could via the staircase and the narrow corridor to the street. There wasn't much protection from any PSB agents who might have been in the cafe. Richfield assumed he would be under surveillance at least until he left Manhattan—and possibly beyond. He was worried that Ponomarev might rely entirely on the PSB for all surveillance. From his own experience and from what Ponomarev had said, he feared that their clumsy tracking procedures would be detected easily by the Constitutionalists' own people. If that happened, he would have to sweat his way through an explanation to Fred and Willy and possibly others of why the PSB was following him. It was a serious worry.

Back on the street, he checked to see if he could spot a tail, but no one seemed to be following him. He ducked into alleyways or moved into and out of subway stations to throw anyone off. He concluded that either he was not being followed, or, if he were, his trackers were skillful enough that the Constitutionalists wouldn't be aware of them, or he hadn't the foggiest notion of how to play this game. By

11:30 P.M. he had already walked past the rendezvous point twice, each time coming from a different direction.

He made one last stop at the subway before he headed for Barrow Street. Number ninety-six was a three-story brick building with an apartment on each floor, an outside fire escape, and railings at the ground level.

It wasn't exactly deserted. A young couple shared a plastic rain poncho and were entwined on the front steps as Richfield walked up to press the buzzer for 4C. Neither paid him any attention as he passed them, but something suggested that they might not be there by chance. They might be a kind of early-warning system to ensure that a PSB raid didn't take the house by surprise.

Several seconds later there had been no response from the people in 4C. Richfield impatiently buzzed again.

Another minute went by. Douglas worried that he hadn't gotten the address right. He felt awkward. To add to his stress, a militia team—a black couple and a white man—was approaching from the opposite side of the street and talking animatedly among themselves. Just as they drew even with Richfield, a strong, female voice boomed out of the speaker above the buzzer. "Who is it?"

"Uh, Diego," Richfield shouted back, momentarily caught off guard, but remembering to mimic a Latin accent.

"Who?" The same voice, still booming.

"Diego!" This time Richfield was irritated.

"Wait."

Douglas's heart was pounding now. It was just the sort of scene the militia might want to look into, a young man whose entry seemed to be in question by the occupants. But the militia team was so deep into its own conversation, having fun, with broad cackles of laughter, that it ignored Douglas and continued walking up the street.

The buzzer sounded, and Douglas gratefully pushed the door open and headed up two flights of creaky stairs to apartment 4C. The smell of cooking and a single naked light bulb in the corridor gave a seedy feel to the place. There was a doorbell, but a sign on the door said "Knock," so Douglas rapped three times with his knuckles.

The door opened quickly and Douglas faced a woman, probably in her thirties, with short, well-trimmed hair, a sharp, thin nose, and piercing gray eyes. She was wearing a blue work shirt tucked into a nondescript pair of gray pants. Even in these clothes something about her immediately smacked of the military. She was too crisp. She'd probably been an officer in the pre-civil war U.S. Army.

"Come in," she said. "I know who you are." The tone was pleasant but authoritative. Douglas followed obediently into a rather large room with white walls, a large sofa, three armchairs, several smaller chairs, and a dining table. Two posters of Manhattan were pinned neatly to one wall. Two windows, presumably overlooking the street, had their blinds drawn and dark brown curtains pulled shut. The room was brightly lit by a neon strip light in the center of the ceiling. A nearly full coffee pot was steaming on an electric hot plate atop an elegant side table. Two cups and saucers, teaspoons, paper napkins, sugar, and coffee creamer were arranged neatly next to it. Whoever was in charge of this apartment had a sense of order.

"You can call me Meg," the woman said. "I'm currently in charge of this transit point, and in case you get any ideas, I'd better let you know that I'm not alone. Give me your windbreaker. You're probably cold and wet. Sorry it took so long to let you in. That's a standard precaution. Have a seat while I pour you some coffee."

Douglas didn't particularly want any more caffeine, but the liquid was hot and he was cold, so he acquiesced. Meg went on talking while she poured the coffee for him, her voice almost unbearably matter-of-fact.

"I'll come to the point quickly since there's no reason to keep you in the dark. Your request is being processed. It may take a few days to clear you and make the arrangements, so during that time, for our sake and for yours, it's important that you stay here out of sight."

"Willy said that I needed to be ready in forty-eight hours."

"Did he say you 'needed' to be, or did he ask if you could be?"

"Well, he asked if I could be."

"Forty-eight hours is our minimum turnaround time, but it's not standard. There's some priority in your case, I understand, but, even so, we aren't going to move you until everything checks out." She smiled slightly as she sat down on an arm of the sofa.

"Meanwhile," she went on, "there are some rules of the house you're required to follow. Rule number one needs no emphasis

137

because it's so obvious. You are to mind your own business, ask no questions, and obey the duty officer. Today that's me. You will not be permitted to leave this apartment until we say so. At that point we will supervise your transfer to wherever you're going. The front door, though it looks normal enough, is operated by a remote, key-code system separate from the door itself. Naturally, you will not have access to it. The windows are also sealed, just in case you feel like launching paper airplanes onto the street below. And you won't have access to a telephone.

"Your living arrangements will be comfortable, but basic. You'll have a room to yourself. You'll share a bathroom with other guests who may be passing through. And there are plenty of books and magazines for you to read. There is no television for reasons I won't go into, but there is a radio. As long as you keep the volume at a reasonable level, you can listen to it during the daytime hours. You won't have to cook your meals—that's the job of the duty officer—but if you miss a meal, we don't allow anyone to raid the refrigerator. All food is strictly accounted for.

"Different people may come and go from time to time. When this happens, you will be told to stay in your room. If it is necessary for you to be out and around the apartment when outsiders are here, we will have you wear a face mask to obscure your identity. We will do our best to keep you from being bored, and we may ask you to perform some clerical tasks from time to time. You can consider that a goodwill gesture to defray some of the expenses of your stay here. Do you have any questions?"

"Sure. I don't want to be rude or ungrateful, but it looks as though I'm a prisoner here. Is that correct?"

"Well, we don't like that term. Let's just say 'special guest.' After all, you didn't come to us under duress. You volunteered your services and we took you at your word. It's just possible that you're a PSB spy, and we have ways to check that out. We just need time to do it. If you're clean, we'll also need to make arrangements for your travel." Meg delivered this chilling lecture while tidying up the dining table and then turning her full attention to Douglas.

"Do you really uncover PSB agents trying to go west?" Douglas asked, almost compulsively.

"Oh yes," she said with her chilling matter-of-fact tone. "But not yet in this apartment. At least, not while I've been here."

"What happens to them?" Douglas followed up, trying to stop his voice from squeaking as his throat tightened.

"It depends." The matter-of-factness again. "We caught a woman once. She claimed that she wanted to join her fiancé, a lieutenant with Hodges. But when we checked her out, we found that her father and her brother were PM officials. It didn't take long to discover that her fiancé wasn't out west at all; he was right here in Manhattan in charge of a PM reconstruction project in the South Bronx. Legally, we could have shot her. Fortunately for her, she had only seen two of us and was apparently untrained. We were also using a safe house. We gave up the house, transferred the two agents, and let her go. Basically, nobody wanted to kill an eighteen-year-old kid."

"PM?" Richfield asked.

"People's Movement." Douglas had never heard this abbreviation before. Perhaps it was Constitutionalist jargon.

"She was lucky," he said nervously, hoping to draw Meg out.

"Yes."

There was an awkward pause. Meg wasn't in a chatty mood.

"Other than kids like her, what have you done with the spies that get caught?" Douglas asked, trying to break the silence.

"We shoot them, of course. There are too many lives at stake. Besides, they knew what they were doing when they tried to infiltrate us."

"Yeah, I guess they did."

Richfield's throat was dry. He barely squeaked out the last comment. Meg didn't look bloodthirsty, but she spoke as calmly about shooting spies as she would have about killing insects. Douglas was at least grateful that she didn't seem to notice his shaky voice. He was furious with Ponomarev for the spy catcher's odious and manipulative ways.

"Well, I've got things to do," Meg said briskly. "I'll show you your room and the adjoining bathroom. I'm afraid we'll have to lock you in at night for everybody's peace of mind," she said as she led him to a small hallway and to the first door on the left. "If nature calls, you'll find a chamber pot—no kidding—in the lower part of your night table. The bathroom's next door. You'll find pajamas on the bed and a clean set of clothes for tomorrow, some basic toiletries, and a copy of the house rules. We'll wake you up at seven tomorrow and let you out to brush your teeth or whatever. Breakfast here is at eight, lunch at noon, and dinner at six. You can put your clothes in the wicker basket outside the bedroom door. If you don't mind getting yourself ready for tonight's lockup, it's already late and I'd like to close up around here."

Douglas shrugged as he went to the bathroom with a toothbrush and a tube of toothpaste. He was more than a little on edge, not just because he was under lock and key so unexpectedly and at such a high risk, but also for having to show up for breakfast on time and get to bed when told to like a ninth-grader in summer camp. For that matter Meg wasn't talking to him much differently than a camp counselor would.

"Pleasant dreams," she said, not waiting for his reply and closing and locking the door briskly.

Irritated and sour, Douglas turned his attention to his room and methodically searched every nook and cranny, much like a convict might explore his cell. When he found the chamber pot, a touch of good humor returned. It was an ornate, porcelain vessel with a flowery pattern. At least someone had a sense of proportion, he thought, smiling to himself for the first time since entering the apartment. Somehow he couldn't imagine Ponomarev's thinking up this detail.

He'd intended to browse through the well-filled, ceiling-high bookcase, but fatigue overwhelmed him and it was all he could do just to get into bed. Sleep washed over him like a spring tide.

Douglas floated through canyons of risk and recollection: the library surged toward him with false walls and little kitchens that had to be entered before a book could be checked out for the reading room. Gusev monitored the reading room and demanded that everyone stop talking. The Russian was rapping books on the table, and Esther approached and asked if Richfield were all right. The rapping grew louder, as did Esther's voice. "Are you all right? Are you all right? Are you all right!"

Douglas awoke with a start, drenched in sweat and disoriented. Someone was banging on the door and asking "Are you all right? Are you all right?"

"Yes, fine. Who is it?"

"It's me. It's seven o'clock. I've been knocking for a while and I was beginning to get worried. You can come out now. We eat breakfast in fifteen minutes."

There was the sound of a bolt being thrown and a key turning in the lock. Richfield got up and groped for the light switch. He felt alert, but he was still tired. He put on a bathrobe and went out to the bathroom. There was an inviting smell of coffee and toast coming from the kitchen and the sound of a voice on the radio.

He showered and changed into the clothes provided for him. They didn't fit badly, all things considered. Some dark brown pants, a blue denim shirt, and fresh underwear.

Meg was sitting at the long table, eating a piece of toast and reading the *New York Times*. She was dressed in the same clothes as last night, or at least, clean versions of the same. She looked as though she had been born in a uniform.

"Sleep okay?" she asked pleasantly.

"Yeah, not bad, thanks. Where did you find these clothes?"

"I think an oversized shirt beats smelling like a tramp," she snapped.

"Look, I'm not complaining. I'm just curious."

"Yeah, and I think I mentioned last night that we don't encourage questions."

"Okay, okay. Sorry. I'm not a robot. I was just trying to make conversation."

Meg looked at him coldly but didn't follow up with any comment. Richfield's enthusiasm for going west had cooled by several degrees. Good Lord, it was bad enough coping with people like Bremer in the People's Movement. Was the other side populated with different versions of the same basic chip-on-the-shoulder, step-on-anyone personality?

Richfield took a plate and helped himself to two pieces of toast and some margarine and jelly. He poured himself some coffee, sat down across from Meg, and tried to make sense of a front-page editorial in the *People's Voice*. His guard scrutinized his every move, though her expression was no longer unfriendly.

"I'm sorry," she said simply. "I didn't mean to snap at you. It's been a bad week. We lost a couple of people recently in a PSB raid, and I think it was because some jerk wanting to join us was asking too many questions in public and got reported."

"The raid was here?"

"No, the Bronx. They were good soldiers, had worked for intelligence in the eighties. They were killed because of someone's loose tongue. It just makes you really mad when you see that happen."

"I can't argue with that."

"What's the *People's Voice* say? Anything on the Japanese invitation?"

"What Japanese invitation?"

"Ushida has invited Rutledge and other senior members of the PM to Japan to discuss developing mutual relations."

"You're not serious?"

"Why not? Nothing is static in war, especially in a civil war. France and Britain came pretty close to backing the Confederacy in the last American Civil War. Know whose fleet dissuaded them by showing up in New York harbor?"

"No."

"The Russians. The czar sent the fleet for moral support for the North against the South. What the Japanese are doing isn't a whole lot different. Ushida's been in bed with the Russians ever since Tokyo got the Kuriles back, and Zhelenovsky will do almost anything to get his hands on the latest microchips. The Russkies don't stand a chance of catching our subs until they get some decent anti-submarine equipment. The Japanese don't have it yet, but it wouldn't take them long to work it up. Inviting Rutledge and a few other cronies is all part of the process. Anyway, when you're done with the *People's Voice,* toss it my way, please."

"Sure."

Richfield scanned the paper briefly and found a small item about the Ushida invitation on the front page. He folded the paper and handed it across to Meg.

"You don't want to read it first?" she asked, surprised.

"No, go ahead. Even where I worked we used to laugh at it sometimes." Meg looked at him intently but made no comment.

They read along in silence for a while until Richfield had had enough breakfast and was bored with reading. "No offense to the present company," he said, "but do you mind if I go back to my room and look at some of the books there?"

"Sure. The next item of the day is lunch, and that's not till noon. By the way, we may have company then. I have some things to do this morning, but you're free to do what you want. Later, if you like, I can promise you a good game of chess. There's a set in your room. From what others have experienced before in this transit process, if I were you, I'd try to pace myself. Get too uptight about the waiting and you'll be a nervous wreck before it's time for you to move on. That's when you'll need all the nerves you have. Sleep too much and you'll be useless if you need your wits to get out of any tight places on the way west. You don't have to give up on exercise—there's a folding exercise bicycle in your room under the bed. I'd strongly advise you to use it at least once a day."

"Okay, I get it. Keep the chimps fed, fit, and not too bored. Only the healthy specimens are selected for the San Diego Zoo. For the rest it's strictly the Bronx."

Richfield was surprised at the bitterness that crept into his voice. Meg, who seemed to have his measure much better now, watched him for a moment, then laughed. "You've forgotten one thing," she said. "Chimps never volunteer to leave the city. You did."

It was said with a smile, but there was a hint of accusation and warning in it. Richfield decided to back off.

"Yeah," he said, "I did. See you later." With that he went back to his room and browsed among the book selection there. He quickly settled on Tom Clancy's second novel, *Red Storm Rising,* the only one he hadn't read, and was soon immersed in the complexities of the Soviet attack on Iceland. Politburo, NATO, Backfire, ATLINT, KGB, Spetsnaz, SACEUR—the old Cold War jargon that rolled off the pages seemed as archaic as an account of the Battle of Trafalgar during the Napoleonic Wars. But there was an intensity to the issues set before the reader and a briskness of narrative and decision that harked back to a more bracing era of international polarization.

Nowadays people seemed to decide whose side they were on from purely expedient motives, not from political principle at all.

He also took the trouble to look up the Almond reference in the Book of Ecclesiastes that Rachel had mentioned. He found it in chapter 12, a rather forbidding exhortation to the people to think about the Almighty. "When men are afraid of heights and of dangers in the street; when the almond tree blossoms . . ." Richfield suddenly understood. Project Almond would be blossoming precisely when the streets were dangerous places to be because of foreign invasion or civil war.

The morning rolled by. Lunchtime came—and with it came two familiar faces, Willie and Fred. They seemed to know Meg well as they joked easily with her. To Richfield they were friendly enough, but they were also professional. Fred's backslapping style at Jake's had been replaced with a low-key humor. Willie was more outspoken now, openly mocking Rutledge and mimicking other Executive Committee members, especially Leanna Greene, whose hobby horse was helping the Third World countries. "'And we just ain't gonna let no country, including this so-called former United States, this so-called de-mo-cra-tic nation,'" he piped in cruel mimicry, slowing down and rolling the syllables like an old-time preacher, "'exploit the sweat and the toil of our brr-oth-ers from Africa and South Am-er-ica and As-i-a.'" It was a devastating imitation, and everybody roared with laughter. Richfield joined in, but he felt that several taboos were being deliberately attacked during the meal. Fred said little and let Willie do the talking while he carefully watched Richfield.

As she had promised, Meg and Douglas played chess that afternoon. She beat him easily the first game, but he held her to a stalemate in the second. Fred and Willie lingered after lunch for coffee and watched the duel with obvious interest, applauding each player after a good move. Douglas grasped that he was being scrutinized in a variety of different settings. But after the two men left, there was nothing to do but read until dinner. He wasn't sure if he preferred having company, even though it meant being inspected, or being left alone and having time to read.

Meg left before dinner and was replaced by a large, surly African-American in his fifties. His name was Leon and he had an unpleasant habit of belching over his food. He barely talked to Douglas except to indicate that meals were ready, and he seemed to resent having a babysitter-like function. Richfield quickly assumed that Leon was another variation of the good-cop-bad-cop routine, that he wasn't really a bad fellow, and that the Constitutionalists were still testing him. He changed his mind when neither Meg nor Willie nor Fred turned up for the next two days, and Leon made every communication seem like an excruciating pain. Douglas decided that Leon was a churlish, sour person and that would be his personality regardless of which side he supported. It was a tremendous relief when he welcomed Meg back Friday evening after Leon's shift was over.

Meg brought a young African-American couple with her. They greeted Richfield but didn't introduce themselves. Douglas, well trained now after three days in the safe house, didn't volunteer anything about himself either. Over dinner, though, Meg steered the conversation to music, and it was evident that the two newcomers were blues performers. He half-wondered whether they were new volunteers preparing to go through the same background investigation that he was currently experiencing. Next morning when he arose for breakfast, however, they were gone.

"That was a quick turnaround," he said to Meg over his coffee.

"Yeah," was all she said, but she grinned slightly. "By the way," she added as an afterthought, "your two friends from the Village will be coming over tomorrow. They may have some news for you."

News for me? That was an odd way of putting it. Even a little chilling. He wondered if they had learned of his contact with Ponomarev and if they would shoot him immediately or have some sort of trial. He was not terrified of dying so much as of dying without anybody knowing where he was or what had become of him. He had thought of Rachel on and off during these long hours of enforced idleness. Their last encounter had been frustrating. Hurried, too public, tense. She had shown that melting kindness he had first seen in the coffee shop, but she had also been brusque, almost suspicious. Since he had not contacted her, she must know that he was being checked out by the Constitutionalists while being under virtual house arrest. Just how deeply was she connected with the Constitutionalists? Why had no one asked him about his past? They hadn't even been curious about how he knew to ask for Classic Coke at Jake's.

He didn't feel much like chatting with Meg and went back to his room to work out on the stationary bike and read. The book collection was rich and eclectic: everything from Clancy to Thomas a Kempis's "The Imitation of Christ," all six volumes of Gibbon's *Decline and Fall of the Roman Empire*, Machiavelli's *The Prince*, "The Federalist Papers," Carl Sandburg's *Life of Lincoln*, an obscure biography of George Washington, Marx and Engels's *The Communist Manifesto*, Isaac Walton's *The Compleat Angler*, and Fulleylove and Kelman's *The Holy Land* (a rare and fine blue leather edition with a bookmark from "G. David, Bookseller" in Cambridge, England), several paperbacks by Ludlum, Fowles, and Stephen King—to name just a few. Whoever had stocked the shelves wasn't the average community college sophomore. Douglas had dipped into Gibbon, skipped Walton, and devoured Machiavelli and Clancy's *Red Storm Rising*. Tonight, though, he turned to Fulleylove and Kelman. "The secrets of satisfactory travel are mainly two," he read at the opening of the preface, "—to have certain questions ready to ask: and to detach oneself from preconceptions, so as to find not what one expects, one desires to find, but what there is."

He was reading late the following morning when the doorbell rang and Fred and Willie arrived. One part of him was eager to see them again. Perhaps his review was complete and he would be free to move out of the city. He was surprised that he'd never been asked to put on the mask as Meg had indicated he might have to, and that no one else had stayed in the apartment, apart from his keepers, while he was here. He had guessed that the trip west, if he were approved, would be challenging and risky, but he was eager now for any freedom after being cooped up indoors for four days.

Incredibly, Meg had scrounged up four good steaks. It was almost impossible to get them except at certain privilege stores open only to higher-ups in the government. She had also acquired fresh lettuce, tomatoes, and cucumbers—rarities indeed in early December in New York—and some new potatoes. In fact, the lunch had a festive air to it, as though it were a farewell occasion.

They talked about some of the stories that had been in the papers that morning, particularly about Rutledge's decision to go to Japan and some rumored personnel changes on the Executive Committee. The New Age representative, Shirley Metaxas, had been an off-and-on embarrassment to the regime from the outset with her breathless public pronouncements about planetary alignments and the political virtues of carrot juice. But she hadn't been removed for a simple, basic reason: her fellow committee members couldn't agree on a replacement. "Why don't they just bring on another white female, maybe an attorney or something?" Fred asked.

"Because they don't want to admit that they have serious problems agreeing on policy," replied Richfield, whose Protocol job had provided him with a working knowledge of all the members of the Executive Committee. "Shirley was out to lunch a lot of the time, but she had the virtue of not being in anybody's faction. Whoever replaces her will be bound to have political ideas a whole lot more realistic. In other words she'd belong to one faction or other. That would upset the balance that currently holds the committee together. It's a lot like the old Supreme Court."

"What factions are you talking about?" asked Meg, entering the conversation for the first time. "How many can there be when there are only eleven people on the committee in the first place? A good portion of every freakish thought pattern in America seems to be represented."

"Not really; there are only two groups," said Douglas authoritatively. "The largest group, led by Rutledge, stands for a multiethnic revolutionary front dedicated to the basic redistribution of wealth and a largely classless, racially integrated society. That would be Rutledge, Daniels, Greene, Gomez, Muzzio, and—usually—Metaxas. Greene is African-American, Gomez is Hispanic, and the other three are white.

"The other faction consists of Vice-chair Robinson, Secretary Northwood, Jamil al-Baraka, Wu, and Roseanne Great Bear. That's two African-Americans, an Asian, a Native American, and a white. They don't mind redistributing the wealth, but they favor a society structured around ethnic separateness rather than broad social integration. Metaxas sort of floats between the two, settling like an

147

unpredictable butterfly on the classless revolutionaries once and on the multiculturalists later."

Fred guffawed at Richfield's analysis. "Hey," he said with a booming voice, "that's not bad! Wait till the political types out west hear about this."

There was an awkward pause around the table. Meg looked at Richfield and then at Fred. Willie looked enigmatic. Douglas broke the silence.

"Does that mean I'm moving on?" he asked.

"What do you think, Meg? Should we shoot him now or after the dessert?" And Fred roared with laughter yet again.

Willie even chuckled this time. "Yeah, you check out okay. I was going to get to that, but you might as well know now. They're a little worried about you back at the Municipal Building. That's a good sign. You obviously weren't going around threatening to defect. You move out at 5:30 tomorrow morning. Meg, you'll have to be up for that, I'm afraid, since you'll need to identify the fellows who come by for Diego."

"Can I ask how I'm going to get there?" Douglas asked, suddenly energized with the anticipation of the trip.

"You can," said Fred, "but we're not going to tell you. You've done well here, Meg tells me. You even managed with rude ol' Leon. That was just as good—we wouldn't have let you go if you'd gotten him riled. Now there's just one thing you still have to do. The G-2 boys out in Montana want some raw-meat proof that you are who we say you are.

"There are four lines of Shakespeare you'll have to memorize from *Richard II*. When someone on the other end asks what your favorite lines of poetry are, you don't tell 'em Walt Whitman or Allen Ginsburg. You tell 'em this"—and he leaned back in his chair as though projecting to a vast auditorium—

> Not all the water in the rough rude sea
> Can wash the balm from an anointed king;
> The breath of worldly men cannot depose
> The deputy elected by the Lord.

"Okay? In simple terms that just means that I vouch for you. I'm not going to write it down, so repeat it after me until you've got it."

Richfield did so and found it much easier and more pleasant to memorize than the phone number Ponomarev and Gusev had forced upon him. What had that been? Yes, 109–1224. It wasn't especially strange that two intelligence officers—for that is what he deduced Fred was—had both required him to memorize details for security purposes. But how much richer was the Constitutionalist code.

With the uncertainty that had been hanging over Douglas now removed, a mood of real joviality enfolded everyone. Meg in particular looked relieved that Richfield would be moving on with the Constitutionalists' good housekeeping seal of approval. Douglas wondered if her matter-of-factness, so unnerving at first, wasn't a defense mechanism.

Fred and Willie left, and the rest of the day passed slowly. Douglas was impatient to move on now that the safe house was becoming oppressively confining. He persuaded Meg to play two games of chess after dinner, which helped move the evening on, and then he went to bed early.

At 4:30 his alarm clock went off, and soon afterward Meg knocked on his door. He dressed quickly in a pair of pants and a blazerlike blue jacket, with a dress shirt open at the collar. Meg gave him a thick gray parka to carry. Breakfast was just as it had been every day since he had been in the house. At 5:25 the doorbell rang three short times. "Who is it?" Meg asked through the intercom, and a male voice crackled back, "Mike." She buzzed the downstairs door open.

"Mike" was a well-built man about Richfield's age but some four inches taller, giving him an imposing presence at about six foot four. He had a crewcut. Richfield imagined him as a phys ed high school instructor or an Army Special Forces volunteer. He brought two identical-looking soft nylon carry-on bags and gave one to Richfield. "Most of what you'll need is here," he said, "at least for the first part. For obvious reasons you can't take much. We have some identification papers for you, and you must leave all of your current I.D. here. They'll be kept safe for you."

As Meg served them both some coffee, Mike outlined the day's procedure. "We're going to La Guardia first to catch a flight to Minneapolis. You're a maintenance engineer with USAir on assignment to the Minneapolis airport. I'm your supervisor, and I'll do all the

149

talking unless they specifically speak to you. Your name is Joe Field-ing, and you're from Jersey City. The address is on your I.D.s, including your driver's license.

"We'll have to leave by the usual passenger terminal, but we have special tickets that indicate we're airline personnel and don't require advance booking. The flight isn't full, and since they don't permit regular standbys, we won't have any trouble getting on the plane. The only danger is that we may have separated seats, and you might have to sit next to someone who wants to know your life history. That could be a problem. If it happens, claim a toothache, nausea, headache, or anything that gets you out of having to talk about anything. Probably the best thing, since it's an early flight, is to fall asleep, or at least pretend to.

"When we get to Minneapolis, just follow me out of the plane and to another area of the airport. Whatever happens, don't try to talk to me—either at the airport, on the plane, or anywhere else—until I say it's safe to talk. That will certainly seem unnatural, but it's essential for my security and yours.

"One final thing, and I'm sorry to have to say this. You can treat it like the standard safety lecture at the start of every flight. If you're thinking about double-crossing us, I advise you to forget it. I won't hesitate to kill you if I think that's what you're up to. I know you've been cleared through a comprehensive background check, and you ought to be just fine. But this isn't a game, and we don't take risks with the lives of patriots. Got any problems with that?"

"Or with putting my tray table up and my seat in the upright position?" Richfield said sarcastically. "Listen, you're calling all the shots. I'm grateful for the ride. Do what you have to do." But he felt as though he were saying, *Yeah, shoot me as soon as you find out about my Russian connection.* It was like living under a permanent, suspended death sentence.

"Okay," said Mike, "let's move out." When Douglas turned to say good-bye to Meg, she gave him a long hug, which touched him more than he would have guessed. "Have a good trip, kiddo," she said warmly. "Hope to see you back here some time."

"You bet. Thanks for putting me up. I'll get even with you in chess next time."

"We'll see," she said with a laugh.

Mike told Douglas to remove his shoes as they went downstairs. His arrival had hardly been secret, but the building had other tenants who didn't need to know that two men were leaving long before most people in New York left for work. They put their shoes on in the lobby and headed out into the cold morning.

By prearrangement Mike went out the front door first and stood there for a few seconds. He looked carefully in both directions and seemed to be listening, his head cocked like an animal alerted in a forest. Then he raised his right hand slowly to the back of his neck and rubbed it. On cue a dark gray, unmarked van moved out from the spot where it had been parked some thirty yards to the left and drew up to the curb in front of them. Mike signaled Richfield, who came quickly out of the house and followed him to the van's rear doors. Both men got in and the van drove off.

The van had an extra row of windowless seats behind the driver, and this was where the two of them sat. The driver was a gray-haired African-American man who, to Richfield's surprise, chatted constantly as he drove. He had a lot of opinions on the People's Movement, most of them irreverent and unprintable. There hardly seemed a Manhattan landmark that didn't, in his view, demonstrate the wickedness of the regime. "See that block down there?" he said, indicating a burned-out segment of Hudson Street. "It's a year after the riots and shooting in New York, and they still haven't fixed half the city up. Look at it, man, it's a total mess. They've got these damn silly political billboards all over. Think they're gonna fix the economy? Who they trying to kid? 'Work for peace,' they say. Sure. Who's gonna work for anything if all you get is ration coupons and the stores don't even have anything most of the time?" As he rattled on, Mike merely punctuated his stream-of-consciousness commentary with a few "yeah's" and "you're right's," grinning sideways at Richfield as he did so.

It was still before six o'clock, and since it was a Saturday there were few vehicles of any kind on the road. They were taking the quickest route to the airport from lower Manhattan, across the Brooklyn Bridge. It was much less likely to be patrolled than the East Side Drive and the Triboro, or the Midtown Tunnel for that matter.

Both the tunnel and the Triboro presented additional problems because the traffic, slowing down to a crawl as it funneled together from many directions, could more easily be monitored, especially where the tollbooths were equipped with television cameras to record every vehicle's license number.

The route to the Brooklyn Bridge took them close by the Municipal Building and it made Douglas uncomfortable to be so close. He half-feared, absurdly, that Bremer might be looking out one of the windows for outbound traffic, just in case Richfield was in one of the departing cars.

"Uh-oh. Better watch this one." It was the driver, suddenly tense. Peering ahead of him, Richfield saw two city police cruisers, their red and blue lights flashing, stopped in the right-hand lane of the bridge about midway across.

"They stopping anybody?" Mike asked anxiously.

"Well, let's see." The van had slowed down and allowed other traffic to pass as it approached the police cars. "No, looks as though they're busy with something else," he said with relief after a few seconds. As the van drove by, Richfield saw the policemen questioning two men and a woman who had gotten out of a badly banged up Toyota that had stopped, or been forced to stop, about mid-bridge.

Once out of Manhattan the van followed the Brooklyn-Queens Expressway up through Queens to where it joined the Grand Central Parkway. In Brooklyn, the landscape of decay and destruction was striking. Even before the civil war Douglas had always thought the BQE really belonged more to the Third World than to an industrialized nation. The huge potholes, the broken-down masonry, and the graffiti evoked the image of life after civilization had ended. Much of the masonry was still pockmarked from semiautomatic fire during the street fighting that had brought the People's Movement to power. Work crews had at least finally found all of the hundreds of bodies who fell during the struggle for control of Brooklyn. It was obvious that, even if all of the People's Movement's reconstruction programs got under way as hoped, it would take years, perhaps two generations, before the damage was repaired in America's major cities.

As the van approached La Guardia, Mike moved forward to sit in the front seat beside the driver and told Douglas to do so too. Both of them held their carry-on bags on their laps. "Even maintenance engineers generally don't get out of the rear doors of a van when arriving at an airport," Mike explained dryly. They both thanked the driver and quickly went toward the departure gates.

Mike seemed to know the gate number of the flight without looking, and Richfield followed him. But at the security checkpoint he tensed up again. A guard was checking travel documents before passengers were permitted to pass through the metal detector. What if he asked for I.D.s as well? Douglas could barely remember his alias, Joe Fielding, much less his Jersey City address. Mike wordlessly produced the two airline tickets, yawned as though life in general was tedious and filled with trivial checks, and looked in the opposite direction. The official merely glanced at the tickets, looked at Mike and Douglas, and waved them through.

Probably because it was still early and few people were up, the security presence also seemed thinner than usual to Richfield. Normally, every departure lounge had at least one militia person on duty and often a plainclothes PSB agent too. Today, though, as far as he could tell, the only people around were the airline ground agents. The Constitutionalists, evidently, had planned Douglas's trip carefully.

There seemed to be barely two dozen passengers booked for the flight: two elderly couples, four young men and two women in the khaki officer cadet uniforms of the American People's Army, three young civilians who looked as though they might be off-duty militiamen, and the rest an equal number of men and women in civilian clothes in their thirties and forties. Mike had evidently timed their arrival so that they would be in the middle of passengers checking in.

"Have a good flight," the gate agent said pleasantly, perusing both their tickets and their I.D.s adding oddly, "Many happy landings." Mike permitted a brief grin and responded, "Thanks. Same to you." Douglas, alerted to hints and gestures after four nights of confinement in the safe house, assumed this was a Constitutionalist coded greeting.

They began to call for a general boarding just fifteen minutes before the scheduled departure time of seven o'clock. The plane, an old Boeing 727, was airborne within a few minutes of being pushed back from the gate and climbed in a sharp, sweeping curve back over Manhattan and New Jersey on its way toward its assigned cruising altitude. Douglas's eyes were heavy with sleep, but he forced himself to take in the urban panorama of New York before the aircraft soared upward into the low overcast.

Richfield had looked at it and pondered it before at least a dozen times on Protocol trips up and down the East Coast. Yet the extent of the devastation from the previous year's fighting still amazed him. The economic crisis and the regime's own varying priorities had delayed rebuilding in the city, although the South Bronx and Harlem were well underway toward rehabilitation—which the regime had promised its priority would be. The South Bronx, even in pre-civil war times, had always astonished him by its grimness. He remembered hearing how visitors from China in the 1980s, heading north out of Manhattan by train, had sometimes asked politely if there had been a war in New York. What struck Richfield now was the extent of the devastation in other parts of the city. Block after block, the black shells of buildings stared up like missing teeth in the face that Manhattan turned sadly toward the sky.

Nearly three hours later the flight attendant nudged him awake saying, "Put your seat back up, please." His ears were popping as the plane descended into its final approach into Minneapolis Airport. He hadn't even awakened for the snack. Across the aisle Mike was eying him carefully, perhaps worried that, in a moment of disorientation, Richfield might blurt something out on awakening. But Douglas merely nodded at him and rubbed his eyes.

"This is the captain," a deep voice crackled out over the speaker system. "We're on final now for Minneapolis-St. Paul, which is the termination of this flight. I am instructed to remind all passengers that government regulations forbid the taking of any photographs from the plane from now until we have landed and you have departed the passenger terminal. Flight attendants, prepare for landing."

Curious, Douglas looked out his window as the aircraft descended toward the runway. He could see nothing that suggested any security problem. But as the 727 touched down and continued its landing roll, he caught sight of a dozen humpbacked fighter jets in mottled camouflage colors lined up on the apron in front of a hangar at the far side of the airfield, their cockpit canopies open in neat and identical array. He didn't know what kind of aircraft they were, but they didn't look like any American planes he had seen before. He turned slowly and caught Mike's eye, nodding toward his window. Mike followed his glance and narrowed his eyes. Then he glanced around to see if anyone was looking at him. Confidant they weren't, he silently mouthed the word "MiGs."

Richfield was stunned. Could the Russians—or perhaps the Cubans—have dared to introduce combat aircraft into the American civil war without anyone's knowing about it?

Inside the terminal it was thick with militiamen and with newly minted American People's Army officers in their khaki uniforms and blue-and-gold collar tabs. The officers seemed to be leaving Minneapolis after some kind of visit. The dozens of militiamen may have been there as part of security measures to protect the visiting fighters. Yet it puzzled Richfield why military aircraft of any kind would have landed at a major commercial airport unless the Constitutionalists had succeeded in disabling all the military airfields in the area.

Leading the way, Mike took a side door out of the baggage claim area and down a corridor to another door that read: "Administrative Offices. Authorized Airline Personnel Only." They took an elevator to the third floor. Two doors down the corridor Mike stopped at a door with a plastic nameplate that read: "Interline Office."

Mike opened it without knocking and came almost face-to-face with a balding, dumpy little man sitting behind a metal desk facing the door. White wisps of curling hair tracked hesitantly down the back of his neck and along his temples. He couldn't have been a day younger than sixty-five.

"Can I help you?" he asked.

"I'm Mike Rainer," Richfield's companion said, "and we're looking for Warren Phelps." It was the first time Douglas had heard Mike's last name.

"You're talking to him," said the man, his eyes sizing them both up through bifocals.

155

"This is Joe Fielding. We're from the Aurora Travel Service in New York and understand you can help us with transportation. We've got documentation."

Mike took out two plain manila envelopes and handed them to Phelps, who removed the papers and spread them out in front of him.

"The Aurora Travel Service . . . , eh?" Phelps said noncommittally, twiddling a wisp of white hair at his temples. "Let me see your I.D.s."

Mike handed over a driver's license and some other local New York I.D. Douglas produced the fake New Jersey driver's license and a health club membership card. He hadn't had time to scrutinize them in the van or on the plane, but as he handed them over, he was surprised to see that the photographs were indeed of him. He couldn't remember anyone taking his photo at the safe house.

Phelps carefully lined up each photo I.D. of Mike and Douglas with the documentation neatly lying in front of him. He looked more like a professional stamp trader perusing a newly acquired collection than a crucial link in a complex chain of civil war espionage.

Standing slightly to one side in front of the desk, Douglas could make out the letterhead of the Aurora Travel Service, another photograph, three paragraphs of text, and a large signature.

"Young fellow," Phelps now said quietly to Richfield, "would you please go and slide the bolt shut on that door? . . . Thanks."

Phelps fingered the documentation carefully with both hands, almost if he were deciphering a Braille message. Then he pulled a small traveling iron from a bottom desk drawer and he plugged it into an outlet on the wall beside him.

"I've got a couple of questions I'd like to ask you," he said gravely. "Mr. Rainer," he said, turning to Mike, "tell me what Leon is like." Mike frowned, looked confused, and stammered back, "I'm sorry, I don't know any Leon." Phelps looked at him coldly. "Well isn't that a shame," he said sarcastically. "Are you sure?"

"Yes." Douglas looked at him and Mike shrugged back, as though indicating that Phelps was confused. But Phelps now turned to Richfield. "Do *you* know Leon?" he asked.

Richfield looked questioningly at Mike, wondering if he was allowed to respond. Mike nodded.

"Yes, I know Leon," Douglas answered. "He's a middle-aged African-American man with graying hair and an unpleasant temperament."

"Good," commented Phelps. "Someone's at the plate who can hit. Now let's see what kind of vacation planning your friends at Aurora have in mind."

He then picked up the iron and placed it heavily in the middle of the sheet of paper. When he removed it, Douglas was surprised to see dark handwriting between the regular lines of the letter. Phelps examined the writing through a portable magnifying lens, appeared to read it several times, and then looked at his watch.

"Eleven-thirty," he said. "We don't have much time. You have to be in Bismarck by eleven tonight."

With that he handed the I.D.s back to Mike and Douglas, picked up the travel agency letters, and casually lit them with a cigarette lighter. Douglas watched in fascination as the pages quickly melted into ash and dropped in fluttering fragments onto the metal desk. Then the older man neatly swept up the ashes with a napkin onto a newspaper, crumpled it all up into a tight ball, and put it in his coat pocket. He smiled cherubically as he silently shook the hands of his two visitors and led them out of the office.

At a pay phone in the corridor he dialed a local number and asked, "Can you get a pickup here in fifteen minutes?" There was a pause, then, "Bismarck. By eleven . . . Yes, I know, but it's an urgent business trip, and my clients have to be there on time . . . Good, thanks."

He hung up and turned to Mike and Douglas with a grin. "Your limo will be here in fifteen minutes," he said. "Many happy landings."

"Thanks," said Mike. "And to you too."

The pickup showed up in less than fifteen minutes at the arrival area, a green, battered old Ford that had probably spent most of its life on a farm. The driver was a fresh-faced, blond and freckled youth who might not have been eighteen years old, but who drove with the air of someone used to moving vehicles and people around quickly. Mike and Douglas sat with him in the cab, their bags squeezed into a space behind the front seat.

"Hi, I'm Daryl," he said, offering a friendly hand to his new passengers. Mike and Douglas introduced themselves and settled down for the long ride.

Daryl exited the airport to I-494 and followed it around south Minneapolis until it hit I-94 heading northwest toward North Dakota and Fargo. He drove confidently—and fast, the speedometer hovering around seventy-five miles per hour. "Don't you worry about a ticket?" Douglas asked as casually as he could.

"You kidding? Where've you been for the past year? I doubt if a single speeding ticket has been given out on a Minnesota interstate since the civil war began."

"Why not?"

"You figure it out. Hardly anyone can get the gas for long-distance driving anymore. Then, when the People's Movement took over the Twin Cities, just like everywhere else, one of the first things they did was put all the squad cars under lock and key. They didn't trust the cops not to hightail it to Montana or even Canada. There's hardly a handful of patrol cars operating in the state, and pretty well all of 'em are in the Twin Cities area for normal police work there.

"What we're gonna have to watch out for are unmarked militia and PSB sedans. They like nothing better than to set up makeshift checkpoints along the interstate and hassle anyone driving by. With our CB network we generally get a good warning. The truckers are especially helpful at alerting everyone on the road. If you see a police cruiser at all, it'll either be a medical emergency or an escort for some big shot heading into North Dakota. The highway patrol, or maybe a PSB detail, if the visitors are important enough, picks them up at Fargo and takes them on to Bismarck. That, of course, is the end of the line."

"What do you mean?" asked Richfield, forgetting for the first time his instructions not to ask questions.

"I mean the end of the line for the PM," said Daryl. "The Missouri River is the border for the People's Movement, aside from Denver. The Slope—that's what North Dakotans call their state west of the Missouri—is enemy territory, ruled—at least by night—by Hodges's boys. Until recently, the Connies didn't venture much on the other side of the Missouri either. I guess they weren't geared up for it. That's all been changing the past few weeks. They've been popping up all over the state after dark, east of Bismarck, ambushing PSB convoys, stealing weapons, kidnapping, even doing some recruiting."

"How do they break in?"

"By chopper sometimes, or small boat across the river. Sometimes they fly in by small plane. North Dakota's a big state, and the PM hasn't figured out how to watch it all. There's plenty of room."

Mike was frowning now, apparently uncomfortable with the amount of information Daryl was handing out to both of them. Catching his look, Daryl clammed up. Douglas quickly figured that Daryl enjoyed chatting but he would need to be coaxed. Mike would have to get used to the fact that they weren't in public now.

"There's a couple of bottles of water in the back if you guys get thirsty," Daryl said after they'd driven several minutes in silence. "I also brought along some sandwiches. We can't risk stopping at a diner or fast-food place because they're always crawling with militia and PSB. You're in big trouble if you're not locally known or have out-of-state plates. We'll stop for gas at some private pumps I know on the way. If you guys need to take a leak, just let me know.

"By the way, if we get stopped, I'm just the driver. If you think your travel agency stuff will work, give it a shot. I've got a workable alibi, but you guys are on your own if they don't buy your stories."

The interstate rolled on slowly through the rich farmland and the tidy little towns. For the first few miles the Mississippi flowed languidly by to the right, but after St. Cloud, it turned north and split off from I-94. Albany, Melrose, Sauk Centre, West Union, Brandon, Pomme de Terre Lakes—the small communities and landmarks rushed by as the pickup pushed west. The heater in the cab and the body heat from the three men made the air stuffy. Richfield and Mike both dozed off several times.

When Richfield awoke after one doze, Daryl had a small ear piece in his ear, the wire disappearing into his shirt and reemerging at his belt to connect with a socket on the dashboard.

"What's that?" inquired Richfield.

Daryl looked back, glanced at Mike, who was asleep, and grinned. "CB," he said. "We're getting into the area where the PM operates helicopter patrols, and the militia or PSB make sudden, unannounced checkpoints. Sometimes they'll just cruise the interstate into North Dakota looking for suspicious vehicles, unmarked trucks or vans, big limos, you know, the oddballs. Traffic is so light it's pretty easy to know who just about everybody is on the road. Fortunately, we've got a pretty good warning system, but you've got to listen and keep changing the channels or you miss it."

They'd been driving for three hours and both Mike and Douglas had reached back for the water and the sandwiches more often then they'd thought they might. The thick forests of eastern Minnesota had given way to the farmland of the West. They were approaching the Red River Valley and the state line with North Dakota. Shortly after crossing the Buffalo River, Daryl turned off the highway and stopped for gas at a farm. A lone farm hand seemed to know who he was and unlocked the pump, but he didn't ask any questions. Richfield, cramped and headachy, was eager to feel the bracing cold air and stretch his legs. Mike, it seemed, was increasingly detached from the transit operation as the truck headed further west. He also seemed bored. Richfield much preferred Daryl, since he was less uptight and his openness was refreshing.

Dusk approached as they crossed the Red River into Fargo. Lights blazed from the city and the headlights of oncoming cars glared uncomfortably off pavement wet with a just-melted sprinkling of snow. Mike was asleep and snoring lightly. Douglas, uncomfortable in the middle, was dozing lightly when Daryl nudged him awake. "Take a good look at what's in the trucks and start counting," he said quietly.

At first, Douglas didn't understand what was going on. The late-afternoon traffic seemed to be at a normal volume for the time of day. There didn't seem to be an accident or a blockage on the freeway. But suddenly Douglas grasped what Daryl had meant. A gigantic military convoy and what looked like school buses, stretching as far as the eye could see ahead, was lumbering slowly westward. The trucks wore the standard dark green of traditional U.S. Army vehicles; the APA had not bothered to repaint them. But the school buses had been repainted in a mottled green-and-brown camouflage scheme. And they were packed with troops.

Military police humvee were interspersed among the convoy at regular intervals. Counting carefully, Richfield noted every truck and humvee until, after several minutes, they had overtaken the lead vehicle, which was a humvee mounted with two armor-protected, heavy-caliber machine guns pointing to each flank. The troops were all wearing the khaki field uniforms of the APA, and they sat without much animation, staring out the windows. They had been on the road for some time.

"How many d'you think?" asked Daryl.

"Forty-seven," Richfield answered.

Mike woke up, saw the convoy, and quietly exclaimed to the wind.

"I'd say we're all headed for the same place, or somewhere pretty close," Daryl said.

"That doesn't make a lot of sense," said Mike, forgetting his practiced vow of silence. "The serious fighting has been farther south, around Denver. Why would the APA make a big thrust up here?"

"Because if you were one of Rutledge's generals, why would you fiddle around in Colorado? You'd go for the jugular—Montana—where Hodges has the bulk of his forces. You wouldn't waste time with small potatoes to the south."

"Colorado isn't exactly small potatoes," Mike corrected him. "Denver has nearly been cut off a couple of times so far. It's pretty strategic."

"Sure it is, but if the PM loses Denver, it hasn't lost the war, unless maybe the Army of the Southwest suddenly makes a breakout from New Mexico. If the Connies lose Helena, then it's major finito. Simple as that. But the PM isn't nearly ready for a big push into Montana. There must be another explanation."

"Well, assuming you're right that they're headed for Bismarck, maybe the PM is having trouble defending itself there. The Missouri River is the beginning of no man's land, and Hodges has been able to mount a pretty effective guerrilla movement throughout much of the eastern half of the state. They've even blown up stuff on this freeway. My guess is these new troops are being sent to protect Bismarck itself. It wouldn't take a whole lot of effort right now for Hodges to cut off Bismarck and hold it. It's already pretty much a closed city because of the number of checkpoints you have to get through to get in there."

The trio lapsed into silence. Richfield didn't want to sound like the new kid on the block, and Daryl didn't seem to enjoy having something to say to Mike. The thick vegetation of the Red River Valley gave way to a prairie of gently rolling hills and large-scale farms, although in the darkness Richfield could only pick out the vaguest silhouette of the landscape. Night descended swiftly on the wintry landscape and the temperature dropped quickly. The sparsely populated settlements and small towns along the interstate bore the names the settlers had brought with them barely a century earlier—Casselton, Valley City, Jamestown, Medina.

They'd been on the road, including stops, nearly five hours now and they might well make the 193 miles from Fargo to Bismarck in another four. Daryl had said they'd stop one more time for gas closer to Bismarck. Richfield guessed that they would probably not enter the city directly because of the area's numerous checkpoints.

Three hours later there was hardly another vehicle on the road, just the occasional eighteen-wheeler or pickup. Douglas, alone in his thoughts and half-dozing, wondered what Rachel would think if she knew where he was. She had been so beguilingly well-dressed both times he had seen her; he couldn't imagine how she might look here in farm country. Her face was easy to remember, especially the way her sternest expressions would give way to impish humor or melancholy or annoyance. He'd never encountered a woman so profoundly alive.

"My God!" Daryl suddenly exclaimed, jolting Richfield fully awake. He was braking the pickup hard, letting up after a second or two to keep from locking the brakes, and staring at a flickering glow two or three hundred yards ahead of them.

"What is it?" Douglas asked.

"It's a truck . . . and it's on fire," Daryl replied.

An eighteen-wheeler had jackknifed across most of the westbound width of the highway, and the weight of the container had pulled both it and the trailer over. Nasty, long flames were licking their way through the cab. About twenty yards beyond the truck were two more destroyed vehicles, apparently regular sedans, one of them crushed horribly into the rear passenger area of the other.

As Daryl slowed the pickup to a crawl to find a way around the twisted wreckage and debris, he whistled in dismay. The side of the cab seemed to have taken a direct hit from either a grenade or rocket. Both sedans were pockmarked with bullet holes. "Poor devils," he muttered. "They didn't stand a chance. I wonder if there are survivors."

"Who cares," Mike hissed brusquely. "It's none of our business. Just get us out of here."

"And leave somebody to bleed to death by the roadside? Not me, man. That may be okay in Manhattan, but we don't do that out here."

"So what are you going to do?" Mike asked angrily. "Spend half the night playing doctor and wait for that convoy to come along and blame us for what happened? We're in the middle of a war, and I've got a delivery to make in Bismarck. Let's get out of here. For all we know, the PM has already figured that this truck isn't where it's supposed to be and has sent a chopper out to track it down."

Daryl ignored Mike and stopped the pickup near one of the smashed sedans. He got out and trudged toward it through the wind and snow.

"You idiot!" Mike shouted. "That car may be booby trapped."

"Yeah, it might," Daryl said with an edge of anger in his voice, "but in this part of the world, if someone's hurt on the highway, you stop to help him. If they're all dead, we go right on, but if someone's alive, we help."

"Oh no we don't," said Mike, out of the pickup and following Daryl to the wrecked car along with Richfield. "I'm in charge of this transfer operation, and I say we keep moving."

Daryl turned around to face Mike. "You can say what you like, but I'm not driving until I'm satisfied there isn't someone we can help."

"Even the enemy?" shouted Mike in fury and disbelief.

"Yeah, even the enemy. They're human too, you know. Have you lived in New York so long you've forgotten that?"

"You'll regret this," said Mike coldly, and he turned to walk back to the pickup. Richfield guessed what Mike might do and gestured to

Daryl that there could be a weapon. Daryl nodded and pulled out a small nine-millimeter pistol. He took a firing position and aimed it at Mike, some twenty-five feet away.

"Okay, your choice," he yelled. "Now freeze where you are."

Mike stopped instantly.

"Douglas, take his gun, give it to me, and keep him covered with this one."

Richfield walked up to Mike and patted his jacket below the armpit. The pistol, also a nine-millimeter, was in a holster just under the right arm. He took it and walked back to Daryl, who had not taken his eyes or his gun away from Mike.

"I'm going to cuff him," Daryl said. "Doug, you'll find some handcuffs taped below the glove compartment. Bring them to me."

As Richfield walked back to the pickup, Mike called out, "Don't be a fool, Douglas. If you side with him, you'll be in breach of military discipline in wartime and be liable for a court-martial. If our people get hold of you, you'll almost certainly be shot."

Douglas couldn't resist retorting, "Our people? Isn't Daryl on our side, Mike? You talk about military rules, but what about the Geneva Convention on prisoners of war? Doesn't that have something to say about caring for wounded enemies? Besides, if there is a survivor, maybe he'll tell us something useful."

Mike snorted contemptuously and kept silent.

They handcuffed him and tied him flat to the bed of the pickup, using drainage holes in the side to keep the rope in place. He shouted a few obscenities at them, but when they didn't reply he became quiet.

They found four bodies in and around the cars. The cab of the truck was burning too fiercely to see if the driver was there, but the left side had been so badly smashed in by the explosion that it was unlikely that anybody had lived through it. They made a rapid search of the roadside on both sides of the freeway, looking for signs that anyone might have crawled away from the accident.

They found a survivor some twenty yards from one of the cars. He was on his back in the roadside grass and moaning quietly. By the faint and eerie light of the flames from the truck, he appeared to be a man in his forties or so with a big, droopy moustache. The right side of his face was badly cut, and blood had trickled from the wound matting the grass around him. When Daryl swept his flashlight over the man's body, it was clear he also had a wound in his upper right thigh.

"Hold on, man, we'll get you out of here," said Douglas. "Can you put your arm around my neck? Here, Daryl, can you give me a hand?"

They carried the groaning survivor back to the pickup and seated him on the tailgate. Daryl unlocked a metal chest that was mounted in the truck bed and pulled out a sleeping bag and a small first-aid kit. He cut away part of the wounded man's jeans and cleaned the wound with swabs. Between Douglas and him they managed to bandage the leg. Next they eased the man into the sleeping bag and placed him in the back of the truck next to Mike.

"What's your name, pal?" asked Daryl.

"Matt. Matt Andersen," he answered in a whisper. "Thanks. My leg hurts real bad. Did the militia send you along?"

"No, we were just on the road," Daryl said quickly. "What happened?"

"The Cornpickers set up an ambush. They seemed to know we were coming and blasted the truck with some kind of antitank round. The cab took a direct hit. The driver and his buddy didn't stand a chance. They hit us with small arms from somewhere off the road here. I was in the back seat and threw myself on the floor as soon as the shooting started. It probably didn't last more than a minute."

"Cornpickers?" Richfield asked involuntarily. Daryl gave him a look but said nothing.

"Yeah, Cornpickers. Who else would shoot up an eighteen-wheeler in the middle of North Dakota on a dark night? They knew what they were hitting all right."

"What was that?" asked Daryl.

"Can you believe it? Coffee. They haven't seen it in Bismarck for weeks, and people are going crazy. The PM authorized a special shipment and sent two cars along to guard it."

"Why didn't the Cornpickers steal the cargo?" asked Richfield getting into the argot.

"'Cause they don't have the means to move cargo away from the roads. You guys don't sound like locals. Where ya from?"

"Minneapolis," Daryl replied. "Now, you've lost a lot of blood. We'll get you to Bismarck as quickly as possible. It shouldn't be more than an hour from here now. We're going to lash you down beside this guy. Don't mind him, he's harmless, just a little excitable. He can't hurt you."

"Who is he?" Matt asked, taking note of Mike for the first time.

"Never mind. Now let's make tracks." With that, Daryl slammed the tailgate shut and he and Richfield ran around to the cab.

"You think he's okay back there with Mike?" Richfield asked, as Daryl accelerated to seventy miles an hour.

"Sure. Mike's not going to do him any harm. He's hard-nosed and a little obnoxious, but he's not a sadist. Matt'll fall asleep soon enough. I reckon he'll be okay for three to four hours, but if he doesn't get medical attention by then, he's in trouble."

"And what do we do with Mike?"

Daryl frowned. "That's a problem," he answered. Hodges's boys are sticklers about picking up the wounded, but they shoot you for sassiness—or what they think is sassiness—quicker than you know what's happening. I think that may explain why some folks call them Cornpickers."

"Hey, I've never heard that one before," said Richfield.

"I guess it's local. It's not politically correct to say 'Constitutionalist' anyway when you're around PM hardliners. But getting back to Mike, I think we have a real problem on our hands. He's sore as a cow elk after calving."

"Fine," said Richfield, getting irritated now and wondering if he'd made a huge blunder by taking sides with Daryl. "We've got a badly wounded man on our hands who needs immediate hospitalization and an angry Constitutionalist agent, both of them trussed up like turkeys in the back of our pickup. Can't you just see the first full-service gas station guy saying: 'Check your oil? Water your prisoners?'"

Daryl didn't say anything. He just grinned at the image of a full-service station and kept driving. The buildup of housing made it clear they were coming close to Bismarck.

Suddenly Daryl started. "Holy smoke" he said under his breath, looking intently in the mirror. "Someone is either late for a funeral or wants to make our acquaintance very quickly."

"Can you lose him?" asked Richfield.

"Are you kidding? In a pickup? Anything over eighty and we're dead meat. This thing'd fall apart."

"Then what do we do?"

"The only sensible thing—keep going. If he's not after us, it makes no sense to slow down. If he is, let's just hope he's on the same side."

Through the rear window of the pickup, Richfield watched the pursuing car quickly catch up and then close to within some twenty feet of their tailgate, its headlights full on and flooding the pickup's mirrors painfully. Daryl took a hand away from the vibrating steering wheel to angle his driver's mirror away.

"That's great," he said sarcastically. "Could you just give me a little more of your brights up here?"

After a few seconds the pursuing vehicle suddenly dropped back, dimmed its brights, and stayed with the pickup. Daryl slowed down a tad and readjusted his mirror, but he kept looking back in it.

"What was that all about?" Richfield finally asked after things seemed to have returned to normal.

"Beats me, man," replied Daryl. "War produces weirdos all the time, but this one's an oddball for sure. I won't be happy until I'm in Bismarck and this guy's on his way to the Little Bighorn or wherever."

"And here I was thinking that the real screwballs operated only in Manhattan."

"Is that where you work?" Daryl quickly asked. "Manhattan?"

"I'm not supposed to say," Richfield replied lamely.

"No, I guess you're not, just as you're—" he interrupted himself now as he glanced in the mirror again. "Uh-oh, here comes the hot rod again."

Richfield turned back and saw the same bright headlights roaring up behind the pickup again. This time, though, the pursuer didn't dawdle. Instead, it drew up alongside the pickup in the slow lane. Richfield quickly looked out and felt his adrenaline suddenly surge into his chest. A man with a black ski mask was just a few feet away, pointing an M-16 automatic rifle with a silencer right at his face.

8

Discontent at Sea

Aboard the USS Massachusetts

Aooga! Aooga! Aooga!

As the *Massachusetts*'s klaxon sounded battle stations and the submarine plunged like an angry sea monster beneath the gray Atlantic, the crew tensed throughout the ship, responding instinctively to years of training. At any moment the boat could come under attack from the Bear reconnaissance bomber, that is, if the plane had spotted it. The procedures for escape and evasion were etched in the subconscious of every man aboard. Rush had ordered this particular drill practiced until the crew was sick of it, but his judgment, as usual, had been sound; of all the emergencies the submarine was most apt to face, attack on or near the surface was the most likely.

Gresham, panting with tension and exertion after hurling himself down the aft hatch into the air regeneration room, didn't bother to change out of his foul-weather gear before rushing forward to the con to join Rush for the crucial first minutes of evasive action.

"Maneuvering, con, all ahead flank," said Rush, his voice deadly calm.

"Con, Maneuvering, all ahead flank, aye."

"Helmsman, left forty-five degrees."

"Forty-five degrees. Aye, Sir."

"Diving Officer, make your depth three hundred feet."

"Three hundred feet. Aye, Sir."

"Do you think he saw us?" Rush asked Gresham, who was following the captain's orders minutely.

"I don't know, Captain. He certainly wouldn't have been expecting to see anything so close to the coast, and he may not have even been looking. The guy might just be on a milk run to Cienfuegos."

"I guess we'll find out soon enough. Sonar, any contacts?"

"None, Sir."

"Not that we'd know at this speed. We must be making a hell of a lot of noise. Chris, take her down to three hundred, stop all engines, and rig the boat for quiet. If they're on to us, we'll know by then. You have the con."

"Aye, Captain." As Rush left to plan the submarine's navigation with Williams, Gresham watched intently as the diving officer read off the depth changes of the boat. At first the *Massachusetts* at flank speed seemed to be descending like a rock, but as the boat approached three hundred feet, it leveled off.

"292 . . . 294 . . . 296 . . . 298 . . . 300 . . . 302 feet—"

"Diving Officer, make your depth three hundred feet!" Gresham interrupted, annoyed that the diving officer hadn't allowed for the inertia of the sub's descent in giving instructions to the two planesmen.

"Three hundred feet, aye, Sir," said the diving officer, flustered.

"Maneuvering . . . con, all stop."

"Con . . . Maneuvering, all stop."

Then, on the MC, the communication channel for the whole boat, Gresham ordered: "Rig the boat for quiet."

All over the submarine men stopped their conversations in midsentence, crept, rather than walked, and tried to stay as still and immobile as they could. Propelled forward for several minutes at more than thirty knots by the power of its reactors, the *Massachusetts* continued to move rapidly under the sheer inertia of its forward momentum. But as the resistance of the seawater to the passage of the sixteen-thousand-ton hull built up, the sub slowly settled into an eerie hover off the New England coast.

The sonar operator needed no additional instructions from the con. He scoured the Atlantic with the boat's passive listening devices for any human-made noise, especially the deadly ping of an active sonar from an air-dropped buoy or, much worse, from a Russian fast-attack submarine that might, by chance, have been lurking in the area before the *Massachusetts* crash-dived into the Atlantic.

But there was nothing, not even the ghostly singing of "biologics," or whales and porpoises. The alert radar operator had picked up the Bear far enough away for the sub to crash-dive before being spotted. For several more minutes the Trident hovered, listening to everything in the ocean around it.

"Sonar . . . con, report any contacts on the three MC," Gresham said after a few minutes' pause. Then, dialing up Rush on another channel, he reported: "Captain, the boat is rigged for quiet. No contacts or sign of pursuit."

There was a pause at the other end of the intercom. "Very well," Rush finally said wearily. "Let's move ahead two-thirds on a heading of one-one-five. I think we're through the net."

They were. Rush knew that the quadrant of the North Atlantic they were moving out of was often thick with Russian boats. Russian President Zhelenovsky himself had ordered this deployment at the very beginning of the civil war. He appeared to believe that the renegade submarines, out of frustration, might launch their missile against one or two American cities in the hope that the Russians would be blamed. If this happened, Zhelenovsky reasoned, there would be nothing his regime could do to assist the People's Movement in its consolidation of power. In America itself only a handful of the most rabid People's Movement Maoists believed this was a plausible scenario. Yet the effect of Zhelenovsky's order was to tie down a large number of Russian fast-attack submarines in a confined sector of the North Atlantic and North Pacific when they could more usefully be searching for the Tridents elsewhere.

The *Massachusetts's* emergency dive and evasion procedures had been performed well, but the crew skills were maintained at a high price in terms of overall stress for the boat as a whole. To maintain combat preparedness and technical skills over months required endless vigilance over the morale of the boat. Not even Daniel Marcus, in devising the Almond strategy, had been able to calculate how long crews would have to operate without relief in wartime conditions and avoid accident, errors of judgment, or even mutiny. The average pre-civil war patrol had been 90–105 days.

During that time, even in peacetime, each crew member was allowed to receive only eight very short radio messages from family members. Nothing could be sent back in reply. Fresh fruit and produce taken aboard at the outset of the patrol gradually ran out within a few weeks, and the overall quality of the food served on submarines—much celebrated in navy lore—steadily diminished toward the end of the patrol. Sometimes even the traditional Saturday night pizzas didn't last out the cruise.

Boredom and frustration also inevitably took their toll, even in peacetime with patrols of predetermined length. Partly to combat this, there was built-in pressure within the submarine service to pass ever-higher levels of technical examinations essential for promotion, and the submarine itself was ergonomically designed so that there was a constant awareness of the necessary procedures for safety and survival. Pipes, wires, gauges, dials, and switches were not hidden away, but met the eye in all directions. Humans needed reminding of the complexity of the machinery essential for survival in the unnatural environment of life several hundred feet beneath the ocean surface. Routine was also constantly interrupted by procedure drills to test the sub's response to everything from a damaged reactor to an actual missile launch.

Enormous thought had also gone into providing entertainment and diversion in a way that, somehow, might compensate for the deprivation of the joys of family life and loving relationships. The lower level of the missile deck provided a surprisingly long stretch of corridor around the missile canisters wide enough to run on. The area was known as "Sherwood Forest" because the missile canisters, painted brown, rose like great trees from the sub's floor. There were exercise machines and free weights available to help the crew relieve their stress through healthy physical activity. Both fast-attack and missile submarines had nearly inexhaustible video and audio libraries and an impressive collection of books. There were the usual pot boilers, but they also had serious works that could challenge a crewman's intellect at a high level. For all these carefully devised distractions and the thousands of hours of research that had gone into making life aboard a submarine as psychologically healthy as possible, there was no escaping one fundamental truth—there would be a breaking point for even the best-trained and the most-disciplined crew.

As soon as Project Almond had been set in motion, after the signing of the Treaty of Paris in September of the previous year, all peacetime guidelines for the length of a patrol by three of the Tridents had been abandoned. The patrols were now extended to six-month periods between home port visits to Chile or New Zealand. Early on in the first of these extended periods, Rush and Gresham realized that if there were not some morale-boosting system to keep the men focused on positive experiences, they might be facing a mutiny even faster than had been predicted at the outset. Accordingly, at Gresham's suggestion, the sub introduced "Club Med" packages. Once a month eight crew members and an officer were chosen to enjoy a two-day vacation at a remote atoll, far removed from the shipping lanes or inhabited areas. The men were left sufficient rations and water for their time of rest, sun, and swimming.

The program was so popular with the crew that occasionally Rush would add two crew members to the group whose performances had been exceptional in the intervening period.

Between home port visits and aside from the "Club Med" packages, the *Massachusetts* didn't surface or make its presence known to anyone. Food was carefully rationed, not doled out liberally as in the past, and, of course, it was much worse than in peacetime. Worst of all, though, the home port visits lasted barely a week, a time so brief as to constitute merely a blip in the endless procession of eighteen-hour days and six-hour watches. Marcus and the other planners of Project Almond had understood that any liberty period longer than a week could both erode the crew's battle skills and make them far less willing to resume their patrols when the home port visit was over.

The term "home port," in fact, was hardly an accurate one in the context of Project Almond. The seven days, not all of which could be physically spent ashore, were barely enough time to get used to sleeping in a real bed, to go for a run in the open air, to smell the vegetation, and to feel the touch of the wind. The two clandestine ports the *Massachusetts* had visited were in southern Chile and on the south island of New Zealand. Entry was a harrowing operation, requiring precise navigation submerged in deep-water fjords to locations within the channels far enough into the wilderness to be out of touch with normal human activity. The "covert ingress" operation meant that the submarine remained underwater until it was literally alongside the docking pier.

"Pier," in fact, was something of a misnomer. It referred to a temporary, floating dock that, when not in use, was kept hidden with other essential loading and unloading equipment in a giant, skillfully camouflaged sea cavern blasted out of the steep sides of fjords in Chile and New Zealand. The submarine surfaced just outside the cavern, then nudged its way in so that nothing was visible from the air or from space. The only serious concern was that a satellite might detect unusual wave patterns in the enclosed fjord areas as the submarines first arrived or departed. Otherwise, the principal worry was hitchhikers, geologists, or others who might stumble into the barbedwire perimeter of the twenty-acre sites standing on top of the caverns. Once the submarine was safely docked and the repair and resupply procedures were underway, the crew could at least venture out on terra firma.

Yet the shore leave in the traditional sense was not shore leave at all, since the crews couldn't leave the area, and social life outside of each other was nonexistent.

Shore leave did, however, provide a vital component in morale in the form of mail from family members. Marcus had himself devised a mail-forwarding system so that crew members could keep in touch with their families without divulging either the whereabouts of the family or the destination of their mail. There were newspapers, books, and magazines to catch up with, a small video arcade, even a game center with table tennis and a racquetball court.

Despite the best efforts of the Project Almond designers, there was nevertheless no avoiding the fact that the challenge to the submarine crews was an extreme one. During patrols of six months at a time, even the eleven million square miles of the Pacific and the five million square miles of the Atlantic often seemed to be terribly confined spaces.

The "Club Med" packages helped for the first several months of Project Almond. But even the glamour of these wore off the second or third time, and swimming or snorkeling in the middle of nowhere, with nobody new to talk to, had lost its appeal. The fact was that after months on patrol the best and steadiest men in the crew—the African-American Reynolds, Chief of the Watch Rodriguez, Rush, Gresham—found their last reserves of patience and forbearance strained past the breaking point in the confined quarters and amid the continuing uncertainty of the civil war.

Rush was no less aware of the problem than Gresham, who occasionally served as a sort of unofficial onboard chaplain and counselor to different crew members. Rush had readily agreed to the "Club Med" idea. Gresham, more cerebral, had concocted trivia contests, elaborate card games (cribbage had remained one of the favorites), guessing games about internal dimensions within the ship, even grade-school-style essay-writing contests with discouraging titles like "My Favorite Summer Vacation." The prizes for the winners of these contests were desserts or candy the captain kept in his safe, along with the nuclear codes, to ensure they were always available.

It all helped, but both the captain and the executive officer knew that it merely keep the wolves of anarchy and mutiny at bay for a few more weeks each time. Sooner or later, each man knew, though none admitted it to the other, some of them were going to snap, and the entire safety of the ship and the crew, not to mention the viability of Project Almond, would be compromised.

Rush convinced himself that the six-month patrols, with one week's leave, were no more than extended versions of the peacetime three-month cruises. But he quietly increased the frequency of the formal roving patrols by designated seamen throughout every nook and cranny of the 650-foot-long submarine. He was on the lookout for possible sabotage that might not actually endanger the lives of the crew but might force the submarine to the surface and even to surrender if it became impossible to continue operating the boat. He wanted to prevent any potential plotters from skulking together in remote corners of the boat. He was determined to stem even the slightest hint of sexual activity among the crew.

The fact was, if the crew held together, the submarine could evade the Russian navy almost indefinitely, provided it took the normal, prudent precautions and they didn't have any exceptionally bad luck. What the ship could not survive was even the slightest weakening of the morale of the crew. As the weeks turned into months, and the months had now rounded off into more than a year, Rush wondered how long morale could hold up. The moment it fell apart was the moment Project Almond starting collapsing.

Then, one evening in mid-December, Rush's fears suddenly approached reality. It happened in the enlisted men's wardroom during the evening crew's mess. Electronic Technician William Byron was eating with three of his friends, Machinist Hank Planter, Machinist Mate Bill "Bosco" Henry, and Torpedoman Joe Galateo. Byron had been reprimanded by the officer of the watch for cutting corners on the prescribed procedures for a simulated reactor failure. The drill required the submarine to go to periscope depth so that the auxiliary diesel engines could breathe air. Byron in Maneuvering had ignored the orders sequence during the drill in a way that was clearly insubordinate. Williams had called him on it in front of the men. Now Byron was seething.

"You know what I'd like to do with these officers? I'd like to assist them in rapid egress from the starboard torpedo tubes. Who does that scupperhead think he is, anyway? He's some two-bit Okie with a waitress mom who slept with every fat businessman in town on Saturday nights to send him to college."

"Hey, Bill, take a look at your stew. You must've already got to Williams. There's bits of him in it!" Planter and Galateo laughed conspiratorially.

"Shut up!" shouted Byron. "Just shut up!" And he flung the bowl as hard as he could against the opposite wall, narrowly missing young Fairweather Planesman Mikulski, but splattering him and two companions at his table.

"Hey, chill out, Byron!" Mikulski shouted back.

"Why, you little jerk!" Byron responded and got up from the table as though he were as going to lay into the younger man. But Planter and Galateo held him back.

"Hey, Bill, cool down, will you? The kid's just sore you splashed him with your stew. He doesn't mean anything."

"Oh no?" Byron began his famous and often deadly sneer. "Then how come he's always brown-nosing Williams and the other officers? You'd think he's the officers' little toy boy or something. Why're you sticking up for him, Joe? You know this whole patrol stinks as much as I do. What crime did we commit to get stuck as prisoners inside a toilet just so some nickel-plated general can play George Washington in the Rocky Mountains? Did we volunteer for Almond? No way! Did anybody ask us if we wanted to stay on, unpaid, for fifteen months to keep this stupid war going? No way! I say the enlisted men should have a conference—no officers or petty officers—and vote whether we want to keep this charade up."

There was a silence as his words sank in. Byron was proposing mutiny at sea, a military crime considered so heinous that it carried a possible death sentence. Byron had now put all the enlisted men in the wardroom in the dangerous situation of either tacit complicity in his crime if they broke the military honor code by not reporting him or potential treachery to a combat colleague if they did.

"I didn't hear any of that," mumbled Mikulski as he wiped the stew off his khakis with a napkin and quickly headed toward the door.

"But I did," said a cold voice at the door. It was Rush, accompanied by two seamen on an unscheduled roving patrol of the ship. "Mancini, Diederich, arrest Seaman Byron and confine him until I convene an officers' panel in an hour's time."

For a split second Byron looked as though he would attack the captain and try to take over the ship on the spot. His face and body went completely taut. But Rush's eyes locked on his and checked him. He relaxed and smiled tightly at Galateo and Planter, who were still holding his arms, and said, "Very well, Captain, you win this one. My goose's cooked as long as you're in command of this ship. But don't take it for granted that you always will be. I'm not the only person aboard who thinks this way. Sooner or later others are going to get together and do some planning, and there won't be a thing you or any of the officers can do about it."

"Be sure he's cuffed when you take him to confinement and feed him punishment rations for three days," the captain said tersely to Mancini and Diederich. "The rest of you men, get back to your posts or your cabins. Mikulski, get me a list of everyone in this wardroom and report to Commander Gresham in thirty minutes." And he left.

9

Montana

Daryl kept on driving. He was terrified that any other move would unleash a stream of bullets into both of their heads.

"Pull over! Pull over immediately!"

The command seemed muffled and remote, but it was obviously coming from a bullhorn from the other vehicle. Their pursuers dropped back and raced up to menace the pickup from the other side. Needing no further persuasion, Daryl slowed down and pulled the pickup onto the shoulder. The pursuers slowed down with them, staying parallel and keeping them covered with the M-16.

"Now get out of the car, put your hands on top of your heads, and move in front of your vehicle. Face front." It sounded like an order from the highway patrol in pre-civil war days, but the bullhorn and the silencer-equipped M-16 lent far more lethal menace to the instructions.

Wordlessly, Daryl and Douglas got out of the pickup and moved some five yards in front of the pickup. A spotlight from the other car held them in its glare. Two men got out and walked carefully toward them. One, presumably, still held the M-16. "Just stand there," said what sounded like the bullhorn voice, with a faintly Southern twang, "until we tell you what to do next."

Well, thought Richfield, greatly relieved, *at least they aren't going to shoot us on the spot.* He assumed the PSB or a militia unit had finally caught up with them. But visions of an icy cell in Fargo, beatings maybe, or even worse crowded into his mind. Daryl, by contrast, seemed strangely placid in the glare of the spotlight. His breath steamed out into the chilly night.

One of the two men went around to the back of the pickup and came across Mike and the wounded man. "Hey, Pete, come take a look at this. They've got some guy in a sleeping bag—looks injured—and another guy tied up. I'll watch these two."

Pete inspected the two in the back and barked at Richfield and Daryl, "Who are these guys?"

Richfield decided to speak up. "The wounded man is called Matt. We picked him up a few miles back at the scene of an ambush. He was the only survivor of a truck and its two escort vehicles."

"Who's the other guy?"

Douglas bit his lip and looked at Daryl, who shook his head. He didn't reply.

"I said who's the other guy? Suddenly lose your tongue?" The tone was demanding but not angry or out of control.

Daryl spoke up. "Before we get into who we are, maybe you could tell us who you are. Do you make a habit of hijacking cars on the highway after dark?"

"Listen, punk, watch yourself. Who are you, anyway, and what's with the toy cop routine? That guy you've got tied up could get frostbite if he's exposed to much more of this weather. Are you Joe Fielding?"

Douglas gasped. So they'd caught up with him. The PSB, most probably, or the militia. Now he was in trouble. If they knew his Constitutionalist code name, they must know virtually everything about him. The question remained—was Ponomarev involved in this scenario?

"I said—are you Joe Fielding?" the man repeated impatiently.

"No," said Daryl.

"So the other guy is?"

Daryl said nothing, so Douglas, convinced it made no sense to play dumb on a cold night with two agents of the regime, spoke up.

"Yes, I'm Joe Fielding," he said. "If it's me you want, why don't you just let these guys go? Matt needs a hospital. He's lost a lot of blood, and he could go into shock. If he doesn't get medical treatment soon, he may not make it at all."

"We'll take care of him," Pete said. "There's no need for anyone to get hurt in this operation. Now will someone tell me which one is Rainer?"

From somewhere in the back of the pickup, Mike called out in a weak-sounding voice, "I am."

"What the hell are you doing there? Are they turning you in or something?"

Daryl now answered. "Let me explain," he said, "since I'm the guy who put him there. I picked these two guys up at Minneapolis-St. Paul Airport this morning. I'm a contract driver, and I was paid to take them to Bismarck. We came upon a truck jackknifed on the highway and on fire. There were two wrecked cars nearby, smashed up real bad from some kind of ambush. Everyone was dead except Matt. I wanted to make sure there weren't any wounded lying around, but Mike there insisted we go on to Bismarck. He was getting ready to pull a gun on me, but I drew mine first and told Joe here to disarm him. He did what he was told because I was holding the gun. If we hadn't found Matt, he'd probably be dead by now."

"Is that true?" Pete asked Mike.

"I don't have to answer to you guys any more than I have to explain myself to these two. If you're going to arrest us, why don't you just get on with it?" Mike replied harshly and more than a little strident.

"Listen, pal," Pete said, "don't get smart with me or we'll leave you out in this freezer till your fingers turn black. Now let's get moving. We don't have much time. Fielding, you and what's-his-face, the driver, put the injured guy in our van. If he needs any more blankets, there's a couple in the back. Chip, check out Fielding's I.D. and call in Wombat as soon as he checks out."

Pete kept the flashlight on Richfield's face as he and Daryl went to the back of the pickup to move Matt. Douglas briefly considered making a run for it, but he wasn't sure which of the two hijackers was holding the M-16. If it was Pete, he wouldn't get farther than ten yards. Daryl said nothing as they carried Matt to the thickly carpeted floor of the minivan and placed a folded blanket under his head. He was barely conscious, but muttered what sounded like a weak thanks.

"Okay, you, driver, what's your name?" demanded Chip, now in charge of the shakedown, as he looked in from the driver's-side door.

"Daryl."

"Okay, Daryl, you get back to where the captain is and don't try anything on the way." Chip kept his gun and his flashlight pointed at

Daryl as the young man walked back toward the other hijacker at the pickup's tailgate. He turned back to Richfield, who suddenly felt enormously tired, just as he had in Ponomarev's office almost a week ago.

"Okay, just routine. You'll have to get out of the van while I frisk you."

Forcing himself to go through the movements, Richfield climbed back out of the minivan and spread-eagled himself against the side of the vehicle. Chip patted him down and ordered him back inside the van. "Okay," he said, "what's your name again?"

"Joe Fielding," said Douglas.

Hand over your I.D.s, all of them."

Douglas complied but wondered why there was such a hurry. All they had to do was get on the radio and a PSB or a military chopper would back them up within minutes.

"Who's your favorite poet?"

"Shakespeare," Douglas said. He shuddered. Had they broken Willie and Fred down? What had happened to Meg? Cantankerous old Leon? Had the safe house been cleaned out? If these people knew who he was, why were they bothering with the verse code from *Richard II*.

"Okay, so let's hear your favorite lines from Shakespeare."

Richfield took a breath, wondering whether he should try an alternative Shakespeare quote—if he could think of one. Nothing came to mind, so he groped in the back of his mind for the unusual four lines of blank verse from *Richard II*. He'd made a point of remembering "water," and as he pivoted his mind around this mnemonic point, he found that the haunting verses returned easily to his memory. He said them slowly, in an almost melancholy manner:

> Not all the water in the rough rude sea
> Can wash the balm from an anointed king;
> The breath of worldly men cannot depose
> The deputy elected by the Lord.

Chip paused for a few seconds before switching off the flashlight and turning on a dim roof light in the van. Douglas could now see his interlocutor clearly: a slim, neat-looking man with dark hair and a carefully trimmed moustache. There were laugh lines around his eyes. Richfield estimated him to be in his mid-thirties.

"Good man," he said quietly. "It's an interesting play, *Richard II*, examining the clash between power and moral idealism. I'm glad we found you before you got to Bismarck. We've cut the city off, and you'd have had a hell of a time explaining to our boys in the suburbs who you were or what you wanted. We couldn't risk that. You'd probably be flattered to know the general himself ordered us to extract you. Welcome to the Army of Western Montana."

"The general? Extract me? You mean—" Deep inside Richfield's fatigued brain a light suddenly went on. "You mean, you're not PSB?"

Chip guffawed. "Do we look or sound like them? No way. I'm Chip Rawlings. My partner is Captain Pete Gaines, United States Army. We were sent to find you before you got tangled up in Bismarck. We're supposed to get you to Helena as quickly as possible. They're kind of eager to see you, I think. Now excuse me while I get back on the net. I doubt we have more than seven minutes before the PM wises up to what's going on. We're not using a chopper because they're noisy and drink fuel like an Irishman on St. Patrick's Day. We've got a STOL plane waiting for you less than two minutes away. I reckon we've got about five minutes to get you out of here, eight at the outside."

As Douglas groped his way through this sudden development, his whole body seemed to sag beneath him in relief.

Chip clicked on the mike of a hand-held, shortwave transceiver. "Wombat Two, Wombat Two, this is Groundhog," he said. "Come in, please." There was a crackle over the speaker and a low background purr.

"Groundhog, this is Wombat Two, over."

"Wombat Two, we are ready for extraction. Our position is approximately six miles west of point alpha. Terrain is good for an approach in either direction for about two hundred meters. We're on the shoulder of the westbound lane. Traffic should be clear for about two miles on each side of us. We'll illuminate for normal landing. Do you read me? Over."

"Affirmative, Groundhog. ETA in five minutes. Over."

"Wombat Two, can you get here any quicker? We've got a wounded man to take care of and a possible prisoner. Over."

"Groundhog, negative. Is the passenger wounded? Over."

"Negative, Wombat Two. The passenger is fine. See you in five. Over."

"Groundhog, roger."

Back at the pickup, Pete had untied Mike and was holding Daryl and him at gunpoint. "Okay, let's get this straight or you'll both be in big trouble. Daryl, you're a fool for pulling a gun on a fellow agent and then tying him up. You could be court-martialed for it. Rainer, for someone trained as a Ranger, you directly contravened the standing orders of the Army of Western Montana in seeking to evade your responsibility to enemy wounded."

"The man was a civilian," said Mike. In a surly way he added, "Hodges's regulations don't cover civilians."

"They do in combat situations, which is where Matt, whether he wanted to be or not, found himself. I'll recommend you for a court-martial too, if you push me to it. But what I'd prefer to do, as the senior military officer here, is use my discretion and overlook the incident since you were both at fault. But if either of you tries to double-cross the other, believe me, we will impose the full weight of military law on you. Now shake hands and get out of here and back to Minneapolis. Lieutenant Rawlings and I will take the wounded man with us."

Daryl and Mike turned reluctantly toward each other and shook hands. "Does Mike get his gun back?" Daryl asked as an after-thought.

"You bet he does. Right away," said Pete. "What kind of a hand-shake would it be if he didn't?"

With Pete still carefully watching him, his pistol lowered but still ready to fire, Daryl went back to the cab pickup, retrieved Mike's nine-millimeter pistol, and gave it to him, the grip end first. For the first time in a long while, Mike smiled. "Okay, let's make real peace," he said and extended his hand again to Daryl. The two then said good-bye to Pete, got back into the cab, drove the pickup across the grass center strip, and were soon roaring back along the freeway toward Minnesota.

Douglas and Chip meanwhile strung two lines of low-amp, battery-operated green lights, each about forty yards long, on either side of the westbound lanes of the freeway. Pete was talking to the pilot.

"Wombat Two, this is Groundhog. What is your position? Over."

"Groundhog, Wombat Two is about two miles southwest of you at about twelve hundred feet. Please give us a wind condition."

"Wombat Two, surface winds are 290 at 10. Suggest a westbound approach and landing."

"Groundhog, westbound, roger, coming in now."

Richfield could hear the purring and whistling noise of a single-engine plane making a power-off approach to the highway. The wheels chirped slightly as the plane touched down, but then the plane seemed to come to a complete stop almost immediately. In the beam of Pete's flashlight, briefly directed at the plane as the pilot throttled forward again to turn round and taxi over, Richfield saw a tall, gangly looking, high-wing aircraft with long, spindly legs, and an extended, narrow cockpit. The aircraft was completely black.

The pilot kept the engine running as Chip and Pete rushed Richfield out to the plane and helped him climb into a single rear seat directly behind the pilot. He shook hands quickly with each of them and closed the canopy.

The pilot, whose helmet was equipped with night-vision glasses, turned around to ensure the canopy was closed, showed Richfield where the seatbelt was, and handed him a headset and mouthpiece. Without a word he throttled the engine and was airborne again.

"You okay? Can you hear me?" the voice asked through the headset.

"Sure," Richfield replied into the mouthpiece. "Thanks for the ride. What kind of plane is this?"

"A Fieseler Storch. It's a German World War II observation plane that was designed in the 1930s. This one's a replica that some patriotic soul brought out west and has let us use. For short takeoffs and landings, the only thing we have that's as good is the four-seat Polish Wilga. It's much larger, more comfortable. and has greater range. We'd be flying in one tonight, but it's being repainted for day-time winter operations.

"We're going to head west over the rest of North Dakota to Montana. We'll make two stops to refuel, maybe three, depending on the wind and other conditions. At one of our stops we're going to have to stay on the ground for three hours or so to catch some sleep. The trip will take about six and a half hours in the air, and we should be in Helena by dawn tomorrow.

"It's not going to be comfortable, especially for the first hour or so until we're past the Missouri and no man's land. We'll have to fly very low, and I'll be changing course frequently in case someone is trying to track us. Once we're well into our territory, it should get a bit easier. But I have to warn you, this isn't going to be a joyride. Have you ever been in a small plane before?"

"No," said Richfield, who was rapidly losing his sense of excitement about being whisked from one side of the battle line to the other.

"Well, you'll find three or four barf bags tucked into the pocket by your right knee. Please don't wait until it's too late. This is the only Storch we have, and other people don't like the smell of vomit any more than you do."

Douglas acknowledged and settled himself as comfortably as he could into the seat. As the pilot had warned, the plane bucked and pitched, sometimes alarmingly, as the pilot hedgehopped his way across North Dakota toward the relative safety of Montana. But Richfield was so tired he found the constant motion soporific rather than sickening, and he slipped into an almost permanent doze.

The plane set down briefly on a narrow farm road a few miles the other side of the Missouri. With Douglas reluctantly rousing himself to help with the operation, the pilot refueled from a truck parked in a shed and cunningly disguised as a fertilizer spray tanker. There was no one in sight. Some two hours later the Storch landed at a regular airfield in Miles City, Montana. This time a well-trained and apparently forewarned ground crew expertly refueled the aircraft and carefully inspected it. They were now obviously in Constitutionalist-held territory.

They had come in after midnight, and Richfield could barely keep his eyes open. He couldn't imagine how the pilot was managing.

He was relieved when the pilot said that they would be here for four hours and to get some sleep. The two of them sacked out on bunks in an underground shelter that was obviously in frequent use.

A sergeant awoke them both shortly after 4:15, and the Storch was soon on its way once more. This time they no longer followed the contours of the ground, a severe flying challenge at night for any pilot, even with the terrain-avoidance equipment aboard the Storch. Instead, the pilot followed I-94 all the way to Billings and then pursued I-90 up through Bozeman Pass and down into the depression between the Bridger Range in the east, the Gallatin Range in the south, and the slow ascent of the Missouri River north toward Canyon Ferry Lake. They flew past Bozeman, Belgrade, Logan, Three Forks, and turned right, following Route 287.

Night was rapidly retreating. Exhausted as he was, Douglas felt an exhilaration as he watched the low rays of the sun shoot over the tops of the Big Belt Mountains and peel away the shadows from the Elkhorn Mountains. The great green forests, dappled with deep snowfalls, seemed to preen themselves in the chilly light of a new day. Looking down over the side of the narrow plane at the freeway below him, Richfield was surprised at the amount of traffic, almost all of it military. Humvees, jeeps, tank transporters, gasoline trucks, school buses, and several automobiles were moving in long convoys in both directions. As he gazed down in wonder, the pilot turned around and grinned at him.

"You're probably wondering why we're following the freeway," he said through the headset with the tone of a man close to home after a long trip. "Well, it's pretty simple. We have radar and identification friend-or-foe systems along every major road system in the state. If you follow the road and squawk correctly on your altitude-reporting transponder, they know who you are and leave you alone. If you stray off into the mountains, you're almost certain to be shot at. Of course, Helena knows that we're coming, but we still follow the approved way in. The PM tried sending in some tactical aircraft at medium altitude a couple of times. They were shot to pieces before they got anywhere near Helena."

As they approached Canyon Ferry Lake, there was even more activity on the roads. Richfield was surprised that he couldn't see any obvious gun emplacements, but when he asked the pilot about it, the man laughed and pointed out three spots on the hillsides that were well camouflaged. It would have been difficult for an expert to have spotted them. At Canyon Ferry Dam the antiaircraft positions and defensive positions could not be concealed. They gave the dam a strange appearance; it looked like a medieval fortress.

Approaching the southern outskirts of Helena, the Storch descended gradually. The pilot was in contact with the tower at Helena airport, though he used a verbal code to describe his position and approach from references he read off a clipboard. The plane made a standard turn onto base and then began its final approach. But the pilot landed so close to the beginning of the runway that he was able to get if off the active runway onto a taxiway within a few seconds of touchdown.

They taxied over to a small, structurally reinforced hangar. Heavily armed troops were everywhere. Douglas noticed that a couple of them even had their weapons trained on the plane from a nearby roof.

As the pilot opened the canopy, a sergeant came over and helped them out of the cockpit. "Welcome back, Sir," he said to the pilot, and to Richfield, "Welcome to Montana, Sir. Major Larson has asked me to escort you. Do you have any baggage?"

"Only a small overnight bag in the plane. I'm sorry, I forgot about it."

"That's all right, Sir. I'll get it for you." The sergeant deftly climbed back into the Storch, retrieved the bag, and jumped down.

Richfield looked around. The first thing that struck him were several American flags mounted atop buildings on and around the airport. It was both thrilling and frightening. He had ingested enough People's Movement propaganda about Old Glory ("a symbol of reaction, racism and belligerence," Chairperson Northwood would often say at the rallies) to feel slightly nervous. Yet he couldn't undo his years of childhood training, the Pledge of Allegiance, the sense of belonging to something bigger and nobler than himself. He felt undone, naked, a stranger in a universe he had consciously rejected during the days of the Chicago uprising. But he now felt inexorably drawn back.

The airport was heavily sandbagged and fortified against both aerial and ground attack. Hodges appeared to have thought through his military needs carefully. It looked as though the Constitutionalists were prepared for full-scale fighting from hangar to hangar, if necessary.

The second thing that struck him was the large number of African-Americans in uniform. Intellectually, he knew that in pre-civil war days the U.S. military, for all of its other faults, had one of the better records for racial integration and opportunity advancement than other American institutions. African-Americans enlisted in numbers disproportionate to their demographics in the U.S. population, and they did well. Yet one of the triggers of the civil war had been nationwide urban uprisings of young, embittered, jobless blacks. When the People's Militia was formed, inner-city African-American youth had enlisted in record numbers. Most PM partisans assumed that African-Americans would support their cause overwhelmingly. Yet, to judge from what he was seeing here, that was not true, at least not in the military.

"How did you like the Storch?" the sergeant asked cheerfully.

"Noisy," said Richfield, "and not exactly the most comfortable plane I've ever been in."

"But it got you here in one piece, didn't it? That's not bad for something the Germans used to rescue Mussolini."

"You mean this actual plane?"

"No, but the same type."

They walked toward a small trailer. The sergeant knocked rather unusually, Richfield thought. After hearing a high-pitched "Come in," the man led Richfield into a warm and neat office, somewhat utilitarian in decor.

A wiry, thin-faced man in his forties almost sprung up from behind his desk and extended his hand to Douglas. He had a closely cropped crewcut of gray hair and the lean, almost sallow features of a long-term runner.

"Harry Larson," he said briskly and amiably. "Call me Harry unless the general's around, then it's Major Larson. You must be

Douglas Richfield, alias Joe Fielding. Sergeant, that will be all, thank you. I'd like you to keep the jeep handy until we're ready to move again."

"Yes, Sir." The sergeant, implacably cheerful, saluted smartly and departed.

Douglas spoke. "Well, I guess you know just about everything there is to know about me."

"That would be an exaggeration. But we do know a lot. Now just the formalities. Your social security number, home address, phone number, and those elegant lines from a certain poet you were supposed to remember, please."

Richfield obliged.

"Good, excellent. I'm quite sure you're the right fellow," he said, bursting into a high-pitched laugh. "Now you're probably exhausted and hungry as a horse. Unless you feel really alert, I suggest you have a bite to eat, sleep for a couple of hours, and then come back to us a little freshened up."

"Well, I am hungry, but I'm pretty alert now. Could we start with whatever you want to do after I've eaten something? Sleep can come later."

"Yes, of course. I'll take you over to the cafeteria. I think you'll be quite impressed."

Douglas was. A concealed door in what looked like a small metal shed of fire-fighting equipment opened to an escalator that descended below the airport. At the bottom were shops, a corridor leading to a hospital, and a very large cafeteria that probably doubled for an auditorium. It was doing a thriving business, and both officers and men seemed to be patronizing it.

At Larson's urging Richfield helped himself to a large breakfast of scrambled eggs, sausage, and pancakes. He had not had a proper meal since breakfast the day before and was famished.

As Richfield ate, Larson sipped from a large cup of coffee and chatted about the weather (little snow and very bright, sunny days), the fighting (all of it farther south, toward Denver), and the small inconveniences of daily life (hardly any fresh fruit, rationing for meat, sugar, and dairy products). He seemed to have no interest at all, for the time being, in his guest. Richfield, wearier than his excited state of mind allowed him to acknowledge, was slightly annoyed that Larson seemed so uninterested.

But the major seemed to know what he was doing. Back above ground the sergeant materialized and drove them out of the airport in a jeep. The modest, pre-civil war Helena Airport was now a full-fledged air base. Though there were no fighter aircraft that Richfield could see, Apache and Cobra helicopter gunships were parked in concrete revetments, and several C-130 transport planes were lined up on the apron. Douglas saw half a dozen tanks around the perimeter and three ancient-looking armored personnel carriers were patrolling the eastern side of the airfield. No jets were in sight, but several small, propeller aircraft were taking off and landing, apparently coming from or going to the west.

Richfield was surprised how small the town was. Minuscule, in fact, for a state capital, except that even in pre-civil war days the entire population of Montana had been just eight hundred thousand. Yet the streets were thronged. Most of the people seemed to be in combat fatigues, but there were plenty of civilians too. Douglas had noticed a large temporary housing area on the eastern approach to the city. He now saw masses of trailer homes and temporary-looking, hutlike structures, presumably accommodating tens of thousands more people than the city had held previously, crammed into what had once been considerable, open areas of the city.

Almost every building seemed to be sandbagged at its corners or on the roof, whether as a protection against bombing or as a tactical infantry position, Richfield didn't yet know. There was heavy traffic, which surprised him, considering the obvious gas shortages, but almost all of the vehicles were military, and every civilian car had a colored strip atop the license tag.

"What do the different license plate colors mean?" Richfield asked Larson.

"Exactly what they denote is classified, but you might say that they indicate different civilian or military affiliations."

Douglas decided not to ask any more questions. As he looked at the pedestrians, he was struck by the cheerful expressions on most people's faces. This contrasted starkly with the PM cities he had visited. He wanted to talk to these people, ask them if they were locals, and if not, why they had come here. Did they really expect to win the war with the vast weight of industrial resources on the PM side, similar to the Northern industrial advantage over the South in the first Civil War?

They drove up Montana Avenue, the broadest street in town, toward a cathedral and what looked like a mosque to the right.

"Does Montana have a lot of Muslims?" Richfield asked naively.

Larson chuckled at this. "No, no," he said. "First-time visitors, especially from the East, always ask the same question. It's the civic center. It used to belong to the Shriners."

Montana Avenue entered Last Chance Gulch at an angle, and the jeep continued until what had once been a jumbled street of mining claims offices changed into a pedestrian mall for the last few hundred yards. The sergeant stopped and let his two passengers out. Larson led Richfield up to the end of the mall. At a heavily guarded nineteenth-century office building inscribed with the name of the Western Insurance Corporation at the entrance, the major showed his pass to two sentries.

"He's with me," Larson said, nodding at Richfield just behind him.

"That's fine, Sir," said one of the sentries, "but he won't be allowed beyond main security unless he can identify himself positively."

"I understand, Sergeant," Larson said with a slight smile.

At the opposite end of the main floor was a flight of stairs leading down to a corridor that led deeper into what was probably the hillside. "S-2 Directorate" read neatly printed signs on both sides of the corridor. Another central notice warned: "Authorized personnel only. This area under surveillance at all times. Visitors required to submit to random I.D. checks." Two civilians just inside the corridor were being questioned by military police officers.

At the end of the corridor, Larson identified himself in front of a video camera beside a formidable-looking steel door, much like a bank vault. He produced his I.D., holding it in front of the lens, punched in a numerical code on the keypad next to the monitor. "Your turn," he said, turning to Richfield. "Just tell the camera who you are and show it any I.D. on you."

"Even if it's fake?" asked Douglas.

"We *assume* it's fake," said Larson.

The comment was sharp. Larson was still cordial, but as they got closer to the nerve center of Constitutionalism here in Helena, he seemed to want Richfield to know how much they already knew about him.

When the heavy steel door finally opened, the two of them were admitted to an airlock-like, metal-sided antechamber. The outer door closed behind them as they waited for another electrically operated door to open at the other side of the airlock.

Finally, they were in. A Marine guard registered them and examined their I.D.'s. He dialed an extension on his phone and then turned back to Larson. "Colonel Trinh will be here shortly, Sir," he said.

"Thank you, Corporal."

After witnessing the generally surly exchanges between officials or militia personnel within the People's Movement, Richfield found the elaborate military courtesy here in Montana almost theatrical.

The Vietnamese-American colonel who soon arrived to meet Larson and Richfield was surprisingly broad-shouldered with a round face and a ready smile. Somehow Richfield immediately liked him. He and Larson exchanged greetings, but it was clear that Larson was not close to the colonel and was somewhat uncomfortable around him.

After their introductions, the three men walked down the central aisle of a large, open office area where officers and soldiers were either huddled over computer terminals or engaged in intense discussions in quiet voices in small groups of three or four. Despite the starched Marine at the entrance, the atmosphere was calm, relaxed, and almost academic. There was little background noise other than the hum of air conditioning, the muted clack of fingers at computer terminals, and a low murmur of conversation.

Down a side corridor to the left of the office area, there was a large office, comfortably furnished with a polished cherry-wood table in the middle of the room. A tape recorder was set up in the middle of the table. There were three chairs on one side and one chair on the other side. Richfield knew where he was expected to sit. Each place, including his own, had a yellow legal pad and a pen placed neatly on the table. A stenographer, in uniform, well into her forties, sat quietly at one end of the table, ready to operate the tape recorder by remote control.

Douglas's euphoria at having arrived successfully and with such drama right in the middle of the Constitutionalists' main lair in the continental U.S. had worn off a little by now. But he was beginning to feel his fatigue. He didn't object to an intensive session or questioning—after all, that was what he had come to Montana for—but it only now struck him how exhausting his ordeal might prove to be. He noticed with gratitude that there was a coffee urn on a sideboard next to the table.

Larson said, "Colonel Trinh will be in charge of your questioning, but I will be a full participant too. The third person will be Mr. Stokes."

"Mr. Stokes?" Richfield asked, with a laugh he couldn't suppress. Was this some kind of joke? He sounded like a character from a Dickens novel.

Larson was irritated. "I think you'll find Mr. Stokes an indispensable member of this interrogation panel," he said with a hint of menace. But Trinh was chuckling. *Thank God someone's got a sense of proportion,* Richfield thought.

Stokes now burst in, a long-haired, disheveled man in his early thirties with a crumpled sports jacket, an ill-tied, red-plaid tie, and a bad case of acne over much of his face. Like an overzealous fifth-grader he shook hands with everyone, including the stenographer—to her embarrassment—mumbled an apology for his lateness, and sat down in the chair to the right of the one opposite Douglas. Trinh invited everyone else to sit and immediately began asking questions.

"Why did you decide to come over to us?"

"I was fired from my job at City Hall and became disillusioned with the People's Movement."

"Why?" It was Larson now, just a tad aggressive.

"I couldn't stand the hypocrisy, the backbiting, the posturing we all had to do. I couldn't stand working for my supervisor—"

"Was that Bremer?" Larson brusquely interrupted.

"Yes, but there were others too—Maynard, Bugatti, Lukacs. They'd been on my case for months, chiefly because I took the PM changes in ideology and doctrine lightly."

"But what made you want to come over at this particular time? Why, if things had gotten so bad, didn't you make your move earlier?" It was Larson again, doggedly pursuing a line he seemed to suspect as unlikely.

Trinh interrupted. "Major, I'm sure we can come back to that later. Because of the realtime nature of Mr. Richfield's special information, I think we should get on to that subject first, unless Mr. Stokes thinks differently."

Stokes, who had been scribbling furiously during the first exchange, his long brown hair flopping down over his pimpled forehead, nodded quickly up at Trinh. "No, Colonel, please go on."

"Would you tell us, please," Trinh continued pleasantly, "what you saw following during the Thanksgiving parade in New York ten days ago?"

How many times had Richfield told the story? To Rachel, to Ponomarev, partially to Fred and Willy. His memory was becoming confused.

He went through the story again of leaving the parade, of seeing an elderly couple with the woman limping, of the militia confrontation and the shooting. It was almost too well rehearsed.

As he came to the point where he had seen Marcus trying to escape and then thrashing blindly through the air before crunching down agonizingly on the sidewalk, he began to sweat. Perhaps he was giving too much detail. Perhaps he'd left insufficient room to improvise with the questions that would be sure to come raining down on him.

". . . I was close to where Marcus fell," he concluded his tale, "but the militia threatened to get nasty with me if I stayed around once the PSB and the militia closed off the street."

Stokes interrupted without asking permission from Trinh. "A very interesting story," he said rapidly, pushing away a flop of hair from his face, "but what do you think happened to Marcus after they blocked off the street?"

"I didn't stay around to find out. I suppose an ambulance took him to the hospital."

"Did you see the ambulance actually arrive?"

"No. There were lots of police cars with flashing lights. After my I.D. had been checked, I got out of there as quickly as I could."

"How badly hurt do you think Marcus was?"

"Well, he had at least one bullet wound in the upper back from fairly close range. Maybe more. He fell heavily. But maybe he could have survived."

"Are you sure?" Trinh asked, speaking for the first time, and all three of them were watching him intently.

"Look, my medical knowledge is limited to first aid. Some people survive some pretty bad shootings."

"Are you aware that there was a *New York Times* report on the incident?" Stokes asked.

"Yes, I read that."

"And you know, don't you, that it wasn't said in that story whether both men died in the shooting?"

"Yes."

"Doesn't that seem odd to you? I mean, what could explain the failure to say what had happened to two suspected Constitutionalist agents after a serious shooting in the middle of New York?"

"I suppose the editors—or the authorities who cleared the story for the *Times*—didn't want people to know whether Marcus was alive or dead."

Stokes held his flop of hair on his forehead. He looked piercingly at Richfield.

Trinh now asked, "What do you know about Marcus?"

Douglas was sweating again. He could tell them what Bremer had said, but he was becoming fuzzy now about how much he had learned about Project Almond from Bremer, from Rachel, and how much from Ponomarev. He didn't want to drag Rachel into the story, but it would require his best concentration to ensure that he related only as much about Project Almond as he had learned from Bremer. His fatigue wasn't helping much.

"Not much," he found himself saying, stalling. "Bremer said that Marcus was connected with a program to hide Trident submarines in the event of a strategic surrender of the U.S."

"What was the program called?" Larson asked.

"He didn't say."

Stokes spoke up. "Have you heard of Project Almond?"

Richfield blinked, then answered: "I don't think so."

Even as the words came out of his mouth, he knew they didn't believe him. In fact, it wasn't the words themselves that let him down; it was the one-second pause between the question and his answer.

Larson positively gloated. Trinh, with an amused shrug like an indulgent parent permitting a showoff son to perform for his guests, let him run with it.

"Let's get back to the timing of your decision to come over to us," Larson began. "Was it connected with the events on Thanksgiving Day?"

"Yes," answered Richfield, grateful to have a chance to tell the truth.

"Then why did you wait five days before seeking out our people in New York?"

"Look, you don't make a decision like defecting on five minutes' notice. It wasn't until Monday, back at the Protocol Department, that the ugliness of my work really hit me. That and the impact of the killing finally just got to me."

"How did you know where to contact our people?"

"I didn't know exactly, but you don't have to be a genius in Manhattan to know the political sympathies of the Village. Besides, even in my lowly Protocol position, I've had access to some estimates of political opposition in Manhattan. I'd have been noticed by someone sooner or later. I was just lucky out at Jake's."

"You were, weren't you? I'm wondering if you had some help with your luck. Maybe the PSB just eased you on your way in our direction?"

"I've had no contact with the PSB either before the Marcus incident or since! I despise them." Richfield was so heated and earnest that Trinh raised an eyebrow at Larson, who momentarily looked nonplussed. From what they now sensed of Richfield's personality, he was telling the truth. Yet it obviously didn't jibe with his hesitation in denying any knowledge of Project Almond.

"Let's go back to something else," said Stokes, adopting a can't-we-all-find-a-way-out-of-this-unpleasantness tone. "If you had to bet your life on it, would you say that Marcus was alive or dead?"

Richfield paused again—a pause all three of them noticed. Stokes scribbled away with his pencil. "I wouldn't want to bet my life on someone else surviving three bullet wounds at thirty yards distance," Douglas replied, not unreasonably.

"You may not want to, but you're in a rather precarious position, and you just may have to," Larson replied maliciously.

Richfield was getting angry. These people weren't much better than Ponomarev. About the only thing they hadn't yet done was threaten to gang rape his sister.

"Just what do you mean, 'I may have to'? And what am I supposed to have done that makes my position precarious?" His prickly heat, his fatigue, his sense of unbearable stress were all getting the better of him.

"Look, I put my life and my liberty on the line by coming to your guys in New York and letting them know I had seen Marcus just before he was shot. I didn't have to do that. There was no way they would have known I knew anything about the Marcus shooting. I think your people would have taken me in even without that on the basis of my Protocol Department position and my Kommandatura pass alone."

Stokes involuntarily whistled under his breath, drawing an annoyed look from Trinh. "You had a Kommandatura pass?" he asked. "Why didn't you tell us that at the beginning?"

"Because you had your own agenda and never bothered to ask," Richfield replied tartly. But he felt relieved to have some maneuvering room in the interrogation.

Trinh interrupted. "Major, Mr. Stokes, I have to make a phone call that will require a brief interruption in our conversation. I'd like to call a fifteen-minute adjournment while I do that. Would you both accompany me? Mr. Richfield, you will be free to relax here or visit the facilities through that door over there. I'm sorry, but you will not be allowed to leave this room. Gentlemen, this session is adjourned until noon."

Trinh, Larson, and Stokes rose from the table and filed out of the room without so much as a nod at Richfield. The stenographer busied herself with her equipment and the paper roll and took both out of the room with her. As the door opened and closed, Douglas saw an armed Marine with a military police armband standing at ease in the corridor outside.

The minutes ticked by slowly. After he came back from the washroom, Richfield looked at the pictures on the wall, rather bland landscapes of Montana, and stretched out his legs while leaning against the wall, like a runner warming up, and swung his arms up and down a few times. He was tired of sitting. He was tired of answering questions. In fact, he was tired of the whole charade into which he seemed to be plunging further and further, like Alice falling down the rabbit hole into Wonderland.

The stenographer came back first, exactly a minute before the appointed fifteen minutes had expired. She was a mousy-looking woman, kindly in a prissy sort of way. She smiled nicely at Richfield as she entered, which cheered him up a bit.

Then Trinh, Larson, Stokes, and a fourth man, also in civilian clothes and carrying a large suitcase, reentered the room. While the first three were settling into their chairs again, the fourth man opened the suitcase in a corner of the room and set out wires, electrodes, straps, and other frightening-looking equipment. It was almost too much for Douglas. He had already decided that if he were threatened with torture, he would tell anyone anything he could to forestall the pain, but he couldn't be sure that he would have the luxury of confessing first.

"Don't be alarmed," said Trinh, with a sympathetic smile, observing his expression. "That is not electric shock equipment and we have no intention of torturing you. The general has banned torture of any kind in the Constitutionalist areas for any purpose whatever, including tactical military intelligence. This equipment is completely painless, and we don't even rely absolutely on its results. But we think this is the right time to submit you to a flutter test."

"A what?" asked Richfield wearily.

"A lie detector test," said Trinh flatly. "After we've evaluated that, there is someone who is eager to meet you."

10

A Second Interrogation

Are you now working for the PSB?"

"No."

"Have you ever worked for the PSB, the People's Militia, or any other security organization of the People's Movement?"

"No."

"Are you here in Montana in order to help the cause of the People's Movement?"

"No, no, and again, no!"

Richfield was irate. Over and over they had asked him the same questions, and over and over he had given the same answers. It was obvious that the polygraph operator regarded Douglas's answers as truthful. The equipment backed him up. His three interrogators, their chairs now placed in such a way that he couldn't see them all at the same time, were observing him intently and taking notes. They also appeared to believe his denials.

Yet it perplexed them. They were certain—and they believed that Richfield intuitively sensed this in them too—that he had lied to them when he denied having heard of Project Almond. They had hoped that the stress of the polygraph test, his fatigue, and their steady questioning would break down his resistance and reveal the PSB connection they suspected him of having.

But it wasn't happening. Though a phlegmatic and restrained person most of the time, Douglas could summon surprising bursts of energy and aggression. He had demonstrated resilience under their questioning, sidetracking them briefly with the revelation of his access to the Russian Kommandatura on Governor's Island in

New York. (Curiously, they had not come back to that question yet.) They questioned him relentlessly on his supposed PSB ties, causing him to become angrier and less cooperative by the minute.

Trinh took over. "All right, we're getting nowhere. Mr. Williams, we're going to resume our earlier conversation with Mr. Richfield without polygraphing. Can you stand down your equipment? Thanks."

The polygraph operator muttered something in response, removed the electrodes from Douglas, and left the room.

"Let's go back to your Kommandatura information," Trinh resumed. "I find that interesting. Mr. Stokes, would you like to develop this line of questioning?"

Stokes, hair flopping back and forth, was obviously eager. Richfield presumed him to be an intelligence specialist on PSB affairs and perhaps on Russia as well.

"Thank you," he said briskly. "Mr. Richfield, will you tell us why the Protocol Department gave you a Kommandatura pass?"

"Very simple," Richfield responded cockily, pleased that the infernal polygraph was temporarily out of the picture. "Several of us in City Hall—maybe nine or so—and three of us in Protocol had passes so we could move back and forth to Governor's Island whenever a visiting Russian needed an escort in Manhattan or whenever we were arranging meetings or social events between the PM and the Kommandatura. They issued the passes within a few weeks of the arrival of the first Russian military observer and adviser contingent last January."

"How many times have you visited Governor's Island?"

"Maybe twenty or so."

"Did you ever have conversations with Russian officials or military officers on politics or security matters?"

"Never. We were always too busy with the events to hang around and chat, and the Russians were always very professional, very reserved. They never even tried to approach us."

"How many Russian officers, soldiers, and civilians are based on Governor's Island?"

"I've no idea, and anyway the numbers vary. I think they must have increased the number around two weeks ago. I'd guess between one hundred and two hundred."

At this Trinh raised an eyebrow at Stokes, but the civilian paid no attention to him.

"When did you first hear of Project Almond?" Stokes went on. The question was launched like a javelin.

But Douglas had been expecting it, and deflected it easily. "You asked me earlier whether I'd heard of Project Almond, and I answered then that I didn't think I had. But I'm not going to swear away my life on it. In Protocol we constantly hear about all sorts of different programs."

"Colonel, I think we can break this logjam with Mr. Richfield quite easily." Stokes seemed excited now, his flushed face temporarily hiding the pimples as he addressed Trinh. "I know it may be inconvenient, and I'm sure you and Major Larson have other questions. However, I think you'll agree that it's essential that we settle the issue of Mr. Richfield's veracity on Project Almond as soon as possible. Could we please put Mr. Richfield back on the polygraph?"

Trinh frowned, grunted, and then reluctantly agreed. Once more Douglas found himself wired to the machine.

"Go ahead Mr. Stokes; you have the floor," Trinh said.

"Thank you, Colonel." Very slowly, deliberately, and staring him directly in the face, Stokes asked, "Are you aware that there is a connection between Project Almond and Daniel Marcus?"

Richfield was sweating, and he silently cursed his uncooperative body for revealing his emotional stress.

"No," he said flatly. Sitting just behind and to the side of Richfield, the polygraph operator studied his data and silently shook his head.

"Did the PSB tell you about Project Almond and Daniel Marcus?"

"Steve Bremer told me about Daniel Marcus, but not about Project Almond."

"I didn't ask about Bremer. I asked about the PSB."

"For God's sake, Bremer is the only PSB-connected American I've ever had close contact with!"

"Why don't you ask him about the Russian Foreign Intelligence Service?"

The voice was deep, clearly enunciated, and with a hint of humor in it. It came from the door behind and to the left of Douglas and caught everyone by surprise. No one had heard the door even open. Richfield's three questioners, instead of spreading themselves out as they had during the first polygraph session, were seated opposite him, as during the ordinary interrogation, either making notes or watching his every expression. The official transcriber, though facing the door, was peering intently through her glasses at her fingers. As for the polygraph operator, he had been too busy with his own equipment to notice anyone entering the room.

A split second after looking up at the intruding voice, Trinh and Larson were on their feet. Somewhat slower, Stokes stood up as quickly as he could and reflexively brushed his hair out of the way. The stenographer and polygraph expert pushed back their chairs and also rose. Only then did Richfield, weary and fatigued though he was, grasp that the intruder was a person of considerable importance. He, too, now stood up.

"Excuse me, General," said Trinh immediately, "we would have briefed you in advance and rescheduled this interrogation if we'd known you wanted to attend."

"There was no need," the newcomer said pleasantly. "I was just impatient to meet this visitor and curious what he could tell us about poor Daniel Marcus."

Lucius Hodges was impressively tall, perhaps six foot three, by Richfield's reckoning. Apart from the three general's stars in black trim on his collar and the exceptionally neat appearance of his dark green field uniform, there was nothing about his clothes to denote his importance. He had a lean, almost aquiline face with bushy gray eyebrows. His hair had receded in front, but at the sides it was gray and cut quite short. His overall expression was that of a person accustomed to being listened to and obeyed.

It was his eyes that riveted Douglas. Even though they had dark patches of fatigue beneath them and were slightly bloodshot from—presumably—lack of sleep, they had an extraordinary energy and alertness to them. To Richfield they suggested someone difficult if not impossible to distract from whatever task he had at hand. This was the famous General Hodges, commander of the

Army of Western Montana, the most dangerous and implacable foe of the PM in America.

The general extended his long arm toward Richfield in a move that was somehow both deliberate and relaxed. With such a large frame, he seemed to have learned over a lifetime how to economize his movements.

"You must be Douglas Richfield," he said evenly. Then, with a warming smile, "Welcome to the Constitutionalist forces. I hope they're treating you well. I'm Hodges."

"Thank you, Sir," Richfield replied, shaking the extended hand firmly and trying to get over his surprise.

"Sit down, everybody," Hodges said, settling carefully into a chair against the wall and behind the three questioners. "I'll spend a few minutes here if you don't mind, Colonel. Paul, you can dispense with the polygraph right now. It won't be necessary."

"Very well, General." Williams was polite, but he was now impatient and frustrated. He disentangled Richfield for the last time from his equipment, carefully packed it away in the case, muttered a quick "good-bye," and left the room.

"Now, perhaps, Major," Hodges resumed, turning toward Larson as though he had been sitting in on the entire interrogation session, "you'd like to ask Mr. Richfield the question I suggested?"

Douglas was inwardly racing to adjust his inner defenses to the new psychological element of the interrogation. It was now in the hands of a person with a formidable ability to lead, control, inspire, and certainly—when necessary—to intimidate men. Richfield's responses to Hodges could not be double-checked against the polygraph, and Hodges was hardly infallible. But what the general could do—and Richfield grasped this immediately—was to penetrate the heart of Richfield's convictions. Hodges operated out of the immense emotional advantage of knowing and totally believing in his own cause.

Richfield, however, was only in Montana under duress, even though he had been ambivalent about ultimate loyalties since coming into contact with the Constitutionalists. Richfield, essentially, had no cause. He was an everyman threading his way through the conflicts that others had set up without consulting him.

Larson leaned forward eagerly. He was now on stage in front of his commanding general, and he felt his own suspicions of Richfield's loyalty were being vindicated.

"What do you know about the Russian Foreign Intelligence Service?" he asked.

It was a clumsy softball, and Richfield whacked it out of the ballpark.

"Major, I know virtually nothing about the Russian Foreign Intelligence Service."

Hodges laughed loudly at this, embarrassing Larson, but amusing Richfield. "No, no, Major, that's not at all what I had in mind," the general said. "You might as well ask a captured mugger what he thinks of street crime. Richfield"—and the form of address was itself a deliberate intimidation—"have you had any contact whatsoever with Russian intelligence officers in New York?"

It was the "whatsoever" that pushed Richfield over the edge. That and the look of pitiless concentration and willpower on Hodges's face. For a millisecond Douglas wondered if he might be able to beat around the bush long enough to deflect Hodges, to cause him to change the subject, or simply to tire of the chase. But the eyes of his questioner burned into him. Like that handful of people in life who are incapable of lying, Hodges had developed an almost infallible intuition for spotting dishonesty in others. The force of his personality, the intensity of his expression, and the way that he had learned to project his own obsession with truthfulness disarmed Douglas's unpracticed deceits easily.

Everyone was looking at Richfield.

"Yes, General, I did have contact with one officer, or two to be precise." Richfield spoke slowly and in a low voice.

"Exactly when was that?"

"Last Monday."

"You mean the week before last?"

"No, last week."

"Stokes," Hodges inquired, "what's the name of that new arrival from Moscow you wanted us to keep an eye on?"

"Alexei Ilyich Ponomarev, General. He arrived from Moscow late last week. He is deputy director of the Russian Foreign Intelligence Service, in charge of foreign espionage operations."

"Good. Now, was Ponomarev the Russian intelligence officer you met in New York?"

"Yes, General, he was."

Hodges continued to look intently at Richfield for a few seconds, his eyes beneath the bushy gray brows holding the attention of everyone in the room. Then he relaxed but continued to look at Richfield.

"Carry on, Colonel," he said quietly. "I think you'll find our visitor from New York will cooperate fully. But I would like to see him later myself." With that he rose from his chair and left. He had been in the room less than five minutes.

Trinh looked crumpled. "This is a serious issue, Mr. Richfield," he said with a sigh. "You have already lied before this tribunal and, as a result of your latest admission, must now be considered a potential espionage suspect under Articles 104 and 106 of the Manual for Courts-Martial. As you know, the penalty for being found guilty of this crime in wartime is capital. You may, if you wish, request an officer from the judge advocate general's office to represent you."

The word capital sunk into Richfield like an icicle. Was this how it was all going to end, a firing squad in Montana, and all for being an eyewitness to the death of a man he hadn't even heard of until that afternoon?

"Colonel," Richfield rasped out, his mouth dry, but his wits fully at work, "I'm grateful to you for offering your legal services, but you may have forgotten that I'm not a soldier; I'm a civilian."

"You may be a civilian," Trinh said coldly, not appreciating this response, "but by freely choosing to make contact with representatives of the Constitutionalist armed forces—the legitimate military authority of the U.S. government—in time of war, you have implicitly submitted yourself to military jurisdiction. The defense of being a civilian or a noncombatant has never, to my knowledge, been upheld."

Richfield shivered. He felt out of place and cornered. They probably didn't *want* to shoot him, at least not right away, because they would be eager to get whatever information they could about Ponomarev.

He needed to change tactics. He would let them come to him. He didn't want to die, but he suspected that spilling out the whole story—the parade, the library and Rachel, Ponomarev, and then Rachel again—would only arouse contempt among his interrogators.

"You seem to have your mind on other business," Trinh said curtly, interrupting Richfield's reverie. "Perhaps we can return to the matter at hand. Mr. Stokes?"

"Why were you in contact with Alexei Ponomarev?" Stokes's excellent Russian pronunciation delivered the Russian's name with verve and even a certain linguistic pleasure to Richfield. Po-no-mar-yov, with the stress on the final syllable. That had been exactly how Ponomarev himself had pronounced it.

"Let's get the sequence right," said Richfield, becoming resilient again. "He contacted me. The militia and PSB had closed off the area where Marcus was shot and questioned everyone in the net. Because I had a Kommandatura pass and therefore was sort of official and because I'd seen the shooting at close hand, he called me in from the Protocol Department."

"But didn't he have to go through the PSB to do that?" It was Larson, riding his favorite hobbyhorse again.

"Yes, of course." Richfield successfully overcame the temptation to be sarcastic.

"So the PSB knew that you were meeting with a Russian intelligence officer?"

"Well, if you mean it was part of their day book, no, they didn't. Bremer knew. I suppose Ponomarev liaised with someone to get to Bremer. In fact, a PSB agent escorted me to Ponomarev's office, so obviously Ponomarev wasn't a freelancer."

Larson was about to pursue this line, but Trinh cut him off curtly and asked Stokes to continue. The young man was hitting his stride now, flattered by Hodges's visit and interest and excited that there was now direct evidence of Russian participation, at least at the intelligence level, in the civil war. "Where did your meetings with Ponomarev take place?"

"In the RCA Building. The thirty-fourth floor."

"How many meetings did you have?"

"Just one. It could be considered two, because I thought I'd finished with them and was waiting to be escorted out and they dragged me back in. That's when they coerced me into working for them."

"You say they coerced you. How do we know that? Everyone says he was forced into something bad when he's caught." It was Larson again. This time Trinh became angry.

"Major, I must ask you not to interrupt Mr. Stokes in his questioning! Is that clear, Major?"

"Yes sir." Larson's face was a blank mask against the anger boiling up in him.

Stokes went on as though there had been no interruption. "Who else was in the room when you met with Ponomarev?"

"A bald man, a bit older than Ponomarev." Stokes laughed as though at an inside joke and turned toward Trinh. "That must be Gusev," he said. "He's a sort of gofer-cum-butler to Ponomarev. Loyal as a retriever, unfortunately for us."

"Yes, Gusev was his name," Richfield noted. Trinh raised his eyebrows in acknowledgment of Stokes's expertise.

"Mr. Richfield," Stokes went on, "there are several questions we need answers to in connection with Ponomarev. But let's begin with the first one. What were Ponomarev's instructions to you?"

Richfield looked down, sighed, looked up, and said nothing. Trinh became irritated. "Mr. Richfield, I think it's clear enough to you what kind of trouble you are already in. I suggest you answer the question."

Douglas had been waiting for this and had his response ready. "You've already told me that I could be brought before some sort of military kangaroo court. What's the point of cooperating with you at all, since you seem to have selected the firing squad already?"

"I told you earlier that you could have an officer from the JAG's office if you choose," said Trinh, exasperated, "but you declined to accept that then."

"I'm not sure it would make the slightest difference. You'll shoot me if you want to, even if you pack the room for protocol's sake with military lawyers. Hey, that's a good one, 'for protocol's sake,'" he added bitterly.

"For someone in a perilous situation," said Trinh caustically, "you seem to have a cavalier attitude toward these proceedings."

Now Stokes was getting angry. Like a bloodhound chasing an ever-warmer scent, he believed he was on the verge of the greatest Constitutionalist counterintelligence coup to date in the civil war. In front of him sat a man who could not only confirm Russian intelligence involvement on the side of the People's Movement, but who could provide priceless insight into how much the Russians knew about Project Almond or the Constitutionalists in general. But Trinh and Larson were turning him into a cornered animal.

Flicking his hair back in annoyance, Stokes turned quickly to Trinh. "Colonel," he said, "this is all extremely important for people like yourself with legal considerations, but couldn't we pursue our common interest in Mr. Richfield's story without frightening our guest?"

Trinh glared back for a few seconds before answering. "My job, Mr. Stokes, is to ensure the smooth functioning of this hearing—"

"Has it already turned into a legal process?" asked Richfield, becoming sharper by the minute.

"Dammit, Richfield, keep quiet until you're asked to speak!" Trinh snapped. Then he turned back to Stokes. "My job is to ensure the smooth conduct of this debriefing," he resumed. "Yours is to ask whatever questions you need in order to do your job. That doesn't include second-guessing my judgment."

Richfield was grateful for this exchange because it gave him precious time to think. He decided to play peacemaker. "Colonel, forgive me for interrupting again," he said placatingly, "but this is important. I do have information that is of immediate concern for Mr. Stokes, but I am under instructions to make it known only to the very highest authority."

"Why didn't you tell us earlier?" snapped Trinh.

"I would have, but when you started getting into all that legal stuff about espionage, I began to wonder whether anything I said would be of any use. At least Mr. Stokes understands," he said, somewhat condescendingly. Stokes beamed, reddened, and flicked his hair back.

Trinh sighed with frustration. There was now a risk that his handling of the interrogation might later become an issue. He had discovered that, though an amateur in espionage, Richfield was slippery and difficult to deal with when cornered.

"Mr. Stokes," Trinh said, "you have heard Mr. Richfield say that he is unwilling to continue with this line of questioning at this level of authority. What do *you* propose?"

"That we request a meeting with General Hodges at the earliest possible moment."

"It's certainly true that the general said he wanted to see Richfield," said Larson.

"Very well, we'll consult further outside this room. This meeting is adjourned for fifteen minutes."

Douglas remained in his chair as the three interrogators and the stenographer filed once more out of the room. He poured himself some coffee, rubbed his eyes, put his feet up on another chair, and leaned back. He fell promptly asleep.

He was awakened by a brusque shaking of his shoulder by Larson, who was standing over him and looking quite annoyed. Richfield was drenched with perspiration.

"You'll have more than enough time to sleep later," Larson said harshly. "General Hodges wants to see you immediately."

Only Larson and Stokes had returned. Richfield gathered himself up from the chair, shook his head to clear it, and followed the two men out. He felt badly in need of a change of clothes, and now he wished he had accepted Larson's earlier offer of sleep before his interrogation. He was punchy, almost drugged. If only he could get some rest, he was ready to tell anyone virtually anything.

They followed the corridor out to the central office area and moved through yet another set of airlock-like security doors. If Douglas's sense of direction was accurate, it seemed as though they were heading farther into the hillside. The new corridor was narrower than the others and the sides were rough, unfinished concrete. The corridor had no doors or other passages leading off from it either. It seemed to be sloping gradually down.

Finally they came to a stainless steel door with a video camera and a speaker above it. "Identify yourselves," said a terse voice through the speaker. Larson and Stokes did so, facing the camera in turn and inserting a coded I.D. card into a slot next to the steel door. When Richfield's turn came, the speaker asked him to say his name. "Douglas Richfield," he said, unthinkingly.

"No match, say again," said the voice. Larson now prompted him, "Try your alias."

"Joe Fielding," he said after scrambling mentally for a moment to recall it.

The steel door now opened into a small anteroom in which several soldiers were busy at computer terminals, photocopying materials, and looking over long name lists. The walls were lined with huge maps of the western states, with the locations of Constitutionalist and enemy forces indicated by stick-on labels. Directly in front of the steel door, the other side of the anteroom opened up through two large double doors into an elegant, spacious office. It was furnished in colonial American style, except for a collapsible military cot that lay against the right-hand wall. There was a handsome mahogany desk with a sloping top in the left rear of the room, facing the door. A small teak and brass campaign desk lay over to the right rear of the room. In the center was a knee-high table of thick cut glass, like an extra-large coffee table, and around this were seven Windsor armchairs.

Except for the very rear of the room, the walls were painted in a pastel shade of green Richfield thought he had only once seen before, in a room of George Washington's home at Mount Vernon. Portraits lined the two side walls: Washington, Lincoln, Grant, Lee, Sherman, both Theodore and Franklin Roosevelt, Pershing, Eisenhower, Patton, and Schwartzkopf. Highly polished mahogany side tables, almost certainly antiques, were elegantly placed close to the armchairs. Only the rear wall was not painted or wallpapered. Instead, the entire surface was a huge map of the United States. It was brilliantly successful both as cartography and as a design for the room.

Douglas took all this in from the anteroom as the three of them waited to be shown in. Only after a few seconds did he notice that the almost immobile figure looming above the desk was Hodges. Standing next to him was an immaculately turned-out captain, handing him documents for his approval.

The three of them waited in silence. Hodges was not a person one interrupted. He didn't lose his temper, but he turned upon those who distracted him without good reason, the expression of someone for whom concentration was almost a form of personal piety.

Those who didn't know the general but who had heard about his famous stare assumed that it derived from arrogance. The general, however, was neither haughty nor consumed in any way with his *persona*. In a way he was completely unconscious of his style, much less the impact of his natural gravity or demeanor.

Yet Hodges had a definite sense of humor, and when he employed it, it glittered. He was witty, often bitingly so, but no one could recall hearing him tell a joke. That would imply a familiarity with his peers and his subordinates that was simply alien to him. Hodges projected a quite unconscious sense that he didn't have peers, that he belonged in a category by himself. At West Point this combination of unapproachability and innate authority had earned him the monicker "the General," not as a mockery but as a mark of respect. It had stuck with him all through his extraordinary career.

He'd been fifty-three when the civil war broke out, a lieutenant general in command of the U.S. Army's Third Corps, based in Fort Hood, Texas, one of the largest U.S. Army posts in the world. The base was home to the First Cavalry Division and the Second Armored "Hell on Wheels" Division, a natural location for the man whose career had always been associated with the U.S. Army.

Hodges by then was already a legendary figure, though for reasons that virtually guaranteed he would never be appointed to the Joint Chiefs of Staff in Washington. He was independent, and the combination of his self-confidence and sense of authority offended many. He thought more deeply about the nature of war than any other military man of his era—about its contradictions, triumphs, and squalors. To him war was more than force against force between and among nations; it was seamlessly woven into the complex fabric of human existence. He had poured his reflections into tightly written essays that were well received inside and outside the U.S. military.

His accuracy in predicting the importance of high-tech weaponry in combined operations had been prescient in the 1970s, and his stubborn conviction that tanks would remain absolutely vital elements in land warfare annoyed both nonarmor officers of the airborne "elite," and trendy careerists. Despite the rancor caused by his self-confidence and tendency to be right much of the time, his career arc through the U.S. military firmament had already been dazzling.

Hodges had entered West Point a year older than most of his classmates. On the advice of his father, a tough-minded, retired World War colonel, he'd spent the intervening year between Choate and the academy on a sheep ranch in Australia. The experience had hardened him physically and broadened him culturally and socially. The egalitarian-minded Aussies had not only liked him, they showed him uncustomary respect. Was it his height, his physical temerity, the authority he exuded, or—more prosaically—his well-known capacity for downing pints of Aussie ale in ten seconds flat? Who knew? But on entering West Point, he was both more mature and more self-confident than most of his fellow plebes, a fact that infuriated the upperclassmen and made him the target of some vindictive hazing. His apparent equanimity under this pressure only heightened the regard in which he was held by his classmates.

Before choosing armor as his specialty, he'd gone through the tough Airborne and Ranger schools at Fort Benning and then Armor Officer Basic and Advanced Courses at Fort Knox. He then had two tours of duty in Vietnam. He'd experienced the fury of the North Vietnamese and Viet Cong Tet Offensive in February 1968 in Quang Tri Province and had earned the first of several medals for gallantry, the Silver Star and the Bronze Star with "V" device for valor. As a reward for his performance as a first lieutenant and company commander, and as an experiment, the army had sent him to Oxford for a year after his first tour. There he read in history and philosophy, taking a B.Phil. in history with a thesis on the Roman general Scipio Africanus, who had defeated the Carthaginians in 146 B.C. He also rowed crew. As with all of his activities, he threw himself into this with such energy that he earned an Oxford blue by rowing in the university eight in the annual race against Cambridge on the Thames. In the year that he was there, Oxford won.

It was his solid reputation as an oarsman that helped redeem him in the eyes of many of his fellow undergraduates for his strikingly unfashionable political views. In the late 1960s and early 1970s at Oxford a fiercely radical and openly anti-American mood, largely due to the unpopularity of the Vietnam War, made life uncomfortable for the American students there. Most of the Rhodes scholars were themselves antiwar and thus deflected this hostility by participating in a generalized disenchantment with America. But Hodges, who supported the goals but not the tactics of the war, despised this approach.

He liked to confront his often bitter English debate opponents head on, skillfully picking on the complacency, class consciousness, and laziness of much of English society to undermine the moral authority of their arguments. In the cut-and-thrust of argument carried out late at night in college rooms, in student lodgings, or "digs," as they were called, or in pubs in and around Oxford, Hodges honed his wit and acquired his skill in debate with the aggressively outspoken and often sarcastic English.

Hodges enjoyed these exercises, but he was genuinely pained by the deep alienation of many of the American undergraduates, especially the best Rhodes scholars, from American society as a whole. It baffled him. Here were the very Americans whose abilities, despite their sometimes humble origins, had been generously rewarded by the society that reared them. Yet they seemed to hate their country. Hodges could easily grasp principled objections to war in general by conscientious objectors and to the Vietnam War in particular on the grounds of proportionality. The classical just war theory he embraced required that violence to counter violence must not pass the point where it undermined the moral basis of the original decision to resist. But he was openly contemptuous of the handful of his fellow countrymen at Oxford who declaimed, in all seriousness, that North Vietnam's repressive and regimented Communist society was a more attractive model for humanity than American democracy.

Back in Vietnam in 1973 for the last actions of the ground war involving American advisers, Hodges was wounded in a mortar attack in Quang Ngai Province and only survived because of a heroic rescue effort in the face of enemy fire by a steel-nerved South Vietnamese helicopter pilot. He never forgot the bravery. Later, when the young man and his family managed to escape Saigon during the chaos of the South Vietnamese collapse in April 1975, Hodges personally sponsored them as they sought asylum in the United States. The pilot, Nguyen Van Duong, settled down comfortably if unglamorously as a shoe salesman in Salinas, California. Every year thereafter Hodges would fly Nguyen and his wife at personal expense on the anniversary of his rescue to wherever he was currently based. The couple would spend a weekend as Hodges's guests and would be guests of honor at a dinner Hodges's wife would arrange. The general's sense of indebtedness went beyond Nguyen. He went out of his way to help the careers of Vietnamese-American officers under his command, in any way that he could. Trinh was but one example of this kind of assistance.

During his inevitable Pentagon postings Hodges soldiered through the quagmire of bureaucratic inanity and corridor backstabbings. He served as a major during 1973–76 in the prestigious Office of the Deputy Chief of Staff for Operations. This particular Pentagon niche was responsible for updating the U.S. military doctrine and war contingency preparations. It was a testing time. The collapse of the South Vietnamese regime in Saigon in 1975 and the debacle of the final American military evacuation brought the reputation and morale of the U.S. Army to its nadir in the twentieth century. Hodges grieved angrily over foolish decisions that had been made long before he came into his new assignment. He was responsible for many of the improvements in training and assignment that came about as a result of the post-Vietnam evaluation. Later on, though it had been an unhappy time for him both professionally and as a patriot, he was grateful for the hard thinking he had been forced to do as the military struggled to improve the system that had failed it in Vietnam.

Both at the Pentagon and in his commands, Hodges's outspokenness and confidence in his own judgment frequently antagonized his superior officers. He detested both incompetence and careerism. He very seldom lost his temper, but he treated laziness, dishonesty, or stupidity with an undisguised scorn. In someone of lesser ability or integrity, this attribute might have sidelined his career at an early stage. But promotion board after promotion board had been forced to swallow its pique at Hodges's style in the face of the overwhelming evidence of both his patriotism and his brilliance.

During Desert Storm in 1991 he was a major general in command of an armored division. His ideas for outflanking the Iraqis drew the favorable attention of General H. Norman Schwarzkopf. Yet after the medals had been handed out and the encomiums distributed, Hodges himself wondered if his assignment to the army's Third Corps at Fort Hood, Texas, might not be the last significant posting of his career. Although this was a prestigious assignment, the fall of the Soviet Union had diminished the importance of large armor commands. He was at the point of his career where the attitudes of a handful of superior officers would determine by the flick of an eyebrow whether he would add another star and move toward being selected as chairman of the Joint Chiefs of Staff or retire at his current three-star rank.

Fort Hood was hardly a backwater. Despite its largeness no segment of the army had taken more draconian cuts in manpower and funding during the economic collapse of the 1990s than armor. Hodges's command was a fraction of the size it had been in the plump 1980s. With characteristic determination, within months of his arrival there in the spring of 1997, he had improved morale and performance enormously and turned the base into a landmark of pride and efficiency in a U.S. military that was entering a new period of decline and national neglect. He alone, of all senior U.S. Army commanders in the fall of 1997, had both the trained, motivated troops and the brains and nerves to respond to the collapse of constitutional rule across America's cities.

"Gentlemen, please, come in and take a seat," Hodges said without looking up or interrupting the rhythm of his work with the papers before him.

Waiting for him to finish, Richfield, Larson, and Stokes sat awkwardly in the chairs arranged around the coffee table. After another two minutes the general handed the last of the papers to his aide and sat down in a fourth chair that faced his three visitors. The aide sat behind the campaign desk.

"I'm told that you have information from the Russians that you can pass on to us only at the highest level," he said, facing Richfield. "Is that correct?"

"Yes, General," Richfield replied.

"Then proceed." His tone was pleasant and even, almost avuncular.

"Ponomarev wanted the highest authorities among the Constitutionalist forces in Montana to know that Daniel Marcus, the originator of Project Almond, is under arrest in Manhattan after a shooting incident."

Hodges watched Richfield expressionlessly and was silent for half a minute. Douglas felt uncomfortable.

"It seems clear that you've never worked for the Public Security Bureau," Hodges went on in an even voice. "So the question is, why would Russian intelligence send an amateur to inform us about something we had obviously figured out already, namely that Marcus was shot while resisting arrest in New York?"

"General, I was the only closeup eyewitness to the Marcus shooting, and I was considered a reliable courier because of my Kommandatura clearance. Ponomarev wanted it known, from the mouth of an eyewitness, that Marcus was now in the hands of the People's Movement."

"Obviously, Ponomarev wants us to believe that Marcus is alive. We'll come in a moment to the question of whether or not he is. But first tell me, Mr. Richfield, why you agreed to work with an espionage service that is in alliance with our opponents? Major Larson, I assume you or Colonel Trinh have informed Mr. Richfield of the consequences of a conviction for espionage in wartime under the Code of Military Justice?"

"Yes Sir, I have. I don't think he quite grasped what he was involved with when he got here, but he sure does now," Trinh replied.

"Very well. Mr. Richfield," said Hodges, turning back to Douglas, "just why did you agree to cooperate with Russian intelligence?"

"Because, General, they threatened to kill my mother and gang rape my sister."

"Typical Ponomarev," Stokes blurted out. "A complete bastard."

Hodges's still-bloodshot eyes flickered quickly at Stokes, but he didn't rebuke him for his interruption. "Stokes," he said, "knowing what you do about Ponomarev, why do you suppose it was so important for him that an eyewitness—an untrained agent at that—pass on to us confirmation about the arrest of Marcus?"

"I'd say that Ponomarev is on a fishing expedition. It's typical of him to have several lines in the water just to get one bite. One of his skills is exploiting chance pieces of information that come his way."

"So you think he may have sent Richfield here knowing full well that he would quickly be uncovered, but expecting that we would immediately try to turn Richfield, and that, in this process, Ponomarev would subsequently acquire vital intelligence information about us?"

"Yes Sir, though I suspect that there is one particular piece of information he's pursuing."

"So do I, and we'll come back to that. In any event you agree with my surmise that the Marcus issue, important as it is, is also bait for another big fish—or several of them—that Ponomarev wishes to land?"

"Yes Sir."

Douglas, following all this closely despite his fatigue, was dazzled by the speed of Hodges's mind."

"Okay, Stokes, glad you're with me. You too, Larson?"

Larson wasn't but he wasn't about to admit it. As far as he was concerned, Richfield was a spy and that ended any further discussion. Regulations were regulations and spies were shot.

"Okay," said Hodges, shifting into a breezy, informal dialect, "let's deal with the first and immediate question, whether Marcus is alive or dead. Mr. Richfield, look at me when you answer this question. Is Marcus still alive?"

Douglas was already convinced before he came into the room that it was pointless to lie to Hodges and had decided he would be as truthful as he could be without, if possible, giving away anything about Rachel.

"General, I can't produce a death certificate or tell you I felt his pulse, but I haven't the slightest doubt that he is dead."

"My God," Larson said under his breath.

Stokes pursed his lips and gave a low whistle.

Hodges almost bounced in his chair with elation. He was as unaffectedly open in expressing joy as he was restrained in displaying anger.

"Fascinating, quite fascinating. Now, please, give me three evidences in support of that assertion."

"Well, first, the militiaman who dropped him got in three shots at his back from a good aiming position about thirty or so yards behind him. Second, one of the militia checked his pulse but made no effort to summon an ambulance or medical help. Third, just before my I.D. was checked, along with about a dozen other people, I looked back at the body and saw that it was unattended. Blood had seeped all over the surrounding sidewalk. The militia are not known for their caring ways, but I've never heard of them deliberately abandoning a wounded person after arrest. I'm positive he was dead."

"What did Ponomarev tell you about Marcus?"

"That he was under arrest and would eventually be able to talk."

"How did you respond to that?"

"I made no comment."

"Why not?"

"General, I didn't volunteer to spy for the Russians. They forced me into it under pain of savage treatment for my sister and mother. If Ponomarev thought I'd fall for his line that Marcus was alive, that's his problem."

"What is Ponomarev like?"

"He gives me the creeps. He comes on real smooth. You know, a sophisticated traveler. He has this thing about being a bird-watcher. I suppose he thinks it'll impress people. Gusev, his sidekick, is a real toad, one moment pretending to be a nice guy, the next kicking your legs out from under you."

"Good, we're making progress," said Hodges. He turned to his aide. "Dick, get us all some tea, will you? It's about that time." Larson smiled slyly at Stokes as the aide scurried off to obey. The general was notorious for eccentric Anglophile mannerisms that he'd picked up at Oxford.

The aide came back with a tray in less than a minute; Hodges's staff had obviously been expecting the order and had already prepared it. The general, momentarily assuming the role of host, poured out the tea for his three visitors.

"All right," he continued, turning back to Douglas, "you seem convinced that Marcus is dead. If you're correct, this could quite simply win us the war. If you are not—you could be lying, but I don't think you are—it becomes an absolute priority to ascertain where he is being held and what his condition is. Stokes, I want you to stay here after this discussion. We've a lot of work to do in a hurry. Now, Mr. Richfield, what other things did Ponomarev have on his mind?"

"He said he was worried about the Chinese. He thought they might try to intervene in the war on the Constitutionalist side."

"Did he now?" Hodges almost managed to raise his two bushy gray eyebrows at the same time as he said this. Richfield looked at Stokes, who in turn was watching him like a panther ready to pounce.

"And what else?"

Douglas sighed. Should he hold back on the suspected Constitutionalist mole or let the information out now? Something in him desperately wanted to negotiate, to trade his last remaining piece of information for an assurance that he wouldn't be shot. He decided to take the initiative. "General," he asked, "may I ask a question myself?"

"Of course," said Hodges, genially. He felt elated at what he had heard from Richfield so far.

"I've tried to show good faith here by being completely open with you about my conversations with Ponomarev. But is there some benefit for me in all this? I mean, am I going to be shot whether I cooperate or not?"

Hodges looked grave. "Mr. Richfield," he said slowly, "by your own words you have admitted to collaborating with a foreign intelligence service in alliance with an illegal regime that rules much of this country. That is an extremely serious act with appropriately heavy penalties. If you can prove that you acted under extreme duress, as you claim, I can assure you that the legal authorities will deal with your case with sympathy. And if, as part of our war effort, we asked you to cooperate with us against the enemy and you consented, we would certainly waive all charges against you. But that must remain a hypothetical situation for the time being.

"Meanwhile, how your case is resolved depends entirely on the candor with which you work with us. I will make no promises whatsoever to you in relation to what you tell us now. But I am a man of my word and you will discover that in due course."

Richfield sighed again. He felt his emotions stretched to the breaking point, swung this way and that over the past week by threats to his family or himself. Why couldn't he make his own decisions about which side to support instead of being coerced by first one and then the other? But then another thought came into his muddled brain; hadn't he already chosen one side back when the Chicago rent riots first broke out? Could you choose sides twice in a civil war? Did he even want to?

He was perspiring, whether from fatigue or stress he didn't know.

"All right," he said wearily, "I understand. I'm damned whatever I do."

"No you're not, for heaven's sake, man!" said Hodges with great force. "Are you so dull-witted that you no longer see what's up and what's down? Larson, make sure that while Richfield is under detention pending further investigation someone takes the time to sit down and explain to him what this civil war is *really* all about. No, on second thought, I'll think of the person myself.

"Now, Mr. Richfield, you're not damned and what you have to say is very important. Please continue." Hodges was once more friendly, avuncular. The effect of this on Richfield was almost hypnotic: good-cop-bad-cop in one and the same person.

"Ponomarev asked me to find out what I could about a suspected Constitutionalist mole working at the very highest level of the People's Movement."

"You mean Russian Foreign Intelligence is getting into American domestic counterespionage on behalf of the People's Movement? Did he say why?"

"Yes. He seems to think that the PSB is both incompetent and heavily infiltrated by Constitutionalist agents."

"He's right about both things," said Stokes spontaneously. Hodges laughed. He liked Stokes and saw beyond the pimples and nervousness to a brilliant and extraordinarily knowledgeable mind.

Hodges looked at both Larson and Stokes now. "You know what this means?" he asked. "It means they're really getting spooked by the leaks out of the National Executive Committee in Manhattan, and it means that Rutledge is at his wit's end how to deal with it all. Still, it astounds me that he's called in the Russians to help him. He must be desperate." Then he looked at Douglas. "Mr. Richfield," he said, "you may have an opportunity to redeem yourself for earlier, misplaced loyalties sooner than you think. Now just one other thing. Is there any living person other than Ponomarev and his sidekick or some PSB flunky who can corroborate your version of events at the Thanksgiving Day parade or thereafter?"

Douglas sighed deeply. It was becoming a habit. Of course there was someone. But what ugliness or danger might she now be subjected to if he dragged her into this mess? And would she ever forgive him if he did?

He sighed yet again. "Yes, there is," he said in a low tone that Hodges struggled to hear.

"Say again."

"I said, yes there is. Her name is Rachel Silverstein, and she works for the Caleb Foundation."

"You know her personally?"

"Yes, I do."

"And my guess is that you are rather fond of her?" Hodges said with a warm smile that lifted Richfield's gloom slightly.

"Yes, I am," he said forlornly.

"That's a very good thing," replied Hodges brightly, "because so are we."

11

Cellmates

*S*enior Lieutenant Oleg Yurevich Basmanov had only one really annoying habit, and that was his constant sniffling which he did quite loudly. The noise was getting on Douglas's nerves. For some reason the Russian was louder when he was on the floor, a place where he seemed to spend much of the day, his back propped up against the wall, his feet sprawled out into the middle of the room.

Cell, actually. A tolerably sized, even rather grand cell for two people, about seventeen by eight feet in size, quite clean, with a small, high window that let the sun through in generous doses from mid-morning to mid-afternoon. Richfield deduced that it probably faced due south. Ominously, in his opinion, the two beds, instead of being placed a spacious distance from each other, were piled one above the other, bunk-style, and the other furniture, if that is what it could be called, was crammed into about half the size of the overall area. It looked like whoever designed this accommodation had intended it to hold six people overall, perhaps more.

There was a porcelain basin with no sink stopper, a toilet with no seat (they could make a weapon out of it, after all), a stainless steel mirror (glass might be used to cut things), a stainless steel table large enough for four people if they were crammed around it, and two plastic chairs. The door had a thick glass window and a small, two-way speaker through which the guards could communicate with the prisoners without being exposed to any aggressive actions (spitting being particularly dreaded because of infections). A half-dozen or so books, all of them paperback, including a dog-eared copy of *The*

Book, a 1980s-era modern English version of the Bible, lay scattered in one corner. Coffee stains spotted the table and the floor.

Basmanov cleared his nose again with an offensive honking noise. Douglas winced. The Russian was a small, wiry man, in his mid to late twenties, probably the same age as Richfield, with crewcut hair and a large scar across his forehead. He had been very nice to Douglas ever since he'd been brought into the cell the night before. Richfield had already been there three days without talking to a soul. There had been several interrogations with nameless intelligence officers, usually relating to political information Richfield had about the People's Movement. But many of them meant going over and over again Richfield's account of the parade, of his meeting Rachel, of his talk with Ponomarev, and of his trip west. He felt that everything he had ever learned, including entirely trivial information, had been methodically mined from him. There had been no further communication from Hodges at all.

When he was not being taken out of his cell to a nearby room for the interrogations, the rest of the three days had turned into a dull routine of reading, eating, and waiting for the lights to be turned out at ten o'clock each evening. Thus when Basmanov had arrived, Richfield had welcomed the company.

Now he wasn't so sure. The Russian had been cagey and uncommunicative, telling Richfield almost nothing about himself except that he was a senior lieutenant in the Airborne Assault Force of the Russian army and had been taken prisoner while on a mission in Montana. That revelation alone had been enough for Douglas's jaw to drop in disbelief. Basmanov wore a mottled brown-and-tan camouflage uniform with the pale blue shoulder insignia of the Airborne Assault Force (VDV in Russian) and the characteristic blue-and-white striped undershirt showing at the neck of his tunic. He still wore his combat jump boots. Unless the Constitutionalists were laying on an elaborate charade for some devious purpose, Richfield thought, Basmanov seemed to be exactly what he said he was.

If the little Cossack were a Constitutionalist plant sent to smoke out Douglas he was taking his time getting to the point. If anything Basmanov seemed suspicious to the point of being fearful. That alone, after a few hours of watching each other warily and exchanging inconsequential comments about the food and the furniture, prompted Richfield to be bolder in addressing the Russian prisoner.

"You said you were a senior lieutenant," Douglas tried again, as much to ward off boredom as to learn anything particular about the Russian. "Call me ignorant, but what is that equivalent to in the American army?"

"First lieutenant, of course! Don't they teach you anything in the American army? Or maybe you didn't consider Russia a serious opponent after the Cold War was ended?"

Basmanov's English was surprisingly good, better in fact than that of any other Russian native speaker he had met. Even his accent was slight. But his sneering tone caught Richfield off-balance. Why was he so hostile? "I've never been in the American army," Richfield replied levelly. "I haven't the slightest idea what they teach there."

"Then what are you doing here? Did you get drunk or insult a Constitutionalist officer?"

"Drunk? I haven't been in Montana long enough to know where a bar is, much less get drunk in one. As for Constitutionalist officers, I've met a few, but we didn't exactly spend the time making polite conversation."

Douglas felt a bitterness rising within him as he said this, and Basmanov picked up on it quickly as a sentiment similar to his own. He was curious.

"Then why are you here? Are you a spy for the People's Movement?"

Richfield laughed bitterly at this. "No, I'm not," he said with a big smile, "but you're not the first person to ask me that."

Basmanov lapsed back into silence, thinking things through. Douglas took the initiative. "Since we're asking each other such intimate questions," he said, "what the hell is a senior lieutenant of the Russian army doing in the wilds of Montana?"

"Well, as you can see, I am no spy," Basmanov replied, a bit more cheerful now, "because spies don't dress up like soldiers. It's too much risk. Maybe they think you are a real soldier and shoot you." His English was beginning to slip, and Richfield noticed it. Basmanov was either tiring or relaxing. Now he seemed to want to talk a bit.

"Well, I think you already guessed why I am here. Maybe you know that there are Russians helping advise your People's Movement in the East to form their own army. I am one of them."

"Sure," Douglas said sarcastically, "and the main training bases of the American People's Army are here in Montana within easy shelling distance of the Constitutionalist forces. Just for the sake of greater realism in the training."

Basmanov seemed offended by this and became silent for a few moments. But Richfield wouldn't give up so easily. He was grateful for the conversation. "Okay, okay, that was uncalled for. I'm sorry," he said, "but you've got to admit that Montana is just about the other side of the moon in relation to Governor's Island or Fort Dix."

"How do you know we are at Fort Dix?" Basmanov asked sharply.

"Because if you live in Manhattan you'd have to be in a coma not to know where the Russian training base is."

Basmanov looked but he was wary again. "I will tell you why I am in Montana, if you will tell me why you are here. Obviously we both did something that our hosts didn't like."

Richfield couldn't risk letting out the details of his own complicated story. But an idea began to take shape. "Okay," he responded. "We both have reasons not to give out information on why we're here, so let's try a different approach. Like, can you tell me what you were doing a year ago?"

Basmanov brightened and he quietly hitched himself up from the floor and sat at the table opposite Richfield.

"I will tell you exactly what I was doing a year ago," he said with distinct pride in his voice. "I was guarding twenty thousand American prisoners of war in Kerman, Iran. Perhaps you have heard of the Gulf of Oman disaster?"

Douglas winced. He'd heard the barest fragments of what had happened to the U.S. expeditionary forces in Iran. It had been the greatest American military disaster since the fall of Bataan in the Philippines in 1942. One part of Douglas wanted to justify his own position on the Iranian operation; he'd opposed it from the beginning. But something inside him hurt. Decent American service personnel had died by the thousands or had gone into a brutal captivity.

"Yes, of course I've heard of it! I've just never met anyone who was there," he said wearily.

"Would you like me to tell you what it was like?"

This was getting humiliating, but something inside him wanted Basmanov to continue. "Sure," he said as casually as he could.

"Well, first, I think you know," said Basmanov, like an eager first-year teacher, "that your defeat in Iran was what really started the civil war. Your forces were so badly beaten that your president had to go to Paris to negotiate with our president. It was supposed to be about the return of your troops we held captive. But the POWs, as you say, were small potatoes. What counted was that you would have to give up your nuclear forces, all of them. Unfortunately, your Senate didn't seem to understand that and wouldn't agree to the terms of the treaty. That's when your People's Movement made the big riot in Washington and decided to push for power."

Douglas ignored what he considered Basmanov's clumsy attempt to rub things in. "Tell me more about what it was like in Iran itself," he said levelly.

But Basmanov was in a sententious mood. "History will one day judge your president very severely," he said irritatingly, "for making the decisions that led to the Iranian operation. It was a very foolish mistake to think that just one branch of the Iranian military forces, the air force, would be enough to overthrow the Islamic regime. Our people have always had very good intelligence in Iran, and they knew early on that the plotters had contacted the CIA and were asking America for help. Some of our senior people told me that Moscow should publicize what was happening beforehand so the coup wouldn't happen. But others, perhaps more clever, said, 'No, let it happen, let America come in. Then we will show them that even if they won the Cold War we can still win the Cold Peace.'

"Just think about it. It took half a year for the U.S. and its allies to prepare the troops and equipment to fight Saddam Hussein during your Desert Storm in 1991. Did you really think you could do the same thing in Iran, where the geography is terrible, in just a few weeks with fewer troops? Even your own intelligence people had played those computer war games in the 1980s, with Soviet troops coming through the Zagros Mountains. And in the war games one of your prisoners told me, the Soviets almost always won. Everything was against you, but still you went forward with the operation."

Richfield listened glumly and said nothing. His silence seemed to signal Basmanov to continue.

"Anyway, why was Iran so necessary to you? You didn't need its oil. It was not threatening to attack you. Sure, the people were always calling you 'The Great Satan,' but it is—how do you say it?—the fate of a great power, especially of a superpower, to be hated some of the time by someone. The trouble with you Americans is that you always want to be liked by everybody. We Russians don't care about being liked. Nobody has ever liked us very much anyway. We only want to be respected. And now we are," he concluded smugly.

"Look, I'm not defending the Iranian operation," Richfield interrupted testily, "but you're forgetting one very important item. Iran had acquired nuclear weapons and the means to deliver them and had started threatening to use them against Israel and the West. The American operation in Iran may have been stupid, but at the time it didn't seem like such a bad idea to take the nuclear button out of the hands of a bunch of crazy mullahs. Besides, the American military wasn't unanimous about the operation. The chairman of the Joint Chiefs himself opposed the military expedition, was overruled, and resigned in protest."

"Oh, such a heroic, charming gesture," commented Basmanov cynically, but when he noticed how quiet Richfield was, he softened his tone. "I think you should be proud of a few things," he continued soberly. "Your landing points were well chosen. Your generals were competent, brave men who did the best they could. What they couldn't have known was that we already knew where you would land, what forces you would have, and much of the operational planning."

"How did you know that?" Richfield asked, shocked.

"Because our intelligence penetration of your government was better after the Cold War was over and we were no longer Soviets, just Russians, than it had been when we were Communists. We knew almost everything we needed to know."

"It's never been very clear to me how much fighting there actually was."

"There was a lot, and it was very bitter, especially in the first few days," said Basmanov soberly. "Your men fought very bravely, very professionally. Even when they had exhausted their ammunition, water, and food, many units fought on in defiance of the surrender order. Some survived off the land for weeks, as a sort of guerrilla force. A handful even made their way into Pakistan, where they were interned at first.

"Your position was militarily impossible from the beginning. But it became hopeless after we sank your two carriers. I don't think you expected we could, or would, do that.

"We had a very good plan. Part of our forces came through the Zagros Mountains, and part of them landed as four divisions of airborne troops at Kerman and Isfahan. Our main ground forces reached Isfahan in a week and Kerman a few days later, before your forces were even properly secure on the beachhead. We carefully closed the net, even having a lot of our troops wear Iranian uniforms. Since you didn't think much of the Iranian troops, you underestimated the forces against you. You also weren't sure whether we were in Iran as a deterrent or to fight with you directly. By the time you realized that you were confronting Russian forces, it was too late. Of course, we already knew that your president had decided there was the possibility of using nuclear weapons against us. During the depression you had fallen behind again in nuclear equipment."

"Why did so many Americans die in the POW camps?" Douglas asked after a pause. "Was that deliberate?"

"No it wasn't. You have to understand. Here we were in the dry mountains of Iran in mid-summer at the very end of our supply lines and in combat. We hardly had enough food and water to keep our own soldiers alive. All of a sudden, we have fifty thousand American POWs to look after, about twenty thousand of them where I was. We were completely unprepared for this and we did our best. It was not like the death march at Bataan. We did not choose to let them die. I also was very sad about this."

A silence grew between the two men. There was much for Richfield to ponder. After a few moments he turned away from the wall and faced Basmanov directly.

"All right," he said, "you've accounted for the military disaster during the Gulf crisis. But that doesn't explain why your government, which is ultranationalist and by our terms, well, fascist, now wants to lend support to the People's Movement. We have a completely different view of the world from you."

Basmanov laughed again and cleared his nose with the unpleasant honking noise. "You Americans are so naive," he said. "What do we care what kind of government America has, just so long as we are stronger? Didn't your own people say the same thing about Russia when we were at our lowest point with Gorbachev and Yeltsin? They said, 'Who cares whether Russia is democratic or not, just so long as it isn't a world power anymore?'

"As for us we found out that democracy couldn't put food on the table, couldn't stop the crime wave, and couldn't stop the international bankers and Zionists from bullying and lording it over the Russian people." Basmanov was gathering indignation now, and his face was red. "Every nation needs its sense of destiny. Yours was to glorify democracy and to try to spread it everywhere around the world. Your problem was, when the problems got too big in your country, not even democracy was working anymore. You were hating each other and blaming each other all the time for the things that went wrong. So now you have a civil war. And when it is over, what kind of system will you have? Will you go back to democracy? I think now that you will have to learn the rules all over again.

"But as for us Russians, we never really had illusions that democracy would solve everything. Yeltsin tried for a while to allow democratic politics, but he discovered that people were too selfish and corrupt. Anyway, just when he really needed it, your own government wouldn't give him enough support. Actually, we think he was taking orders, as Gorbachev had, from the CIA. And then there were the international bankers. They were sticking their noses in every part of our country, telling us what we could do and not do. It was disgusting. Finally, we started listening to what Zhelenovsky and others had been saying all along: Russia must bring an end to the foreigners' domination, must unite her people once more, smash down crime and lawlessness at home, and stand up against foreign conspiracies abroad. Russia must reestablish her flag on three continents, must recover her military greatness, and rediscover her moral destiny. Especially, Russia must show the world how to defeat the international Zionist conspiracies."

"What are you talking about?" Richfield interrupted, almost shouting. "What Zionist conspiracies? That's only ugly, anti-Semitic drivel, the stuff that Hitler used to peddle!"

"Hitler was right about some things. The Jews, for example. Sooner or later even your own, so-called progressive government, the People's Movement, will discover that."

Richfield felt a rage boiling up within him. How could you deal with this irrational hatred, this lunatic conspiracy paranoia? It wasn't just that he thought of Rachel and how vulnerable she would be to the rantings of Basmanov if they gained a foothold in America. It was that Basmanov's world-view—or more importantly, Zhelenovsky's—cut to the very bone of the idealism about tolerance and fairness that Douglas, as an American, thought to be virtually his birthright. He'd joined the People's Movement because he was outraged that African-Americans, at the bottom of the economic pile in his country, were overwhelmingly the victims of the economic depression and its harsh side effects.

He wasn't naive about the composition of the power center of the People's Movement. He knew there were some flaky, even sinister, elements within it. But he believed that most of its leaders shared the same fundamental American idealism about racial tolerance that he did. But now, apparently, some of those progressive idealists were so determined to defeat the Constitutionalists that they didn't mind enlisting the assistance of a Russia that was in the grip of a messianic and anti-Semitic xenophobia as virulent as that of the Third Reich.

As Richfield's anger welled up, something changed at the very root of his being, something so deep that it touched loyalties within him at a much deeper level than ever before. He had never believed in the talk of good and evil. That was all just a cultural metaphor by his reckoning, a means to explain the irrational, the unexpected, and the extreme in human behavior. Sooner or later, he had always assumed, scientists would be able to account for almost every human action, however strange it might seem in the light of today's knowledge.

But now, in an intuitive way that surprised him because it went beyond logic, Richfield felt himself confronting something primevally wicked; not Basmanov himself nor the amazing and in so many ways admirable country that he came from. What Douglas felt was evil was a pulsating energy of destruction and hatred that somehow emanated from the core of this paranoid and anti-Semitic ideology. It was as though the idea itself had come into being from a source of living malice. There was no other way he could put it.

This conviction was itself a surprise to Richfield because it went so far beyond the familiar impulses of his idealism. Basmanov, in a perverse sort of way, was an idealist insofar as he subscribed to the mumbo jumbo about Russia's messianic global destiny of smashing down foreign conspiracies. Richfield felt as though a new moral eye, one whose very existence had hitherto been unknown to him, had been set in place at the center of his being. The eye had been forced open by his proximity to the sheer horror of the Zhelenovsky doctrines.

With it Douglas now understood something he hadn't previously considered. There was a sense, it seemed, in which an individual's will, whether realized or not, actually made choices with moral consequences much of the time. The daily, the trivial, the inconsequential might not be so ephemeral and unimportant after all.

This wasn't just sobering to think about—it was terrifying. What if there were some kind of moral judgment at the end of it all, never mind who did the judging—the mountains, the oceans, the trees, or even a deity? Any sane person would have to make choices every day to avoid lending support to evil, however complicated and uncertain those choices might be. Some tectonic shift in Richfield's grasp of things told him that now—after meeting Basmanov—everything he did in the context of the war would have consequences far beyond their immediate setting.

There was something else too. If evil existed in some tangible, personal sense, what about good? If some sort of ultimate good existed, did it have a name? It was maddening to have to deal with all this; he thought he had safely finished with metaphysical questions by his first year in Chicago. Now they had come roaring back like a long-lost prodigal.

"Did I offend you?" Basmanov asked, surprised by the impact of his last remark. Douglas had pushed his chair back in his indignation, spread his legs out in front of him, and fixed his gaze somewhere above his cellmate's head.

"You didn't offend me personally," Richfield said calmly, "but your ideas shocked me. Of course I knew of them already. I had just never met anyone who expressed them openly and with the sense of conviction as you just did."

"Then it's clear that you—"

He got no further before a loud buzzing noise from the two-way intercom drowned him out. "Prisoners Richfield, Basmanov!" the electronic voice barked. "Move away from the table and stand facing the wall at opposite sides of the cell, hands above heads! Now!"

The rude interruption brought them back to earth with a thud. They might in one manner be mutually antagonistic philosophers, but they were also cellmates, sharing the routine humiliations of captivity. They grinned at each other, breaking the tension, then rose from the table to obey the command.

Another buzzing noise followed, and the cell door swung open to admit two guards brandishing nightsticks. A third stood blocking the open doorway. The guards patted them down brusquely for weapons, then rifled through the cell quickly in a random search. They left as soon as they had come in. But the third guard, who had stepped aside to let them pass, waited behind in the open cell doorway. "You, Richfield," he ordered coldly, "put your hands on top of your head and walk this way." This was different from his normal summons to interrogation. They usually called him to the door, opened it remotely, and had him exit. Was this it, then? Surely they'd tell him if his case were quickly decided . . . even in a negative way.

"Good-bye," Basmanov called after him cheerily. "Hey, I never heard what you were doing last year."

"Quiet, you!" the guard out in the corridor shouted at him. Then the door, buzzing electronically once more, swung back and closed again.

Strangely, Douglas didn't feel fearful as he obeyed the guard's orders to walk down the long corridor outside the cell. If this was the end, he certainly didn't want to die. But if he did, in a way he had cheated his cynical spymaster in New York out of something. Ponomarev would have to explain to his superiors Gusev why the agent he had chosen to run had failed him.

"You can put your hands down now, but don't even think of doing something stupid. At this range my pistol would turn your spleen into wallpaper." It was a different voice and one he recognized. Major Larson, his erstwhile prosecutor during Douglas's original interrogation, had silently taken over as his escort, wherever they were going. The voice was cold and detached, but it was nevertheless heartening to Richfield. If Larson alone were assigned to escort him somewhere, it was unlikely that the Constitutionalists were going to execute him. Ordinary soldiers would have escorted him for that. And, there hadn't been any pretense of a military tribunal. Hodges was strict, but Douglas had come to learn that the general was a stickler for due process.

"Can I ask where you're taking me?" Richfield asked.

"You can ask, but I'm not going to tell you," Larson replied smugly.

They turned left at the end of the corridor and followed another long passage down a slight incline. The walls were rough, unfinished concrete, and the ceiling was lined with wires and pipes. Occasionally, an officer or soldier would scurry purposefully by, looking curiously at Richfield. They stopped at a checkpoint where Douglas was blindfolded, spun around a few times, and then led off with Larson guiding him by the arm. Douglas knew that there had been mining tunnels in the hills behind Helena, but he seemed to be in an underground city. There were turns and changes of direction, but it wasn't clear to Douglas whether these were meant to disorient him or that the journey was that complicated.

"Okay, blindman's buff is over. You can remove the blindfold," Larson said somewhat less gruffly than earlier.

Untying the heavy dark cloth, Richfield found himself standing in front of an electronically operated checkpoint and door identical to the one through which Larson had first brought him just three days earlier.

"Joe Fielding," he said at the required electronic identification prompt. The thick, steel door obeyed Larson's final instruction to open. Beyond the apparently standard security anteroom in the entryway lay a cavernous operations room. Midway up the walls was a gallery that provided an excellent view of all that went on at the main level and that, presumably, could greatly increase the operations center's occupancy. A large screen at one end of the room was blank; Richfield surmised it was either for projecting computer information or video images.

The area had been divided in two. One held computer terminals, maps, and other equipment, and the other side was occupied by a massive round table of highly polished wood large enough to accommodate about twenty comfortable armchairs.

The table immediately drew Richfield's attention. Sitting on it, his legs dangling almost to the floor, was the tall, unmistakable figure of Hodges. He was talking to a dozen or so senior officers who stood in a tight semicircle around him. For years afterward the image was locked indelibly in Douglas's mind: Hodges, speaking with few gestures, and the officers listening with infinite respect and attentiveness. Authority seemed to emanate effortlessly from the man. Richfield wondered if there were any elements in the man's life that balanced this power with a sense of weakness or vulnerability. Watching him now, it wasn't apparent that anything did.

Larson stopped Richfield at a polite distance so that the two men couldn't eavesdrop on the conversation. But when an officer facing Hodges noticed them, the general looked back over his shoulder to see who it was.

"Ah, Larson, Richfield," he said briskly. "Please sit down and we'll begin."

Hodges seated himself across from Larson and Richfield. To Douglas's surprise Stokes was at the table but in the uniform of an army major. He looked even more ill at ease than when Richfield had first encountered him. His face was almost completely obscured by flops of hair, like a Belgian sheep dog. Larson and Richfield, were surrounded by six empty chairs.

"How was your time in stir?" Hodges asked cheerily.

"It was a revelation, General."

"That's what I anticipated. Interesting fellow, Basmanov, isn't he? Our scouts found him with three enlisted men—two PMs and a

Russian—about thirty miles from here, just the other side of the Big Belt Mountains. We've got a pretty good idea of what they were up to. I didn't think it would take long for you to understand him and come to the appropriate conclusion. We'll come back to that. Right now I want to tell you why we've brought you here. It's very simple. We're not sure yet what to do with you."

Richfield grimaced involuntarily, sending a ripple of laughter around the table.

"Don't worry," Hodges went on, joining the laughter, "we're not going to shoot you. Your story has been verified. In fact, before we go any further, we've managed to bring in someone to confirm this. Sergeant, bring in our guest," he called out to an MP standing guard at the door behind him.

Before the general had finished speaking, Richfield knew who it would be. Until Basmanov came into the cell, he had spent much of the last three days thinking of nothing but Rachel and speculating about her connection to the Constitutionalists. For Hodges to have referred to her with such warmth suggested she was no mere run-of-the-mill Constitutionalist agent in Manhattan, but someone of immense importance to their war effort. He remembered how uncomfortable she had been talking about the People's Movement during their first conversation in the coffee shop. The second time they had met, she had known exactly which cafe to send him to so that he could make contact with the Constitutionalists.

Why had she trusted him? Had he been so clumsy and naive in his efforts to come out west that she had seen through everything he said? How did she know that he wouldn't lead a busload of PSB thugs to the cafe? How did she read him: as someone to whom she owed an obligation, or as a person of potential value to the Constitutionalists? More importantly, she seemed to like him. He knew that he liked her, maybe too much.

Douglas watched the door expectantly. He tried to control the moment with an act of indifference, especially in front of Hodges and his senior officers, but he knew he wasn't carrying it off very well. Already he felt his ears burning. He knew he was blushing.

And then she came in. She was wearing blue jeans, black cowboy boots, a cream cotton shirt, and an unbuttoned blue-denim jacket. Her hair was pulled back in a way that enhanced her delicate features. She looked beautiful, and Douglas couldn't help but smile at her entrance.

Everyone else around the table was equally struck by her, turning their heads in unison as she came into the room. Hodges looked slightly annoyed over the diversion her appearance had created and rose to greet her.

"It's good to see you again, General," she said.

"And you too, Rachel. I congratulate you on getting here so quickly. It must have been quite hazardous."

"No, Sir, not really. Our people have a remarkably efficient pipeline across the Midwest."

"Good. Gentlemen, I'd like to introduce a very important element in our overall effort within Manhattan, Miss Rachel Silverstein."

The other officers nodded as the general continued. "I think you may want to sit with Major Larson and Mr. Richfield."

As Rachel came around the massive table toward an empty seat on his right, Douglas remembered again the first time he had seen the extraordinary grace of her walk. She rather formally, perhaps for the sake of the others in attendance, extended her hand to him before she sat down. In spite of his normally egalitarian ways, Douglas stood and helped her with her chair. As the attention returned to Hodges, who was slightly impatient to move on, Rachel rested her hand on his arm and squeezed it. He noticed the same delicious fragrance he had detected in the coffee shop half a continent away. If what he felt could be channeled to a generator, he was sure he could light up half of Montana.

Douglas wrenched his attention back to the general. "We have one thing we have to consider today," he was saying, "and that is what to do with Mr. Richfield. I have my own views, of course, but I didn't bring you here for a monologue, gentlemen."

"General Baum," Hodges continued, "would you present the case I think you have in mind?"

Four seats to his left General Daley Baum, a gray-haired African-American looked up from the table. "Yes sir," he began. "First, let's look at the facts of the case. By his own admission Mr. Richfield came to us under instructions from a senior official of the Russian Foreign

Intelligence Service, or to be more direct, the KGB. Second, there is no doubt that he was coerced into this. Third, he brought us some absolutely crucial information, namely, that Daniel Marcus is dead. I believe he could be of immeasurable service to us if he returned to New York under our instructions, appeared to be still under Ponomarev's control, and acted as our ears to what Zhelenovsky's people are up to. Right now we have virtually no access to them at all."

"Admirably concise, Daley," commented Hodges, with a pleased smile. "General Parsons, I believe you don't agree with General Baum."

"No sir, I don't," said a trim-looking brigadier in his early forties with a brush cut and a moustache that gave him the appearance of the stereotypical outdoorsman. "I agree with only one of the alleged facts of this case as provided by General Baum, namely that Richfield is, or at least was, under the control of a foreign intelligence service. As to whether he was coerced, we have only his word. I think I should remind everyone also that Richfield at first lied about what he knew of Daniel Marcus and Project Almond.

"Nor do we know that Marcus is dead. Again we only have Richfield's word for it. Even if he sincerely believes this to be true, there is no independent confirmation. It's plain enough that he doesn't have the background of a professional agent, but that hardly makes him less potentially dangerous to us. If we send him back to Manhattan, this Russian will squeeze him dry about our operations. I think we should hold Mr. Richfield here for the remainder of the war. Certainly he can be useful to us, perhaps as a training resource for our own agents."

Douglas thought he saw Hodges's bushy gray eyebrows lift a little at this, but the general's face, as usual, gave away nothing of his own position. There was a brief silence while Hodges flicked through a sheaf of papers in front of him, scribbled a note on a legal pad to his right, and then looked up to his left and right. "Anybody have anything to add?" he asked.

"General," said a colonel with untidy blond hair and gigantic hands, who sat to the right of Parsons, "it may be that we won't determine the facts until the end of the war as proposed to us by General Baum and as challenged by General Parsons. But I suggest we don't have the luxury of waiting. The information Mr. Richfield has provided, if true and skillfully exploited, could give us a very significant advantage over the enemy in both the short and the medium term. It is in this timeframe that we still hold some advantages of initiative. I am wondering if there is some way we can reexamine the issue of Mr. Richfield's veracity. If there is a reasonable probability that the story he has given us is true, then I think we have no alternative but to send him back east."

"Thank you, Hank," said Hodges. "In fact, there certainly is a way we can get closer to the facts about Mr. Richfield. Miss Silverstein is one person to whom he gave an account of what happened following the Thanksgiving Day parade before he met Ponomarev. Rachel, what impression did you have of Mr. Richfield when you first met him?"

"I thought he was a brave and decent man," she replied. She turned to him to smile and added, "He was little naive and confused. What he saw happen to Daniel Marcus obviously made a big impression on him."

"And just what did he say he saw happen to Marcus?" It was Parsons, boring in skeptically on Richfield's reliability.

"He saw Marcus shot down on the street. He described three wounds, two in the back and one in the neck."

"From what range was he shot?"

"Douglas didn't say. But I think it's clear it was close. How far can a limping man run in three or four seconds?"

"Why that time period?"

"I'm speculating, but Douglas said that Marcus's companion was shot and only then that Marcus tried to run for it. I suppose it would take three or four seconds for a militiaman to re-aim his pistol at a fleeing man once he had already shot someone else."

"There's no need to speculate, Miss Silverstein, we can ask Mr. Richfield directly. Mr. Richfield?" Hodges asked.

It was probably less than three seconds. The shooter barely had to move to take aim."

"May I continue, General?" asked Parsons persistently.

"Of course, Bill," the general said.

"Mr. Richfield may have been impulsive in telling you what he saw after the parade, but I think that could be explained by his

meeting a very pretty woman. A lot of men would do as much."
There was a ripple of laughter among the officers. "Even so, how
do you know that he wasn't working for the PSB? I've seen the
transcripts, and Mr. Richfield now admits—though he didn't at
first—that this man, Bremer, who also works in the Protocol Department had told him about the PSB search for Marcus before the
shooting. It's pretty obvious that Bremer is PSB, or at least close to
them, and why not Mr. Richfield too for that matter?"

General Baum spoke up, eager to vindicate his original position.
"Colonel, we already have some impressive independent evidence
that, whatever Mr. Richfield's connections with the Russians, he is
not PSB. I refer to the polygraph test results. All of the other polygraph data are confirmed by information that we can independently
verify. But the polygraph indicated not once, but several times, that
Richfield was telling the truth when he said he was not a PSB agent."

There was another pause while Hodges looked intensely at the
sheets in front of him, apparently transcripts of the various interrogations of Richfield. The silence was broken by Larson, sitting on
Richfield's left. "Excuse me, General, I know that I'm here only as
the prisoner's escort"—the word *prisoner* gave Douglas a shudder—
"but I was the officer who met him when he first arrived at the airport, and I was present throughout his first interrogation, including
the time he was on the polygraph."

"You may certainly comment, Major Larson," replied Hodges
dryly, "but let's not refer to Mr. Richfield as 'the prisoner.' I think
that term prejudices our discussion. Please proceed."

"Pardon me, General, I'm not trying to prejudice anyone. I'm
speaking only as an officer with experience in counterintelligence
and who has had extensive opportunity to observe Mr. Richfield. I
simply don't think anyone is trustworthy who agreed, without the
duress of torture, to work for a foreign organization against the
United States. Isn't it less important to know whether Mr. Richfield
worked for the PSB or the Russian Foreign Intelligence Service than
to determine his ultimate loyalties?"

"That's a valid point, Major, and I certainly take it. Fortunately,
we have one person here who knew Mr. Richfield before his encounter with Ponomarev and who can thus give us some insight into his

personality before threats were made to the life and health of his mother and sister."

"With respect, General," said Larson, riskily interrupting Hodges, "we have only Richfield's word for it that threats were made against his family. How do we know that he didn't volunteer for this assignment?"

"General Baum or Colonel Gutmacher, do you have any response to this?" Hodges asked.

Gutmacher spoke up. "Yes, we have only Mr. Richfield's word for it that he was coerced into spying rather than volunteering. But what other possible motivation could he have? Certainly he had met many Russians through his contacts with the Kommandatura on Governor's Island. But I think you'd have to have very strong motivations indeed to spy for a foreign regime which, though it was allied to your own, was completely at odds with it philosophically. Can anyone imagine a Nazi *volunteering* to work for the Soviets, even assuming Hitler approved of such altruism? Certainly the Gestapo or the Abwehr might have designated specific cooperation, but even then the Nazi agent would have been ultimately under German, rather than Soviet, control. But I think there is now a consensus here that the analogous situation didn't occur with Richfield. That is, the PSB didn't send him to the Russians. Ponomarev could have accessed any PSB professionals if he had wanted to. He chose not to, and not surprisingly being short of volunteers in the street to work for him, he simply applied a thumbscrew. That's the way the KGB used to work in the old days, isn't it?"

He had intended to continue, but the question was immediately picked up by Hodges. "We've got someone here who can answer that better than anyone else. Major Stokes, what characterizes Ponomarev's working style?" Hodges badly wanted Stokes's participation in the conversation, but he knew that the talented civilian, despite the courtesy uniform and thus not a civilian in appearance, felt intimidated by the presence of so many of Hodges's senior staff officers. Stokes needed to be led out of his shell.

"Ponomarev is an old-school spymaster," he said, flicking back his hair. "His willingness to apply coercion to recruit agents comes from the old KGB manuals. I haven't the slightest doubt that he applied coercion to Mr. Richfield, and it would be typical of him to threaten harm to his mother and sister.

"How can you be so sure?" It was Parsons again, not giving up so easily.

"Because there are only three ways a normal person will spy: conviction, coercion, or cash. Whatever else Mr. Richfield is, he doesn't strike me as a man of great conviction, certainly not the kind of conviction compatible with Russian ultranationalism. Cash? Possible, but I'd say marginal. Manhattan is a hotbed of Maoist-style egalitarianism. You'd be in deep trouble, no matter how legitimately you got the money, if you started flashing around a load of extra dollars. That leaves coercion, the most unpleasant, but usually quite reliable form of recruitment. It's typical of Ponomarev."

"Thank you, Major Stokes," said Hodges briskly. "I think you have convinced us that Ponomarev did indeed threaten Richfield directly. Perhaps it's time to turn to the question of what might be called Mr. Richfield's 'ultimate loyalties,' to use Major Larson's term. I'm not convinced, however, that Mr. Richfield has ever had any. He obviously joined the People's Movement out of a misguided idealism. But I have the definite impression that even this has faded as the regime's nature has become clearer to him. Colonel Gutmacher, you propose sending Mr. Richfield back to Manhattan. But would you do so if you weren't sure about his convictions or what they were?"

"No, General."

"Nor would I, so we shall have to try to determine that. Rachel, I think you said your first impression of Mr. Richfield was someone who was 'decent and brave.' Had you ever met him before?"

"No, General."

"Then on what do you base that impression?"

"General, Douglas rescued me from a very dangerous situation in the New York Public Library. I got into it through my own stupidity when I argued with one of the clerks. The only reason I wasn't arrested was that Douglas used his credentials to impress the man. I don't think he'd ever seen a pass like that before, and he wasn't sure enough to challenge it. It was certainly decent of Mr. Richfield to intimidate an ill-mannered bureaucrat, but nobody required him to risk his career, and perhaps even his liberty, to get me out of trouble."

Douglas almost glowed as he listened to Rachel's recounting of their first meeting. But Parsons wasn't yet finished.

"That's very touching, I'm sure, Miss Silverstein," he commented dryly, "but as I've already suggested, quite a few young men—and maybe many who aren't so young—might try chivalry if they thought it would be a way to meet you. I'm sure a Protocol I.D. is impressive, but it doesn't strike me as requiring great heroism to flash that in front of an officious library clerk in an attempt to invoke authority."

"General," Rachel said, her face showing a controlled impatience, "it wasn't a Protocol I.D. that Mr. Richfield produced. It was his Kommandatura I.D."

"Are you sure?"

"I saw it, General."

There was a brief silence, but Hodges once more was on top of it. "Major Stokes," he asked, "what would happen to a person who was found using a Kommandatura I.D. for entirely personal purposes?"

"It is, first of all, a major breach of regime security. Ordinary people aren't even supposed to know that there is such a pass. Mr. Richfield would certainly have been arrested if a PSB agent had been present or if the library clerk had grasped what the I.D. was."

"General Parsons?" Hodges was pushing for a consensus now.

"I concede that Mr. Richfield was brave—foolhardy, perhaps—and that he was acting at great risk and on his own. Miss Silverstein, there's one thing I'm still curious about. When Mr. Richfield approached you the second time, asking about ways to come west, weren't you suspicious of him? Why did you give him rather sensitive information about where to contact our people in Greenwich Village?"

"General, it was so incredibly stupid of him. You don't approach anyone in the People's Movement areas and ask for that kind of information unless you're desperate. I suspected that someone had gotten to Douglas, though I assumed that it was the PSB. As I thought about it, though, it didn't make any sense. They hadn't known about my meeting Douglas, so they were hardly likely to have used him to set me up. I realized that Douglas was being coerced and that he was absolutely desperate to follow his instructions. For that reason, and because of the risk he had taken to get me out of trouble, I didn't feel I could turn him away. I was confident I could get information to you about him before he could do any damage, intentionally or otherwise. I didn't report that Douglas thought Marcus was dead because I wasn't sure who he was and he seemed confused himself about the whole incident. I thought we could discover who was controlling him. There's one other thing too." She paused.

"Yes, Rachel," Hodges said patiently.

"Perhaps it's now my turn to admit naivete, but I had, well, an intuition that Douglas wouldn't try to harm any cause to which I was loyal."

There was an awkward pause around the table. Gutmacher broke it. "General?" he said.

"Yes, Hank."

"I think we already have one ingredient of a conviction." Hodges looked at him impenetrably, then addressed Douglas as though he hadn't heard the comment. "Mr. Richfield," he said, "what was your impression of Basmanov?"

"General, in my job, you sometimes run into some real hokey types. But Basmanov made me angrier than I've ever been at someone's political ideas. I found his anti-Semitic conspiracy rantings repulsive. I think the only word to describe those kinds of ideas is simply evil."

Hodges once more said nothing, busying himself with tidying up the papers in front of him. Then he looked around the table. "Gentlemen, perhaps we now have the beginnings of two rather strong convictions." Then he looked at Douglas with the same relentless intensity that the former Protocol officer had experienced during his first encounter with the general. "Are you willing to return to Manhattan and work for us, under the guidelines of military discipline?" he asked. "You must understand that if Ponomarev finds out that you're on our side, he will be absolutely merciless. There will be nothing we can do to help you."

Douglas didn't take his eyes away from Hodges. "Yes Sir, I'm prepared to go back," he said quietly. Out of the corner of his eye he saw Rachel watching him. She moved her hand over and again squeezed his arm.

Hodges now smiled broadly. "Your timing is helpful," he said briskly. "We'll need you here for a while before sending you back. There are some important visitors coming tomorrow, and they may need some Protocol assistance.

"I'll do whatever I can, Sir."

"Good," said Hodges, "I thought you'd be willing. It's only a pity that you don't speak Chinese."

12

Visitors from China

Douglas and Rachel ate at Carpaccio's that night, the best and virtually the only good restaurant still operating in Helena after the ravages of the depression and the civil war. Rumor had it that Hodges himself, who was partial to Italian cooking, had given instructions to the quartermasters of the Army of Western Montana not to let Carpaccio's ever run short of the key ingredients for its cuisine. The general was seldom there, but night after night the restaurant was packed with his officers, and the noise of the conversation and the bustle of the restaurant was legendary. Sometimes you had to shout to be heard.

Colonel Gutmacher had arranged the meal, letting Douglas and Rachel know that they were to be the guests of the Army of Western Montana. That idea, Richfield figured, though he was too polite to ask, was obviously Hodges's, not Gutmacher's. But why?

Rachel smiled slyly at the question, and Douglas looked at her again as though for the first time, astonished that a woman could look so beautiful in so many ways. She was wearing a beguiling black cocktail dress, rather short, with a black choker and a Wedgewood medallion around her throat.

"I'll let you in on a little secret," she said coquettishly in response to a barrage of questions from Douglas. "I've been here a few times before, and I have a very good friend in a very high place, General Hodges's wife Helen, to be precise. I've brought outfits before, which Helen keeps for me. But she also lets me borrow from her wardrobe."

"Is there a connection between the two of you?"

"Let's just say that I'm trying to help her find someone."

Douglas assumed this would be intimate family business relating to the Hodges and dropped the subject.

Almost bellowing at each other to be heard over the noise of the restaurant, they peeled away more layers of their lives. Douglas told Rachel about his parents' divorce and his dreary childhood in New Jersey. He felt compelled to explain why he had been drawn into the People's Movement, and as he relived his early excitement and idealism about it, Rachel listened gently. Now it was his turn to be grateful. He looked at her for a moment and smiled.

They lingered over dessert and the hubbub abated as the night came to an end.

"Does everyone here go to bed at nine and get up at five?" Douglas asked.

"It certainly looks that way," Rachel said. "Trust us Manhattanites to show people what nightlife is all about." Now they both laughed.

As it grew quieter, they found themselves wanting to be more serious. Rachel, who had said almost nothing about herself so far, told him of her love for Israel, where she had been born. She spoke of Jerusalem, a golden city, a place of such compelling presence and beauty that on seeing it for the first time, she felt she had belonged to it all her life.

Douglas, whose life had never intersected with people of deep esthetic, much less religious inclination, listened in both fascination and wonder. Had he been looking for something? He didn't think so, yet Rachel had brought more than just an irresistible femininity into his life. She had demonstrated how narrow and one-dimensional much of his attitude toward life was.

"Attention! Attention!" A deep voice crackled through a speaker in the restaurant's ceiling. "Thirty minutes to curfew. Thirty minutes to curfew. All military personnel must immediately return to base."

"Curfew!" Richfield looked at his watch in disgust. "It's only 9:30!"

"There's a war going on," Rachel said and shrugged. He looked at her a moment longer. "Let's go," he said.

The sky was clear and as he walked along the sidewalk Douglas looked up at the stars overhead. Orion's belt, the Pleiades, the Big Dipper—these great, silent witnesses to history stared down impassively from the heavens as his breath steamed out into the cold. It was well below freezing, and his ears were beginning to sting. Rachel, more chic tonight than practical, shivered in the same raincoat she had carried at the library.

They were driven first to Rachel's billet in a large, opulent-looking house on Dearborn Avenue in the mansion district above the city, and then to an officer's residence on Lawrence Street, where Douglas was staying. It was not quite ten o'clock, but the streets were empty and silent except for MP humvees making slow patrols through the city and the occasional chatter of radios on the open security net. "Three-thirty, Sir?" asked the broad-shouldered Hispanic corporal who dropped him off.

"What do you mean?" asked Richfield in surprise.

"Wake-up time, Sir. We have to be at Chopper Base Alpha at exactly 4:15 tomorrow morning, Sir."

"Good grief," said Douglas. "I'd completely forgotten about that."

"I'll be picking Miss Silverstein up first, sir, if you don't mind."

Douglas was startled. "I didn't know she was going," he said, a bit flustered.

"Yes Sir. Excuse me, Sir, but I think she's been asked to keep an eye on you. Excuse me again, Sir, but I think you're very lucky. Good night, Sir." He grinned a comradely grin and sped off before Richfield could say anything. By then, despite his tiredness, Douglas too was smiling to himself.

❖   ❖   ❖

The grip on his arm was firm, but the hand behind it was moving like a piston. Douglas was so tightly wrapped in the coils of his dream that the powerful tugging at his arm didn't penetrate his sleep. Finally he was yanked into consciousness by Corporal De Soto, true to his word, at 3:30.

"Morning, Captain," the voice said, and Richfield struggled to put the disparate pieces of information together. Morning? Who was captain? Then it slowly came to him as he hauled himself into a sitting position. Of course, he was the captain; Hodges had given him this courtesy rank so that he wouldn't have to identify himself constantly to those around him in Helena. He even had a uniform, complete with a captain's shoulder tabs. He mumbled a thank you and lurched into the bathroom.

Twenty minutes later he was showered, shaved, and feeling surprisingly fresh. It was even colder outside the billet than when Douglas had gone to bed. Great clouds of steam were pouring out of the humvee's muffler. Douglas never wore headgear, but he was grateful for the patrol cap that came with his uniform.

He knew that Rachel would be in the vehicle, and a wonderful sense of happiness came over him as he slid into the seat next to her. He greeted her with a quiet "morning."

She smiled warmly back at him, her eyes once again glittering with a spirit that he was only beginning to know.

He turned to take in the other three passengers, soldiers in full battle gear. Their faces were young, but when they nodded silently to respond to his greeting, their expressions seemed older than their years. War, he thought, the perennial thief of youth.

The humvee thundered off at breakneck speed, and as Richfield struggled to balance himself, he didn't notice the warm mug of coffee that Rachel was offering. "Coffee? Real coffee?" he exclaimed theatrically. "Where d'you get this stuff?"

"Oh, I have a few connections," she said with a laugh.

"I'll bet you do."

The humvee reached the Helicopter Base Alpha in just a few minutes. The army had taken over a high school football field, and about a dozen Blackhawks, Apaches, and Cobras were neatly lined up on three sides of the field. Refueling trucks, tents, antiaircraft artillery, and missile batteries filled much of the space around the fourth side of the rectangle. Despite the early morning hour and the careful blackout, there was a sense of bustle around. A ground crew was fueling, arming, and preparing a Blackhawk at midfield. Two Apaches were also preparing for departure on each side of the Blackhawk. In the Blackhawk's cockpit the two helmeted pilots were going through final pre-takeoff checks in the eerie red glow of night-flying illumination.

As the humvee drove onto the middle of the field to the left of the Blackhawk, two officers were bent over a map inside the portside door of the helicopter, discussing the flight plan with the crew chief. With a slight shock Douglas recognized one as Brigadier General Parsons, the inquisitor of the previous day's round-table hearing. The other man was Asian.

At first Douglas wanted to walk over and greet or somehow signal that he wanted them to start the new day on a different footing. But just in time he remembered that he was, at least nominally, a junior officer, and junior officers weren't supposed to approach general officers without first saluting. Awkwardly, Douglas did so. Without any expression of surprise or amusement, Parsons calmly returned the salute and went on with his conversation. For Douglas it was a relief, and he was glad to be introduced to the Asian, Chinese-born Colonel Tony Chang.

Within minutes Rachel, Parsons, Chang, the three escorting soldiers, and Douglas were strapped into their seats on the Blackhawk and listening to the crew chief explain the emergency procedures required for a forced landing. To his surprise Douglas noticed that the soldiers pointed their M-16s toward the floor rather than the ceiling. Halfway through the flight he realized that a weapon accidentally discharged in flight through the ceiling could do damage to either the rotors or the engine. An accidental shot into the floor, however, was unlikely to cripple the chopper.

With the Apaches flying escort on each side and slightly behind their chopper, the Blackhawk took off from the football field and headed back over the city in a westerly direction. To Richfield, whose outward-facing seat was closest to the left-side sliding door, the helicopter seemed to be following one of the main highways through the city, flying barely more than two hundred feet above the tallest buildings and moving fast. It was a scary experience. The city was almost completely blacked out, and he had no idea how the pilots were navigating across it so low and at such speed. Parsons, sitting in the left-hand, forward-facing seat on Richfield's right, was deep in conversation with Chang. Rachel, despite the noise and excitement, had dozed off next to him and had rested her head on his shoulder. The three soldiers were motionless.

The chopper followed Route 12 around Mount Helena, which loomed above them to the left in the dark, then rose with the road up toward Missoula. In less than five minutes, at MacDonald Pass, they reached the Continental Divide. The Blackhawk then pursued the road down the other side of the slope until it joined up with the railroad tracks of the Burlington Northern line.

At Avon, a tiny railside hamlet fifteen miles or so beyond the pass, the three helicopters broke north along Highway 83 up the Swan Valley. The tree-covered slopes and the broad, clear-cut areas were dusted with a recent snowfall. Salmon, Seeley, Lindbergh, and Holland lakes squinted up at the choppers as they raced along with flashes of night sky reflecting off the water. There were few houses, just the occasional campground and recreational area, all filled with the civilian refugee influx.

"Now listen up; this is General Parsons." His voice crackled clearly into Richfield's headset. Rachel stirred and gave the general a look to let him know that she was listening.

"In twenty minutes we'll reach the rendezvous point to pick up the Chinese. We'll be landing at Chopper Base Yankee on the golf course at Grouse Mountain Lodge in Whitefish. The Chinese came in last night through Vancouver and some backwoods routing across the border.

"They were on foot part of the way to avoid detection, so they'll probably be very tired. We expect that they caught a few hours' sleep. There'll be seven of them, and we'll be splitting our group and theirs for the return flight, using a second Blackhawk already on the ground at Whitefish.

"I don't know who's in the group, except that the delegation leader is Chen Faxian. Colonel Chang informs me that Chen is the eldest son of Chinese Premier Chen Rongguo. This means that the reform faction in the Chinese leadership is totally committed to the success of this mission. But the stakes are high, people. If anything happens to the Chinese while they're here, heads will roll both here and at the very highest level in Beijing. The rest of the group will be an interpreter, a senior state security operative, and at least two bodyguards.

"Miss Silverstein, gentlemen, it's absolutely vital that this operation succeed. We don't have to worry about concealing our weaknesses because they'll figure those out regardless of what we do. Most are obvious enough. What we do have to do as impressively as possible is show them our strengths, which are not always obvious.

"I want every one of you to focus on impressing the Chinese in every way you can. If Chen reports that we're holding more than our own against the PM, China will likely remain neutral or maybe tilt toward us. But if they think we're losers, they'll be very polite, thank us profusely for our hospitality, and go back and ask for a meeting with Zhelenovsky. We have our work cut out for us.

"Captain Richfield, Colonel Chang is well acquainted with the standard formalities of meeting with senior Chinese officials, but there may be some items of recent vintage we need to know about Chinese delegations. You've had experience with them quite recently in New York. What can you tell us?"

"Well, General, it's important to remember that the few Chinese delegations that have come to the People's Movement areas have all at some point run into American Maoists, who are angry with them for deserting the socialist revolution. That makes the Chinese furious. They don't like having to listen to some Maoist gobbledygook from a Brooklyn sociology professor."

"So you're saying to lay off Chinese politics, right?"

"Yes Sir."

"Okay. Here's the rest of the sequence. After we're on the ground, we'll go straight to the lodge. We have a battalion headquarters there and that's where the initial welcoming will take place. Colonel Chang has advised us to arrange the introductory meeting in the Chinese manner, with tea and polite, formal speeches of welcome. This will allow us to control most of the agenda and make them feel a little more at ease. General Hodges has already seen my opening remarks, so there will be close coordination between what I say at the outset and what he says in his discussions with them.

"The entire welcoming session should take half an hour, unless Chen is a little long-winded during his part of the proceedings. The general has asked me to keep this portion of their visit short. It's vital that they spend as much time in and around Helena as possible. They have a window of four days before they're missed in Vancouver. We want them to see as much of our military preparedness as we dare without letting too many people know they're here. We've brought along Constitutionalist uniforms so they won't stand out quite as much. Let's just hope that the PM doesn't choose this week to start any kind of push against us."

It was a jolting idea to Richfield. He'd felt strangely secure since arriving in Montana, perhaps because everyone's motivation and confidence was so high, perhaps because the main body of PM forces seemed too far away to mount anything this deep into Constitutionalist territory. True, APA planes sporadically bombed Helena and its environs, but more as morale builders for the PM itself than as serious military exercises. Even that had stopped once Hodges sent three F-16s in a precision attack on the PM headquarters in Denver. Since then lack of spare parts and fuel shortages had grounded most of the aircraft on both sides. But then Douglas remembered the Russian aircraft parked on the tarmac at Minneapolis-St. Paul and the convoy of APA troops heading west in Minnesota. He wondered what his interrogators—and Hodges himself—were inferring from this information.

"One final thing," Parsons was saying as the Blackhawk and the Apaches began their landing, "remember that we have to work through interpreters. Give the interpreters time to do their jobs before you rush through a conversation. Good luck."

Richfield's ears were popping as the Blackhawk settled down into a small, neatly marked landing area on the fairway of Whitefish Lake Golf Course. While he'd been listening to Parsons, he hadn't noticed how visibility had deteriorated amidst the swirling tiny flakes of snow. It was still dark, and the three helicopters were guided into their locations by heavily wrapped ground crews signaling with light batons. Rachel was fully awake now and looked serious, expectant. Douglas felt a little nauseous.

The crew chief pulled back the Blackhawk's left-side door while the rotors were still turning, and this lent a sense of urgency to their arrival. Everyone quickly tumbled out. Despite his parka Douglas felt whipped by the wind and stung by the small snow particles as the party moved toward three waiting humvees. Whip aerials gyrating wildly in the snowflakes, the small convoy moved off toward the lodge.

The Chinese, rested, breakfasted, and dressed for the chopper ride to Helena, came down the main staircase about ten minutes after Parsons's group arrived. Richfield took off his parka and picked up a cup of coffee and a danish. He was a little surprised that things were moving faster than he was warming up.

Chen entered the room first. He was a slender man of medium height and prematurely graying hair. Douglas had imagined he might be in uniform, but he wore a well-tailored pale gray suit, a white shirt, and a silk tie.

He seemed to be in his late thirties, but his unusually refined features conveyed a sense of his family's belonging to the gentry class for hundreds of years before Communism came to China. Chen's forebears had maintained their position in Chinese society through the generations by training their children to succeed in the examination system. This feat not only provided a talent pool for China's imperial bureaucracy, but it ensured that China's ruling classes were synonymous with education for some two millennia.

Chen had a slow, confident walk. In a distinctly un-Chinese manner, he looked into the face of each person he walked by as he came into the room. Obviously he had gained more from his four years at Cal Tech than a Ph.D. in biogenetics.

Leading him into the room, General Parsons introduced him to two colonels who had come to Whitefish Lake independently of the Blackhawk. Then he introduced Douglas and Rachel. As he stretched his hand out to Rachel, Chen's eyes seemed to twinkle noticeably and a smile twitched at the corners of his otherwise grave-looking mouth.

Directly behind Chen was a smallish, wiry man with almost crewcut gray hair who could have been anywhere in his fifties. He wore a crisply pressed uniform of a two-star general in the People's Liberation Army, complete with gold shoulder tabs and three rows of combat and campaign ribbons. The American officers present were very curious as to which engagements he had seen.

Almost at his elbow was a slim, rather tall, and very pretty Chinese woman in her late twenties or early thirties wearing a gray business suit and ice-blue blouse. She translated Parsons's words of introduction almost as soon as they were spoken.

"This is General Ma Fanmei," she said before Parsons could ask. "I am the delegation interpreter, Li Meiling." The general for whom she was interpreting responded both to her Chinese and to the English words of welcome spoken to him as though the only safe facial expression in this setting was a fixed grin.

"It's a pleasure to meet your delegation," Rachel volunteered to Li. "Welcome to the United States. I hope you are not too tired."

Douglas was a little impressed; that took class and a certain brazenness. Officially, the Chinese no longer recognized the United States, insisting on referring to the entire country, whether controlled by the People's Movement or not, as People's America. Rachel, however, referred to the Constitutionalist-held areas as though there were no civil war at all.

Li may have missed the subtlety, but she responded warmly to the greeting. She smiled broadly and thanked Rachel for the welcome. General Ma, his grin in place, was relentlessly being moved on past Douglas through the small receiving line, always looking at the person in line beyond the one he happened to be shaking hands with.

The rest of the group were more polite and wore slightly serious expressions. Xu Xilian, an infantry colonel, spoke excellent English. Ruo Baotong, a civilian wearing round-rimmed eyeglasses, was introduced as a "ministry official," but Colonel Chang later identified him as a senior intelligence analyst in the Ministry of State Security, China's foreign espionage department. The junior members of the delegation were conspicuously young and tough-looking civilians introduced blandly as "technical support." Including Chen, there were seven in all.

"Welcome to the United States of America," General Parsons said pointedly after the Americans and Chinese had settled down around the rectangular table and tea and coffee had been brought in.

"Thank you," said Chen immediately in English. "It's nice to be back. I visited Montana in 1993 just before I returned to China." He spoke with a strong northern California overlay, emphasizing the r's more than a native speaker, but making it clear he knew the idiom.

Parsons, a little wary, was about to respond when Li, giving him a trace of a smile, rapidly translated the opening dialogue for the

258

benefit of the others in the Chinese group. She was quick and collo-quial in her command of English.

"I know that General Hodges is eager for us to get you to Helena as soon as possible," Parsons said, stopping after each sentence or two for Li to translate. "But he did want me to welcome you on his behalf and to those areas of the United States still governed by the U.S. Constitution.

"Let me give you a brief orientation. General Hodges will offer you a much more detailed political and strategic assessment of our civil war, as well as his views of its relationship to the overall international situation.

"The armed forces that you will be seeing on this visit belong to the Army of Western Montana, the largest of four army groups loyal to the Constitution. The other groups are the Army of Colorado, the Army of the Southwest, and the Army of the Missouri. All four army groups are subordinate to Acting President Verazzano and the National Command Authority on Oahu in Hawaii. General Hodges is the Supreme Commander of U.S. Ground Forces on the American mainland. There are smaller units consisting of reservists, National Guard troops, and civilian volunteer enlistments operating with substantial independence as guerrilla units in parts of Texas, Oklahoma, and the South.

"As you will see from this map, Constitutionalist forces control approximately the westernmost one-third of the American mainland up to a broken coastal strip in the Far West connecting the major Pacific Coast cities. All of these cities are currently in People's Movement hands, but substantial areas of the coast itself are under our control."

There was a burst of Chinese from General Ma, followed by the interpretation in English by Li. "Excuse me for interrupting, General Parsons," she said, "but General Ma wishes to know if this means that you have military access to the Pacific Ocean."

"We have access," said Parsons tersely. But as Li started to translate this, Chen turned irritatedly on Ma, presumably rebuking him for the interruption. Parsons, slightly amused and wanting to help the interpreter out of her embarrassment, gave a subtle half-wink with his left eye. Without changing her expression, Li half-winked back.

"Mr. Chen," said Parsons diplomatically, "this is not the detailed military briefing that you will receive in Helena itself, but only a general orientation for the purposes of your visit. I have no objection if your delegation prefers simply to ask questions of me."

"Thank you, General, but we would prefer to hear your introduction first," Chen replied.

"Very well. So far there hasn't been a major offensive by either side in this war. The People's Movement has only recently put into the field the first of its newly organized combat units, which it calls the American People's Army. They are far inferior to us so far in training, experience, and numbers. But they are building up and they have a much larger population base to draw from. On the other hand, we believe that the people in the areas they control will increasingly turn against them and will overwhelmingly support us when we initiate our major offensive toward the east."

After Li had interpreted this last section, Chen turned to Ma, Colonel Xu, and the civilian Ruo and started a rapid conversation among them. Parsons waited patiently, glancing at Li while she waited for her compatriots to finish.

Chen turned back and said, "Excuse me again, General Parsons, but our delegation believes it must acquire some crucial information before we continue, just in case our visit is inadvertently cut short. May we now ask some questions?"

"Of course," Parsons replied. Li now smiled slyly at him as she continued her translation. Chen switched into Chinese too, which Li translated. "How many Americans are under the control of the People's Movement and how many under the control of the Constitutionalist forces?" he asked bluntly.

"We estimate that, including refugees from other parts of the country, we have approximately ten million civilians in our areas."

General Ma laughed openly at this, as did Colonel Xu. There was some almost derisive shoulder-shrugging between them as they listened to the figures.

But it was Chen who responded. "Forgive a naive question," he asked, once more in English, "but how can you expect to fight and win this war against such overwhelming odds?"

"It is not a naive question, but a very good one," Parsons replied levelly. "First, we could triple the number of civilians within weeks if we encouraged them to come to us. But we don't. We do not have the resources to feed, house, administer, and protect millions more civilians in these largely wilderness areas of the United States. We are confident that, as the People's Movement becomes increasingly authoritarian—and this is already happening—the civilians in the enemy-held areas will turn against them and will openly work to ensure the enemy's defeat.

"Second, it is not our doctrine to control large numbers of civilians. Our objective is to reverse the unconstitutional seizure of power achieved last year by the People's Movement. To do that we need only to defeat the armed forces of the illegal People's Movement regime."

Now it was Ruo's turn to came in. "What makes you so sure," he asked, "that the masses of the people will support your side rather than your opponents? Did they not seize power with broad support in all of the major cities in a mass revolutionary uprising to overthrow your traditional constitution? Did not almost all of the progressive intelligentsia come over to the revolutionary side, along with the broad masses of the national minorities?" The heavy jargon suggested years of propaganda work in China's shadowy security ministries.

"As you well know," Parsons replied patiently, "and I admit with sadness, America's cities were notorious for their poverty, drugs, and high crime rate even before the depression four years ago. The people living in these cities found their circumstances so desperate that they were willing to follow any leadership that offered what they considered the order and the economic equity necessary for survival. The People's Movement certainly offered them this, and we should have focused far more attention on these urban problems than we did.

"You are also correct that what you call the 'progressive elements' did indeed support the People's Movement from the beginning, along with large numbers of African-Americans, especially the youngest generation, who lived in the cities.

"But the fact is neither African-Americans nor any other minorities abandoned the constitutionally designated armed forces of our nation when the civil war began. You will see African-Americans,

Hispanics, and Asians everywhere you go on your tour today and to-morrow. Ask them why they haven't joined the People's Movement. They'll tell you openly. Colonel Chang, would you like to respond to that?"

"Yes Sir," said Chang, caught slightly off balance. "It's very simple, Dr. Chen," he said in Chinese, rising to the theme as Li translated. "There are two ways to solve our social problems. One way is coercion, the other is freedom. For most of world history rul-ers ruled, sometimes well, more often badly, and their subjects obeyed. But more than two hundred years ago this country began an experiment unique in the history of humanity, the entrusting to ordi-nary people of the most important decisions of national life. That is why I chose to remain with the Constitutionalist forces rather than go over to the People's Movement."

"But that does not explain," said Ruo, with the persistence of an experienced interrogator—which he had probably been at one point—"why not just so many of the national minorities, but many others too supported the overthrow of the old regime. Perhaps your 'way of freedom' was no longer working?"

Sensing a debate about to break out, Colonel Chang looked at Parsons inquiringly. He knew time was running out.

"Mr. Ruo," General Parsons said calmly. "You are completely correct in your assumption. The way of freedom was not working under the conditions of economic collapse, military defeat, and the overwhelming social problems, especially in the big cities, that we failed for far too long to pay attention to. Many Americans believed that only a new kind of political power, pushing through radical solu-tions very quickly, could restore justice and equality among our people. Many still believe that, and I think most of them are sincere. But what they will sooner or later discover is that all dictatorships end up worse than the conditions they are set up to cure. It will not be long before most everyone in the People's Movement areas comes to this conclusion."

There was more animated discussion in Chinese, with Colonel Xu apparently disagreeing with Ruo over the direction of the conver-sation. Chen finally ended the deadlock with an imperious wave of his hand. He returned to English.

"General Parsons, let me return to your last remark, which I know my delegation wants to hear more about. Why should most everyone, to use your expression, in the People's Movement areas conclude that an enforced equality and justice is worse than the uncertainties of your freedom?"

"Very simple, Dr. Chen. The People's Movement has had to turn to a foreign power not just to train its armed forces but to fight some of its battles.

"What do you mean?"

"I mean that some Russian units have already begun deploying close to our positions in support of APA operations."

"Can you prove that to us?"

"We have a prisoner."

"One prisoner?" said General Ma, almost rudely. "He could be anyone. He could be an actor. Why should we believe that?"

"You will have to decide for yourselves whether he is genuine. Unfortunately, we do not have the luxury of assuming either that he invented his own role or that someone else set him up for this drama. We have other evidence, but it is of an intelligence nature, and I am not authorized to reveal it to you. Perhaps General Hodges will do that."

"Very well," said Chen, taking over from his senior general and continuing in the same skeptical tone, "let us assume that you are not mistaken and that Russian troops have entered the field against you. Let us suppose that this is an embarrassment to the People's Movement. If that is the case, you still have a lot to worry about. President Zhelenovsky will not hesitate to use his strategic ICBM dominance to rain down nuclear, or at least chemical, devastation upon your positions. He will feel even more justified in doing so because, in effect, the rump of the armed forces of the United States failed to live up to the terms of the Treaty of Paris." He sat back and paused.

But Ma was ready to wade in again. "Let's be very blunt about this, shall we?" said the Chinese general. "If Zhelenovsky chose to finish you off with nuclear weapons, here in America, not even the leaders of the People's Movement, who invited him in, would be able to stop him."

263

Ma was not just impolite but almost bullying. He thought he had succeeded in punching large holes in Parsons's logic and was becoming contemptuous of the Americans because of it. But Rachel now intervened.

"Excuse me, General Parsons," she asked, "may I say something?"

Parsons looked irritated and was about to brush her aside, but Li was smiling at him as she translated the request into Chinese. Parsons had come to enjoy his interplay with Li. He didn't want her to stop smiling at him, which he suspected she might if he turned Rachel down. So he allowed her to speak.

"Very well, Miss Silverstein."

Rachel was nervous and took a deep breath before beginning. "Are the Chinese aware that there are three Ohio-class nuclear submarines armed with Trident missiles that are loyal to the Constitutionalists and are providing a deterrent against the use of nuclear or chemical weapons in our civil war?"

There was a sudden hush around the table. This topic had not been authorized in the opening discussions with the Chinese. Even Li looked at Rachel in amazement.

Now Colonel Xu jumped in, *and* speaking perfect English. "We have heard this talk," he said calmly, "but this is another thing that you claim but cannot prove. Why should we believe you on this any more than your alleged captured Russian soldier?"

"Because we have a photograph for you." It was Parsons, recapturing the initiative now that the discussion had moved in yet another unexpected direction.

"General," said Xu, almost kindly, "are you asking us to believe that, just because you have a photograph of a Trident submarine, three of these warships are actually still free and supporting your side? How can you possibly prove that the photograph is recent?"

"Very simple, Colonel," said Parsons, his cheeks beginning to quiver with the tension of the challenge. "The photograph clearly shows the front page of the *Boston Globe* of November 25. General Hodges asked me to bring along the photograph, just in case your visit was cut short and you had to depart before he could show it to you. Your researchers can confirm the authenticity of that issue of the *Boston Globe*. But we also have a copy of the paper here too. Major Stockwell, please show our guests the two exhibits."

As Li completed the translation of Parson's last comment and Stockwell left his seat to bring in the evidence, there was an explosion of discussion among the four senior Chinese, including Li. Ruo and Colonel Xu seemed to want to dismiss this sudden new evidence out of hand, but both Chen and Ma were more open to seeing it. From what Richfield could tell, Li was siding with the two senior Chinese. Colonel Chang now spoke to Parsons, confident that none of the Chinese would hear him. "General, there's a serious division of opinion among them, and I'm not sure even the photograph and the *Boston Globe* will convince them."

"We'll just have to see, Tony."

Stockwell returned and laid out the *Boston Globe* and six fine-quality, eight-by-ten color prints of the *Massachusetts*, two of them with the front page of the *Globe* clearly displayed against the sail of the submarine by two sailors. As they were looking at them and talking animatedly, Chang and Parsons continued their own conversation. Glancing with a shrug at Douglas, Rachel reached over to look through the newspaper. She opened it to page two.

"Well," she said with an uncustomary cynicism, "if we forged the submarine pictures and this edition of the *Boston Globe,* we at least did a convincing job. We even forged a story about a Chinese delegation visiting Boston."

Douglas, who had wondered what Rachel was up to with the paper, perked up.

"Let me see that story," he said. Taking in the particulars while both sides of the table continued to examine the photographs, Douglas turned to Rachel and said, "I think I worked with this group."

Resenting the distraction, Parsons turned to him and said, "This better be something good, Richfield."

"Sorry, Sir, this is important," Richfield answered brightly, attracting the interest of the Chinese. "I can prove that this newspaper is genuine, and that in turn should authenticate the submarine photograph."

"How?" asked Parsons.

"General, there is a story in this paper about a Chinese delegation visiting Boston. Sir, they came to New York first, and the Protocol Department showed them around. I remember them well. The three senior members of the group were political figures that our visitors will almost certainly know. One was the mayor of Hangzhou, one was the new Chinese deputy governor of Hong Kong, and the third was a former Chinese ambassador who has some kind of senior advisory position now in Beijing, I don't know exactly what."

Chen was listening intently now, but he waited until Li had finished translating before saying anything. "Tell me about the mayor of Hangzhou," he said to Richfield.

"Well, he'd been educated in the U.S., somewhere in California, I think."

"Can you recall anything special about him?" Chen watched Richfield intently, as did everyone else around the table.

"Yes, he was absolutely crazy about American basketball. He wanted to know how the Celtics were doing and how the Lakers were going to fare next season. He was crushed when I told him that the league system had collapsed with the outbreak of the war. He couldn't believe anything would bring pro basketball to a halt in America."

"*Dui le, dui le. Jiu shi ta! Bu keyi bu shi ta! Hao ji le!*" In his excitement Chen had broken out in Chinese, prompting another cascade of discussion from his compatriots. Li, catching the urgency of it all, asked him a couple of questions in Chinese and then went back to English. "Dr. Chen says that's correct," she said. "You see, Dr. Chen was good friends with the mayor when they were both students in California."

Pandemonium broke out and the tension around the table dissipated quickly. Both delegations took on a friendlier tone. Even Ruo's tightly controlled features relaxed into something resembling a smile. Rachel put her hand on Douglas's shoulder and gently squeezed it. Li and Parsons shared a mutual look of relief. The Chinese were again talking among themselves, but this time Chen adopted what seemed like an I-told-you-so expression.

Major Stockwell caught Parsons's eye and pointed to his watch. Richfield noticed and looked at his own. It was after six o'clock.

Through the fogged-up windows the first auguries of dawn had succeeded in nudging away the night sky. The snowing had stopped too.

Douglas's mind began to wander from the meeting. He thought about Basmanov, about how he would surely have some ranting to do about the Chinese, something about the "yellow peril," no doubt. He doubted Parsons, much less Hodges, would let the Chinese anywhere near the Russian in case, by some fluke, Basmanov should escape and report his sightings to his superiors. Then he realized something else, something quite wonderful, despite his early morning daze. Rachel had her hand on his arm.

"Gentlemen, I think if our visitors have any more questions, they may want to save them for our briefings in Helena and their meeting with General Hodges. Dr. Chen, may I suggest that we move out and board the helicopters?"

"Of course, General," said Chen affably. "We have certainly had an interesting beginning. All of us look forward to our remaining meetings."

Everyone rose from the table and left the meeting room for the humvees that would take them to the helicopters on the fairway.

In the morning light Richfield saw the second Blackhawk, apparently armed and fueled, for the new passengers. Prominently displayed on temporary-looking flagpoles, though hardly fluttering in the still morning air, were the Stars and Stripes and the flag of the People's Republic of China.

They boarded the two helicopters, mixing the Chinese delegation in with the Americans. Douglas stayed on his original helicopter with Parsons, Chen, General Ma, and Li, while Tony Chang, Colonel Xu, Ruo, and Rachel were in the other craft. Two of the Chinese security men and two American escort soldiers went in the first chopper, and the others went with the second.

The Blackhawks quickly rose and gathered speed, then turned back over Kalispell Airport and Blaine Lake before nosing off down the Swan Valley once again. They were about half a mile apart, with the Apaches riding shotgun above and in front of the lead Blackhawk.

Talking to each other through the intercom with the aid of Li, Parsons, Chen, and Ma compared notes on mountain and guerrilla warfare. The atmosphere was congenial and casual. Ma, after deciding he had been wrong about both Parsons and the Constitutionalists in general, was jovial and surprisingly open. Resuming his own seat facing the left side of the chopper, Richfield lost interest in the conversation, turned the speaker volume down on his headset, and began to nod off. Despite his three days in a cell, he still needed time to process the extraordinary rush of information, emotions, and impressions he'd been subjected to in the past two weeks. He wondered how Rachel was doing in the other chopper. He tried to imagine what life might be like . . .

"General Parsons, this is the pilot. Echo One, our lead Apache, has spotted incoming targets at ten thousand meters, Sir. I don't think we've been compromised, but they're closing fast with us."

"Can we outrun them?" Parsons asked.

"Negative, Sir, if they see us. I recommend a 180 and descending to ground level in case we can defilade somewhere here in the valley."

"Go ahead, Pilot."

Shocked awake, Douglas turned up his headset to listen to the pilot-to-pilot conversation.

"Echo One, this is Milk Run One, we're changing heading to three-three-zero and descending to fifty AGL [above ground level]. Where are the targets and how many are there?"

"Milk Run One, Echo One. Three bogeys at nine o'clock, eight thousand meters and still closing. Echo Two has gone into cloud cover to try and get a jump on them. We'll maintain present heading as long as possible to draw them off you. Tell Milk Run Two to go high. They're moving too fast to go hunting for him in the clouds."

"Echo One, roger."

The Blackhawk executed a steep bank to the right into a 180-degree turn and descended rapidly toward the valley. The aircraft shuddered and shook with the stress of the turn, and Douglas wondered if it wouldn't fall apart. Chen looked pale. Li looked green and nauseated.

Richfield tried to find the other Blackhawk, but there was no sign of it. His own chopper was moving at close to its maximum speed of two hundred miles per hour, and it was vibrating heavily.

Telegraph poles, trees, and an occasional building flashed by at terrifying speed as the pilot tried to hug the terrain in an effort to pull
the chopper out of danger.

"Echo One, Milk Run One, I'm on three-three-zero at fifty
AGL. Milk Run Two's gone high. Where are the targets?"

"Milk Run One, Echo One. They've spotted me and have broken formation. I'm going low on the same heading."

"Echo One, can you identify the aircraft?" The Blackhawk
pilot's voice was tense now as he hauled his straining craft up the
Swan Valley and tried to stay up to date with the rapidly changing
situation.

"Milk Run One, they're choppers. But not Apaches or Blackhawks
or even Hueys. It's crazy, but they look like—"

He didn't finish the sentence. As everyone in the Blackhawk listened with horror, the intercom crackled with the noise of a sudden
explosion followed by total silence.

"Is he gone, Pilot?" Parsons asked after a few seconds.

"I'm afraid so, General. He must not have seen it coming. Had
to be a missile."

"Pilot, just who are *they?* It's important to know if this is just a
raid or a major offensive. Can Helena give you a read on this?"

"I'll try, General." Through his headset, Richfield heard the pilot contact Chopper Base Alpha in Helena.

"General," the pilot's voice came back more urgently than ever,
"Helena reports an attack in progress on Canyon Ferry Dam and
some outlying parts of the city. They think it's some kind of raid. The
sky's thick with choppers. They've instructed me to get you on the
ground as soon as possible, but I'll have to do a hot offload."

"Very well, Pilot."

"Crew chief, brief the passengers for emergency hot offload."

"Roger, Captain."

The crew chief now turned back to face the passengers.
"Ma'am," he said looking at Li, "will you please translate for your
people?" She nodded, her face no longer green but still very pale.

"When I've opened both doors and given this hand signal"—
he raised both hands high to his head and then swung them down
sharply to his side—"I want everyone out of the chopper by the

nearest door. Don't wait for anyone else to go before you. Just move. It'll be about a three- or four-foot jump to the ground, and the chopper will be moving forward at about five miles per hour. When you hit the ground, go prone or roll to get out of the chopper's way, then run to the nearest available cover, a tree, a bush, anything that can conceal you, as far away from the road as you can get. We'll send another chopper for you as soon as things have cleared up."

The Blackhawk throttled back and reared into a nose-up position, gaining altitude quickly and bleeding off airspeed. It gradually settled down and slowed. The crew chief slid back both doors, signaled, and shouted "Go! Go!" into the intercom.

Everyone scrambled out and landed with varying degrees of adroitness. They somehow went through the motions of a roll on the ground to get away from the chopper. Then they scrambled toward a wooden construction hut about thirty yards from the road amid a snow-sprinkled, muddy clearing.

Douglas paused briefly, panting, to watch the chopper drop its nose down and claw the air to regain airspeed as quickly as possible. Then he sprinted after the others.

The two American escort soldiers assumed point positions. Another soldier carried a backpack radio and was down on one knee adjusting it. He fumbled through his patrol cap for a scrap of paper listing the combat frequencies. "Damn!" he muttered. "Gary, what's the frequency? Is it seventy-five twenty-five or sixty-five twenty-five?"

"Try the first push, then the others if that doesn't work," the other man shouted back. The radio operator, his fingertips peeping out of the fingers of his gloves, spun the dial and pressed. The radio replied with only static and squawks.

Parsons, General Ma, and Li had meanwhile clustered around the radioman while the Chinese security team, prompted by Li, joined the American squad in scanning the valley for any sign of the enemy.

The radioman spun and pushed the dial again, and two voices came up chattering loudly. But they weren't speaking English.

"Where's that coming from?" asked Parsons.

"It sounds like pilot talk, sir," the radioman answered.

"It sounds Russian," Parsons said, a look of astonishment on his face.

"It is," said Li grimly.

13

The Raid

Well, who are they?" Parsons, his gloved hands on his hips, was both angry and puzzled as he stared at the radio.

Li rapidly explained what they had just heard to the rest of her group. General Ma responded with a slew of orders to his men.

"What's he saying?" Parsons demanded, irritated as much at being second guessed by his Chinese counterpart as he was at the precariousness of the group's position.

"He says he wants to hear this conversation."

"Okay, so let him. Lipman, give us maximum volume. General Ma can use the headphones if he wants."

The Chinese general squatted down on his haunches and put the headphones on. He listened for a full minute without saying anything. Finally, he stood up and turned to Parsons, grinning maddeningly but holding out his hand to the general. Still smiling, he rattled off a speech in Chinese and pumped Parsons's hand a second time. Standing almost between them, Li was nodding her head in agreement with the Chinese general.

"General Ma says that he congratulates you for standing up to the Russians. He says he knows for sure now that everything you have told him is true, and everything you will tell him is sure to be true too. He also says he understood the Russian pilots. He spent four years in the Soviet Union in the late 1950s, so his Russian is very good. He says they were the pilots of the three combat helicopters that your Apache pilot saw too late. From the conversation it seems they are supporting a raid in or around Helena, but one

273

that is limited in scope. He thinks they may be part of an infantry extraction group—I think that is the correct translation."

"That certainly makes sense," Parsons said. "The only thing we've got to do now is find Milk Run Two and make sure he knows what's going on and keeps out of the way. Then we can find out when Helena thinks it's safe to get back."

The Chinese were talking among themselves. Li passed on Parson's last comment which General Ma and Chen seemed to be weighing.

"Lipman, Johnson," Parsons said, energized by the crisis, "you better raise Helena on this net in one minute flat or you'll be in the firewood detail until Christmas. When you've done that, raise Milk Run Two and let them know everything we've heard. For all we know, they may know more about what's going on than we do. Captain Richfield, you stay outside and keep your eyes on everything that moves in this valley. If anything comes toward us or looks suspicious at all, inform me immediately. The rest of you people move into the hut."

Though it was fully light now—nearly eight o'clock by Douglas's watch—the low overcast made the sky seem darker than usual. It looked as though it might snow at any point. Peering up the valley toward Kalispell, he spotted a car about a mile and a half away driving fast down the road in their direction. He was about to run past the two Rangers into the hut when Lipman, who was kneeling beside the radio with Johnson, stopped him and handed him a pair of binoculars. Douglas ran back to the corner of the hut and focused the binoculars on the speeding vehicle.

What he saw shook him. There were six heavily armed soldiers crammed into a black Volvo, automatic weapons pointing out of all four windows. Even from three-quarters of a mile away it was obvious that the rifles were Kalashnikovs.

"Quick, get out of sight, the car's heavily armed and jammed with Russians!" Douglas yelled to the Rangers as he sprinted into the hut. "Pardon me, General," he said in a breathless rush, "armed Russians in a Volvo are approaching us fast from the north! They'll be on us, or by us, in less than a minute!"

"How do you know they're Russians?" Parsons said calmly,

"AKs, sir, bristling out of the car windows."

"Good, we could do with some extra guns. I'll have the fire team prepare an ambush. Richfield, run as fast as you can across the road and dive for cover as soon as you're in the trees on the other side. That should distract them and give us the time we need. NOW GO!"

He shouted so loudly that Douglas's nervous system seemed to leap into overdrive. He was more terrified of disobeying Parsons than of the oncoming Volvo. Sprinting as fast as he could, he hurled himself out of the hut, across the clearing and the road, and up a shallow slope into the tree line. He had galloped half the final distance, his heart heaving, when he heard bullets whiz past him, followed by the rattle of semiautomatic rifle fire.

He was a rapidly moving target, and the Volvo was a poor gun platform. When he hurled himself to the ground into the underbrush behind the first fir trees he could reach, something terribly hot slashed across the back of his left forearm.

After rolling over twice, as much out of panic than out of a sense of dodging more bullets, he reached over with his right hand and felt where his arm had been hit. There was no pain at all, but a thin trickle of blood was coming from the hole slashed through the parka by the stray round.

He was aware that the Volvo had stopped and that a few more shots were searching the undergrowth around him. He didn't dare look up, but he heard the sound of car doors and of someone shouting in Russian.

A new level of terror swept over him, much deeper than the wild, instinctive, animal-like fear he'd experienced while sprinting across the road. He was being stalked by people intent on killing him. The terror began to envelop him when the air was suddenly rent with the deafening clatter of automatic weapons from farther away and two brittle, deafening bangs from grenades that landed somewhere between him and the Volvo, although he prayed they were much closer to the car than to him.

There was answering fire from the soldiers who'd gotten out of the car, but for just a few seconds. The Rangers had almost immediately cut down four of the Russians intent on pursuing Richfield. A fifth was wounded and a sixth surrendered.

The shooting stopped. Douglas found himself panting almost hysterically, his face buried in the wet, icy undergrowth and the accompanying mud, his arms covering his head. Someone shouted from the other side of the road, "Captain Richfield. Captain Richfield. Are you okay?"

Douglas wasn't okay at all. He was in a state of near shock; his whole system was overloaded with adrenaline. His fears were turning into resentment and rage. *They'd used him as bait!* What if he'd slipped? Fallen? Had been mowed down by the Kalashnikovs?

True, they'd used him as a diversion, but if he hadn't run across the road, the Americans would have lost the element of surprise and they might all have been killed, including him.

He pulled himself up from the ground just as Lipman came jogging up the shallow slope to look for him. "Oh, thank God," the Ranger exclaimed. "You're okay."

"Yeah," was all Richfield could think to say, wiping the mud from his face and holding his left arm. More blood ran out from his wound, making it look worse than it really was.

"Captain, you've been hit," Lipman said, as though this would be a revelation to Douglas. "Okay, now, take it easy, let me give you a hand."

"It's okay," Richfield said. "I can still walk just fine." No sooner were the words out than a cloud of nausea enveloped him. Black spots seemed to swim slowly in front of him. His knees buckled. And he was flat on his face in the snow in a dead faint.

Douglas was out just a few seconds. He came to as Lipman carried him back to the hut. On the way in he was conscious of passing Li, her face ashen. The American and Chinese soldiers had set about disarming the two prisoners and removing weapons, papers, and other forms of I.D. from the dead and the Volvo.

Li had been assigned the role of front-line medic. After her initial shock at seeing Richfield's arm thoroughly bloodied, she began to nurse him calmly and competently. She helped Richfield out of his parka, cut away the surrounding clothing with a knife, and cleaned and dressed the wound with medication and bandages from a medical pack.

"Where did you learn this?" Douglas asked.

"Oh, school somewhere," she replied with a laugh. But it wasn't convincing. Li looked as though she had not only been trained in first aid but had handled similar wounds before.

General Parsons returned and stood for a moment in the doorway. With his hands on his hips he looked seriously at Richfield for a moment and grinned at Li. When he saw that Douglas was awake, alert, and in no serious pain, he smiled at him too.

"Douglas," he said, using the name for the first time, "I took a big chance that you'd come through for us, and you did, in real style. Your wound has already earned you a Purple Heart. I'm also going to recommend you for a Bronze Star for exceptional bravery in combat. I'm not sure how all this will square with your civilian status, but we'll find a way. You got away by the skin of your teeth, but that's exactly what we needed to draw their attention away from our side of the road long enough to neutralize their advantage in firepower. They fell right into it."

He paused, listening. Approaching very fast, with its ominous and telltale thud-thud-thud, was another helicopter, maybe two. Richfield and Li instinctively ducked, even though they obviously couldn't be seen. Parsons didn't flinch but cocked his head slightly as though listening for something in particular.

When it was clear the choppers had gone, Richfield propped himself up and asked, "General, just what is going on here?"

Parsons narrowed his eyes a little and frowned. "I can't tell you yet, Douglas. We don't know the dimensions of it. We've raised Helena on the net and all they'll say is that parts of the city and suburbs are under attack by a chopper-borne force of less than a brigade."

"Maybe they're after General Hodges," said Richfield.

"What makes you say that?" Parsons asked sharply.

"Because Basmanov was obviously Spetsnaz. He'd never have spoken such good English if he wasn't. Anyway, what was he doing sniffing around western Montana, which is apparently where you picked him up? He asked me a lot of questions about Hodges, which I ignored at first, though I told your interrogators about it. The point is that the one area where the PM would be absolutely out of their league in military skills is special operations. It would be natural for them to ask for Spetsnaz help in mounting the kind of operation the Russians are known for."

"Excuse me," Li interrupted, "but what is Spetsnaz? I do not know this term."

"Spetsnaz are Russian elite special operations forces designed to penetrate enemy lines and engage in vital sabotage or assassination activities," Parsons answered.

"If they are Spetsnaz," he went on, resuming his line of thought with Richfield, "and if infiltration into Helena was their objective, they may have Constitutionalist uniforms with them. Also, it's possible the two prisoners speak some English."

Coming up behind Parsons, Chen said, "They do have Constitutionalist uniforms, General. And high-level identification cards. One of your soldiers found them in the trunk. And the wounded one speaks English rather well."

"Have you talked to him, Dr. Chen?" Parsons asked.

"No, General, but as we were moving him off the roadway he was obviously in great pain. He swore in English and asked us to be careful as we moved him."

"Thank you, Dr. Chen, that's very helpful." And he left the hut for the cluster of soldiers guarding the prisoners.

Chen turned to Richfield and said, "I also want to congratulate you. You probably saved all of our lives."

"Thank you, Sir," Douglas said.

Outside, one of the captured Russians, wearing a camouflage uniform of the Airborne Assault Force, was sitting in the mud with his back against the hut, his hands and feet bound, and Johnson guarding him warily. He hadn't said a word since surrendering. The Volvo, miraculously, was still drivable, despite the fusillade of automatic fire that had hit it. Lipman had moved it off the road with the wounded prisoner in the back seat. When Parsons came up, the man was groaning, and Lipman was trying to make him more comfortable.

"He's an American, Sir," he said. "APA. He says his name is Ron Thompson."

"Thank you, Lipman. I'll speak to him now. Ask our guests to remain inside the hut for security reasons until we make a definite move out of here."

General Ma, who was genuinely fascinated by everything that was happening, finally responded to Lipman's polite tap on his arm and followed him back to the hut.

"How're you feeling, son?" Parsons asked the wounded prisoner.

"Not good. My shoulder hurts real bad, and I can't feel my right thigh at all."

Parsons frowned and looked at the ugly, gaping wounds. "We'll ensure you receive good medical treatment just as soon as we can get out of here. Now give me your name and rank."

The wounded man was a tall, gangly youth with red curly hair. He seemed barely out of his teens. His expression was a combination of fear, dislike, and uncertainty. Parsons seemed to know exactly how to speak to him.

"I don't have to tell you anything," the prisoner replied, breathing heavily and in pain from the wounds.

"No, you don't, young fella, and that leaves us the option of merely guessing whether you're an American dressed in a Russian uniform, which makes you a prisoner of war and protected by the Geneva Convention of 1949, or a Russian posing as an American, in which case we'll be forced to treat you as a spy. The penalty for espionage in wartime is death by firing squad. When we're not sure, and if the prisoner doesn't cooperate, we sometimes flip a coin to determine which category he falls in. Think about it." And he started to walk away.

"Ron Thompson, sergeant, First Division, American People's Army," the prisoner recited breathily and as loud as he could to catch Parsons before the general was out of earshot.

Parsons stopped and sauntered back. "Let's see some I.D. And don't stop talking," he said dryly.

"My APA I.D. is in the glove compartment of the car," said Thompson." We were going to get Constitutionalist I.D. before reaching Helena."

"You're lucky we intercepted you first," Parsons said bluntly. "If you'd been caught with that, the Law of Land Warfare would have had you catching bullets within twenty-four hours. Now who are these other guys and what's your mission?"

Thompson stopped, bit his lip, and breathed heavily again. "How soon can you get me medical help, General? I'm getting weaker all the time."

"Soon young man, but even sooner if you tell us what your mission is and where the rest of your forces are. I'm not about to call a chopper in here if it's going to be shot down by your buddies—whether they're Russian or American."

The prisoner closed his eyes and grimaced again. He seemed to be trying to gather his strength to talk.

"Our mission was to find General Hodges and bring him out, alive, if possible. We've got two battalions of the APA's First Division, the Lincoln Steffens Brigade, and a company of Russian Spetsnaz working as advisers and infiltration specialists."

"Where's your exfiltration point?" Parsons asked fiercely.

"Lake Helena," Thompson said, gasping now.

"Lake Helena? How can you get a chopper in there?"

"Not choppers . . . flying boat . . . Russian." He was having trouble getting out more than a phrase at a time now, panting with every word. But Parsons was relentless.

"How many choppers?"

"Sixty."

"Where?"

"Please, please . . . get me some painkillers . . . hurts so bad . . ."

Parsons ignored his request and kept boring in.

"Where are the choppers?"

"Canyon Ferry Dam . . . Deer Lodge . . . Canyon Creek . . . Ranch . . . Lake Helena."

"Anywhere else?"

Thompson closed his eyes now and seemed to have passed out. But Parsons wouldn't let him go. "Answer me," he shouted at Thompson, bringing his face close to the prisoner's. "I asked is there anywhere else?"

"No, no . . . please get me help . . . hurts so bad . . . please." Thompson's voice faded off into a whimper. But Parsons wouldn't relent. "Okay, we'll get you help," he said, speaking slowly and deliberately as though to someone who understood English poorly, "but there's one thing I need to know. How many groups like yours are operating in this valley?"

"One . . . just one . . . behind us." And then he fell into unconsciousness.

"Good boy," Parsons said, more to himself now as he removed his head from the car. "You just got yourself a medevac chopper and honorable captivity. Lipman!" he shouted to the Ranger who had reemerged from the hut, "get those bodies off the road and out of sight. Then drive this car as far away from the road as you can, without getting it stuck if possible. Johnson, come here and write down these details and get them on the net to Helena right away: Ranch, Canyon Ferry Dam, Deer Lodge, Canyon Creek, chopper set downs—flying boat exfiltration from Lake Helena—sixty choppers and two battalions—plus Spetsnaz advisers. Tell 'em we intercepted a vehicle that six Spetsnaz had commandeered and we have this information from a prisoner. The prisoner says there's another group at large in the valley and Helena ought to know about that. And find out what's going on in Helena itself."

"Yes Sir." Fumbling inside the cargo pocket of his pants as he kept an eye on the bound prisoner in front of him, Johnson came up with paper and pencil and hastily scribbled the information down. Then he dialed in the frequency for Helena.

Back in the hut, Ma, Chen, and Li were all subdued. The excitement of the ambush had given way to some sober reflections. They were very vulnerable. Richfield's arm was stinging badly, and it was all he could do to keep from groaning. "It's a raid on Helena," said Parsons without ceremony as he strode in. "There's another enemy combat team somewhere in the valley behind this one and we can't take the risk of pulling off another ambush. We'll hole up in the tree line, keep in touch with Helena, and wait for a chopper to come and get us. We'll have to move fast. The bad guys could be around here any moment."

"What are you going to do with the two prisoners, General?" It was Ma, not missing a detail.

"Lipman will stay in the car with one, and we'll take the other one with us."

"But that will be dangerous. He could escape. He could give our position away if other Russians are in the area. Why don't you just shoot them both?"

Parsons looked at him for a moment, biting back a harsh retort about "civilized values" that sprang into his mind. But instead, he said, "The U.S. Army, General Ma, doesn't shoot prisoners. Captain Richfield, can you walk with us?"

"Yes, General," Douglas said weakly.

"Good, then let's go."

With Parsons leading the way and looking in all directions for the other Spetsnaz team, they left the hut in a group and quickly walked to the tree line. Lipman, listening on his headset to Helena, nodded at Parsons as the general indicated for him to follow with the walking prisoner as soon as he could.

It was bitterly cold under the trees, and the snow was much thicker here than around Helena. They managed to find some protection from the wind behind a six-foot-high log pile. The location wasn't visible from the road and offered some protection if the situation turned into a shootout. Lipman joined them after twenty minutes. He had bound the prisoner's hands behind his back with plastic handcuffs and had cunningly hobbled the man's feet with some rope he'd found in the hut. The man could walk in short steps, but he couldn't run.

It seemed to be the last straw for the Russian—or American, if that was what he was. He was boiling with rage. As he trotted in an undignified mincing gait, prodded firmly by Lipman, he glared at Parsons. General Ma laughed as Chinese often do when they are embarrassed. This was too much for the hobbled Spetsnaz soldier.

"You bastards!" he yelled out in English. "You think you can hold up history out here in the mountains! Well this is just the first of some nasty surprises People's America has in store for you. All of America hates you for what you are doing, dragging the country into a civil war. You're war criminals, do you hear!"

There was a shocked silence from everyone. Parsons, however, looked at the flailing prisoner coldly. "You're not worthy of the title soldier, behaving like that," he said in a voice ringing with contempt and eying him relentlessly. "Walk properly, in silence, as a dignified prisoner, or we'll tie your feet and drag you through the snow."

The prisoner stopped his shouting and lowered his eyes. He was still furious, but he was subdued.

The wind was getting up, blowing flurries of snow off the trees and pulling the wind-chill factor down below zero. They'd found some extra clothing and two sleeping bags in the car's trunk. The wounded prisoner was wrapped up in one of the sleeping bags and the other was given to Li, who was weakening as the temperatures dipped.

For the next half-hour, Lipman dialed in several different frequencies to monitor the fighting as it developed. They learned that Milk Run Two had made it safely back to Whitefish Lake with its passengers and was waiting for things to quiet down in Helena before coming back down the valley. They also let Helena know their position, using a hand-held satellite navigator. A few minutes later two more helicopters roared overhead followed by the sounds of strafing. "Sounds like Apaches, Lipman," said Parsons. "See if you can raise them."

"Echo leader," Lipman said, "Milk Run One on the ground, do you read me? Over."

"Milk Run One, Echo Three, affirmative. Just picked off some bandits in a pickup a mile north of your position. Hope that's the last of the Spetsnaz in your neck of the woods."

Parsons took the microphone. "Echo Three, this is Phoenix Six at Milk Run One. What's the status of fighting in Helena?"

"Milk Run One, General. Sir, we've stopped 'em short of Last Chance Gulch, but there's a bunch of 'em still holed up in Carroll College. It'll take a while yet to flush them out, but we ought to be able to get a Blackhawk to you soon. Over."

"Echo Three, Milk Run One, Phoenix Six again. We've got a badly wounded prisoner who needs evacuating fast. Can you get one in before the Blackhawk? Over."

"Milk Run One, Echo Three. Negative, sir, but I'll make sure the Blackhawk hightails it and brings a medic and a litter."

"Echo Three, Milk Run One. Thank you. Roger and g'day."

The Blackhawk arrived twelve minutes later. As it descended

into the muddy construction area, the chopper's downdraft threw up a blizzard of snow from the nearby drifts and trees. A medic jumped out and helped Lipman and Johnson bring the wounded prisoner aboard. After loading the healthy APA captive, bound hand and foot, and securing him in a seat to the rear of the chopper, Parsons helped Li, frozen and exhausted, into the chopper. Chen, Ma, Richfield, the two Rangers, and the crew chief finally climbed up, and the Blackhawk rose and nosed down for the flight back to Helena. After setting the two prisoners down at a field hospital in the mansion district, the Blackhawk returned to Chopper Base Alpha.

Hodges was at the base to greet Chen, his laugh lines wrinkled up in anticipation of the visit. "Welcome to Helena," he said, stretching out his hand to Chen as the Chinese wearily climbed down from the Blackhawk. "I see that you had some excitement on the way here, but I'm delighted that nothing untoward happened. You must be tired, frozen, and hungry. We've selected a large, fine house in a nice part of town as your quarters during your stay. Unless you want to do something else, I'll see that you're taken there right away. When the second Blackhawk arrives in a few minutes, the rest of your party will join you too. As agreed, we'll meet at eighteen hundred hours for our initial discussions, then adjourn for dinner at twenty hundred hours. Is there anything special that you need?"

"Thank you for coming to welcome us, General," said Chen in Chinese, with Li interpreting. "We consider that a great honor. There is only one important thing that I must ask to do. Because my government may have heard from a variety of sources about today's fighting, it is imperative that I communicate with them immediately."

"Certainly, Dr. Chen. I can arrange for that before you leave the base. You should know that we have already told them you're safe and that we will be fully responsible for your security during the remainder of your visit."

General Ma came forward, his grin in place, and pumped Hodges's hand warmly. He spoke to Hodges in rapid Chinese, looking up at the much taller American. Hodges smiled, somewhat embarrassed, his thin gray hair ruffled by the wind. "General Ma says that he has read a great deal about you and is very honored to meet such a distinguished soldier," Li explained. "He says that, as a military man, he admires the way your General Parsons and Captain Richfield performed this morning. He thinks they should be rewarded for their competence and bravery."

Hodges smiled wryly at this. "Please tell him thank you for his warm compliments," he replied. "Brigadier General Parsons is a little new in his rank for promotion, and Captain Richfield has only been an officer for a day, so perhaps we'll delay his elevation just a while too. Maybe to honor their performance, I'll have them learn Chinese."

At this Ma laughed and clapped his hands together at the joke. Parsons surreptitiously rolled his eyes at Li, who had suppressed her own laughter. Douglas was too tired to appreciate the joke and his arm was beginning to throb. Hodges sought him out after seeing the Chinese off in their humvees and speaking briefly with Parsons. The general placed both hands on Richfield's shoulders and said. "You've done exceptionally well," more like a father would speak to his son than a general to a suspected enemy agent. "I know that you still haven't sorted everything out. That's understandable after what you've been through. But later you'll look back on today as one of the finest in your life." With that he patted Douglas lightly with both hands and walked back to his own humvee. Douglas had to fight hard to stop the tears running down his face.

Night came on quickly and the temperature dropped still further as the low overcast gave way to a brilliantly moonlit night. Douglas's wound was examined and redressed at Helena's main civilian hospital. He'd wanted to see Rachel, but he was too exhausted and his arm throbbed so much that he could only think of returning to his billet. He stretched out as soon as he got to his bed and fell into a deep sleep. That's where Rachel found him a few hours later when she came round to visit him.

"How're you feeling?" she said softly, wiping the perspiration from his forehead.

It was such a contrast with the way he'd been awakened earlier that day that he wasn't sure where he was.

"I understand from certain sources," she said teasingly, "that an Oriental Florence Nightingale was tending your wound this morning. We won't allow *that* to happen again. Next time you save half the general staff of China and the United States from annihilation, let me know in advance, will you? *I'd* like to be there." Her flirting made Douglas laugh. He wanted to say something, to do something, to let her know what she had come to mean to him. But Rachel placed a finger across his lips to keep him from speaking.

She looked at him for several seconds and bit her lower lip. "I've watched you. I've seen you under a lot of pressure, Doug. I've come not just to like you but to feel something a whole lot stronger. But there's something you have to understand. When we get back to New York, we won't be able to see each other at all. Zilch. Nada. There's a whole lot I'd like to say and do, but I have to leave it like that."

Douglas felt dead. A thousand protests wanted to be heard. She couldn't just shut the door like this. She was feeling the same thing he felt. If it was political, they could go to Canada, anywhere. It didn't have to be like this because of a sense of duty or a job left undone. They could go anywhere. Even help Hodges from outside. "So this is good-bye?" he half-asked.

"No," she said. "The Constitutionalists are going to win the war. And when they do that we can . . . date . . . or something."

Douglas looked at her lingeringly, trying to photograph her mentally. "I wish I had your faith," he said. "I've no doubt whose side I'll be working for when I get back to Manhattan, but the odds look pretty long to me against the war ending any time soon."

Suddenly Rachel had tears in her eyes. "Douglas, kiss me. Now. Right now."

Richfield stood and held her. His hands caressed her, pulling her to him and kissing her with every ounce of energy in his body. She opened herself to his embrace. They paused for a moment and then kissed each other hungrily again. Douglas wanted to say something, but she gently put her hand over his mouth and turned and left.

That night, Parsons, who arranged the seating for the dinner, ensured that Rachel and Douglas sat next to each other. Apart from

Hodges and his wife Helen, the Chinese delegation, and Tony Chang, the guests included several senior staff officers, a professor of Chinese literature, and the governor of Montana and his wife. Parsons had naturally arranged to be close enough to Li for the two of them to banter from time to time and to exchange glances in what was becoming an increasingly conspicuous flirtation. The rest of the seating was made up of other senior commanders and two senior officers from the Army of the Southwest, Stokes (again), and a handful of civilians from different walks of life who had either been to China or had some contact with the Chinese.

Parsons had wanted the dinner to take place in the Capitol, but Hodges vetoed the idea on the grounds that it would be impossible to prevent news of the occasion from leaking out. In a private residence security would be simpler to maintain.

Colonel Chang had suggested that the speeches take place at the beginning of the meal, rather than at the end, in the Chinese manner. After that, he said, the discussions could get down to business. Hodges had disagreed. He argued that the predinner discussions had been long, detailed, and tiring. The last thing the Chinese would want to do, whatever their cultural traditions, was to proceed immediately to yet another session of formal discourse. "Let's feed them as well as we can," said Hodges. "Give them some wine, if we can find any, and allow the natural conviviality of the occasion to set the tone of the evening. The Chinese are good givers as well as good receivers of hospitality," he added. "I don't think they will object if we order our formal toasts in the American manner." Of course, his arguments prevailed.

It was a wise choice. Hodges looked tired and spoke little either to Chen or anyone else for the first part of the meal. The direct threat to his own life and liberty posed by the morning's Russian-American raid seemed to have wounded him. It represented a transgression against the unwritten code that neither side aimed from the outset to decapitate the other's leadership. As the excellent dishes came by—Senate bean soup, beef Wellington, and a very traditional pumpkin pie—washed down by some excellent Washington State merlot, the general apparently recovered his energy a little. He began to joke with Chen and filled him and General Ma in on the final hours of the raid, when the last elements of the attack force finally surrendered. "I talked with some of the prisoners," Hodges said, "and most of them were okay kids, fine soldiers I'd happily have under my own command. A few of them were heavily politicized, however, and spitting hatred and anger toward us. It's a wicked thing, ideology, when it's deployed in the service of total war."

Ma nodded his head eagerly, his grin once again absent. "I know what you mean," he said, with Li interpreting. "During the Cultural Revolution in the 1960s I was subjected to the same kind of hatred at the hands of a Red Guards assault upon our regimental headquarters. Under instructions from Defense Minister Lin Biao, who was himself acting for Chairman Mao, we were forbidden to offer any resistance to these terrible teenagers. I still have scars from that experience."

Chen nodded, though he evidently wasn't altogether pleased at Ma's analogy between China's Red Guards and the newly formed elite units of the American People's Army.

Finally, when a mood of mellowness had descended upon the guests, Hodges went to the small dais set up behind his seat. "I will be very brief," he said, "because we have a lot of work to do tomorrow, and we have already had extensive and detailed discussions on what each side considers a desirable relationship between the government of China and the Constitutionalist side in our civil conflict. Also, of course, representatives of the Chinese government have had meetings in Hawaii with Acting President Verazzano.

"Dr. Chen, you and your delegation will obviously draw your own conclusions about our ability and will to fight this war to a successful conclusion. I won't presume upon your good manners by trying to persuade you additionally. But what I do want to persuade you of, if I may, is how different your country and your civilization is from that of the nations who are trying to draw you into a new imperialistic axis with them.

"Let us start with Russia, the most powerful of them. I have always admired the Russians, Russian culture, Russian talents. During World War II they demonstrated an almost superhuman courage against a powerful and unspeakably cruel enemy. But despite some very promising interludes, most recently the Yeltsin years, Russia for most of the past three hundred years has been tormented by an inability to recognize her natural destiny. She has been unsure whether she belonged to the East or the West. She has not known whether she wanted to be a partner with the rest of the world or a sort of moral and political teacher. As you know, we in the West missed our opportunity after the Cold War to provide the same moral and material boost to a defeated nation that we gave to the defeated opponents of World War II. Today we are paying for that failure in the form of a virulently anti-Western and indeed paranoid national leadership and ideology.

"Toward China in particular, Russia has demonstrated at different times the worst instincts of racism and paranoid hostility. Ordinary Russians are wonderful, dignified people, yet Russia as a whole is a politically immature state whose only experience of continuity from one leader to another has been under the heel of a totalitarian ideology. First it was Communism; now it is fascism. Until Russia establishes lasting institutions of political democracy, it will always be a potential danger to its neighbors and of unreliable value to its friends. I say this to you frankly: If you ally yourself with Russia because of the prospect of sharing in the booty of a new world conquest, your loss will be the greatest of all. Russia will eventually turn on you. At that point she will see in the conflict a war for her own survival as a nation, and she will inflict upon your people hostilities of such savagery that all the gains of your old alliance with her will be reversed by the disaster of your newfound enmity with her.

"Then there is Japan. I need to say much less about this country, with whom your own people have had such sad and bitter experiences in the wars of this century. I do not disrespect the Japanese. Citizen for citizen, they are one of the most talented and intelligent nations on earth. But if Russia is now wooing Japan, arguing that a Russian-Japanese alliance provides a natural balance of interests between a large, resource-rich state and a small, technology-rich state, where does that leave your nation? We have a saying: 'Two's company, three's a crowd.' What it means is that there is no room for three major nations in a joint plan for global hegemony.

"Russia needs Japan for its technology and its capital, and it needs you for manpower. You would fit in with its grand plans for a season. But you would never be a partner, and you would eventually find your national destiny subordinated to the strategies of Moscow.

"Do you want this? Is this China's destiny? I think not. Consider your history, your culture, your own entry into the world family of great powers. Is it worthy of the world's oldest continuous culture, of one of the greatest treasure troves of culture and civilization of the human race, to compete with Japan to play second fiddle to Russian fascism? You must already know the answer.

"My final observation goes beyond strategy and to what I may call philosophy, if you'll forgive my use of this term. You in China have a profound respect for history and what, if we can ever find this out, it teaches us. You have had a sense that it is impossible to design a wise course for the future if you do not have a truthful picture of the past. Your classical literature practically starts with history.

"Now consider our history: a small republic of prosperous farmers that 222 years ago embarked upon the most extraordinary success story of political growth and stability in human history, but which fell victim to its very prosperity and success, and which split up, eventually, into two camps in a second civil war.

"We Constitutionalists do not say that everyone in the People's Movement is bad, or that they are not sincere Americans. We do not wish them ill; they are our own flesh and blood. But what we do say is that they are wrong, profoundly wrong, in how they are trying to reconstruct America. We say flatly that their vision of American life is simply not founded on truth. If science consists in basing a conclusion on overwhelming evidence, we also say that their vision is not scientific. That does not mean that all of their policies are uniformly bad, or that they do not have some excellent men and women who are committed to their cause. But it does mean that they are trying to build a new structure of national life, their 'New Era,' as they call it, on foundations that are not humanly or philosophically sound, and that therefore they will ultimately collapse.

"They believe the economic inequities in our national life can be eliminated through a rapid and enforced collectivism, and that wrong social attitudes can be made right through noisy and ubiquitous propaganda. They are convinced that there are 'correct' and 'incorrect' ideas about the good of society, but the term they use for 'good' is 'progressive.' They have persuaded many people that because so many things were wrong in the old days, any change is 'progressive.' To speed up this 'progress,' they have assembled greater political power in their hands than any group has ever had in our land. Eventually, they will realize that they have made some serious mistakes, but when they do they will not permit themselves to be held accountable and they will be too powerful to be dislodged.

"That is why we are fighting them now, even when the odds against us seem very great. It is not that we disagree with all that they are doing. They have made some great improvements in some problem areas of our national life, especially in the cities. We are fighting them because, however slow and cumbersome our political system was under the old Constitution, it was a more humane, safer, and far more stable system than the priestlike political hierarchy that now governs most of this nation's citizens. We do not idolize the Constitution, much less worship it. After all it contains within itself the mechanism for its own modification. But we do not believe, as a way of governing free citizens, that anyone has ever devised anything better, or in the foreseeable future is likely to. In simple terms we say that there is no ill so terrible in American society that it warrants the suspension of society's protection against bad government. And that protection is our Constitution.

"You yourselves are experiencing a time of deep political change after the death of your great economic reformer, Chairman Deng Xiaoping. I will certainly not advise you on how to proceed in this domain. In politics there are very few absolute rights or wrongs that ordinary people will agree upon, except, perhaps, that freedom is both the first and the last axiom of civilized political life. Most people, sooner or later, having tried everything else, will reinvent the wheel of political democracy if they are permitted to. If I haven't misjudged your country, I believe you yourselves are now doing some political reinventing. You also have moved away from a dogmatic ideology of history with its supposed ironclad laws to a more flexible and, we believe, far more humane understanding of politics. I believe you are approaching conclusions similar to the ones we long ago came to: There are absolutely no certainties in politics, and there is no theory yet in existence so wise and profound that it explains all

291

that is wrong, as well as whatever is right, with the world. You are definitely moving away from conspiracy theories of history.

"But that is not true of Russia, which never fully grasped democracy, or of Japan, which had democracy imposed on it from outside and later abandoned it, nor of People's America, which, like a spoiled adolescent, is determined to adopt any system other than the one that it grew up with.

"So I say to you, Dr. Chen, coming from a country that I hold in the highest respect, admiration, and affection, consider not just the wise choice. Consider truth itself."

Hodges stopped, and picked up his wine glass. "I would like to propose a toast," he said, "to China, to your delegation, to the future of American-Chinese relations, and to the survival of truth and honor in both our countries."

There was an explosion of applause from both the Chinese and the Americans as Hodges, observing a Chinese tradition of hospitality, went around the table with his glass, raising it first to Dr. Chen and then to all of the Chinese seated there.

When he had returned to his seat, he stretched out his long left arm and invited Chen to the dais.

The Chinese leader left nothing to chance and had with him a two-page text, which he read with pauses for Li to interpret without lifting his eyes from the page. Compared to Hodges's rhetoric, it was a flat, workmanlike, diplomatic speech that hedged all of its bets on which side China would support in the American civil war. It was a boilerplate that could have been concocted by any foreign ministry bureaucrat trying to present his country's overall policy.

It was also very short, less than a third the length of Hodges's, and had obviously been written in Beijing before Chen's delegation had left China. As Chen droned on, his delegation sat through it impassively. The Americans fidgeted and tried to conceal their disappointment, except for Hodges, who wore an expression of calm pleasure and appreciation on his face.

"Is he acting?" Douglas whispered to Rachel at one point.

"Yes," she replied.

Just when Douglas had decided that the evening had started well but had ended as a disaster, Chen came to the end of the text, picked up his glass, and for the first time looked like the man he had seen close up since early morning. "My government," he said in English now with a broad smile, as Li translated back into Chinese, "has authorized me to make some small comment of personal greeting to you in addition to the words that I have already read. My greeting is this: A salute to brave Americans, a salute to the cause of justice, and a salute to tellers of truth! A toast to your good health."

As everyone scraped their chairs back once more from the table, Douglas whispered in frustration to Rachel, "That's like the old Delphic oracle, 'You the enemy will destroy.' It could mean absolutely anything."

"No it couldn't, my dear," said Rachel, not looking at Douglas and smiling at Chen as she raised her glass along with everyone else. "It means that he's going to go back and recommend to China's leadership either that they stay neutral or that they support us surreptitiously."

"What makes you so sure of that?"

"Because 'brave Americans' and 'the cause of justice' are phrases the PM could happily live with. 'Tellers of truth' is not. That was his signal."

14

The Broadcast

Douglas didn't know what had taken place during the talks between Hodges and Chen's delegation. He inferred from Chen's "personal greeting," as interpreted by Rachel, that the Chinese now accepted the Constitutionalist assertion that at least one Ohio-class submarine was still free. Hodges was not naive; he would not gratuitously show the Chinese too much of the Constitutionalist military position. But he also knew that the Chinese would be more sympathetic to the Constitutionalists if they felt that nothing of major significance about the Constitutionalist position—good or bad—was being kept back from them.

Richfield had desperately wanted to see Rachel one more time before he left Montana, but it proved impossible. She was deep in conversation with Helen Hodges, and the general's wife obviously didn't want to be interrupted. He waved to her as he left, and she waved back. It wasn't a kiss, but it was a consolation, at least.

There'd been quite a discussion about his return trip. It was out of the question for him to return by small plane to North Dakota. The buildup of APA forces had made extraction and infiltration difficult, particularly in and around major highways. Instead, he would be flown down the Rockies aboard a liaison flight between Helena and Albuquerque, headquarters of the Army of the Southwest. From there they would drive him into Texas and get him aboard a train to Kansas City. Once there he would be given a fake I.D. for a flight to Chicago and then back to La Guardia.

It was a long and unpleasant trip. After the excitement of Montana and the heady experience of meeting Lucius Hodges, Douglas found his brief stay with the Army of the Southwest a disappointing, disillusioning experience. Discipline was much looser. The best troops had gone with Hodges, and many units in the Southwest were cobbled together from reservists, National Guard elements, and newly trained civilians. He had to spend a week with a transportation company whose commander, a captain, resented his presence and wasn't impressed with where he'd been, what he knew, or whom he knew. Douglas did manage to make friends with a lieutenant who confided much that was shocking to him. There had been at least one atrocity committed by the Army of the Southwest against captured APA prisoners. Several—the lieutenant wasn't sure exactly how many—had been killed. It was the lieutenant's view that the commander of the army here, Major General Harold Lake, had been more concerned about keeping the details from reaching Hodges in Montana or Verazzano in Hawaii than in investigating the incident and punishing the perpetrators.

The lieutenant was detailed to drive Richfield from Albuquerque into Texas. At Amarillo, one of the most easterly of the Constitutionalist-held cities in Texas, the young officer arranged for Douglas to receive a fake civilian I.D. and air tickets from Kansas City to Chicago and beyond. They shook hands warmly as Douglas waited for the train to leave, and the lieutenant got back into his humvee for the return trip to Albuquerque.

The three days it took him to return to Manhattan were almost surrealistic for Richfield. There was the discomfort and the occasional danger of the train, which seemed to move in and out of areas held respectively by the Constitutionalists or the PM. As they moved farther east, evidence of Constitutionalist control became rarer and rarer. There were also fewer APA troops and more People's Militia, heavily armed, aggressive-looking, and apparently prepared for conventional infantry combat.

Sometimes when the train was at a station, the militia would come into the cars and intimidate the passengers with I.D. checks or even searches of luggage until the next station was reached. Kansas City, both in Missouri and Kansas, was practically an armed PM camp. It was one of the westernmost PM strong points and was heavily defended because the Constitutionalists' Army of the Missouri, originally formed at Fort Leavenworth, Kansas, was operating out of the Ozarks with increasing aggressiveness. From the train there was palpable evidence of recent fighting, with shell-damaged silos and potholed roads. Occasionally there was the chilling sight of a burned out farm. "Who did that?" Douglas rashly asked the strangers sitting near him in the Pullman car. No one replied, but several in the group watched each other expressionlessly.

Richfield felt he was not only crossing the country, but crossing between two radically different cultures and societies. The Constitutionalists stressed freedom and had gone, literally, to the hills to preserve it. Yet they didn't have to cope with the impoverished and desperate cities of America, which the PM, whatever its many faults, had at least worked to try to clean up. Of course there was much less crime and total destitution in the big cities of America than there had been before the civil war began. But there was much more control too. Which was better? A rough egalitarianism with low crime but dreary living standards and culture, or an exciting and flexible society in which the enthronement of individual freedom sometimes made life itself more dangerous? As in all civil wars the choice of sides was often far more narrowly balanced than it first appeared.

Then Douglas thought of Rachel and the incredible risks she took by acting both as a Constitutionalist agent and as an activist pushing to enable more Jews to emigrate to Israel. He thought of Ponomarev, certainly not as an American nor in any way an advocate of PM philosophy, but as a man in whom guile and manipulation had become daily actions. Did Ponomarev's open cooperation with the PM in some way ennoble the Russian because of the ideals that side professed? Or did Ponomarev's involvement cheapen those ideals by implying, despite the lofty PM rhetoric, a commonality of cynicism and dishonesty?

As he boarded the flight from Chicago to La Guardia, Douglas found it helpful to confront these paradoxes head on. With Rachel out of sight and reach, perhaps forever, philosophy was about the only consolation available.

❖ ❖ ❖

Back in Manhattan, at about the time Richfield was finding his seat aboard Boeing 757 in Chicago, Alexei Ilyich Ponomarev had no interest whatever in philosophy. He was, in fact, venting his fury with the world on the thirty-fourth floor of the RCA Building in an inner office within the Educational Programs Administration.

"Those idiots!" he fumed, holding in his hand a cable from Moscow. "I've been in America barely three weeks, and they expect me to have uncovered Daniel Marcus's secrets, located three nuclear submarines, and unmasked a mole in the National Executive Committee who just happens to be the most successful political spy of the past half-century. What do they think I am, a miracle worker or something?"

"Alexei Ilyich, they certainly do think extremely highly of you," said Gusev placatingly, slipping into his golden retriever mode. "That's exactly why they've come to expect you to accomplish the impossible."

"But what do they think I've been doing for the past three weeks?"

"Excuse me, Alexei Ilyich," said Gusev, who hadn't seen the cable but guessed its contents. Do they give you some kind of deadline for accomplishing something?"

"No, Gusev, they are much too subtle to put down on paper anything resembling a deadline. What they say is this, 'We cannot overemphasize to you that uncovering the rebels' submarine home port network and unmasking the Constitutionalist spy in the National Executive Committee is absolutely vital to long-term national interests. It goes without saying that success in this effort would secure permanent advancement in your own career.'

"Let me translate, if I may," Ponomarev added. "What they are saying is: If you catch the Constitutionalist mole or locate their submarines, President Zhelenovsky is sure he'll get Alaska back. If you don't, esteemed colleague, you're looking forward to an early and sudden retirement, maybe cleaning windows in the Lefortovo Prison." He stopped and thought for a while, abruptly changing his tone as a new idea struck him. "Wait, Gusev, maybe we've been looking in the wrong place all along. How many people know that Marcus is actually dead?"

"Well *you* know, *I* know, those two militiamen know, the PSB knows—or at least a handful of them do—maybe four or five."

"And as far as the Constitutionalists are concerned— particularly since we sent that Richfield off to tell them this— Marcus is still alive, gravely wounded in a hospital, and about to tell us the whole story of Project Almond at any moment? Right?"

"Yes, Alexei Ilyich."

"Well, then, I think it's time that Dr. Daniel Marcus revealed to the world the lurid secrets of his criminal Project Almond."

Gusev looked puzzled. "But Alexei Ilyich," he protested, not sure whether he was being made the dupe of an elaborate joke, "you and I both know that Marcus is dead."

"Of course he is you imbecile! But who else knows that? Call Rutledge's office and ask for a priority red meeting with him at 11:30. I'd arranged to see him at noon anyway, so it'll only mean changing the time by half an hour. Have Natalya order up a decent lunch for three people at 1:30 from the commissary. We'll have it here in the office. Something just a little special, maybe that veal they do so well. I'd like some of that excellent cabernet sauvignon we had the other day to go with it. Get three bottles. And some brandy too. I think I know just how to arrange things."

Three hours later Michael Fleetwood, U.N. correspondent of the *New York Times,* was at the entrance to the Educational Programs Administration. He was almost perspiring with anticipation. Had there ever been a precedent for this? One of the highest officials of one of the world's most powerful intelligence organizations had invited him to a private luncheon for a "confidential chat."

Well, almost private. The exquisite pleasure of obtaining what was almost sure to be the story of a lifetime was just slightly sullied by Fleetwood's having to share it with Sally Giordino, a very pretty but very tough and very aggressive New York correspondent of ABC News. Fleetwood's impression of Ponomarev's sagacity had dropped a degree or two when he'd found himself sharing the elevator with Giordino. Sure, she'd gotten a scoop or two on the People's Movement's policies, but what did she know about world diplomacy? Why, Sally Giordino had never even been to Moscow, where Fleetwood had been bureau chief for four years during the Gorbachev era.

As for Sally Giordino the disappointment was even greater. She'd met Ponomarev very briefly at a reception ten days earlier, had found him attractive, and without having a clue who he was, other than that he was some important Russian doing business with the People's Movement, had flirted mightily with him. Not long afterward she'd overheard two other correspondents talking about him at a U.N. stakeout. Ponomarev was running Russian espionage in New York. That was one thing. But now, just before Christmas, she was being invited to a tête-a-tête in the bear's own lair in the RCA Building. At very short notice, and after canceling a luncheon with a source in the People's Movement Secretariat, she'd dressed up for the occasion . . . only to discover she had to share it with pompous, Saville Row-dressed Michael Fleetwood. Not just a fly in the ointment, a cockroach, she thought.

Ponomarev, though, knew exactly what he was doing. Natalya, looking very elegant and charming herself this morning, opened the doors for them and ushered them into Ponomarev's office, converted for the moment into a private dining room. A white-coated waiter was there with a tray of drinks and had time to take their order just before Ponomarev himself walked in.

"I'm so glad you could come and at such short notice," he said charmingly, kissing Giordino's hand and giving Fleetwood's hand a hearty, man-to-man shake. "You must forgive me for not being totally exclusive with one or the other of you. Those bureaucratic rules, you know." He laughed as if it were obvious what he meant. Giordino, assuming she ought to understand, laughed too, which forced Fleetwood to join in the merriment.

"I've not had a chance to get to know any of the media so far," Ponomarev went on. "It's a pity. Of course, in an earlier incarnation it was part of my business to be sociable with the Fourth Estate." He paused and smiled genially at Fleetwood, who rose instantly to the bait.

"Yes, I think in *those* days," he said with a laugh, "that was one of the activities of the First Chief Directorate. But of course, *you* were only a diplomat at the U.N. then, right?" He laughed loudly at his own joke, and Ponomarev obliged him by laughing along.

Giordino managed a half-smirk at this. She hadn't a clue what the First Chief Directorate was (the foreign espionage department of the old KGB), and she was furious at Fleetwood for trotting out his old Soviet Union expertise. Next thing he'd be trying to engage Ponomarev in Russian.

She was right. "I kak vam nravyatsya bolshiye izmeneniye v etom gorode?" Fleetwood asked, a genial smile fixed to his face.

"Oh, Michael, my friend, that's not very well mannered of you," Ponomarev said. "There is a lady here who doesn't speak Russian and you use that language to ask me what I think of the major changes we've seen in this city? I know your Russian is very good, but I don't want to have to translate everything so Sally doesn't miss something." Sally was as ready to shower the Russian with kisses as she was to hit Fleetwood with her purse.

But Ponomarev nevertheless ignored the question. "I thought it was about time to meet with two of the best reporters in the country," he said, "to exchange views on what has been going on recently. First, let's establish some ground rules. You can attribute this to 'diplomatic sources.' Period. Not 'Russian officials' or 'Russian' anything. If you break those ground rules, I'm sorry to say that the consequence will not simply be that you will never have access to any Russian official again in this town. That, unfortunately, would be too lenient." He turned to Fleetwood with an icy stare. "Michael, I am very confident that you in particular will remember the ground rules of this conversation. You recently remarried, didn't you? Is your wife aware of what your social life was like in Moscow? I'm sure she doesn't want to know the details . . . and of course, there's no reason she should."

Fleetwood flushed crimson, but Giordino went white. If that was what Ponomarev would do to Fleetwood for breaking the rules, what might he do to her? What could he know about her?

Ponomarev answered the unspoken question. "Sally," he said, turning on the charm again, "you're such a pretty woman that it's a pleasure just to have you here with Michael and me at lunch. I just know your producer would never believe it if the PSB came to him and said that you were sleeping with your sources, would he?"

Giordino trembled. She could have left the room that moment in indignation. Had she been alone, she would have done so. But Fleetwood was there, and she wasn't going to hand the story over as a sole exclusive to him. Besides, Fleetwood hadn't gotten up and left in indignation either. With a momentary glance at each other, both Giordino and Fleetwood knew they'd stay for the entire lunch, they'd observe the ground rules, and neither would reveal Ponomarev's blackmail on the other.

"Natalya," Ponomarev called out cheerily, as though there had not been the slightest hint of unpleasantness in the conversation so far, "tell Brentwood that we'd like to start lunch right away,"

"Yes, Alexei Ilyich."

"Now, what I'm interested in discussing with you," Ponomarev resumed familiarly, "is what we all think has happened to those submarines. I've heard some interesting theories, and I have some of my own. I'd be interested in your views on the scuttlebutt around town on Project Almond. Personally, I think the whole business has been completely misunderstood. Oh, Sally, please help yourself to the asparagus. It's so much nicer when it's still hot, isn't it?"

After this, and despite the chilly beginnings, the luncheon went surprisingly well. As the first bottle of cabernet sauvignon gave way to the second, Fleetwood became urbane and witty, and Giordino had both men in stitches describing conversations she'd had with higher-ups in the People's Movement. Ponomarev related anecdotes of his career in many interesting places, not revealing anything of significance, but adding to the impression that the two reporters were being let into the confidence of a truly remarkable personage.

The impression had its desired effect. The leaks worked. ABC ran the story as its lead item on the 6:30 news, though hedging it with enough denials from People's Movement officials to let the network off the hook if Giordino had been misinformed by Ponomarev. The gist of it all was simple: Daniel Marcus, mastermind of Project Almond, had been captured by Public Security Agents and had revealed enough details of the project to bring an end to the renegade mission of the pro-Constitutionalist submarines. "Diplomatic sources," Giordino intoned earnestly in a standup in front of the U.N., "say they are surprised that the People's Movement has not publicly confirmed the existence of the renegade submarines since it is now only a matter of time before they are forced to surrender."

As for Fleetwood he wrote a masterly piece that ran below the fold on the front page in the next morning's *Times*. He'd done his homework. He had even dug up some details about Project Almond that Ponomarev had never seen revealed in public before. It gave the Russian a twinge of unease. The new information suggested that the Constitutionalists, or at least their philosophical forerunners in the pre-1997 Pentagon, had foreseen the current world and American domestic situation clearly enough to plan intelligently for a protracted struggle against superior odds. And if they had planned an elaborate scheme to conceal submarines, what else might they have planned?

Ponomarev's presentation to Giordino and Fleetwood had been preceded by one other success, though it had not required the same bludgeon to accomplish. At his meeting with Rutledge the Russian had persuaded the chairperson of the National Executive Committee to authorize a Voice of the American People's official "confirmation" of the essence of the stories that would be reported by Giordino and Fleetwood.

"It's too risky," Rutledge had said at first.

"Stan, I'm sorry," said Ponomarev, "but you don't have any choice. We've publicly sat on the whole Marcus shooting incident too long. If you don't put your own spin on the incident very soon, you'll be vulnerable to all kinds of rumors. Let's break the whole thing open with an official confirmation of the stories Giordino and Fleetwood will run."

Reluctantly, Rutledge had agreed. The statement was an ultimatum to the three pro-Constitutionalist submarines, broadcast the morning after Ponomarev's luncheon with Giordano and Fleetwood.

The statement asserted, quite falsely, that Daniel Marcus had been apprehended by the PSB and, in the interests of bringing the civil war in America to an end as quickly as possible, had cooperated fully with the authorities in revealing the details of the so-called Project Almond. His cooperation made it possible for the security forces of the People's Movement to locate the families of the submarine crew members. The Russian navy, moreover, had been provided with information regarding the home port bases around the world.

303

"Chairperson Stan Rutledge, of the National Executive Committee of the People's Movement," the VOAP announcer said, "calls on all personnel now serving in the submarines *Massachussetts, North Dakota,* and *Arkansas* to surface and make their identity and location known on the frequencies to be listed at the end of this broadcast." Once surfaced, the statement demanded, they should await identification by aircraft or ships of the Russian fleet and listen on the designated frequencies for further instructions on surrender procedures.

"Officers and enlisted men have twenty-four hours to complete this maneuver," Rutledge's gravelly voice proclaimed in the prerecorded statement. "No further military action will be taken against any submarine that complies with these instructions. All military personnel aboard will be treated honorably as prisoners of war.

"Failure to comply with this order will result in an intensification of the global search and the immediate destruction of the submarines once they are located. It may also result in hardship for family members of crew personnel who refuse to comply with this ultimatum. You have until 1500 hours GMT on December 23 to respond.

"Fellow Americans, you have shown great bravery and persistence in pursuing your cause, however misguided it is. Now, for the sake of restoring unity in our land, for the sake of your families and your children, and for the future of our great nation, we on the National Executive Committee say in unison: It is time to come home."

Ponomarev was alternately frowning and smirking as the syrupy, menacing message came to an end. The announcer gave out the radio frequencies for the submarines and indicated that the announcement would be repeated every hour for the next eight hours.

But Ponomarev was still uneasy. It had all gone a little too smoothly—the leak to the media, Rutledge's ready cooperation. Even Gusev, who knew him better than anyone, had been unusually quiet, not coming up with his usual, predictable objections to Ponomarev's brilliantly inventive schemes. Was there anything he'd overlooked? Then, like a blip at the very edge of a radar screen, he remembered the oddly ambivalent account of the shooting of Marcus and his companion in the *New York Times* the day after his arrival. How had the story read? Something like, "two suspected enemy agents, *one* of them shot dead . . ." Did the people at the *Times* know more about the Marcus incident than they'd let on? Had Fleetwood known anything? He certainly hadn't given any indication of it.

And then he remembered Richfield.

"Gusev!" he shouted at the door that Natalya had diplomatically closed, having been warned by Gusev that Ponomarev was in an explosive and volatile mood.

The bald head and bushy eyebrows reappeared swiftly. His poker face gave nothing away. "Yes, Alexei Ilyich?"

"Have we heard anything from Richfield? He's been gone three weeks, hasn't he?"

Gusev went a bit red. "Alexei Ilyich," he said, "I knew how preoccupied you were and how you wanted to listen to the VOAP announcement, so I didn't want to interrupt you."

"So?" said Ponomarev, his irritation beginning to rise.

"Richfield called in about forty-five minutes ago. I said you were very busy but would be very happy to know of his safe return. He's in his apartment, waiting to hear from us."

"Get him here immediately!" The older man braced himself for a torrent of invective for having failed to notify his superior immediately, but it never came.

Ponomarev's annoyance at his failure to be notified of Richfield's return had been eclipsed by a sense of deep urgency about his broadcast gamble. He wanted to be sure he'd left no door open.

Forty minutes later Douglas was sitting in the RCA Building office. Ponomarev was neither charming nor threatening, just very cold and very attentive. He scrutinized Richfield's eyes for several seconds without saying anything, then leaned back in his chair and observed, "You spent quite a bit of time out west, didn't you?"

Richfield, who had been briefed just before leaving Montana on how to respond to Ponomarev in a way that kept his distance without appearing hostile, replied, "I was four days getting cleared for the trip by the Constitutionalists. I spent a total of six days in Montana and more than a week in New Mexico trying to get transportation back."

"Yes, we know about that," said Ponomarev. "I expect they arrested you and gave you a hard time," the Russian went on, knowingly.

"Oh, yes, they locked me up, actually with another Russian," he said almost gaily.

"A Russian? What kind of Russian?"

"Some soldier they'd caught trying to infiltrate the area. He was quite a kook. Gave me this ranting lecture about Jews and anti-Russian conspiracies."

"Why did they put you in with him?"

"I think jail space was at a minimum."

Ponomarev was sizing Richfield up and didn't like what he saw. Three weeks ago the young man sitting in front of him had been a prickly, rather naive bureaucrat. Now the same man seemed a lot cooler, more in possession of himself, not at all as easy to rattle. He even had a slight suntan, no doubt the product of a week in the Southwest. But Ponomarev had many disguises. He put on his avuncular, professorial demeanor. "Did you meet Hodges?" he asked.

"Yes I did."

"What was your impression."

"He's remarkable, very tough-minded, a sort of father figure even to his senior officers, very prudent, and completely unself-conscious."

"What do you mean, unself-conscious?" Ponomarev asked, who had detected what he thought might be a sense of devotion in Richfield's use of the word *remarkable* to describe the general.

"I didn't spend much time with him, but he doesn't seem to waste much time thinking about himself or his own position. He's sort of, well, old-fashioned, I guess."

"Did you like him?"

"You can't like someone you don't get to know. You may have a good or bad impression of his abilities or personality. I may have met Hodges, but I don't claim to have a strong sense of him. I don't think a lot of people know him well. He seems to keep them at a certain distance."

"Did he discuss Project Almond with you?"

"No, not at all. He was with a group of senior officers who questioned me about what *I* knew about Project Almond, but he never brought the topic up."

"What did you tell them about Almond, and particularly about Daniel Marcus?"

"I described to them the same scene I told you about, about seeing Marcus and his companion being shot in the street and then watching the ambulance come and take them away."

"Did you say that Marcus was in detention and being questioned by us?"

"No."

"Why the hell not? What were your instructions from me? Weren't they to say just that?"

"Yes, they were, Mr. Ponomarev, but implicit in what you told me was the principle that I not be identified as having any connection with you. One of the first things they did was flutter me with a polygraph. I'd have been a dead duck, not to mention useless to you, if I'd started inventing stuff about Marcus's arrest."

"What did they ask you under the polygraph?"

"If I'd been recruited by the PSB. Of course, I said no and the machine bore me out. After that they were more friendly."

"But they still jailed you?"

"Yes, because they needed to pick my brain about the comings and goings of top People's Movement people in Manhattan."

"Did you help them out?"

"Of course. You told me that they'd probably want to recruit me, so I had to play along as much as I could."

"But what did you tell them about Marcus? Didn't they ask you where you thought he might now be?"

"I had to be careful about every word I said. I'm not a professional spook. I haven't had psychological training on how to fool a lie detector. If I'd been too dogmatic about Marcus being alive and kicking when the ambulance came, they'd have wanted to know which hospital I thought he was in. They'd have jumped all over me, and when they found out nothing I said panned with anything their guys in Manhattan were telling them, they would have left me in that detention cell until the war was over. A lot of use I would have been to you then."

Ponomarev looked up sharply. Richfield had been sassy during their first interview, but it had been sullen, defensive. Now he seemed to be frankly assertive. The Russian leaned back in his chair, took up his cigar, and went through the laborious process of relighting it. It took about a minute, and it was designed to put his interlocutor off balance; an elaborate power move that said in effect, I'm the one who decides how much time we spend on this topic, not you.

"Okay, I see your point," he said finally, staring coldly at Richfield through the cigar smoke. "Before we change the subject, however, I wonder if you heard anything about the Constitutionalists shooting prisoners in cold blood?"

"I didn't hear that in Montana, but there were a lot of rumors about that sort of thing in the Southwest. Morale was pretty poor among the units I observed."

"You're very observant. Do you think the Constitutionalists are capable of cold-blooded atrocities?"

"Absolutely," Richfield replied without hesitation. "In a civil war it's virtually guaranteed that atrocities are committed, usually by both sides."

"Good. Though it's clear that you've acquired a certain juvenile admiration for the dashing General Hodges, it seems you've still got your feet somewhere near the ground."

Ponomarev's chameleon mood changed again. "Where were you when the raid took place?" he said briskly, almost matter-of-fact now.

Douglas blanched, and the Russian watched him very carefully, his eyelids low, almost closed, like a snake waiting to strike.

"The raid really shook them up," he said brightly, stalling. "If I'd been in the wrong place I could've been killed. By the way, if I had been killed, how long would it have taken you to find out?"

"Maybe twelve hours," Ponomarev said with a shrug of indifference. "But you haven't answered my question," he persisted. "Exactly where were you when the attack took place?"

"I was in the Swan Valley, several miles north of Helena and well out of sight of the town."

"What were you doing there?"

"I was in a helicopter with one of Hodges's generals."

"You didn't see any of the raid at all?"

"We were miles from the city when it happened. The pilot told us what he was hearing on the radio, and Parsons ordered us to land to keep out of harm's way."

"You mean you were with Brigadier General Parsons?"

"Yes."

"Did Hodges or anyone else make any reference to their source at the heart of the People's Movement?"

"Not even a whisper. There was absolutely nothing to indicate that they even had one," Richfield said emphatically.

"I rather suspected that," Ponomarev said, "and that's why I've decided to smoke him out directly."

15

Mutiny

*C*aptain, there's a delegation from the crew that wants to talk to you."

"A delegation! What are you talking about, Chris? This is a U.S. Navy warship. There are established procedures for enlisted men who wish to communicate on disciplinary or other matters with senior officers."

"Captain, it's beyond that now. The whole crew knows about the VOAP broadcast."

"So?" said Rush.

"There're a lot of people saying there should be an open discussion of how we respond."

"Dammit, Commander, this isn't a New England town meeting! It's a warship under the disciplines of war. That's all there is to it."

"Captain, there are several issues involved now. One of them is the breach of operational secrecy."

Gresham was standing just inside the captain's cabin with the door closed. He spoke softly and urgently, as though worried that someone outside the door might hear. Rush, cigarette in hand, was bent over the pull-down table looking at charts and tide timetables of ocean tides. They had extended the submarine's antenna to monitor the hourly VOAP news broadcasts earlier that morning.

"How many of the men had access to the transcript of that broadcast?" Rush asked sharply.

"Just you, me, the officer of the deck, the quartermaster of the watch, and the two radiomen."

"Well, you and Williams obviously didn't go bleating about it to the rest of the crew. That leaves the radiomen. What disciplinary measures are prescribed for them? This is an extremely serious breach of naval discipline."

"It is, Captain, but we have a far more serious problem on our hands now than how to deal with the radiomen. The 'delegation' represents twenty-seven men who have signed a petition for us to surrender. They say it's not so much their own lives and futures on the line, but the lives of their loved ones. It was that reference about not wanting undue 'hardships to family members.' He really managed to kick us in the knees there."

"Hell, Chris, I didn't spend four years at Annapolis and twenty-five years in the U.S. Navy to be the first captain of the first boomer to surrender his ship to the Russian navy. I'm not going to do it. It's just that simple."

"Captain, I'm with you. You know that. But right now, unless we make some sort of nonprovocative acknowledgment of what these people are asking for, they'll physically confine us to our cabins—or worse—and surrender the boat anyway."

"Chris, I know my crew. They're not the surrendering sort. Maybe these extreme conditions have driven the worm out of some of the overripe apples aboard, but most of them are okay. They'll go with us. I think we can come up with a plan to arm part of the crew who'll support us and arrest the troublemakers immediately. It's risky, but it'll stop the rot real fast."

"Captain, it may stop the rot, but there won't be a submarine left to operate. If we have half a dozen men as prisoners, we're going to have to feed them in confinement for several months. Where'll we put 'em? And if we do drop them off at our next home port in Chile, who will replace them? Meanwhile, the rot will start again. First, if even one of the other subs quits, the game's up. Second, even the guys who didn't want to join the dissidents will feel sorry for them."

"Chris, let me get this straight. Are you suggesting we negotiate the command authority aboard this submarine with a bunch of mutineers?"

"No, Captain, I'm not. As of yet, we don't have a mutiny, just an early, clear warning of one. I think if we go to the mat with them

312

right now, they'll feel they've got nothing to lose and will try every hold in the book and some that aren't. We may possibly win, but the combat effectiveness of the submarine will be permanently crippled. If a Russian sub came up close, we'd really be dead meat."

Rush rapped his fingernails on the table half a dozen times and looked straight at Gresham.

"Look," he said, "the only thing we may have in greater quantity is wit. You and I know that this message from Rutledge sounds like a bluff. If they'd really gotten hold of Marcus and found the home ports why didn't they produce him or have a recorded message from him? Or why didn't they at least say, 'We know your ports are a, b, and c? When's our next microburst transmission due?"

"Not until Tuesday at midday. If we try to communicate with Hawaii before then, Zhelenovsky's boys will nail us with a positioning fix. Right now we have less than twenty-four hours to prove that the PM is bluffing about Project Almond. Of course, you realize there's only one way to know for sure whether Project Almond's out?"

"What's that?" asked Rush, surprised.

"Send someone up to the surface to talk to the Russians."

"Send someone up? You mean, negotiate with them?"

"Exactly."

"Chris, once and for all, I'm not going to surrender this submarine. When I signed on in the U.S. Navy, I accepted the possibility of death in combat. Under Project Almond we're in combat whether there's actual shooting or not. The whole point of Project Almond is that the U.S. never surrenders its final nuclear deterrent. While there's a single breath in my body, I'm not going to negotiate with the Russians, the PM, or the Queen of Sheba." He looked at Gresham very hard and became suddenly formal. "Commander Gresham, I need to ask if you are either questioning my command or contemplating disobedience to the orders this ship is under?"

"Captain," Gresham replied, equally soberly, but much more warmly. "I'm as loyal to the U.S. Navy, to you, and to the strictest interpretation of the orders contained in Project Almond as I was on my first day as a plebe at Annapolis. I'm under no circumstances recommending negotiating the surrender of this submarine. What I'm trying to do is come up with a scheme that will gain time and prevent this petition mob from becoming convinced that the only next step is mutiny."

"Well, if you've got some ideas, let's hear them fast. I don't have time to daydream."

"Captain, I think there's a bluff of our own that just might work. It's risky, but I think if we came up with it and presented it to the crew as our response to the broadcast, it would cut the ground from under the people who could cause us serious trouble if we don't do anything."

"Well, what do you have in mind?" Rush was gruff and irritable. Gresham knew that he would only have one pass to explain his proposal and have Rush approve it.

"Please hear me out to the end, Captain. It will only work if all of the pieces fall into place."

"All right, but be quick."

"First, we explain to the crew that we don't believe the VOAP assertions about Marcus's arrest and the uncovering of Project Almond, because they sound like propaganda by a PM that's increasingly desperate over its inability to knock out our side. Second, we are adamant that we will do nothing before the twenty-four-hour ultimatum has expired. We'll make it clear that we expect within the twenty-four-hour time period reliable information that refutes the broadcast. That could be Hawaii, even Hodges, or a foreign news source that we can trust. Third, instead of surfacing and flagging down the first Russian ship that happens along we'll send up one of the crew to feel them out on just how much they know about Project Almond."

"Hold it right there," Rush interrupted. "You mean that someone aboard this boat will surrender to the Russians with my concurrence?"

"Not surrender, Captain. Talk to them. If possible, find out if they know anything. Then have them contact us with a voice transmission."

"Chris, you've been reading too many potboilers. Hasn't it occurred to you that if we send up some poor machinist to talk to Ivan, they'll put his head in a box and bang on it until he coughs up Chile and New Zealand. Then the integrity of Project Almond will be lost forever."

"Captain, first, we won't send up some poor machinist. It should be an officer, and I volunteer. Second, if they pull out my fingernails and I scream Chile and New Zealand at them, what's the difference at that point? At the present rate the whole crew except us and a handful of others seems willing to do that with no torture at all. And believe me, they may well do it unless we preempt them with a counterplan."

Rush still looked skeptical. But Gresham wasn't finished. "That's only the worst-case scenario," he went on. "One that is no worse than what will happen if we take no action at all. What might happen is entirely different. Suppose I tell the Russian navy that our crew is willing to surrender the boat only in return for certain guarantees of personal and family safety and that the only guarantee they will accept is a freely made voice transmission to this effect from me. They'll have to bite. The Russians would do almost anything to get their hands on a live Trident submarine. It's of no concern to Stan Rutledge what happens to the three boats once they stop operating for the Constitutionalists, but it's worth almost anything to the Russians."

"Let's say that you and I agree on a certain wording that I would use in this transmission if I'm convinced that the VOAP broadcast was a bluff and they haven't a clue where we home port. I probably won't have any fingernails left, but at least you'll have the sub and will still have some options. On the other hand, if they really do know everything, and the crew still decides to mutiny, then let it happen on the basis of accurate information."

Rush looked at Gresham with his mouth half open and something approaching a grin on his face. "Chris, why didn't you become a Jesuit instead of a navy officer? You'd have been great counting angels on a pinhead."

"That wasn't a Jesuit who did that, Captain. It was St. Thomas Aquinas. The Jesuits weren't around then."

Both men laughed and the tension dissipated. Rush drew heavily once more on his cigarette while he thought the matter through further, and the smoke swirled around his eyes and his hair. Gresham, who detested smoke, wondered how long he could stay in the confined space being exposed to it without beginning to feel sick.

"I don't think it's going to come to that. There's a confirmation code you don't know about. I have to wait until NATCOM signals us tomorrow. If we've been compromised, we'll know it then. Every man on this boat is committed to this operation until we're ordered otherwise. There is no other interpretation of our objective. Period. COMSUBPAC put us here; COMSUBPAC is the only authority to withdraw us," Rush said.

Chris Gresham turned to leave, but Rush had one last idea. "Those twenty-seven petition signers," he asked sardonically after a silence. "Is any of them a petty officer?"

"Yes, Guiliani is."

"Good. Then make an announcement that I want to see all of the officers in five minutes in my cabin, and all of the petty officers thirty-five minutes after that. That way I can announce what we're going to do without ever acknowledging that the petition even existed. At least they'll put any further mutiny talk on hold for the period. Continue to copy VOAP, BBC, and other world broadcasts around the clock to see if there's any further light on the ultimatum."

"Aye, Captain." Gresham turned around to go out the door.

"And Chris," Rush said, almost as an afterthought.

"Captain?"

"I sure hope somehow someone can come up with a reliable confirmation or denial of whether Project Almond is still intact before we pop you up through the aft hatch. I really don't want you to lose your fingernails."

16

The Mole Hunt

*T*hey were all there, and they resented Rutledge for calling yet another meeting of the National Executive Committee. There had been far too many meetings going on for far too many hours, much longer than the weekly planned meetings every Thursday afternoon.

They'd attended because, while the sky wouldn't necessarily fall if someone missed an NEC meeting, if someone failed to attend two or more of the unscheduled sessions, the political ground might begin to shift—just a little. That had happened early in the PM era. Ray Belkind, a talented movie director, had come to political prominence through the gay movement and wanted to record the progress of the New Era in a series of movie documentaries. Belkind had been away—on perfectly legitimate business—for three consecutive meetings of the NEC. Vice-chair Elroy Robinson, a Maoist African-American, led a successful move to oust Belkind. The director was furious but powerless, particularly since Robinson controlled the People's Militia and was backed by Preston Northwood, a white multiculturalist and the regime's one impressive orator.

Two things were unusual about the meeting about to start. One was that it was additional to the scheduled meeting that day. The other was that a foreign national for the first time would attend part of the meeting.

Ponomarev was a shadowy figure to the NEC, who had invited him to untangle the Project Almond mess. Rutledge and Daniels were the only members who'd met him face to face. The rest viewed him with both fear and suspicion. Rutledge—pudgy, white-haired, a master of deviousness acquired while ascending the academic ladder at Stanford and Duke universities—had no problems with Ponomarev. He knew the Russian was a servant of a fascist regime but the man was a professional and he was good at catching spies. If a person, willingly or otherwise, served the ultimate objectives of the New Era, Rutledge didn't care what ideology motivated the action.

His First Vice-chair, Ellen Daniels, a tough-minded feminist, had a reputation as a stern, incorruptible figure with a strong orientation toward law and order. Partly as an experiment she'd been given the extremely important portfolio of the Public Security Bureau. For that reason alone she had a natural interest in Ponomarev's plans. Daniels was in her mid-thirties and attractive, although she was careful not to offend her constituency by appearing "pretty." Her hair straggled out in all directions as though it hadn't been combed since the Korean War—just to reassure the sisters that she wasn't copping out to patriarchalism.

Preston Northwood was a flamboyant orator, ideologist, and ethnic self-flagellator, but he was more dangerous than he appeared at first. A Marxist with a strong streak of personal vanity, he'd deeply resented not being given the PSB portfolio and for that reason harbored an antipathy toward Daniels. He had formed a sort of unofficial opposition group within the NEC, enlisting Robinson, the highest-placed African-American, a man with a gift for street tactics and organization and the coordinator of the People's Militia.

Robinson was an angry revolutionary who liked to punctuate his speech with phrases like "take a bold stand" and—citing Chairman Mao—"A great revolution must go through a civil war. This is a rule." Robinson, to put it mildly, didn't like white people very much. Though he was ideologically allied to Rutledge, Daniels, and the rest of them in an effort to remake People's America according to the socialist vision, personal emotional forces had brought him into alignment with Northwood and three others: Jamil Al-Baraka, an African-American representing the vast and growing number of Black Muslims, especially in the inner cities; Nancy Wu, an Asian-American Maoist; and Roseanne Great Bear, a huge, angry Native American who seemed to have a special life's mission to undo the work of Christopher Columbus.

The Robinson-Northwood clique voted along ideological lines, usually splitting with the five members comprising the Rutledge-Daniels faction. Rutledge's other backers were Leanna Greene, an African-American community organizer of strong, classical Marxist leanings; Enrico Gomez, a Hispanic farmworker of relatively moderate views; and Bill Muzzio, a representative of radicalized labor that had thrown its lot in with the People's Movement. Greene couched every argument in the soaring, gospel-reformer cadences of a Harlem preacher, which made her sound like part of the anti-white, pro-Third World Northwood group rather than the Marxist, redistributionist Rutledge faction. She'd shown herself to be a firm ally of Rutledge-Daniels in most cases.

The swing vote belonged to Shirley Metaxas, a New Age progressive who sounded radical and rational one moment and totally erratic the next. Metaxas cast her vote to the beat of her own drummer, siding with the Rutledge faction on one issue and with Robinson on the next. Neither group could predict how she would lean on any given issue. This led to the only consensus the factions had forged—Metaxas had to go. No fool, of course, Metaxas quickly grasped that her best chance of political survival was to ensure that replacing her would be more problematic than keeping her.

The committee convened in the grand boardroom on the third floor of the RCA Building. The boardroom had originally belonged to a major mining corporation, and the walls had been finished in the oak paneling style consistent with a men's club of the nineteenth century. Robinson had wanted to decorate the room with portraits of the great leaders of the Marxist-Maoist tradition—Marx, Engels, Lenin, Stalin, Mao, Hoxha, Guzman—but several members had balked at Stalin, Mao, the Albanian Enver Hoxha, and the Peruvian Shining Path founder Guzman. They had compromised with samples of revolutionary poster art from the early days of the People's Movement.

Each place at the table was marked with paper, pencils, mineral water, and soft drinks. Metaxas insisted on providing large quantities of her own concoction of vegetable juice. Rutledge frequently speculated that the recipe included crickets. Northwood wouldn't sit down unless coffee were available on the sideboard.

Rutledge was fanatical about punctuality, one of the few things he and Robinson were in accord on, so just before noon, barely an hour after Richfield had left Ponomarev's office, they came into the huge boardroom and took their regular seats at the table.

Ponomarev was seated at the end of the long table, and Daniels agreed to take the seat at the opposite end. It was a cunning move by Rutledge. From that position Daniels could either oppose Ponomarev dramatically, if this should be necessary, or ally herself persuasively with him. Gusev attended the proceedings too, sitting at a table behind his boss, his black attaché case beside him

"Fellow committee members," Rutledge began as soon as everyone was seated. "I want to thank all of you for turning out for this meeting despite very short notice. We are here to discuss two questions: the procedural issue of what to do when the renegade submarines surrender, and the continuing and troubling question of security leaks at the highest level of the People's Movement.

"As you know, with the concurrence of this committee, I requested President Zhelenovsky to provide us with expert counterespionage personnel who had experience with the former U.S. armed forces to help us unravel Project Almond. He kindly made available to us Deputy Director of the Russian Foreign Intelligence Service Alexei Ponomarev, who has had considerable experience in counterespionage and with life in America in general. Mr. Ponomarev has been with us since Thanksgiving. Yesterday he informed me that he was ready to make a major move toward ending the mutiny of the submarines, and we issued, in the name of the People's Movement, a statement calling upon the submarines to give up. Some of you may wish to discuss this.

"Before that, however, I'm going to ask Mr. Ponomarev to explain the background to that decision and to his further investigations in our behalf on our security problem. But first, Mr. Ponomarev," and he turned toward the Russian, "let me go around the table and introduce my fellow committee members." Rutledge went clockwise around the table, starting with Robinson and Al-Baraka on his left, Daniels at the left end opposite Ponomarev,

Gomez, Greene, Northwood, Wu, and Great Bear opposite him, and finally Metaxas and Muzzio on his right. Except for Robinson and Muzzio, each of them nodded or gave some indication of greeting as Rutledge called out their names.

The introduction was useful for Ponomarev as it gave him an opportunity to size up the people he would be dealing with. He'd noticed the two women right away. Metaxas immediately on his left, wrinkled, fussy, wearing a calf-length purple dress with a silver belt and matching silver stars in purple-tinted hair, and Daniels, watching him with just a hint of a smile. He reckoned he could charm Metaxas, but he wasn't sure of Daniels. Gomez and Northwood looked as though they were amenable to him. Rutledge, of course, was sympathetic, as was, apparently, Leanna Greene. But Muzzio, though nominally a Rutledge supporter, looked inscrutable. Robinson, Wu, Al-Baraka, and Great Bear seemed to resent his very appearance at the committee. He decided to adopt his unaffected and modest persona, a guise that often changed people's minds in potentially hostile situations.

"I'm very sorry to be the cause of a sudden meeting of your committee," he began. "If you're like me, I'm sure you resent being summoned to discuss something on short notice, especially if you haven't been involved from the start. I apologize for the inconvenience. Stan knows that I was nervous about coming and wasn't sure that it was the right thing, but he insisted." First, put the blame on Rutledge, he thought, then let him off the hook gently. "But Stan knew that we have some controversial, tough questions in front of us, and we both knew it would have been contrary to the spirit of the New Era and to ordinary decency not to give everyone a chance to air his or her views on this issue." That was laying it on a bit thick, but they weren't balking yet. Now it was time to flatter Northwood. Gusev had done his homework. "Mr. Northwood, you look as though you are a connoisseur of good coffee. I enjoy it as well. May I have some from your pitcher there?" He allowed his Russian accent to come out a little more strongly than usual, which added to the impression of charming naivete.

On cue Northwood perked up, his vanity flushed. Obviously, Ponomarev was his kind of man. "Mr. Ponomarev, I personally select the coffee beans we use in these meetings," he said with a broad grin, "and nobody has complained yet, that is, nobody who thinks coffee is healthy." He looked, with a dig-in-the-ribs grin at Metaxas, cradling a mug of her juice concoction. "Why don't you try some?"

That was exactly the cue Ponomarev wanted. The break in the proceedings gave him a psychological initiative, and getting up from the table would also give him a chance to try some of his charm out on Daniels, who was closer to the coffee warmer than he was.

So far, so good. He'd established some contact around the table at strategic points, had forced the entire committee to wait until he had poured himself some coffee, and then almost casually strolled back to his chair. On the way he wondered which of the eleven was the traitor. He would have to move fast to find out.

"As you know, Daniel Marcus," he continued, "the architect of this treacherous program, was apprehended Thanksgiving Day in Manhattan. He's been in PSB custody ever since."

Daniels shifted uncomfortably.

Robinson spoke up. "What's his condition, Mr. Ponomarev?" he asked. "The broadcast said that he had been cooperating with the authorities. If that's the case, why weren't we told about it earlier?"

"There were some difficult tactical questions in deciding what to do with Marcus," Ellen Daniels quickly responded. "Stan and Mr. Ponomarev didn't feel free to move on this case until the day before yesterday."

"If Marcus has been cooperating," Robinson continued, ignoring Daniels, "why has it taken three weeks to find out the most basic information about these submarines?"

Ponomarev looked at Rutledge and Daniels. Damn! People were coming to the point much too quickly. He'd wanted them to ponder for themselves that the broadcast about Marcus had been an elaborate deception. Rutledge nodded just slightly.

"Ladies and gentlemen," Ponomarev said, as smoothly as he could manage, "some of you knew this, but for security reasons we couldn't tell all of you. Marcus is in fact dead. He died resisting arrest during his apprehension. We weren't able to learn anything from him before he died."

Robinson, on Rutledge's left, practically shouted at Ponomarev. "You tell us now! Do you know how many of our people have died in the past three weeks? Adding the APA and the People's Militia together, more than three hundred! And sixty of these fighters in the people's war were murdered in cold blood by racist Constitutionalist war criminals in Texas. Now you tell us that while all this was goin' on, you were sitting on a Constitutionalist war criminal corpse in the city morgue and pretending that he was alive? What kind of game is this Russian playing with us, Rutledge?" As he said this, his face quivering and sweating, he turned savagely toward Rutledge, who had kept his head turned toward Ponomarev and didn't move.

Rutledge had heard similar tirades from Robinson before. He was skilled at defusing them. Emotional as he was, Robinson was also sentimental, a weakness that Rutledge knew how to exploit.

"Mr. Ponomarev," he said calmly, "Vice-Chair Elroy Robinson is a man, as you can see, of deep convictions and strong passions. It's important for you to understand the personal losses that he has suffered in this war, including the death of a brother in the uprising in Washington, D.C., at the beginning of the struggle. Elroy also lost an uncle who was killed in Chicago. We all feel profoundly moved by the sacrifice his family has made in the cause of progress and liberation for the American people. I know that—"

"It's not just me I'm thinking of!" Robinson harshly interrupted, though at a lower level of intensity than his first outburst. "Rutledge, you say that this Pony, Poony, whatever his name is, has come to help us catch some big spy and dig up those submarines. Well, turns out the man he's supposed to be trackin' down has been dead since before he got here. Now you've gone along with an insane scheme to tell the world that Marcus has spilled his guts. So all we're supposed to do is get our butts over there with some bombs or somethin' and finish off this little scheme? It's the dumbest thing I ever heard."

Even for the rough and tumble of NEC meetings, this was harsh, and some of the committee members, particularly Daniels, Northwood, and Greene, were embarrassed. Nobody liked to cross swords with Robinson. They wondered if Ponomarev could stand up to him.

But Ponomarev was a skilled infighter, and he had no intention of letting a rabid Maoist get the better of him in public debate. As soon as Robinson began his brief tirade, Ponomarev leaned back in his chair and began talking to Gusev, as though conferring on some matter relating to the meeting. The move, of course, was merely psychological. By depriving Robinson of an attentive target, it all but dissipated the attack. By the time he'd finished, Robinson had begun to run out of steam and sputter.

"Mr. Robinson," Ponomarev said caressingly, deliberately contrasting a low-volume, highly controlled speech with Robinson's ranting. "You are absolutely right; the idea is certainly farfetched. But it is going to work, and I'll tell you why. First, the Constitutionalists have every reason to believe that Marcus was captured rather than killed, since there was no death announcement and they haven't been able to find out what happened to him beyond learning that he was shot. Knowing that we are not amateurs in acquiring information from people in our custody, they must assume that, if Marcus is alive, he has talked.

"Second, when the Voice of the American People announces that it has information about Project Almond directly from its chief designer, Daniel Marcus, everyone will accept that as actual fact. It's simply far too brazen not to be true. And let me tell you this, it's such a harebrained idea, Mr. Robinson, that no submarine crew would ever bet the lives and liberty of their family members that it wasn't true. We have done studies for both our space program and our submarine program on the effect of prolonged confinement and isolation in close quarters on groups of men under conditions of extreme stress. I can assure you, at the slightest face-saving opportunity, those submarines will surrender.

"There is only one way that the submarines could ever be alerted to the falsity of this broadcast, and that is if someone sitting in this room chose to do so. Unfortunately, that is something that can no longer be ruled out."

There was a momentary silence, broken by Shirley Metaxas. "Are you saying that someone at this table might leak top-secret information to the enemy?" she asked indignantly.

"I'm saying not only that he—or she—might, but he or she already has."

"I think that's insane," said Northwood, contempt dripping from his voice.

"That's ridiculous," said Nancy Wu.

"It's an outrageous and contemptible assertion," added Greene.

Al-Baraka, the Muslim, said nothing but eyed Ponomarev with unmistakable contempt. Robinson was strangely quiet, as were Great Bear and Muzzio, but a buzz of annoyance continued from the others.

"Wait a minute, wait a minute!" interrupted Rutledge impatiently. "Before this meeting gets completely out of hand, I think you need to hear from Ellen Daniels. She's in a better position to verify Mr. Ponomarev's assertion than any of us."

There was a silence around the table and everyone looked at Ellen. "I have no absolute proof that there is a traitor in our midst," she said carefully, her New York accent ricocheting off the oak paneling, "but the circumstantial evidence is very strong. The PSB has done its best to cover every possible angle on the leaks for several months, but we've come up with nothing at any level below the NEC itself. One of the reasons we asked the Russians for help is that they have more experience in counterespionage than we do. The fact is, we've come to the inescapable conclusion that someone in this room is giving significant tactical and strategic information to the enemy. Very regrettably, but with the Chair's prior consent, I have authorized round-the-clock surveillance of all of us—including me—for the next week."

There was another explosion of indignation around the table, this time much louder than before. Al-Baraka broke through the hubbub by rapping his knuckles sharply on the table. In the brief hush that followed, he said in slow, contemptuous syllables, "Do I detect here another example of the white man attempting to assert his supposed 'natural' rights to suppress people of color? Or maybe I should say 'white woman,' since your decadent culture likes to make an idol of women—"

"Cut it out Al-Baraka!" Robinson fumed, furious again. "Listen, brother," he said in an urgent, short speech, "this is too serious to play color games. This regime ain't perfect, but do you want to go back to work on the Constitutionalist plantation?"

This temporarily silenced Al-Baraka, who liked to project a mien of implacable dignity in contrast to the choleric revolutionary disposition of Robinson. But the others were all clamoring for the floor, and Rutledge had to bang the table with a gavel.

"Order, order, for God's sake, order!" he shouted above the din.

"What, man, you gettin' religion now, Rutledge?" Robinson asked with a great pealing laugh that helped diffuse the tensions.

"Nancy, do you have something to say?" Rutledge asked Wu, ignoring Robinson.

"How could any of us be spying for the Constitutionalists?" Nancy Wu protested in a voice of aggrieved reasonableness. "Every one of us has risked life, liberty, property, and friendships to move this revolution forward to change America. It's just not possible that one of us might be working for the war criminals."

"In espionage, Miss Wu, the inconceivable is very often the truth," said Ponomarev, continuing in his silky tones. "There is no such thing as the typical spy, physically, professionally, or even emotionally. I myself recommended the surveillance, which will be implemented by the PSB. I suggested to Vice-Chair Daniels that it be for a limited period of time and that it be suspended if it becomes clear that the leaks are occurring from another source than the National Executive Committee. It is especially important that the surveillance takes place over the next few days as the deadline for the submarine surrender approaches."

Robinson, who had been strangely silent during the outbursts about the alleged NEC spy and the surveillance, now spoke up again. He was not angry this time. "I'll tell you something," he said to the group in general. "It's been obvious to me for a long time that someone's been greasin' the skids for Constitutionalist agents here in this city. It happens too often. One of our patrols pounces on a suspected safe house or some kind of conspiratorial gathering, and the criminals have flown before our people get there. Whoever's been doin' it is pretty smart, 'cause we never know who warned them."

"That's very alert of you to have grasped this," Ponomarev said directly to Robinson, his face full of sincere flattery, "and I'm sure the PSB will need all the help they can get from your militia. It's certainly well beyond my scope to offer tactical advice, but I think you ought to strengthen your control over information and communication outlets of every kind: broadcast, print, ham radio. I know you've banned C.B.s, but I doubt you've eliminated them completely. Maybe you should increase your surveillance in this area for the next few days."

He was about to go on, but Daniels caught his eye and he stopped. "Thank you, Mr. Ponomarev," she said. "We've already placed PSB personnel on a twenty-four-hour watch for the next week inside all broadcast facilities. We will expand our phone monitoring and C.B. monitoring coverage to a wider net. We'll catch the traitor, no doubt about that. Don't expect any pity from us when you are found out," she added menacingly as she looked around the table.

The truth was, regardless of the identity of the spy, several in the committee had connections or business that they didn't want the others, and certainly not the PSB, to know about. Nancy Wu was having an affair with a senior militia official. Shirley Metaxas had used the Russian mission to the U.N. to develop contacts with psychics in Russia. Enrico Gomez had a cousin in the U.S. Army who was now with the Constitutionalists. Preston Northwood was gay with a rich variety of lovers, many of them from politically unsavory backgrounds. All of a sudden, national business was intruding uncomfortably, in the form of blanket surveillance, into their private lives.

Al-Baraka was almost certainly in the clear in every sense. He was probably the most incorrupt person on the committee, a former alcoholic and drug addict who'd gotten rehabilitated and converted to Islam while in prison. He had led a very disciplined life ever since. Greene, somehow, also projected integrity.

Great Bear seemed a prime suspect, since she had too many connections internationally. Gomez was equally suspect. And so was Muzzio, the oldest, at fifty-eight, and the quietest man on the NEC.

Rutledge took over. "As you can see," he said, "the second item on the agenda, namely uncovering the suspected enemy agent in our midst, has taken over from the first, which we still need to discuss. The question is, what action do we take once the submarines surrender? As Mr. Ponomarev has made clear, it's only necessary for one of them to come to the surface and identify itself for us to obtain the information we need on Project Almond once we've interrogated the crew. It's more than likely that the home ports, however many there may be, are in foreign countries. If all three subs surrender, the issue is academic. We make strong representations to the countries concerned and ask them to turn over all matériel and information pertaining to the home port visits conducted during the civil war.

"But if even one submarine doesn't surrender, we are in a dilemma. Obviously we can and will take punitive action against family members of the crew, as we made clear in the VOAP ultimatum. But an Ohio-class submarine, even on its own, is an extremely dangerous piece of weaponry. Just one submarine could destroy all the major cities in Russia, or sink a lot of world shipping with its torpedoes. We might be forced to consider hostilities against a host country of the home port facilities if they refuse to cooperate with us once we confront them with information about Project Almond." He paused and looked around the table.

"We are a major revolutionary world power," said Robinson, "and we are fighting a people's war in the cause of revolution not just for America, but for the whole world. It doesn't matter what country these home ports are in, the masses will understand the righteousness of our cause if we bring war against the regimes that have been harboring the Constitutionalist reactionaries. I'm down for the whole thing, war or whatever it takes to bring these renegades to the judgment seat of history."

Greene spoke up, her sing-song preacher's voice coming to the fore now. "That's all very well, my brother, but what I want to know is, what if some other country decides to mess with us, I mean, mess with our civil war? What if the Chinese or some other power doesn't like us throwing our weight around? I mean, that's what we were doing during that Cold War period, and they sure didn't like us for that."

"That was not People's America," said Robinson, correcting her, "that was the reactionary bourgeois regime we've overthrown. The masses will understand the difference."

"Yeah, maybe the masses do," Greene countered, "but there's plenty of countries out there that don't listen to the masses before they come along and give you the big heave-ho. I say we act very carefully, not making any threats until we see exactly what we're up against. Maybe there's only one home port anyway, let's say in Australia. That'd be pretty easy to close down. But we better know how many of these ratholes those submarines have got to run back to before we lay any ultimatums on them."

"Mr. Chair, please," said Muzzio, quietly, drawing everyone's attention for the first time, "I want to propose a vote of thanks to Mr. Ponomarev for his very hard work and dedication in helping us solve this serious security problem. People's America is in his debt."

"I'll second that," said Leanna Greene. "Me too," said Gomez.

"Any objections?" Rutledge said, now sounding as if he were merely preparing the committee for next week's meeting of the Garden Club. "No? Then all in favor say 'aye.'" There was a loud chorus of "ayes" around the table. "A motion to express the thanks of the National Executive Committee to Mr. Alexei Ponomarev for his assistance in security matters, carried."

But Muzzio wasn't finished. "Mr. Chair, I now propose that we request Mr. Ponomarev to withdraw himself from this meeting while we debate national security issues not related to our internal security. What action People's America takes toward certain other states is a foreign policy issue. It would be inappropriate to permit a foreign national, however well-intentioned toward us, to participate in such a discussion."

Ponomarev looked at Muzzio first in astonishment but then in fury. He hadn't expected this at all. He reddened but reined himself in. "Of course. Mr. Muzzio is correct about the foreign policy ramifications of this question," he said briskly, looking directly at Rutledge, "but I trust I am not being rude in reminding you that it is the Russian navy that will oversee the surrender of the submarines, not the navy of People's America, which, forgive me, barely exists. How is it possible for you to put an end to this submarine scourge without Russian assistance?"

Rutledge was embarrassed now and hesitated before replying. But Northwood jumped in. He'd been for several minutes barely suppressing an urge to enter the conversation, but it had been too noisy and too risky hitherto. Now he saw his chance.

"Can we in People's America, building a new society in a New Era," he asked grandiloquently, "permit the ancient divisions of the nation-state era to prevent us from completing our vital tasks? Can we? I say that it is our resolution, our armed people united in a people's war, that will conquer these renegades and their missile submarines, not by alliances with this state or that one, this bloc or that one."

He hadn't quite gotten a focus on his thought, and sure enough, Daniels barged in, eager to defend Ponomarev. "What are you saying, Preston?" she asked cuttingly. "Are you agreeing with Bill Muzzio that we throw Mr. Ponomarev out of this meeting, even though it is Russia that has most consistently defended our revolution?"

"Sure, the Russians have defended it," interrupted Robinson harshly, "but not because they like us. They fought for us because they know that a weak America is no threat to them, and it makes their country the biggest bully around the world. The Russian masses would support our revolution if they had a chance."

This was the moment Ponomarev had been waiting for. He knew that the tide was running against his staying any longer in the meeting, but he wanted to leave at a point when it might seem that he'd been slightly insulted. If he departed with just a little show of injured dignity, it would strengthen his hand when they asked him back, as they surely would at some point.

"Mr. Chair," he said slowly and carefully, "I have been honored by your invitation to attend this meeting, but I can see clearly that it is now time for me to withdraw. I wish you success in your deliberations, and I will certainly be available to you or any on the committee for further exploration of policy options, should you choose. Thank you."

Quickly pushing his chair back, Ponomarev gathered his papers in a sweep and left Gusev padding along in his wake. As the door closed behind them and the sound of angry argument filtered out into the corridor, he shrugged to himself. It was quite obvious to him that there were only four serious suspects for the mole he was seeking: Metaxas, Great Bear, Gomez, and Muzzio. It could be any one of them, he thought. But only one was really dangerous—Muzzio.

❖ ❖ ❖

She'd said not to contact her under any circumstances. But who could he turn to? He'd been told not to return to the Village to contact Willie or Fred. Rachel was the only person in Manhattan he could think of who could come up with a plan to countermand the VOAP ultimatum. There were barely twenty hours left to do anything. Parsons had told him that if the submarines were sunk or surrendered to the Russians, the APA would be in a position to use chemical and biological warfare against the Constitutionalists. Under extreme circumstances they might even use tactical nuclear missiles. That wasn't likely, but it was an option that would seriously inhibit Constitutionalist war planning as to render virtually impossible any ultimate Constitutionalist victory.

Douglas had returned briefly to his apartment and then set off on foot for the Caleb Foundation. He was terribly unsure of himself. If Rachel had foreseen what Ponomarev might do to smoke out the submarines, would she have been so categorical in telling him not to see her? Of course, she was under surveillance—so, very obviously, was he—but might there be a fleeting opportunity to speak to her and see if they could derail Ponomarev's plan? Presumably, the Constitutionalist agents in Manhattan, once under instructions from Helena, would do what they could. But how much did they know about Project Almond, about Marcus, and about the broadcast?

He was still a safe two blocks away from the foundation, walking north on Madison Avenue and wondering how he could best approach her without alerting his own tail—or hers. Before he realized how close he was, he quite suddenly saw her coming out of a supermarket on the other side of the avenue, carrying a plastic bag of groceries and walking across the avenue toward the foundation building.

Douglas's thoughts were machine-gunning their way across his mind. It was vital she not see him before he got close. He abruptly turned around and headed for a newspaper rack. His tail, who'd grown lazy about keeping out of sight, froze in the middle of the sidewalk only thirty yards from him. As Richfield walked back for his newspaper, the man rapidly turned on his heel and walked back away from Douglas.

At any other time this might have been amusing. Richfield took his paper and crossed the street, walking as fast as he could, retracing Rachel's steps.

The paper! The story on the Tridents was on the front page. Douglas paused for a moment to open it. There was a photo of a submarine accompanying the story that drew his eye quickly. Taking out his pen, he wrote "Eccles. 12:5" across the story and looked to see how far Rachel had walked.

Douglas took a minute to catch up to her. Thankfully, he could move faster than her high heels allowed her. When he was just a few feet away, he called out, "Miss! Miss! You left this at the checkout."

Rachel turned around, a little stunned and very surprised. "My paper?" she asked, startled to see Douglas and mixing a frown with a smile at his being there. "Thanks," she said, and Richfield walked on ahead of her.

He crossed the street at the end of the block and paralleled Rachel's route back to her office. He stopped at a bus bench and looked to see where Rachel was.

The light was against her, and she wanted to cross the street. Douglas saw her glance at the paper and look around, probably for him. When she crossed the intersection she spotted him and nodded. She understood! But how were they going to pull it off?

It was blistering cold as he strode down Seventy-first Street, lost in thought. He turned onto Park Avenue. There had to be a way to get the message out. The wind and the cold had a fierce bite today. Partly from self-preservation and partly because he didn't have anywhere to go, Douglas turned the corner to get some shelter.

Richfield wondered if he'd managed to lose his surveillance tail without really intending to. But the man was still there, grimly keeping up but maintaining a more careful distance than earlier.

As he walked, he found himself near St. Patrick's Cathedral. The wind was harsher and he decided to get out of the weather and enter the church. Perhaps the quiet, warm interior would be more conducive to thinking. He'd found in a few churches a remarkable sense of peace that he liked to bask in whenever he could. Whatever explained this, he wanted to catch a little of it now.

Only one of the three front doors of the cathedral were open, the one on the far right, and this was guarded by two regular New York cops. If there were PSB around, it wasn't obvious. Nor was there a militiaman to be seen. As he climbed the steps toward the entrance and the policemen, Richfield took out his Protocol pass to talk his way through.

"What's up, officer?" he asked as cheerily as he could.

"Nothing. They got some rehearsal going on and they don't want no gawking crowds disturbing it."

"Rehearsal? What for?"

"How should I know? Go ask somebody who cares."

Douglas walked to the south aisle. Even before he was fully inside, he heard music, male voices, unaccompanied, joined in such glorious harmony that it caused him to stop in his tracks.

"What's going on?" he asked an official standing just inside the door. The man had also asked to see an I.D., but so politely it was clear he had no police powers.

"It's a rehearsal for tonight's concert," the man replied.

"What concert?"

"Well, in honor of the Christmas season, the National Executive Committee has authorized a VOAP broadcast of a concert Mass by the Renaissance Chorus. We've closed the church to the general public so that the singers won't be distracted during the rehearsal."

"What are they singing?"

"Palestrina, the *Missa Papae Marcelli*."

"It's beautiful."

"It's one of the most beautiful Renaissance Masses ever composed. Since you're on Protocol business, can I help you find someone?"

"What? No, no, thanks, I'm just familiarizing myself with things going on in the city. Sometimes delegations want to see St. Patrick's, so I like to have something to tell them. If it's okay, I'll just walk around and listen for a while."

"No problem. Why don't you take a seat there close to the back? That's where the acoustics are best."

"Thanks." But already Richfield's attention was elsewhere. The exquisite beauty of the music, the sense of worship it conveyed, the

333

grandeur of the interior of the cathedral all came together upon him. He struggled to comprehend the contrast between the tension and stress of his mission and the profound sense of peace he felt now.

Bathed in this glorious tranquility that seemed to ascend from a combination of the music and the words, even though he didn't understand these, Douglas found himself wanting to stay for the entire rehearsal.

". . . *dona nobis pacem.*" As Palestrina's final five-voiced cluster spread itself out in the majestic choral conclusion to the Agnus Dei, Douglas came to suddenly. He hadn't fallen asleep so much as slipped into a sort of rapturous daydream that had cut him off from everything else. He was suddenly aware that technicians were stringing up wiring and microphones across the nave close to where the choir was standing. His mind, still somewhat removed from the present, slowly brought itself back to earth. Of course, the broadcast. Wait. Broadcast? On VOAP?

A small and harried-looking priest skittered by to catch up with two technicians. "Have you decided where you want the control box?" he asked them nervously.

"The announcer is going to be in the Bride's Room," one of them replied, "but the producer wants to be as close to the choir as he can, just in case we need to reconfigure the mikes in midstream."

"Well, that's okay," said the priest, not looking at all satisfied, "just remember that this is a church, not a recording studio. Eating and drinking are strictly forbidden, especially during the Mass."

"Don't worry, Father," the technician responded with a cheerful smile. "If he gets out of line we'll make sure he pays attention." And he strode off with his assistant to the front of the church.

"Excuse me," Douglas said, getting up from the pew and walking up to the priest, who hadn't seemed very sure what he ought to do next. "Aren't you Father Connelly?"

The priest eyed Richfield suspiciously and then broke into a smile. "Yes, of course, and you're Douglas Litchfield."

"Richfield," said Douglas, correcting him. "We met just before Easter. You came to City Hall's Protocol Department for some reason."

"Indeed," said the priest indignantly. Then he lowered his voice and looked around carefully before continuing. "Some bureaucrat told us that we needed permission to hold a service at midnight and then sent us to the wrong department to get it. You were the man who sent me to the right people. Thanks for that."

"Did you get permission?"

"Yes, in the end, though we had to swear that we wouldn't overthrow the People's Movement before they let us. What brings you here?"

"It's a complicated story. I've sat through most of this runthrough of the Mass and the music is gorgeous. Did I get it right that the VOAP is going to broadcast it?"

"Yes, tonight."

"What time?"

"Eight o'clock."

"Live?"

"Yes, of course. Why do you ask?"

Douglas was the furtive one now and looked around carefully to see if his PSB tail had snuck into the church. "Can we talk privately?" he asked.

Connelly sighed, his youthful face already prematurely lined. "I'd take you into the confessional," he said quietly. "That used to be sacrosanct. Not anymore. We think someone has bugged one of the confession boxes, maybe both. As a result we can't trust any of them to be safe. Let's just sit down in the pews and give the impression we're talking about the concert tonight."

"Well, we will be."

They casually strolled through the handful of technicians and organizers to a pew as far removed from any wall or electric outlet as they could get. Richfield came quickly to the point. "Father Connelly, will anyone be introducing the Mass, or will you just get the order to begin and start the performance?"

"As it happens, I'll be making the briefest introduction to Palestrina and the Mass before the performance begins."

"Will that be live?"

"Yes, but it might as well be recorded. I had to have the text approved in advance by the Culture Committee."

"What does the text say?"

"Oh, the usual, the composer was born in Palestrina in 1525, worked most of his life in Rome, was close to Pope Julius II, and so on. That he wrote more than a hundred Masses. That sort of thing. Why does any of this matter to you?"

Douglas answered with another question. "Could Palestrina have had any favorite Scripture passages? Could this Mass in particular leave a scriptural source?" he asked.

"It's certainly possible, but it might take a little research to find out. Why?"

"Kevin—can I call you Kevin?—for your sake as well as mine, I can't tell you right now. You're going to have to trust me. This is a matter of extraordinary importance."

Connelly broke into a peal of incredulous laughter. "We're in the middle of the greatest economic crisis of Western civilization," he replied. "America is at civil war. Jews are emigrating to Israel as fast as they can. Priests need government permission to conduct the Mass. And you tell me it's practically the end of the world if a Renaissance composer didn't have—or maybe if he did have—a favorite Bible passage."

A good four inches taller than the diminutive priest, Douglas firmly placed a hand on the young priest's shoulders, just as Hodges had done to him in Montana. "No, Kevin, that's not what I'm saying at all. I'm saying that it may well mean that you have to get government permission to keep the church open at all if we cannot *broadcast* as part of tonight's concert a very brief passage of Scripture and attribute its selection to Palestrina."

As Connelly looked into Richfield's eyes, a slow light of understanding began to appear on his face. "I see," he said quietly. "That's pretty serious. Just one question. Which passage of Scripture?"

"Ecclesiastes 12:5. Can you package a favorite passage from a handful of chapter 12 verses and make sure five really sticks out?"

"Douglas, I can do all kinds of things. Let's say for now that I don't recall your asking me to do anything, and I don't recall saying that I would do anything. Do we agree on that?"

"Yes, that's understood."

"Then I have just one other question."

"What's that?"

"Do oppositionist priests get sent to a regular prison or to the Alaska camps?"

"To the camps," Douglas said, biting his lip in anguish. "Look, forget I even brought the subject up." And he took his hand off Connelly's shoulder.

"No, Doug, I can't forget that. I owe you one. Maybe I owe Him one too"—and he pointed slyly upwards. "You're probably not at all a man of prayer, but if you think of it, tonight's concert just might be a good time to start. For whatever *you're* about. And for me." And he grinned and winked.

17

The Almond Tree Blossoms

*T*he question of Kevin Connelly's safety gnawed at Douglas. Did he have the right to ask a man to do something that might lead to his permanent incarceration, even death, for a cause that might not be central in his life at all? Yet Connelly, somehow or other, had shown that he wanted to sign on. It was virtually certain that he'd be arrested after the concert, if not before it even got off the ground, unless he had an escape route that the PSB wouldn't expect.

In the four hours or so before the concert, careful planning was essential. The chief question was how to get out of Manhattan and back west after the concert? With Connelly committed to change the text of his introduction, Douglas could presumably go anywhere, if he could just shake his surveillance. But he realized he had to be in the cathedral when it all happened. If Connelly were picked up and sent to Alaska, it was inconceivable that Richfield, who had imposed this fate on the priest, should not be subject to the same dangers.

Obviously he couldn't go back to Rachel again. He just hoped that his own tail had somehow not noticed their twelve-second conversation. It was bad enough having the fate of a virtual stranger, a Catholic priest, on his conscience, without adding to it that of Rachel and the delicate emigration work of the Caleb Foundation.

Douglas wondered where his tail had gone. Connelly had left him to deal with yet another technical problem, and he had wandered off to inspect different parts of the church. He needed a means to draw out his tail. He searched out Father Connelly again and asked him to show him around the church. He wanted the tour

339

to be open and obvious, so that anyone paying attention to them would not view their conversation as conspiratorial.

It turned out to be an unintentionally prescient move. For one thing Douglas had never bothered to spend any time exploring St. Patrick's for himself. The largest Roman Catholic church in the U.S., it was an interesting nineteenth-century Gothic structure in itself. But as his guide Connelly not only showed off the various chapels, the organ loft, the chancery organ, and the ambulatory behind the sanctuary, but also a flight of stairs behind the sanctuary. "Where does that lead?" Richfield asked.

"It goes down behind the high altar and then to the Chapter House on Fifty-first Street."

"Can you get directly out to the street from there?"

"Yes." And looking steadily at him, Connelly nodded his head just slightly. So there was a different way out. Hope—and relief from his troubled conscience—began to grow like a small cloud in his mind.

Richfield had still not figured out whether his tail had followed him into the church or not, but as he was about to leave, the thin man was leaning against the back of the church, an ugly smirk on his face. Douglas's adrenaline surged into his stomach again.

Sleet was falling as he came down the cathedral steps in the fading afternoon light and continued his walk south down Fifth Avenue. The pretzel sellers were out, and the warm smell drew Douglas in hungrily. He hadn't eaten since breakfast and he wasn't sure, after tonight, where he might be getting his meals. He needed to pull himself together, plan his steps carefully, and think of some way of throwing off his tail when he needed to.

He knew of a small, quiet coffee shop on Fifty-second Street where he could have a burger and fries at a counter and keep an eye on people passing by. Stopping there would give him an opportunity to eat and a chance to think as well.

The place was surprisingly full, but the cheerful Greek owner recognized him immediately at the door and called out for him to come to the counter to the one empty stool.

"Heya, Mister Richfield, good to see you again! You been away a long time or something? You don't come here for a while. Whatsa matter? You don't like my burgers no more?" And he laughed at his own humor, catching the eye of some customers who were forced to smile at the joke.

"No, Nikos, nothing like that. Just busy. Anyway, if I didn't like your burgers, why would I be back?" Douglas responded, drawing another laugh from Nikos.

Richfield sat down, picked up a *People's Voice* from the counter, and waited until Nikos could take his order.

"What you want, my friend?"

He ordered a cheeseburger and coffee and was pleasantly surprised by the quality of the coffee.

"Good stuff, Nikos—this coffee. Where d'you get it?"

"Don't ask, Douglas, don't ask. Listen, we all got to survive, right?"

"Yeah, right."

"Hey, my friend, what you think about this submarine stuff?" Nikos asked, bending low and speaking in a softer voice. "You think it's true, they got this Marcus guy? Do you? Hey, my question is this, if they so smart they got this guy Marcus to talk, how come they don't put him on the television or something? I mean, what they have to do to get it out of him, cut his ears off or something?"

Nikos's coffee shop had flourished during the depression and under the People's Movement largely by the proprietor's conveying to everyone that he'd deal with the devil himself to keep his coffee shop running. He was an overweight forty-year-old who looked ten years older and whose gray hair was thinning rapidly. But the man exuded kindness from behind his wheeler-dealer front. He never refused to feed the street people who begged at the back door of the restaurant.

"Hey, Douglas, you know what's going on up there with the big shots?" he asked again in a husky whisper after he'd put Richfield's order in front of him. "You tell me why the militia boys and the leather-coat guys are all over this block. It started last night. Makes you think like there's some kind of spook convention going on, right?"

"Dunno, Nikos, they never tell me when they order up some surveillance or something. You got some big-shot neighbors here or something?"

"Yeah, Metaxas, good Greek girl. She lives here somewhere."

"Maybe that's it." Out of the corner of his eye, Douglas saw his tail walk by the coffee shop, peer through the window, walk back across the street, and lean quite brazenly against a wall, hands in his pockets.

Suddenly an idea came to Douglas. "Say, Nikos," he asked when the amiable Greek had come up yet again for another gossiping session, "you've never had any trouble at this shop with the cops, the PSB, or anything, have you?"

"No," the Greek replied triumphantly. "You don't think they call me 'Nice Guy Nikos' for nothing, do you?" He laughed again. "I know how to keep out of trouble. Nobody even laid a finger on me. City Hall, militia, PSB. I'm cleaner than the plate you're eating from." His laugh was interrupted by a customer retorting, "Well, that's not so hard." Nikos guffawed.

"Why you ask?" he added.

"Oh, nothing. Just wondered if you needed some good words down at City Hall from time to time."

"Hey, that's real nice of you. I let you know if I do, right?"

"Right. By the way, have you got a pay phone around here?"

"Sure, right outside the restroom. Need a coin?"

"No thanks, I'm fine."

He'd learned what he needed. If Nikos's place was politically "clean," there was a good chance none of his phones were bugged. Douglas needed to call, but he didn't want to use a street phone, since his tail could call in the location and trace the call. In the depths of the coffee shop, out of sight of the front window, Douglas gambled he could make a call safely.

He dialed a number and waited for the answering machine to beep. "Esther, it's me, your old buddy. Is there any chance your brother-in-law is heading out of town this evening on his usual itinerary? If not, do you know anyone who is? I need a ride, and a friend may need a lift too. I really need to go tonight or very early tomorrow morning. Please don't call my home or mention this call to anyone else. If you can arrange it, leave a note in the flowerpot where we were standing together a few weeks ago to indicate the time you can meet me. Write 'nine oranges' for nine o'clock and 'three apples' for thirty minutes past the hour. Eleven-thirty would be eleven oranges and three apples.' The pickup point should be exactly ten blocks north and three blocks west of the flowerpot, on the northwestern corner. The earliest we can do it is nine. Esther, forgive me for doing this to you. All I can say is that your dad would approve. Gotta go. If you can't do it, I'll understand. See you, and thanks a million."

He'd no sooner put the phone down than his mind started playing out worst-case scenarios. What if someone else heard the message and became suspicious? What if Esther herself were actually working for the Constitutionalists and suspected a trap? What if, by some fluke, Esther herself had come under suspicion and was under personal and phone surveillance? He'd already imposed a terrible risk on a Roman Catholic priest, and yet the man almost seemed to welcome it. Why were people being so cooperative? It was unnerving after all the months at City Hall virtually forcing people to do for you what they didn't want to.

"Thanks, Nikos," he said, putting a beef ration coupon and the payment for the meal down on the counter. "Hope your plates stay clean."

"Whaaaat?" said the ever-cheerful Greek, but then he understood as Richfield winked, put a finger to his mouth, and walked on.

It was important to get rid of his tail, but at the right time. If he tried to do so now, he might not only fail, but he might arouse PSB suspicions and attract a whole army of watchers. It was better to let just one man believe that Douglas wasn't going to bother trying to cover his tracks around the city.

It was after five now, dark and sleeting, and there were three hours left before the concert. On reflection the least provocative thing to do was to head back to his apartment and grab a couple of hours sleep—he'd certainly be needing it later—and another bite to eat. He wanted his surveillance, no doubt a different person by now, to be as relaxed as possible. But he still wasn't sure whether he should try to give his pursuer the slip before the concert or afterward. If there were an ugly scene in the church once Connelly read the key Scripture, they might simply block off all entrances and put everyone through a dragnet. Then it wouldn't matter whether he'd succeeded in eluding his tail or not.

Back in his apartment, mercifully, his slovenly roommate Kuzmic wasn't home, and Douglas could set the alarm and sleep for nearly two hours without being disturbed.

He was really fresh when he awoke and made a cup of coffee and two sandwiches. He dressed warmly, stuffed a handful of granola bars into his raincoat pocket, and took with him the last of his advance from Ponomarev.

The subway had more uses for Richfield now than merely getting him to Fifty-first Street. For one thing a PSB friend had once told him that the simplest way to find out if you were being followed was to stand by a subway car and wait to the very last minute to get on the train. It didn't always work at the station where you got on the train first, especially if the crowds were huge. But if you got off quickly at the next station and waited until the last minute again before boarding, you could almost always tell if you were being followed.

Sure enough, it worked at the second station. The tail was a woman seemingly in her sixties, not very tall, and dressed in colors so dreary that it was virtually impossible to spot her in a crowd. It was at least possible that she was working with a partner.

The price of uncovering his shadow was that the tail was alerted and wary. Yet not knowing who was shadowing him would make it impossible for Douglas to be sure, once he made his exit from the church, that he wasn't still being followed. Something else struck him. Although Connelly had shown him the stairs behind the altar, what if the PSB knew about them and closed it off or guarded it tonight? If there were only one way out, all his surveillance team need do was watch the main door to the church.

He had butterflies in his stomach as he joined the people mounting the steps of the cathedral. Both New York police and militia were in full force, ensuring that the concertgoers—or worshipers, depending upon one's world-view—didn't block the sidewalk. There were clusters of PSB plainclothes people as well. Richfield wondered if some ranking PM figures might be on hand, perhaps one or two of the NEC.

As he entered the cathedral by the same door he'd used that afternoon, Douglas managed to spot a second tail, another "old person," and saw that she was twenty or thirty yards behind him. It was just half an hour before the concert was due to begin.

"Doug!" said a voice urgently in his ear. Richfield turned around to find Connelly at his elbow. "Don't worry," the young priest said, "I haven't changed my mind. But listen, officially, there's only one way out of this place after the concert, the door you just came in through. I don't know what the reaction to my introduction is going to be. There's a remote chance that if I do the reading right, they won't come after me until the concert's over. But if we have to get out quickly, remember the stairs I showed you.

"The VIPs are going to sit up front on the left side—opposite from the control booth. I've lit a candle in the Lady Chapel at the back of the church and brought some candles for you. If you need an excuse to leave your seat and go behind the sanctuary, hold the candles conspicuously. The PSB will assume you're ultrapious or superstitious. Whatever happens, I've decided I'm going to exit the cathedral through the stairway I showed you. I'll be there either before you or just afterward. Wait for me. If they grab me, go ahead anyway. Go through the first door, lock it with the key on the other side, then go through the Chapter House out onto Fifty-first Street. It's not being watched. I've already checked. If I'm not wrestled to the ground, we've got a chance."

"But what about your cassock?" Douglas asked. "You'll be a dead giveaway in that outfit."

Connelly winced but then grinned. "Don't worry," he said, his face creasing into the smile and worry lines of a fifty-year-old. "I can get out of a cassock and into blue jeans in thirty seconds flat when I'm having a real slow day, faster when I'm cooking."

"Good," commented Richfield soberly. "Because I don't think things are going to be very slow tonight."

Connelly nodded and left him. The choir was already filing into the sanctuary below the high altar. They wore old-fashioned surplices, which lent a strikingly ceremonial air to the concert. In general the People's Movement in New York had discouraged musical performers from wearing the traditional black ties and long gowns, though a few cities had held on to the tradition.

The church filled up rapidly. The only vacancies near the front were at the far end of the fourth row on the left. The first two rows had been roped off for VIPs, and two security officials were there, periodically checking in with their radios. Douglas felt somewhat self-conscious holding the thin white candles until he saw three or four others on the same side of the church with them. Somehow he felt that Connelly had put them up to it.

By 7:50 there were no more seats left among the general audience pews. There was a stirring at the back of the church as several PSB agents escorted in the important guests. The cardinal came in first, resplendent in his scarlet-trimmed black house cassock, the red sash around his waist and the red zuccheto skullcap on his head. He was a physically imposing man, once an All-American linebacker for Notre Dame. A handful of other, slightly lesser church luminaries followed, only two of whom Douglas recognized.

The biggest surprise followed the cardinal's entry. No less than three members of the NEC attended the concert: Preston Northwood, Enrico Gomez, and Bill Muzzio. All three, in a sense, were naturals. Though Northwood was nominally of Protestant background, his multiculturalist zeal had made him something of an unofficial patron of every religious and cultural expression. It didn't matter to him whether it was an Iroquois rainmaker's dance in the Cathedral of St. John the Divine in upper Manhattan, or Buddhist chanting in the Bronx; Northwood was ready to bestow his tolerant presence anywhere and everywhere. He avoided Protestant or Catholic church services or Masses, even if they were also musical events, on the grounds that they belonged to the previously dominant, white, European, patriarchal culture. Now that this culture was thoroughly cowed and on the defensive, he must have thought it safe to pay a visit to its quaint expressions.

Muzzio and Gomez were expected at the concert because of their Latin ethnic origins. Gomez was something of a conspicuous secularist, despite his Catholic origins, but Muzzio had never publicly broken with his Catholic roots, even though he had voluntarily joined the People's Movement as the labor union representative. He looked tired now and distinctly nervous. He motioned with his hand to his colleagues to sit in the front pew toward the middle. Pleading a headache, he opted to sit closest to the nave.

With the arrival of the NEC members, everyone was in place. In the control booth, walled in by soundproof glass, the producer and his assistants were watching a digital timer count down to eight o'clock and monitoring the announcement of the Mass over VOAP from the Bride's Room on the other side of the church.

The cardinal was positioned before a podium and began the broadcast on cue with a welcome to both the cathedral and the radio audience.

It was Connelly's turn. Richfield's mouth went dry watching him approach the microphone with his unrehearsed and unapproved introductory reading. But Connelly looked calm and confident.

"Giovanni Pierluigi da Palestrina," he began, "was born in about the year 1525 in Palestrina and died in Rome in 1594. He was *maestro* at the Capella Giulia and the Capella Sistina and other churches in Rome for most of his adult life. His creative output was prodigious, including several hundred motets, liturgical compositions and madrigals, and more than a hundred Masses. Palestrina's work represents one of the culminating achievements of contrapuntal, unaccompanied choral music of the Renaissance era. It has been described as the most beautiful and moving sacred music ever written.

"The *Missa Papae Marcelli*, published in 1567, was dedicated to Pope Marcellus II, who succeeded Palestrina's first papal patron, Julius II, in 1555. Many regard it as Palestrina's finest Mass.

"Palestrina was a great student of the Bible and sometimes would associate a work with a particular passage of Scripture."

Richfield watched the VIP rows intently. No one among the dignatories reacted, probably because none of them knew anything about Palestrina. But the cardinal knew the approved text that Connelly was supposed to be following and was now whispering intently to the monsignor sitting next to him.

The signs of consternation were more obvious in the control box. An assistant gave a note to the executive producer, and both men's faces were registering their confusion over the priest's deviation from the text.

"For this Mass," Connelly went on, "Palestrina chose a passage from Ecclesiastes in which the preacher enjoins the people to be mindful of their maker. The text reads, 'Remember your creator in the days of your youth, before the days of trouble come, and the years approach when you will say, "I find no pleasure in them"—before the sun and the light and the moon and the stars grow dark, and the clouds return after the rain . . .'"

Though nothing could be heard from inside the control booth, an animated conversation was being worked out between the executive producer and his assistant. The front rows of the audience had an excellent view of the control booth. Several people close to the booth began their own fidgeting and whispering.

"'When the doors to the street are closed,'" Connelly continued, "'and the sound of grinding fades . . .'"

The producer was urgently trying to catch the attention of the three NEC members, drawing a finger across his throat in a cutting gesture and throwing his hands up as though asking for a decision. Muzzio, at the end of the row, nodded toward Northwood and Gomez with an I'll-take-care-of-this gesture and walked toward the control booth.

"'When men are afraid of heights and of dangers in the streets . . .'"

The producer's face was red with anger and frustration, and he watched Muzzio approach the glass door of the booth with an expression of confusion and irritation. Muzzio made some incomprehensible gestures back to the man rather than opening the door to speak to him. For a moment the producer stopped his own gesticulating to try to grasp what Muzzio was saying. That was all that was needed.

Connelly continued, "'When the almond tree blossoms—'"

Suddenly, someone shouted, "Stop the broadcast! Stop the broadcast immediately!"

Richfield recognized the voice immediately. It was Ponomarev. Turning around quickly, he saw the Russian about six rows behind him. He was standing, with Weikert next to him, and pointing at the control booth and Muzzio. "Arrest Muzzio immediately!" the Russian ordered. PSB plainclothesmen sprang to their feet and ran toward Muzzio. Richfield couldn't take his eyes off the spy catcher.

Their eyes met, and Douglas momentarily felt paralyzed by the evil emanating from the Russian.

Ponomarev was distracted by the general pandemonium sweeping the cathedral. A rising cacophony of screams and shouts crescendoed as PSB agents converged from all over the cathedral on the control booth, pushing their way from mid-pews and shoving people aside as they rushed to the front of the cathedral.

Muzzio shouted back. "Don't listen to that man!" he bellowed. "He's a foreigner and has no jurisdiction here! Northwood, Gomez—Ponomarev has betrayed us! Order the PSB to arrest him!"

The two other members of the NEC, surrounded by their own anxious-looking security detail, appeared uncertain for a moment. The agents were also confused, one moment looking at Muzzio, the next at Ponomarev and Weikert. The audience was also divided on what to do, puzzled, some of them scurrying out of the pews and heading for the door, others staying put because it seemed safer to do this.

During the chaos Father Connelly quietly left the microphone, picked up a candle from behind the pulpit, and calmly walked out of the sanctuary toward the ambulatory. He caught Douglas's eye and nodded slightly with his head. Richfield left his own seat, moving as deliberately as possible and conspicuously holding up his candles. Some PSB agents were about to block the men's exit, but others held them back, worried about the general panic seizing the cathedral.

Most of the audience had remained seated, and the choir, though craning their necks to see what was happening, was still in its place. The cardinal took over.

"Everybody please remain where you are," he said in a booming, football-coach voice. "The Renaissance Chorus will now perform the *Missa Papae Marcelli*." The choir director took his place in front of the singers and led the chorus into the first ethereal bars of the Mass's *Kyrie Eleison*.

Douglas, still trying to walk as solemnly and deliberately as he could, caught up with Father Connelly before they'd rounded the back of the sanctuary. His biggest worry was that the PSB might suddenly stop any movement in the cathedral.

Connelly moved ahead of him and down the steps behind the high altar. Once they were out of sight, they both practically jumped to the bottom and through the door to the corridor leading out to the Chapter House on Fifty-first Street. Connelly locked the door and motioned for Douglas to stand still. They both listened. There was some shouting at the top of the stairs and the sound of many feet coming down the stairs.

"Is anyone in there?" a voice demanded, banging on the door. Douglas looked at the priest, who, for a moment, grimaced with fear. They rushed down the corridor into the Chapter House on Fifty-first Street. Connelly practically ripped his cassock off, thrusting it into a cupboard and grabbing a pair of jeans, a sweater, and an out-of-fashion, worn-looking blue-woolen top-coat, crammed himself into the clothes. "Okay. Let's go," he said. From the distance they heard shots fired—perhaps through the corridor door.

The two of them almost leapt out of the Chapter House onto the street. Apart from two regular New York City policemen halfway down the block, there were just a handful of pedestrians about.

They walked across the street, dodging traffic, and moved as quickly as they could to the end of the block. As they approached Madison Avenue, they looked back over their shoulders. Three PSB agents burst out of the Chapter House, looking up and down the street.

His heart now pumping with fear as well as the exertion, Douglas urged Connelly to keep up with his punishingly fast stride. They didn't dare run in case an alert had been sounded for people fleeing the cathedral. But Richfield knew that he couldn't approach the flowerpot he'd planned to use as a pickup point without being sure they weren't under surveillance. They half-walked, half-jogged two blocks and crossed Madison and paused behind a news kiosk to scan the sidewalks and the streets.

"Let's keep moving," he urged Connelly, whose shorter stature and poorer physical condition made it a struggle for him to keep up with Douglas. He was easily winded. Connelly was doing his best to be cheerful despite the tension and the exertion. "You been training for this?" he asked, panting.

"Yeah, in a manner of speaking," Douglas replied. "Unintentionally, though." He thought of the last time he'd been truly terrified and physically exhausted—in Montana with bullets flying around him. "Let's keep moving," he added.

Douglas wanted to approach the building from the other side of Fifth Avenue from St. Patrick's. He wondered if he'd have been smarter to think of a rendezvous farther away from St. Patrick's than just eight blocks.

Even if Ponomarev had insisted on it, Douglas doubted that the PSB could seal off the area around St. Patrick's. Logistically, the task was just too massive. The dragnet would take at least an hour to be put in place, long enough for the fugitives to escape.

Regardless of what happened to them, the damage had been done. The almond tree message had gone out over the air, inadvertently highlighted by Ponomarev's dramatic interruption.

For a moment Douglas's basic instinct to survive made him want to abandon Connelly. Surely the priest had friends or relatives who could hide him until a plan could be worked out to smuggle him into a Constitutionalist area. But Richfield's better instincts prevailed. On quick reflection it became clear to Richfield that the priest's only real chance of escape and survival lay in sticking with Richfield as they both tried to get out of Manhattan.

It was bitterly cold, despite their pace and the beginnings of perspiration Douglas was feeling underneath his windbreaker. The chill forced him to consider the frightening possibility that Esther had either not received his message, had received it and ignored it, or—far worse—the PSB had intercepted it and was waiting for him. There was no other plan of escape if there were no message in the flowerpot.

As they came back across Sixtieth Street toward Central Park and Fifth Avenue. Richfield was glad he'd chosen to approach the drop from the north. The building's proximity to Central Park gave them a chance of getting away if they were being pursued.

The sleet had turned to slush, and both men were frequently splattered as cars swished by. Farther down Fifth Avenue, the constant sound of police sirens suggested that the cathedral broadcast had turned into a real fiasco.

Perhaps they had arrested others in addition to Muzzio. Poor Muzzio, Douglas thought. He wouldn't receive any mercy as the long-detested and dangerous Constitutionalist mole. They'd certainly torture him. They'd want to find out how much he'd already turned over to the Constitutionalists, who his contacts were, what his methods of communication had been. But they would also torture him because his action might decisively alter the course of the civil war. Victory had been stolen from the People's Movement at the last minute.

The two men approached the GM Building on Fifth Avenue, past the Renaissance-style palazzo of J. P. Morgan's Metropolitan Club. At first everything looked quiet. But there were two three-person militia patrols in Grand Army Plaza. It would be hard to do anything on the GM Building plaza in full sight of the two teams.

"Kevin," Richfield quietly asked, "is there any way you can distract them long enough for me to dig into a flowerpot on the GM plaza?"

"Doug, what you're really saying," he replied, "is can I make enough of a fool of myself to distract them without getting arrested at the same time, right?

"You're right, it's much too risky. We'll just have to chance it." But as they walked toward the plaza, all six militiamen moved off briskly down Fifth Avenue. Probably they were part of the dragnet ordered around the cathedral.

The two men strolled over to the flowerpot as casually as they could. Douglas couldn't believe what he saw. Not only was there an envelope in the flowerpot, sticking up from the foliage, but it was plainly visible from ten feet away. Any passerby could have seen it and read it. Had Esther been this careless or had someone else intended it to be so conspicuous that no one could ignore it?

With a deft sweep of his hand, Douglas picked up the envelope and thrust it in the pocket of his windbreaker. He and Connelly then increased their pace, crossed over to the other side of the plaza, and moved quickly down the steps back onto the sidewalk. Halfway down the block, he opened it and read it, "Nine oranges, one apple, two nuts."

"Two nuts? You mean, like almonds?" Connelly asked, chuckling at his joke.

"That's Esther's way of saying that I'm crazy for asking her to do this and she's crazy for agreeing. What she doesn't know is that there are three nuts. Well, Father, we have to meet up with her in fifteen minutes, roughly fourteen blocks from here."

"We'd better move it," Connelly said. "And on the way, we'd better figure out how she's going to pick you and me up without worrying that she's bitten off too much."

They half-jogged, half-walked the distance. En route they decided that Connelly would wait three blocks down from the rendezvous point on Lexington Avenue, giving Douglas time to explain the situation to Esther.

Richfield took up a position on the corner of Sixty-ninth and Lexington with just two minutes to spare. Exactly to the minute, Esther's battered blue Toyota drove up, stopping conveniently as the traffic light turned red. Esther spotted him as soon as he approached the car, unlocked the passenger door, and let him in.

"Thanks, Esther, you're fantastic, and an explanation is coming in just five minutes. But first, we have to make one more pickup."

"Douglas, what is this?" she replied, tense and alarmed. "Who? Who is this other person? I'm taking a terrible risk already."

"Please, Esther, it's absolutely vital. This man made it possible for me to get here in the first place. He's a Roman Catholic priest."

"A priest?" She instantly perked up. "Why didn't you say so? Of course, I'll pick up a priest. I was raised a good Catholic girl. Just tell me when to stop."

Douglas breathed easier. "Two more blocks, Esther. I'll tell you when."

She nearly caused an accident when they stopped for Connelly, because Esther didn't understand Douglas telling her to slow down. Instead, she braked hard in the right-hand lane in mid-block. Taxis and cars hooted angrily as they passed her.

"Esther, this is Kevin Connelly. He got me out of St. Patrick's in a hurry."

"St. Patrick's? How could you have come from there? I've heard they're sealing the whole area off. There was some kind of concert and the radio said some Connies were caught. What do you know about that?"

"We'll explain it all en route. We're going to New Jersey, right?"

"Yes, and you're very lucky. My brother-in-law was not going to be on the road for another three days, but someone got sick and he was asked to take his place. He's leaving at 4:30 tomorrow morning." She looked at Connelly and back at Douglas. "Is he going too?" she asked dubiously.

"If we have to squeeze him into the spare gas tank."

"How come he's a priest?" she asked a little suspiciously, as she headed across the park toward the upper West Side and the George Washington Bridge. "He's not dressed like a priest."

"He changed clothes so we could get away without attracting a lot of interest."

She was silent for a while as they drove, then turned to look at Richfield. "Douglas, you're different," she said quietly. "What happened to you? And why are you on the run?"

"Esther, I'd like to tell you what's happened more than anyone else, but I can't yet, as much for your sake as mine. I'll say this, though, some people wanted me to work for them, and in the process I decided I really wanted to work for the people on the other side. Now I've done everything I can and my only chance of staying alive is to head west. What's your brother-in-law's name?"

"Juan. He's a good man. You can trust him. We've talked politics, and we agree on just about everything. We've even talked about all three of us quitting this place and taking our chances out there, you know, in the mountains. So, in a way, we're putting our plan into operation for you."

"How far west does he go?" Richfield asked soberly.

"Sometimes all the way. It's very dangerous. Once the trucks get into North Dakota, it's like roulette. At night the Connies sometimes shoot first and ask questions later."

"I know," Douglas replied quietly. "I've seen some of that."

Esther looked at him sharply, but she didn't say anything.

They crossed the George Washington Bridge and headed south on the New Jersey Turnpike until it hit the interchange for Interstate 280. In East Orange they briefly drove north on the Garden State Parkway and exited to a small truck depot just north of Glen Ridge.

Juan, alerted by Esther to meet her and a friend later that evening, was waiting a couple of blocks away from the depot itself. A man of great girth, immensely wide shoulders, and slightly bandy legs, his face had the aquiline nose and deep-set eyes of a Mayan warrior. He quickly sensed that Richfield and Connelly were important passengers and needed to get out of the area.

"Hey, don't you worry," he said with only the slightest Mexican accent. "I've been driving out west and coming back safely for months. I know where you need to go. It'll take about a week on my route, but we'll get there."

"Juan, we're just grateful you're willing to take us," Douglas said.

"No sweat. I've got a place for you to sleep tonight, a bed in the house of some friends who are away for a week. I'll be in front of the house at exactly five o'clock tomorrow."

As Douglas and Kevin got out of the car at the house in Montclair where they would stay the night, he kissed Esther on both cheeks, as did Connelly. She seemed to blush a little. "Vaya con Dios," she said very seriously and with a glimmer of tears in her eyes. "Douglas, I always knew you'd come through in the end. Good luck, my friend. Oh yes, and I should tell you, I really did sit under that favorite tree of yours in the spring. The blossoms are pure white and fall like snowflakes. It's magic to sit there when that happens."

Before Douglas could reply, she'd driven off, waving as she went.

18

Mutiny Averted

Quick! Get back! Someone's coming!" hissed "Bosco" Henry to his companions, Hank Planter and Joe Galateo. They were trying to meet in the submarine's missile compartment and avoid the roving patrols. Someone was running, rubber soles smacking down on the polished plastic surface. The three men crowded behind one of the missile canisters, trying not to give themselves away as the unexpected intruder thumped by.

Whoever it was, however, clearly wasn't interested in them. Through the gap between the missile canisters, the men caught a glimpse of someone in running shorts and t-shirt. The missile deck, dubbed "Sherwood Forest," was the one area of the submarine where someone could let off a little steam by jogging.

"What do we do now?" asked Planter. "This guy could be around here for the next half hour. Sooner or later he'll see us."

"There's only one thing we can do," Henry replied. "We're gonna have to get out of here and look as though we're heading aft to the air regeneration room or the reactor room. We may have a chance there before anyone else comes by."

As the runner's steps temporarily grew distant again, the three men emerged and walked to the end of the missile compartment. They hadn't made it out before the jogger was thudding back toward them, requiring them to clear the walkway. The runner was Lieutenant Richard Larkin, a tall Philadelphia blue blood and one of the *Massachusetts*'s supply officers. An elegant, even dandyish person, Larkin was a more languid version of straight-arrow Gresham. His only problem was that he was a natural athlete with an intense need to work out more than most of the men aboard. He consistently ran more laps around Sherwood Forest each week than most of the other joggers aboard managed in a month.

Larkin gave the three of them an odd look as he ran past, but he didn't stop. They were in the air regeneration room by the time he made his next lap.

No one was there, but it was an awkward place to confer. Anyone might come through the doors without warning. If that happened, it would be impossible to hide and very difficult to explain why they were there.

"All right, quickly," said Henry urgently, almost in a whisper. "I think the captain's plan is a trick."

"Why?" asked Galateo.

"What does it matter to him if our families get picked up? He's on his third wife anyway, and he's probably hidden her somewhere overseas. It's easy enough for him. I never trusted him from the moment that VOAP broadcast came on. I knew he'd refuse to accept their terms. Even if Gresham does get picked up by a Russian freighter, what's to keep him from calling in some allegedly coded message to say that the VOAP announcement's a fake and the Russians have nothing on Project Almond, when he knows well and good that they've got everything?"

"Even if they didn't know anything about Almond," added Planter, "when they made the broadcast, they'd sure know plenty once they'd hung Gresham upside down for a few days. The Russians would nuke the home ports to start with."

"No, they wouldn't, you fool," said Henry. "Not if even one of our subs is still operational. But they'd close 'em down one way or the other just the same. The captain would probably find some remote island to get food and supplies, scare the natives into keeping their mouths shut, and then take us down for another six months."

"No way," said Galateo. "If he tried to do that, even Larkin would be begging us to mutiny."

"Aren't you guys forgetting something?" said Planter. "This is all supposing that nothing happens in the next fourteen hours or so. But suppose the scheduled contact with Hawaii got through saying that Marcus was safe, had escaped or something? The captain wouldn't put Gresham up on the surface, and we'd be back to square one. You think anyone would want to take over the boat then?"

Henry answered sharply. "Hank," he said, "why would you believe a message from Hawaii saying that Marcus was okay?"

"Well, why would anyone trust what the VOAP says?"

"Because not even the NEC is so dumb that they'd announce that Marcus had been caught when he hadn't. I can't afford to blow that off. I've got a family out there, and the PSB may have them under lock and key by now—all because I take up so much space on this boat. We're not doing anything down here. I thought you were with us. You getting cold feet or what?"

"Listen, Bosco," said Planter irritatedly. "Mikulski took my name down just like he took yours and Joe's when the captain hauled Byron in. We're all in this together. I just don't want us to start something we can't finish. If we do mutiny, what do we do next? And I'm sure not going to mutiny unless Project Almond is blown. Nobody else has confirmed the Marcus arrest, you know."

"What do you mean, nobody else? Who the hell do you expect to confirm it? Hodges?"

"Look, Marcus's capture is the biggest intelligence breakthrough that either side has so far. Where is the guy? It's six hours since the original broadcast, and all they've done is repeat the Rutledge statement. No details about the home ports, no comments on Marcus's condition. Nothing. If they have him, why haven't they propped him up in a hospital bed so he can say how well he's being treated and what a big mistake he made by working for the Constitutionalists? The BBC says that no one else has confirmed that Marcus is in custody. Charlie copied their broadcast less than an hour ago and told me that."

Henry looked at him with a mixture of contempt and amazement. "What does the BBC know about Marcus?"

"Maybe nothing," Planter retorted, "but they've been pretty accurate on everything else that's happened so far. And their broadcasts have made it clear they think we exist."

"Hank, you make me wanna puke. You think the PM is going to go blabbing everything they know about Project Almond across the airwaves? Maybe the Russians have already sent Spetsnaz to Chile and South Island to give us a warm little welcome. They sure aren't going to tell us that in advance."

"Listen, quit it, you guys, will you?" interrupted Galateo testily. "We don't have time for bickering. We've gotta figure out what to do if the captain goes ahead with the plan to put Gresham up. Do we move as soon as Gresham makes contact? Do we do it earlier? Or do we lie low until the captain's asleep again?"

"I say we wait until Gresham contacts us from a Russian ship," said Henry. "That'll give us time to get organized and build support. If we make it clear we're not gonna believe anything Gresham beams back, we raise the stakes high enough for everyone to understand that they'll probably never see their families again unless they come along with us. What do you think, Joe?"

"Yeah, I'll go along with that if absolutely nothing happens to disprove the Rutledge ultimatum."

"Just what *could* disprove it, Joe?" asked Henry, exasperatedly.

"Well, if the Constitutionalists can produce Marcus himself, or if they can prove that the Rutledge statement is a bluff. Maybe if the PM makes some stupid follow-up statement that shows they really don't know anything."

Planter, still smarting from Henry's contemptuousness, hesitated and said, "Look, we're all in deep as it is, so the only question remaining is what's best for our families. If they're safe and the broadcast was a hoax, the last thing we want to do is hand Gresham over to the Russians so they can learn every detail about the project. I say we let the deadline go by, then wait until we find out if any of the other subs has surrendered, or if the PM and the Russians really have a clue where the ports are. If they haven't, I say, let's not risk everything in a mutiny."

"What's wrong with you?" Henry asked bitterly. "What about the twenty-seven people who signed the petition? What about poor old Bill in the brig?"

"There are 157 men on this boat, not just 27, Bosco," Planter said in a low voice. "Saying we'll hold our horses doesn't mean we abandon Bill. It just means we're not gonna rush into anything until we're sure what we're up against. Anyway, let's get out of here. Someone'll be in here any moment."

"Hold it, Hank. You're forgetting one thing. What're we going to say to the rest of the twenty-seven? They signed the same petition we did."

"We'll tell 'em what we've agreed on here. We don't want to take the next step until we're totally satisfied we have no alternative."

Bosco merely grunted, and the three of them made their way out of the air regeneration room and back to their quarters through Sherwood Forest where Lieutenant Larkin was still flailing his way around the missiles at a respectable eight-minutes-per-mile pace.

❖ ❖ ❖

"How many days will it last?" Rush asked anxiously.

"A month at most, maybe less," Lieutenant Junior Grade Michael Watkins replied.

"Does anyone else know?"

"Just the chief and two seamen. But they're both smarter than some of the other men on the boat. They won't talk."

"They'd better not. News that the boat's going to be out of food in thirty days is worse than a reactor leak. Chris, we've never accessed any of the emergency stockpiles in the Pacific. Find out how far we are from the nearest one. Lieutenant," and he eyed him with a big grin, "you just may be up for the Navy Cross if this information stays quiet and you can push four weeks to six. I'll—"

"Captain, con," the speaker in Rush's cabin squawked,

"Con, Captain here."

"Captain," the speaker continued, "Radio has copied a BBC report that there was a big disturbance at St. Patrick's Cathedral in New York a couple of hours ago."

"Con, get to the point."

"Captain, the BBC played part of a live VOAP broadcast of a music concert. Some priest was reading a passage from the Bible, and when he got to the point 'When the almond tree blossoms,' he was cut off and the whole broadcast suddenly stopped. On the tape you could hear someone shouting 'Stop the broadcast! Stop the broadcast!'"

"Con, anything else?"

"Captain, there's an unconfirmed report, also from the BBC, that Bill Muzzio has been arrested by the PSB on charges of espionage. He was apparently at the same concert where the broadcast was made."

"Con, very well. Inform all of the officers and petty officers that I want a meeting with them in the seamen's dining room at 0630 hours. Ensure that the room is clear of all enlisted personnel five minutes before that."

"Captain, aye, Sir."

Rush put his microphone down and looked at Gresham. "Muzzio?" he said. "Working for our side? That must be devastating for them."

"Yes, the damage he must have done is incalculable," said Gresham soberly. "Heaven knows what they'll do to him unless Hodges can set up an exchange. That priest was gutsy too. I can't believe they've still got priests who can put their fingers on a scripture in which the almond tree flourishes."

"Blossoms," Rush corrected him with a sly smile. "'Flourish' is the King James translation."

Gresham just looked at him. "Captain, why do you know this verse so well?"

"I'll answer that as soon as we hear from Hawaii. It may even save your fingernails, Chris," Rush replied.

19

Chinese Reflections

*L*ooking out the curtained window of his chauffeured Mercedes, Chen Faxian felt a surge of pride as the car entered Tiananmen Square and drove up to the east side of the Great Hall of the People. The square was the heart of China, originally laid out during the Ching dynasty in 1651, but enlarged during Mao Zedong's Great Leap Forward in 1958 to its present gargantuan expanse of a hundred acres. None of the new buildings around it was at all attractive. Here on Tiananmen Gate itself Mao had proclaimed the foundation of the People's Republic of China.

Every time Chen looked at the Imperial Palace, he was filled with a deep sense of completeness as a Chinese. It was not simply the most magnificent set of buildings in China, it rivaled any palace in the world in proportion and splendor.

It was a perfect north China winter's day—cold, but dry and brilliantly sunny, with a sharp wind filling the flags proudly in Tiananmen Square. Chen's car was not the first black Mercedes to pull up in front of the Great Hall, but he did seem to have beaten most of the others. The meeting was scheduled to begin at ten, and it was only 9:25. This would be a very demanding session, and he wanted to spend a few moments with his father, Premier Chen Rongguo, before the others filed into the Sichuan Room for the meeting. It would be awkward if the others saw the father and his son talking immediately before the meeting. He knew where his father stood on the issue, but America would be only one aspect of the immensely important decision China had to make, a decision that could affect its future not just for the decade, but perhaps for a century or more if the wrong choice was made.

Chen walked up the serried flights of steps at the front of the Great Hall, identifying himself formally to two officials just outside the main entrance. The two were in their thirties and wore dark blue topcoats. They checked his name off a long list, knowing perfectly well who he was. The premier, however, had instituted a draconian policy to root out the age-old curse of Chinese political life, rampant nepotism. Even his son had to submit to the standard processes of identification upon entering government buildings.

Chen smiled amicably as the embarrassed officials asked for his I.D., examined it, and then directed him toward the huge, red-carpeted staircase to the second floor. At the top of the last flight of steps, other officials were also on hand to direct him. He could have found his way in the dark, but after his happy experience of how unnepotistic America was, he approved of his father's steps.

White-coated stewards hovered around the huge Sichuan Room ensuring that every place was correctly laid out. Chen Rongguo, as befitted the premier, had not yet appeared and wouldn't until he had been assured that all other attendees were in place. He chose to work on some final notes in a small office off the meeting room. Chen left his topcoat with a steward and greeted his father warmly.

The older man, his head unusually bald for a Chinese, looked worried and harassed. He responded to his son affectionately, but almost immediately went back to looking at the papers in front of him. Faxian noticed that his own report on the trip to Montana, neatly annotated and well thumbed, lay in a prominent position among the other papers. It was good that his father had had enough time to read the report. Faxian knew that Chinese policy could go in one or two entirely different directions, depending on how the cabinet members interpreted his assessment of what he had seen and heard in America.

"How do you think they will vote, Father?" he asked.

"Faxian, I'm not a prophet. Defense Minister Zhang made a very powerful case last week for us to join the Russians and the Japanese. From the few serious questions asked, it didn't seem as if anyone much disagreed with his analysis. If I had said anything myself,

I would have exposed my position prematurely. They would not only be looking for a way to discredit me this week, but my action would create two factions within the cabinet. For China's sake I did not want that to happen."

"Then you think they will vote for the treaty?"

"I do not know. We have only three votes committed out of fifteen, while they have four in favor of it. The others have not indicated how they will vote, and I fear that they will act in accordance with the prevailing tone today. A great deal lies in your hands, Faxian. No doubt Zhang will try to bully you and discredit your analysis, but you must be prepared for that. Now I must get back to these papers. Speak well to them!"

As he wandered slowly round the Sichuan Room, thinking of the fifteen cabinet members, including his father, who would be there, he knew there was cause to be anxious. He was not a cabinet member; the only reason he was here today was because of his visit to America. Although he wasn't at the previous meeting, he had heard what had happened. Zhang had made it seem that, after entering into the triple alliance as the junior partner to Russia and Japan, China would somehow dominate the pact through superior diplomatic skills and national self-confidence.

They were an experienced and surprisingly well-knit crew, this cabinet of political and economic reformers who had ascended to power in the wake of Deng Xiaoping's death. No less than three of the fifteen had American Ph.D.s, and one-third spoke passable English. That had been unheard of in China until the far-sighted policy of sending thousands of young Chinese to American universities began to bear rich fruit in terms of technical expertise and breadth of vision in the mid-1990s. Premier Chen Rongguo himself spoke very little English, but the minister of finance, Hu Rengshan, a Harvard Ph.D., was fluent, as was the minister of health, Ding Jingsheng, Ph.D. from Rutgers, and Minister of Petroleum Industries Rui Han, Ph.D. from the University of Texas.

Early on in the great wave of political reforms that engulfed China in the mid-1990s, some Americans had foolishly thought that the presence of so many American-trained Chinese within China's leadership would result in automatically pro-American foreign and trade policy moves. But this hadn't proved true, especially following the 1994 depression and the breakdown of world trade. China's new reform leaders were more humane politically at home, and they no longer spoke of "liberating" Taiwan. Hong Kong, too, had been left almost undisturbed. Yet Chinese maps still claimed much of the littoral region of the South China Sea, including parts, traditionally, of the Philippines, Vietnam, Malaysia, and Indonesia as integral Chinese territory. Some Chinese assumptions hadn't changed.

But the most interesting aspect of China's intellectually enhanced, but thoroughly Chinese and nationalistic, leadership was the ambivalence it seemed to hold toward America. When the civil war broke out after the Washington Uprising in September 1997, the Chinese government withheld recognition of the People's Movement regime for several weeks. On the other hand, it had in no way recognized the Constitutionalists as the legitimate heirs of the U.S. constitutional and legal order. Once it formally acknowledged the People's Movement as the politically sovereign body within America, it conducted diplomatic business in the normal way.

Yet there was another side to the tale. China's diplomats around the world, carrying out the instructions of their leaders in Beijing, made it clear they were not happy with the sudden reemergence of Russia to undisputed military primacy in the world in the wake of the Gulf of Oman debacle of 1997. This delicate balancing act had functioned effectively throughout most of 1998; for one thing, the People's Movement was in no position to dictate to China the terms of mutual American-Chinese contact. But now, suddenly, China was being forced to choose. Russia was all but demanding that China sign a treaty of concord with Japan as a prelude to slicing up the rest of the world into spheres of Russian, Chinese, and Japanese influence. There was no direct threat implied within the demand, but Zhelenovsky's government was prickly and arrogant in most of its foreign dealings. As the sole surviving military superpower, it made it clear to Beijing that China would be ignored in further multilateral negotiations involving Russia and Japan unless the Chinese first signed the treaty.

By 9:50 all of the cabinet members were in the Sichuan Room, and Chen called the meeting to order. "It has been three months," he began, "since Moscow first put forward to us this treaty of concord proposal for a triple alliance with ourselves and the Japanese. They have now insisted that we give them an answer within two weeks, or they will withdraw the offer. You have all read the terms of the treaty. Although they are simple and refreshingly brief, the implications are truly momentous, not just for China, but for the whole world. What we must decide today is whether we should reject their proposal and continue unfettered in the international realm, or if we should become part of what is already a Russo-Japanese military and technological consortium over Eurasia, much of East Asia, and much of Europe.

"Last week, Minister of Defense Zhang Meng put the case powerfully and skillfully for accepting the Russian proposal and signing the treaty of concord. I will only summarize for you the two strongest points of his argument. First, he said, we will fall further and further behind both Russia and Japan militarily, economically, and technologically if we do not align ourselves with them. Second, he is convinced that the Russians and the Japanese will indeed sign a secret annex, permitting us an unlimited sphere of influence over Australia and New Zealand. Xiao Zhang argued that the sphere of influence terms would permit us virtually unlimited freedom of action toward Australia and New Zealand, up to and including investment, military measures, and eventual colonization by China.

"We had extensive discussion of what this could mean at last week's meeting, and all of you came away with your own impressions. This week we will not be dealing directly with Minister Zhang's case for the treaty, but more narrowly with Chen Faxian's report of our military inspection team's visit last December to the areas of America held by the Constitutionalists. As you know, this is the first reliable eyewitness report that we have had from the Constitutionalist side in the American civil war. Obviously, how you assess Chen Faxian's report may influence your decision on the issue of the treaty of concord. I should mention that our unofficial delegation to Hawaii last October reported its findings, but it is now clear from that report, which you have also read, that the Constitutionalists' Acting President Verazzano is only indirectly familiar with the state of affairs on the American mainland.

"You all know that I have pursued a strong anti-nepotism policy in the past two years. I wish to remind you, in case you believe that I may have been unduly influenced by my son's report, that it was signed with full consent by all four political principals comprising the delegation. General Ma Fanmei, the senior military officer on the delegation, has also added an appendix to Chen Faxian's report laying out his assessment of the military strengths and weaknesses of the two sides in the American civil war.

"Following the principles of discussion we agreed upon last week, I will ask Defense Minister Zhang to open the discussion with comments on Chen Faxian's report. Xiao Zhang, please proceed." As a sign of affection and respect, the premier had addressed Zhang as "Little Zhang," an indication that he was older and senior to Zhang, but that he regarded him as a friend and colleague.

"Xiao Chen," Zhang began, looking kindly but intently at Chen Faxian, "I congratulate you on this report. It is lucid and well detailed. It confirms in all major aspects the military analysis prepared for me by General Ma and Colonel Xu after their return with you. They, too, spoke highly of the fighting skills of General Hodges and his senior generals and of the high morale of the Constitutionalist forces in Montana. We have heard different reports, as you know, from the so-called Army of the Southwest, but nonetheless, it seems that Hodges commands a formidable fighting force. So much for the present-day situation in purely military terms.

"If we look at the long-term probabilities of this conflict, though, it seems to me that there are some important trends you have paid insufficient attention to. First, is it not obvious that the predominant weight of population and industrial resources available to the People's Movement will eventually overwhelm the Constitutionalists, however brilliant their top military leadership, just as the superior industrial might of the North overwhelmed the militarily talented armies of the South in the first American Civil War?

"Second, your account and General Ma's put great emphasis on the role played by the Russian advisers and actual soldiers in the strategy of the American People's Army against the Constitutionalists. The Russians have lent some of their best Spetsnaz units to the APA, providing these new forces with powerful tools for deep penetration of enemy areas and sabotage of key installations. This kind of technical and training assistance, it seems to me, is likely to turn the military tide of the war even faster than the long-term demographic and economic pressures will. Thus, though I don't dispute your assessment of the current military situation in the civil war, I think you have overemphasized its impact upon the long-term outcome."

"Minister Zhang," Chen responded immediately, hoping that Zhang was not about to launch into point three and simply steamroll any discussion. "What you say about the long-term economic and demographic advantages of the Constitutionalists is certainly true. But superior numbers, equipment, training, and wealth is still less important than the support of the general population in a civil war context, as our own civil war in the 1940s demonstrated. The Nationalist Chiang Kai-shek had several times more front-line troops and far better equipment than our side—than the People's Liberation Army—had in 1946. His government controlled all of China's cities. He even had the material, moral, and diplomatic support of the U.S. Yet three years later he had lost everything and was in full retreat to Taiwan.

"There are actually some striking similarities in the present American scene to our own civil war, except that, in a sense, the ideological positions are reversed. In our civil war fifty years ago, it was the cities that sought to preserve capitalism and the countryside that fought for the socialist goals of the Communist Party. In America today it is the cities that are fighting for socialism and the countryside that is fighting for capitalism and freedom. Just as the entire countryside of China eventually turned to the Communists and against the Nationalists, so it is at least possible, and in my view probable, that all but the most militantly socialist of America's major population centers will gradually turn against the People's Movement."

"What evidence do you have to argue that?" Zhang interrupted sharply.

"The fundamental philosophy of the People's Movement is social control," Chen replied levelly. "The movement came to power because the collapse of the American economy, the military defeat in

Iran, and the continuing riots in the cities showed that the ruling authorities had lost both political power and political legitimacy in much of America. Americans have always wanted freedom, but even Americans will choose strong central controls when the alternative is complete anarchy. But now that law and order have been reestablished in the major urban areas, more and more Americans are chafing at the social and political price they must pay to ensure this continuity of political power for the People's Movement. We discovered in China after thirty years of leftist experimentation and collectivism that people will work harder if there are rewards for doing so. The Americans, after they have become bored with playing with socialist toys, will rediscover this truth too. When that happens, the People's Movement will be quickly swept aside."

"I do not entirely agree with you," said Zhang briskly. "But let us leave that assessment on the side for the time being. What is your response to my second point, namely that the presence of Russian military advisers will help turn the military tide of the war even before economic and demographic factors come into play?"

"Minister Zhang, I respectfully take the view that the decision to invite Russian advisers will prove to be a political disaster. We are talking, after all, about advisers from a regime whose political flavor is ultranationalist and even fascistic in racial terms. What kind of working relationship do you imagine there can be between hard-boiled Russian sergeants—who think Asians, Africans, and everyone else who is not a Slav belong to inferior species—and agitated African-Americans who are hypersensitive about racism? How long do you think that kind of cooperation can last? And even if the main fighting elements of the APA, which include a disproportionately large number of African-Americans from the cities, are willing to accept Russian help, what about the vast majority of the civilian population itself? Will they welcome that assistance? I do not think so. Excuse me, Minister Zhang, may I ask a question of any of your minister colleagues here who has studied in America?"

"Of course."

"Minister Hu and Minister Rui," Chen said, turning to the ministers of health and petroleum industries, "you both spent several years in the U.S. at different times. May I ask if you think ordinary, middle-class Americans are eager to learn from foreigners, or if they are accustomed to believing that they have something to teach just about every other country in the world?"

Both Hu and Rui laughed spontaneously, as did some of the other cabinet members. Premier Chen, Faxian's father, smiled to himself wryly. To pose a question in a way that made one of the two possible answers sound ridiculous had been one of his own favorite rhetorical devices. The senior of the two, Minister of Finance Hu Rengshan, replied first. "Xiao Chen," he said, "it was my experience that some ordinary Americans, very nice people, thought that, as a foreigner, you were something of a genius if you knew how to turn on a light switch." There was a burst of laughter around the table. "I can tell you this. Never once during my three years in America did anyone ask me about my professional, economic, or political skills simply because I was foreign, not to mention because I was Chinese. Well, maybe there was one exception. The eleven-year-old son of my neighbor in Cambridge assumed that because I came from China, I could show him all the moves of a kung-fu boxer." There was more laughter around the table. "Xiao Zhang, I have to concur with Chen Faxian. Americans are not at all comfortable being conspicuously helped by foreigners."

"All of that may be true in general terms," retorted the defense minister, rattled that Chen had stood up so well to his skepticism, "but you have forgotten one very important point. The Russians hold a nuclear sword over the heads of the Constitutionalists because they have a complete monopoly of nuclear weapons now."

"Minister Zhang, with respect, that view can no longer be supported. You have all seen in the report the photographs of the Trident nuclear submarine. The People's Movement confirmed the existence of this pro-Constitutionalist submarine by making a broadcast appeal for its crew members and the crews of two other submarines to surrender. But none of the crews has done so. That means that the Constitutionalists still have a viable nuclear deterrent in the civil war."

"Or it means that none of the submarines is capable of surrendering. Perhaps one or two of them have been sunk, or are so badly damaged that they cannot even put out to sea."

"But Minister Zhang, if that were so, the Constitutionalists would surely know it."

"So maybe they do know it. If they do, obviously they are not going to broadcast this information."

"Minister Zhang," Chen Faxian patiently insisted, "they did broadcast a message, in a manner of speaking, with that concert that was cut off the air after the priest mentioned almond trees blossoming."

"That was just some eccentric priest," Zhang countered, "trying to propagate religion without permission from the People's Movement."

"Minister, if that were so, why would the Constitutionalist spy, Muzzio, have revealed his identity and hence assured his own arrest in an effort to keep the program on the air? He would not take that enormous risk just for a religious program. We know also that the clandestine submarine home port program was specifically called Project Almond."

"How do you know he was arrested at the concert? The official report never mentioned where he was arrested."

"Of course it didn't. To admit that a pro-Constitutionalist traitor to the People's Movement was arrested for trying to keep a broadcast on the air would only draw attention to the content of the broadcast. Verazzano's people in Hawaii informed us that Muzzio was arrested in the cathedral in New York actually at the time of the concert."

"They could be making it up to have us believe that the Almond Project is still in operation."

"They could certainly be making it up, Minister. But in case they were, I have checked with our Ministry of State Security, and they confirmed, through our U.N. mission in New York, that Northwood, Gomez, and Muzzio all attended the concert and that Muzzio never again appeared or was mentioned in the media until his arrest was announced three days later. More importantly there is every evidence that at least one of the submarines and probably all three of them are still conducting patrols. It stands to reason that, if even one of them had surrendered in response to the People's Movement's ultimatum, a huge fuss would have been made about it."

Zhang was silent for a moment. He'd given up smoking a few weeks earlier, and he became fidgety and restless when he was tense and didn't have a cigarette to draw on. He'd anticipated much easier going on the military front with Chen Faxian, who demonstrated a far more detailed grasp of the current realities of the American civil war than he did. But he had invested too much of his reputation as a strategist in last week's eloquent advocacy of China's participation in the treaty to withdraw now. He was determined to launch one final attack.

"Let us assume, for the time being," he said, leaning back in his chair, "that everything you say about the Almond Project is still true. How long do you think these submarines can continue to operate once the full might of Japanese technology has been exerted in the global effort to sniff them out. Can they hide forever? Who believes that? Maybe they will scurry around, with a photograph here and a photograph there for a few more months, and then they will make a mistake, or the detection skills of the Russian navy will reach the point when it is relatively simple to catch them. When that happens, there will be no more nuclear deterrent on the Constitutionalist side. Then the American People's Army, reinforced with the full might of the Russian military machine and the propaganda and financial support of Japan, will move relentlessly against Hodges and Verazzano, and America will once more be under one regime.

"When that happens," he sneered, "if we have not joined with our two neighboring countries in the alliance they propose, where will we be? Sooner or later it will come out that we sent a military inspection team to the Constitutionalists, that we even contemplated covert aid to them. We shall look ridiculous, not merely not joining in with the victors, but tempted for a while to support the side that was bound to be defeated from the start.

"Premier Chen and fellow ministers, we simply have no choice but to accept the Russian offer. We live in a violent, rapidly changing, and thoroughly immoral world where only the strong and those clever enough to ally themselves at the right time with the strong can survive. I commend young Chen Faxian for his bravery in going into the war zone in America and for his interesting and well-written report. But let us now put the question of this sideshow, the American civil war, behind us, and focus on the main issue. I propose, Premier Chen, that we move to a vote on the treaty as soon as possible."

Premier Chen trembled slightly. Zhang had made a powerful counterattack, and he could not be in the position of publicly defying him without support from at least one other cabinet member. Yet no one seemed eager to join the fray and tangle with Zhang.

Playing for time, the premier tried another tack. Looking at the unaccustomedly quiet men and women in the room, he asked, "Does anyone wish to respond to Minister Zhang or comment on the earlier remarks of Chen Faxian?"

No one moved.

This was awkward. Though deeply alarmed about the proposed alliance, Chen knew that it would be political folly to impose himself so blatantly into the debate without at least prior argument from others no less opposed to the treaty. He thought he might be able to postpone a vote for a few minutes by suggesting they deal with other routine business first.

But as he was about to say something to this effect, someone cleared his throat, as though he wanted to speak. Hua Mingdao, the minister of culture, was in his seventies. He was one of China's most distinguished living painters, and he hardly ever spoke up at cabinet meetings. About the only reason he was in the cabinet was because Chen and others in the reform leadership believed that the presence of a learned and genuinely cultivated, creative artist high in the government would do more to convince the West of China's commitment to political reform than anything else.

Hua spoke softly and slowly at the best of times, and he was making no effort to be heard clearly now. There was a hush among the ministers as everyone strained to hear what he would say.

"I am not an economist, nor a political scientist, as all of you know," he began, looking down slightly as he talked. "I was never a member of the Communist Party, but I was not a dissident either, though I often sympathized with some of the dissidents during the Communist Party period. Apart from art my academic training and my lifelong studies have almost all been in history, the history of our culture and our nation.

"It has always seemed to me that heaven itself has conspired to keep the sons of the Yellow Emperor separate and distinct from the barbarians even when they were trying to force themselves upon us.

374

The cycle of our dynasties included foreign rule—the Mongols and the Manchus—yet within barely more than a generation, the foreigners who ruled us came to be ruled by us. The Mongols could not govern without our scholars to manage the bureaucracy for them. The Manchus, our Ching dynasty, only hung on as long as they did because the Western barbarians were so obviously more alien to China than they themselves were. And each time China was weak and humiliated by foreigners, the sons of the Yellow Emperor stood up and resisted and threw out the foreign devils. Chairman Mao, though he made many terrible mistakes, at least understood this. When he announced the founding of the People's Republic in 1949, do you remember, he said: 'China has stood up.'

"What is now being proposed is that we join a global strategic alliance with two barbarian powers, with ourselves as the most junior partner. But I say, how can we depend on these allies if we join with them? Who knows what will happen in Russia? Perhaps they will tire of their nationalist zeal and sooner or later return to the moderate policies they were pursuing under Gorbachev and Yeltsin. Or perhaps their nationalism will burn itself out in a blaze of aggression against their neighbors. But does it make sense to become allied with a regime whose very reasons for being are to redress national grievances? Russians have forever been confused whether they belonged to Europe or Asia. For sure their history and culture contain elements of both. But can we rely on the word of a regime whose philosophy is so extreme and unstable as the one they have currently adopted? I ask you, can China rest its entire fate on that uncertain entity? Any treaty we signed with them would almost surely be temporary.

"As for the Japanese I am surprised to see anyone at this table contemplating an alliance with them. They raped our nation for ten years before our own civil war. They never apologized. And today, they too, like the Russians, are in the grip of a nationalistic obsession that must only signify instability for them at home and erratic behavior abroad.

"Australia and New Zealand could not defend themselves if we chose to do what Minister Zhang says we will have the liberty to do under the terms of the treaty of concord; that is, intimidate, invade, occupy, and settle those lands. But we who have so freely criticized the Americans for what they did to the indigenous people when the white settlers stormed across the continent, can we now contemplate with a clear conscience attempting an even worse crime against those living in Australia and New Zealand? However cruel the policy of the white man in America was toward those peoples originally living there, at least it was the logical development of an inexorable program of immigration, settlement, and migration over a period of nearly three hundred years. And the natives were far from all being 'noble savages' living in perfect harmony with nature and each other.

"Could our people now contemplate the premeditated and unprovoked enslavement of millions of free people in Australia and New Zealand, living in an advanced state of civilization, solely because, if we do not undertake this, Japan or Russia might? How many Chinese lives would be lost in this endeavor? We are crowded greatly in this land, but we are also no longer in the seventeenth century. We do not have the option of sailing across the sea in a powerful ship, overawing the simple natives in a vast and underpopulated land by our mere presence, and then cowing them at every point in their resistance through our superior technology and organization. No, we are not in that position at all.

"Our only possibility of remaining great, as a culture and as a power, is to remain close to the historical focus of our culture. Many of our sons moved abroad to escape poverty in this country. But they prospered where they landed through hard work and business, never through the gunboat or the enslavement of local and indigenous peoples already there. We have ruled the Tibetans and the Turks, and neither of these like us, and we have made many mistakes in ruling them. They are Chinese, but everyone knows they are not Han, and they never can be. Do not forget, we are not just a culture, we are a civilization with rules of morality and conduct that cannot simply be discarded for reasons, seemingly, of immediate, but temporary political need. Any civilization that abandons its ethical roots for the sake of current political expediency will pay a much bigger price in the long run than what it would have paid by facing without compromise the original threat. The Americans have a civil war today because they forgot this principle, or perhaps because they never fully learned it as they were growing up.

"I cannot make any arguments from economics or military power. I do not know what our GNP will be with or without large investments from Japan or trade with the Russians. I do not know how many tanks they have and we have. But I know that, as frightening as it may seem to us if the two big powers in the world today, Japan and Russia, team up to give orders to everyone else, our culture, our values, our civilization will survive, flourish, and influence the world far more if we do not accept this temptation they are putting in front of us today. That is all I have to say."

There was a total, stunned silence around the room for several seconds. Finally, Premier Chen spoke. He was trembling slightly again, but this time because it seemed as though heaven had opened its doors upon the meeting and made so clear, through Hua's speech, what now needed to be done. In the silence that followed, he simply asked, "Does anyone now not wish to vote immediately?" No one responded. "Then let us now do it," he continued. "Out of respect for everyone present, this will be a secret ballot. In front of each of you are ballot sheets with the words 'approve of the proposed treaty' and 'disapprove of the proposed treaty' on them. Put a line through whichever statement you disagree with, leaving the other statement legible. Then place the ballots in the envelope and pass them up to Secretary Wu."

With the impact of Hua's speech still hovering over the table, the cabinet ministers filled out the ballots in silence and passed them.

The silence continued and was only broken by the sound of Wu tallying the ballots. When the sense of tension was becoming uncomfortable, the premier asked Wu to announce the vote immediately.

"Premier Chen, Ministers," Wu said solemnly, relishing his moment in the limelight and drama, "the vote on this question is as follows. In favor of the treaty of concord with Russia and Japan six, against the treaty, eight, one abstention. The proposal to join the treaty is therefore defeated."

For the first time, Chen permitted himself to smile and the mood around the table relaxed. Even Defense Minister Zhang, though he had lost the vote, felt that the argument had been an honorable one. The remaining time passed in a discussion of how the government should announce its rejection of the treaty, in public, or privately, first, to the Russians and the Japanese. Exercising his leadership confidently now that the vote itself had come down on his side, the premier argued vigorously for a unilateral Chinese announcement. This, he said, would prevent either Moscow or Tokyo from beating China in the rush to explain to the world what had happened. No one disagreed with this proposal. It was decided that China would continue to recognize the People's Movement regime, but they would set up a liaison office in Honolulu, a step or two below diplomatic relations, to develop contacts with the Constitutionalists. "What if the People's Movement objects?" Zhang asked.

"Let them object," Chen replied. "The Americans had a liaison office in Beijing while they still had diplomatic relations with Taiwan. We are merely following precedent." And there was more laughter around the table.

Later, as the cabinet members filed out of the Great Hall, down the steps to their waiting Mercedes, Premier Chen lingered with his son in the indoor warmth as the two of them looked out through a window over Tiananmen Square.

"I am very glad that I sent you to Cal Tech, Faxian," the premier said.

"And I am grateful that you sent me," the son responded.

"Let me ask you one thing. I understand that this is not something you can predict. Yet you have some intuition for the way Americans behave, some 'feel' for their character. We both agree that they have come down far in the world since the days after World War II when everyone did what they said. Now tell me, who will really win this war in the end?"

"Hodges," his son said simply.

Richfield and Connelly made it to Montana within ten days of leaving New Jersey, alighting from the truck at night in North Dakota and moving on foot by dark until they had skirted Bismarck and the APA patrols and were well into no man's land. Once in contact with Constitutionalist units, Douglas was quickly able to establish a link to Helena. A Storch flew out to pick them up, painted white for winter operations.

Richfield had immediately been kept busy, not just undergoing debriefings on his most recent Manhattan experiences, but preparing detailed analyses of urban developments in the areas under People's Movement control. Muzzio's swift execution had cast a pall on his escape—a sobering reminder of just how determined the NEC was to maintain its grip on power and eliminate threats to its authority from within. Increasingly, statements in the name of the NEC were released no longer by Stan Rutledge alone, but by Rutledge and Elroy Robinson together.

The media under People's Movement control also took some hits. Ever since the incident in St. Patrick's Cathedral, broadcast and print journalists had been kept under closer scrutiny than ever. *New York Times* correspondent Michael Fleetwood had been reassigned from political reporting to covering ethnic affairs. ABC News reporter Sally Giordino, amid a fanfare implying a promotion, had been moved to the new program, "Family Affairs," where one of her first assignments was to interview elderly former journalists in a Long Island retirement home.

Douglas was grateful to be out of Manhattan, away from Ponomarev and Bremer and Weikert. He'd found his integration into military life in the Army of Western Montana easier than he'd expected. The officers and enlisted ranks were highly motivated and held for the most part both seasoned and decent people. Many were surprisingly well informed about the People's Movement, and they showed no hostility toward him for his early support of the movement in Chicago. Douglas found himself a frequent and popular dinner guest in the messes of different units, and he regaled his hosts with his impressions of the better-known NEC members. He found the brisk, sunny cold and the brilliant blue skies more to his liking than he'd expected. Although it was constantly colder than Manhattan, he didn't feel it.

Only one thing perpetually ached in his spirit—not knowing what had become of Rachel. At first he had quizzed intelligence officers about her whereabouts or her situation, but their replies were noncommittal. He wondered if she'd been arrested or even killed. Maybe she'd taken advantage of her position at the Caleb Foundation and simply boarded one of the flights to Israel.

He compulsively scanned the personnel lists, wandered into the hospitals to see if there were any new admissions, and read back issues of the *New York Times* and the *People's Voice* to see whether there was something about the Caleb Foundation. But he turned up nothing.

Once his heart nearly stopped when he thought he saw her walking in front of him up Last Chance Gulch. But just as he drew even with her, the woman turned and he saw that it wasn't her.

Early in February Hodges called a meeting of his senior commanders and his civilian advisers and analysts. Unusually, Douglas was asked to attend. Though he'd kept in touch with General Parsons and several other officers he'd met on his first visit to Helena, he was seldom admitted to Hodges's high councils. The general would invariably greet him warmly when he saw him, yet not even Richfield's pivotal role in protecting Project Almond had qualified him for regular access to Hodges.

It was colder than usual, and a wind from the north had brought low clouds scudding across the sky with the promise of snow. Even with his gloves and thick parka, Richfield was shivering.

"Know what this is about?" he asked Major Stockwell, who overtook him on the way in, carrying several maps and charts.

"Yes," Stockwell replied tightly, "but I can't tell you before the meeting." Douglas rolled his eyes sardonically. He desperately hoped they weren't going to try to send him back to Manhattan, even though Ponomarev had long since been recalled (in disgrace) to Moscow.

They were to convene at nine o'clock in the same large operations room where Douglas had first met Hodges among his generals and where Rachel had been reintroduced to him for the tantalizing two days they had been together in Montana. Richfield's feelings were conflicted. The room had wonderful associations . . . a hand on his shoulder or placed on his arm. He shivered at the memories, but pulled himself together quickly when he saw Major Larson in attendance.

"Captain, we have a job for you. I don't mind telling you that you made quite an impression on a select group of people last month," Larson said.

Richfield felt like he was being set up—for what, he didn't know. Larson had never brought him good news.

"So what's the job, Major? I'm beginning to feel like a burden here. If you can use me, I'm ready to go," he said.

"Captain, the People's Republic of China is setting up a liaison office with us. That means that we have to have some people over there too—to represent us. General Parsons will be heading the initial delegation, and he and Chen Faxian have both asked that you be assigned to the group. It seems the Chinese have a lot of respect for someone they think saved their lives." It was the first time Douglas had seen the major smile, and he felt his own grin at the thought of a diplomatic position in China. But what about Rachel? Would he never see her again? Was she dead—like Muzzio? Had she been arrested, tortured, even killed? His buoyed spirits sank. Larson seemed to read his mind as he watched Richfield.

"I don't mind telling you that the China assignment will be something of a try-out for you. The general's high on you, but he's been persuaded by a few voices"—here Larson looked down momentarily—"that you need some seasoning before you're completely integrated into our command structure."

"You mean, someone's going to be checking up on me and giving me a grade—pass, fail, or incomplete?" said Richfield with heavy sarcasm.

"You could put it that way." There was just a trace of ice in Larson's tone.

"How long is this probationary period going to last? Do I get a brownie if I turn in the assignment early?"

"Oh, I wouldn't want to turn in the assignment early," Larson replied, this time with a sly grin spreading over his features. Richfield hadn't anticipated this.

"What do you mean?" he asked, perplexed.

"Because if you do well in China, you'll be joining part of the delegation that's continuing further west on an extremely delicate

381

mission to the Middle East. Israel, to be precise. We won't be need-ing interpreters there because everyone we're going to meet will speak English. But there is a certain young bilingual Israeli intelli-gence officer who's expressed an interest in giving you a personal tour of Jerusalem."

Suddenly, he began to grasp exactly what Larson was getting at. "You don't mean . . . Rachel? She's in Israel?"

"Yes, I'm told that how she got there is a pretty amazing tale. But I'm sure she'd rather tell you in person than have me do so." By now Larson was grinning in enjoyment at the way the conversation had gone. He went on: "Mrs. Hodges, by the way, has a personal message she wants delivered to Miss Silverstein. She hopes you can join her and the general and a few others for dinner tonight. It's at seven o'clock. Don't be late."

"Yes, Major. Yes Sir."